Daniel, My Son

A Father's Powerful Account Of His Son's Cancer Journey

Splendid

PUBLICATIONS

Daniel, My Son

A Father's Powerful Account Of His Son's Cancer Journey

Splendid
PUBLICATIONS

David Thomas

Daniel, My Son
A Father's Powerful Account Of His Son's Cancer Journey
By David Thomas

Splendid Publications Ltd
Unit 7
Twin Bridges Business Park
South Croydon
Surrey CR2 6PL

www.splendidpublications.co.uk

British Library Cataloguing in Publication Data is available from The British Library

ISBN: 9781909109667

Designed by Chris Fulcher at Swerve Creative Design & Marketing Ltd.
www.swerve-creative.co.uk

Printed and bound by CPI Group (UK) Ltd., Croydon, CR0 4YY

Commissioned by Shoba Vazirani and Steve Clark

Contents

Foreword by Debbie Binner   7

Preface   10

Chapter 1:   Diagnosis   24

Chapter 2:   Getting used to cancer   66

Chapter 3:   Summer and autumn of 2006   91

Chapter 4:   Decisions, decisions   127

Chapter 5:   Some light relief   152

Chapter 6:   The battle for IGF   181

Chapter 7:   More opportunities and more worry   214

Chapter 8:   A year without treatment   229

Chapter 9:   Relapse   252

Chapter 10: The nightmare continues   280

Chapter 11: 2011: part one   323

Chapter 12 Countdown   361

Chapter 13: Farewell, Daniel   429

Chapter 14: Reflections   438

Eulogy and tributes by university tutors and students   493

My eulogy   502

Annex A: How to research and advocate for your child   512

Annex B: Compassionate use access to drugs   544

Annex C: Homeopathy and Ukrain   548

Postscript by Allison Ogden-Newton, CEO World Child Cancer   553

Thanks and acknowledgments   557

About David Thomas   560

To Daniel,
Thank you

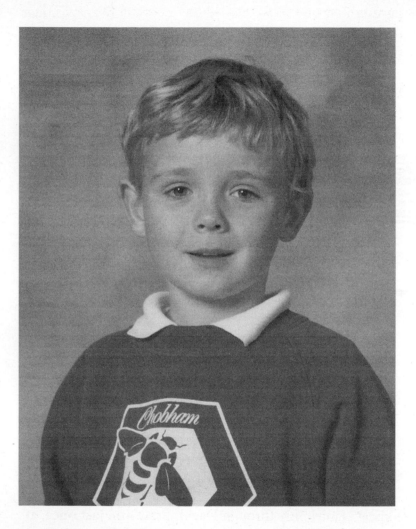

Foreword by Debbie Binner

"A constant source of comfort to me, and sometimes a partner in crime, as we battled the incessant obstacles that blocked our dying children from getting the best possible treatment at the worst possible time."

Words I wrote in my journal in January 2013 about my friend, a fellow 'cancer parent' and the author of this wonderful book: David Thomas.

Drenched in the bitterest of grief after the death of his only child Daniel, David found the compassion and grace to support me as my eighteen year-old daughter Chloë lay dying of exactly the same primary bone cancer: Ewing's sarcoma.

Chloë died on February 28th 2013 - and our family's heart and soul was crushed. Forever.

A lesser person would have run a mile from such similar unfolding misery. But David stayed – just as I knew he would. I'd already witnessed the character of the man. His courage and steadfast spirit as he battled to save, or at the very least prolong, his beloved son's life. He waged a magnificent battle against dismal odds. He left no stone unturned. Not one!

I knew Daniel only through David. I saw him just once, at the hospital. I spotted him instantly as he looked so like David. Those pale blue eyes. Such kind eyes. There he was surrounded by the horrors of the illness: drips, monitors and a wheelchair. So at odds with his youth and beauty. So wrong on many levels.

I prefer my own mental image. Burnished by an Oxford sun, he is sauntering around his University lawns. Surrounded by the "oxygen" of knowledge/education, he is bursting with youthful energy and ambition as he ponders a career in law, government, development….. such endless possibilities for this kind of young man. The thwarted possibilities. So utterly heart-breaking.

David was so proud of Daniel and rightly so. But I suspect that Daniel was equally proud of his Dad. With painstaking precision, born of a lawyer's mind, he dissected every piece of research and evidence for that elusive clue. With his quiet charm and a deeply compassionate soul, he searched the world for somebody to save Daniel.

Many tried but they were destined to fail. While some childhood cancers, such as leukaemia, have seen spectacular breakthroughs in survival (up from 5% to 95% in the past forty years), the picture is way more bleak for many other types. In Ewing's, the drugs used are forty-plus years old and the protocols little changed in twenty years. Doctors sit back helplessly, use "rusty old tools" and watch as the "failed experiment" is repeated time and again. No wonder that survival from Ewing's has hardy shifted in the last few decades.

"Give us hope. Give us new drugs!" we desperate parents scream and nobody listens.

The problem is multi-faceted and, to be fair, complicated to solve. Many try, but the pace is arduous as change agents try to drive new ideas through a deeply resistant conservative culture. A root problem is that the pharmaceutical industry doesn't want to invest in children and young people as they don't represent ROI (return on investment). European regulation stifles innovation further through excessive bureaucracy and the medical world seems unable to organise an effective challenge.

In the meantime our children carry on dying and we parents are tortured by the fact that more could have been – should have been – done.

I roar in anger as I think of Daniel. As I think of Chloë. As I think of all those other young lives lost.

This book is a beautiful legacy to an amazing young man who should have been given a better chance to live. It is also a critical piece of work in raising the profile of childhood and teen cancer and the urgent need for a better system.

Debbie Binner
Teenage Cancer policy advocate
www.facebook.com/createforchloe
www.blogspot.achildofmine

Preface

This is the book I thought I would never write. It's about my son's cancer journey. His journey was inevitably my journey too because I traversed it every step of the way along with Petra, Daniel's mother.

I thought about writing a book early on in the journey. I was learning so much, in so many different ways and wanted to share the lessons. I'm a firm believer that one should learn from life's harsh lessons and, where possible, apply them to make the world just a little bit better. But I didn't think I'd be able to write the book unless Daniel survived and so bad was his cancer that it was extremely unlikely that he would. In any event, when would one know that he had beaten the cancer? His cancer, a rare bone cancer called Ewing's sarcoma, has been known to come back seventeen years after first appearing.

Although I didn't discuss this with Daniel, my idea was to do a joint book, each of us writing chapters about the stages of the journey. I suspect our perspectives would in some ways have been quite different: the same events seen through different eyes. I'm not, in fact, sure that Daniel would have wanted to take part in such an enterprise. His coping strategy was to think about cancer as little as possible. That's not uncommon. One teenager with Ewing's in the US didn't want people to ask how he was feeling, because that would require him to think about his illness.

Sadly, the question of a joint book became academic because

Daniel didn't survive. But when he died, I realised quickly that I should still write a book. I've thought long and hard about why. It was never going to be easy to write, so the reasons needed to be powerful. It has helped me to write it, certainly. Not so much because of catharsis of painful emotion but because it has enabled me to retain Daniel close to my heart, through revisiting so much that we visited together. Doron Weber, an American writer, felt compelled to tell the story of his son Damon, who died following a heart transplant at the age of sixteen. In *Immortal Bird*, Doron wrote: 'It was the only place I had to go for myself. I could not abide living in a Damon-less world.' In the same way, I cannot abide to live in a Daniel-less world. Edward Hirsch, the American poet, who recently published a seventy-page elegiac to his son Gabriel (who died just before Daniel and at the same age), wanted the reader to get to know his son 'through the burden of my poem.' I want someone to pick up this book in a hundred years and say, of Daniel: 'Wow, he sounds like someone worth knowing.' Unusually for someone of his generation, Daniel wasn't on Facebook, so there's no digital memory.

Parental bias acknowledged, Daniel was an amazing individual and inspired many people during his illness. I only really realised this after he died and I doubt he ever realised it. Daniel wasn't inspirational in a demonstrative way, but by example. He just got on with his life, in the face of terrible physical and psychological adversity and achieved some impressive things. More importantly, he kept the purity of his wonderful character. Cancer destroyed his body; it failed miserably to make even a dent on his personality.

I didn't know until he died that Rafael, the Nicaraguan nephew of my friend Maria, had vowed to turn his life around from drugs and teenage delinquency and had gained a place at university, because of Daniel's example. My friend Caterina periodically re-reads my eulogy at Daniel's funeral for inspiration. A woman in the US, a victim of sex trafficking, told me that Daniel's story brought her from the brink of suicide and has inspired many students she knows going through a difficult time. One of Daniel's university tutors, whenever he feels down or demotivated, thinks of all that Daniel went through, uncomplainingly, and is revived. Kieran, then a primary teacher in the deprived East End and a sometime tennis partner, was inspired by Daniel's funeral to inspire his students.

Toru Kaneko, one of the countless doctors around the world who helped me during the journey, wrote: 'The eulogy has to be drummed into the global consciousness forever.' The comment was extravagant and perhaps something got lost in translation, but a number of other doctors have said that Daniel's story has inspired them too. I want his story to inspire others going through a difficult time, to encourage them when the outlook is at its darkest and the suffering at its most unbearable. Because of his story, Daniel was chosen to carry the Olympic Torch, though sadly did not get the chance to do so.

And yes, I want to share the lessons I learnt. Many people have faiths of various types and of varying strength, but none of us knows for certain why we're here or where we're going, just to the grave or somewhere beyond. The phrase 'We are all in this together' has attained a certain flippancy as a catchphrase about austerity measures by the UK Coalition Government. But life: we are all indisputably in it together and it can be a frightening and lonely place. As well as helping and supporting each other, we should be prepared to level constructive criticism where merited. That's how things improve. Criticism includes self-criticism: plenty of that was deserved during this journey. It would have been easy to write a book presenting myself as a father heroically fighting for his son, taking on the medical establishment, handling every situation brilliantly, articulate and reasoned in every discussion, making correct decisions every time. But if I had succumbed to such self-delusion, I wouldn't have learnt any lessons for self-improvement and no one would have been convinced anyway. Memoirists, biographers generally, have a special responsibility to write history as objectively as possible and not as an exercise in self-justification.

Criticism of others, however deserved I may think it, has to be handled sensitively. I have a platform through this book; those criticised don't have the same platform. We only ever see a snapshot of another person, even someone we are close to. We may not get to read their back story. We may not know what else is happening in their lives. We're not privy to most of their thoughts. We cannot fully understand what pressures they might be under. We only get a glimpse into their personalities, their emotional make-up. We rarely get to know about their dreams. Even with the thing which causes two lives to cross, we will not be working to the identical evidential framework and may have objectives which do not wholly coincide if they coincide at all.

Human beings inevitably make judgements about others all the time, even if we try not to be judgemental. That is part of the human condition. But, however clear something may appear to us, we should always remind ourselves that we don't have the full picture and that, if we did, our criticism, or praise, might be tempered. That doesn't mean that our judgements are inevitably wrong. With the intuition which experience and reflection brings, we might, with luck, be pretty close to the mark more often than not. The trick is to try to put ourselves in the other person's shoes, while realising that they may not be our size.

So the criticisms which I level in the book may not be fair, or only partly fair. Those criticised may have a different take on things and may be surprised at the criticisms. I have tried to be scrupulously fair but even notions of fairness can be as much subjective as objective.

Even with these caveats, I have changed the names of certain individuals to protect their feelings and their reputations. That includes Daniel's principal doctor. I have changed his name with regret, because it means that he does not get the benefit of the considerable praise I give. I have also agreed to requests for name changes by certain key individuals for reasons of privacy, with no photographs.

Privacy

I have also struggled with issues around Daniel's privacy. Daniel was quite a private person, especially during the cancer years. To be of any interest or value, this book has to talk about personal matters. Not everything: I have self-censored at times. But to convey the range and depth of emotion, one has to discuss the things which caused the emotion, and to illustrate by example. Would Daniel have wanted me to delve so deep?

I fully acknowledge that this may be self-pleading, but this is how I have resolved the dilemma in favour of telling the story. There are two possibilities: either death is death and Daniel is no more or there is life after death and Daniel, hopefully, is partaking in it. In the first scenario, I am not sure that it makes much sense to talk about privacy. Some philosophers argue that we owe duties to the dead, even if the person isn't aware of harm caused, and not simply to those they leave behind, but I'm not convinced.

But what if Daniel does still exist, as I fervently hope? My assumption – and I accept it's a sizeable leap of faith – is that worldly concepts of privacy do not have much resonance where Daniel is now.

There is, perhaps, a distinction between privacy going to the heart of personal identity and relationships, on the one hand, and the things a person prefers not to share at the time, for whatever reason, but which are pretty innocuous, on the other. As an example of the former, had Daniel said to me 'Dad, I'm gay but I don't want people to know', I would have respected his wish, in death as in life. I hope that now that the story has, sadly, taken a fundamental twist, Daniel is more relaxed about sharing innocuous details, especially if it helps others. I remain uneasy and can identify with the author James Lasdun, who in his recent memoir *Give Me Everything You Have* was troubled about revealing information about his deceased father, a famous architect: 'Sometimes the urge to write these very private things is stronger than the doubts about whether they are worth writing.' All I can do is ask earnestly for Daniel's forgiveness if I have wrongly given in to the urge to tell the world about him.

It's not only Daniel's privacy which is at stake. I share Daniel's instinct for privacy but in writing the book I have to reveal more about myself than I normally would. That doesn't sit comfortably with me, though in truth when one has lost a child such concerns can feel trivial. As importantly, it may not feel comfortable for people who know me. Their view of me may change, perhaps for the better, perhaps for the worse, but it will change as they learn more. However, it's my choice to go public about private emotions and so the situation is not comparable to Daniel's privacy.

There is one final aspect of privacy. Daniel had more than his fair share of talents. Like the rest of us, he loved praise. But he was also exceptionally modest and didn't like us mentioning his achievements to outsiders. The 18th Century theologian William Law wrote: 'You can have no greater sign of confirmed pride than when you think you are humble enough.' Daniel never fell into that trap; his modesty was genuine. As he grew up, I would suggest that it was better to let other people do one's boasting, advice with its provenance in the Book of Proverbs. Daniel took the advice to heart. Not surprisingly, this book contains much praise of him. If I got this wrong as well, all I can do is apologise to him again.

I have on occasion breached my own injunction about modesty, for this reason. I found Daniel's cancer journey incredibly difficult, and the difficulty continues. I frequently languished in the pit of despair. People would often say positive things about how I was dealing with the situation, about the knowledge I picked up, about my relationship with Daniel. The praise came from family and friends and from medical professionals. In one sense, it was just people being nice but it really mattered, especially during the many times when I was struggling. So I have included some examples; it would have created an incomplete picture to have excluded them under a self-promulgated modesty diktat.

Sometimes the unease is not because of what is in the book but because of what I have excluded. If a story is not to be interminable and dreary, inevitably one has to leave out things. Brahms once said: 'It's not hard to compose, but what is fabulously hard is leaving the superfluous notes under the table.' In a strange way, it feels disloyal to Daniel to leave under the table episodes of his suffering, as though they do not matter. But I'm sure he understands.

Truth

Truth is many-pointed, noted Mahavira, Jain contemporary of the Buddha.

This is the story of Daniel's cancer journey as I saw it. It's *my* truth; it's not *the* truth. Nevertheless, I have tried to differentiate between facts and gloss. Accuracy matters and the context in which facts are presented matters so that people are not misled. I remember as a law student, a barrister proudly relating that, although what he had told a judge was literally true, he intended the judge to gain a wrong impression, favourable to his client, from the way he presented the facts. I thought then and think now, that that was as bad as lying; I'm sure the Bar Council would agree.

It's sometimes argued that literal truth is not mandatory; what matters is that the writer conveys the 'essence' of a situation. Ryszard Kapuscinski, the Polish journalist who wrote *The Other*, an eloquent plea for understanding and empathy across different societies, was caught out being economical with the truth, even inventing encounters in Africa. He retorted: 'You don't understand a thing. I'm not writing so the details add up – the point is the essence of the matter.' *Autobiography of a Face* is the story of Lucy Grealy's experience of Ewing's sarcoma, the cancer Daniel had, and the terrible facial disfigurement it caused. At a reading of her book, she was asked whether she was troubled about misremembering details from long ago. Her reply: 'I didn't remember it. I wrote it. I'm a writer.'

Well, I don't agree. History consists of facts ('one damn thing after another', as Henry Ford is said to have remarked). Interpretation of those facts, expressions of opinion, philosophical musing about what the facts mean, all have an important place but should be clearly differentiated from the facts themselves where a book is written as history. So I have tried to present the facts of this story as accurately as possible, and to differentiate between fact and opinion. My expressions of opinion are, I hope, rooted in fact.

Even so, I cannot claim that my account is the only account. In selecting what to include and what to exclude, I inevitably make judgements about significance. In that sense, I am susceptible to what psychologists call confirmation bias – the choosing of facts which support the case one wishes to make. Politicians do this all the time, which is why two protagonists in a debate may seem to be arguing about different issues: they choose different facts to emphasise. I have long thought that politics is the rationalisation of instinct: one reacts instinctively to a given issue and then hones in on the facts which support the instinct.

In any event, the memory plays tricks, or we may simply get things wrong. We mishear, misconstrue, misinterpret all the time; several studies have shown, with the aid of video evidence, that witnesses to a crime or an accident who are adamant about what happened are often simply wrong. Although I documented just about everything, because of the mass of technical information, I may on occasion have misunderstood something.

There is one aspect of recounting accurately which has particularly troubled me. That is the use of dialogue. All memoirists and autobiographers use dialogue. And yet it's almost always a deception. Few of us could recall verbatim a conversation which took place two minutes ago, let alone months or years. I understand why the technique is used: it brings a story to life. And yet the writer knows that a conversation didn't proceed in exactly the way claimed; perhaps it's just the loosest of approximations. And there is a real temptation for the writer to present his contribution as articulate and reasonable and an antagonist's as fumbling and unreasonable, and to substitute the thing he wished he had said for what he actually said. As Wordsworth wrote in *The Prelude*:

> '*I cannot say what portion is in truth*
> *The naked recollection of that time*
> *And what may rather have been called to life*
> *By after-mediation*'

David Copperfield apologised to his readers in case he had misremembered dialogue – and he was only a fictional character, albeit in part Dickens' alter ego. Joachim Fest, writing about his upbringing in Nazi Germany, drew a distinction in this regard between historian and memoirist – he was both – but I am not sure that washes.

Yet for all my misgivings, I have sometimes succumbed to the temptation. On occasion, I *have* been able to remember the precise words used - although not, of course, whole conversations - because they stuck for some reason. That includes amusing things that Daniel, like every child given the chance to flourish, came out with as a young child. I am glad I kept a note of them (the plan was to embarrass him at his wedding). Otherwise, I have used direct quotes only where the exact words or the precise drift of a conversation are not important.

I am writing this book in the three years since Daniel died. Were I to wait until, say, five or ten years – as some memoirists of loss do – the facts would be the same but my perspective might be different. Nothing remains constant in life. The Greek philosopher Heraclitus famously asserted that one cannot step into the same river twice: the river is forever changing. Maybe it would have been wiser to let the river flow some more. But then I would have lost the immediacy of the story and some of the rawness of the emotion. So, for good or ill, this is my perspective at this stage of my journey with grief.

There is one final aspect of accuracy which I should mention. The story contains scientific facts and hypotheses. I have checked everything as carefully as I can. However, I am not a scientist and I may have got things wrong. In a sense, that would not matter, because it would reflect the fact that I inevitably got things wrong during Daniel's illness, as I tried to grapple with incredibly complicated science which no doctor understands completely. So my apology for mistakes is a qualified one. I should note, in addition, that research has inevitably moved on since Daniel died; I have not kept pace with it.

Perhaps with all my introspection and angst about the justification for the book, and about presenting fairly and accurately, it's best to turn to an outsider. In an article in the *New York Times* in June 2010, Dr Abigail Zuger wrote:

> *'After years spent in the company of the sick, I know one thing for sure: there is no story out there that is not a great story. Every single one contains enough pathos, courage, comedy and surprise to power it right to the top of the charts.'*

This sums up what I feel beautifully. Narrative medicine, to which Dr Zuger refers, teaches doctors to listen intently to their patients' stories, to get a glimpse into the real person (I became in the course of Daniel's cancer journey a confirmed and passionate believer in the importance of the human side of medicine).

Daniel's is a story that needs to be told, like all the other stories.

Daniel and I did once write a short story together, when he was seven. He was the hero, inevitably, winning a downhill skiing world championship into which he had stumbled. I used to joke with him in later years that a sentence we came up with – 'He swayed and swerved, swooshed and swaggered' – was the greatest alliteration in literature, involving not just the first but also the second letter of each word (is there a term for that?) and with nouns masquerading as verbs and a dash of onomatopoeia thrown in for good measure.

Until his cancer, life must have seemed a bit like a downhill run for Daniel. The last few years of his life, in stark contrast, were more a trudge up the mountain, until the journey became impossibly vertical and the air increasingly rarefied, before it finally vanished. But the metaphor, like many metaphors, only captures part of the story. The downhill section contained its own major obstacles and the upward climb many extraordinary moments of beauty and accomplishment, with the vista broadened and deepened by new perspective.

This is the account of the uphill segment. There is no onomatopoeic alliteration, but I hope that Daniel's story is rich enough not to require extravagant literary imagery.

Diagnosis

Mum: *I'm going to count to ten and then I want you to go in the bath. One, two, three …*
Daniel (aged two): *I'm not going in, Mummy. Watch my lips*

Some dates are etched in the memory for evermore - 12th April 2006 is such a date. It marked the beginning of the cancer journey with my son Daniel. Another such date is 3rd October 2011. It marked the end of that journey, not in the way we wanted or prayed or at times dared to hope. That was the day when Daniel died, of cancer, three days short of his twenty-third birthday. My life is now divided into three distinct periods: the innocent years before April 2006, the years spanning the cancer journey and the period since Daniel died.

The 3rd October will now always be a horrible day for us, as for others. Among those who died on that date are St

Francis of Assisi and Ronnie Barker (Daniel was a big fan of Ronnie Barker; his views about St Francis are unknown). For some, 3rd October will be a happy day, marking the birth of a child or a wedding anniversary or the all-clear on their own cancer journey. Every year the diarist Samuel Pepys celebrated 26th March, the anniversary of the removal of his kidney stones, a dangerous operation in his day. By contrast, for the parents of Bradley, a young man in the US with the same cancer as Daniel, 3rd September will be especially difficult: it was the day, in 2010, when Bradley died, just a few hours into his eighteenth birthday.

Such are the vagaries of fate. It's slightly unnerving to think that I had lived all these years without appreciating what a black day 3rd October would become for the many people who love Daniel. I did sometimes wonder which date, so innocent at the time, would probably come to hold such significance. Tess of the d'Urbervilles, Hardy's eponymous heroine, put it more eloquently when considering her mortality:

> 'She suddenly thought one afternoon, when looking in the glass at her fairness, that there was yet another date, of greater importance to her than [birthdays and so forth]; that of her own death, when all these charms would have disappeared; a day which lay sly and unseen among all the other days of the year, giving no sign or sound when she annually passed over it; but not the less surely there. When was it?'

In truth, we probably make too much of dates. After all, a day is simply when the Earth is in particular juxtaposition to the sun. Because Daniel died early in the morning, it was actually 2nd October for much of the western hemisphere. But I suppose we need dates to give some structure, some security to our otherwise chaotic lives.

I kept a journal for most of Daniel's illness. It's poignant for me now to revisit the other 3rd Octobers in my journal.

There is no entry for 3rd October 2006 but I recorded elsewhere that I spoke to a leading complementary therapy doctor. On 3rd October 2007, Daniel went to school and his pelvic pain had reduced. We were considering additional radiotherapy following my trip to Germany for a second opinion. Petra, Daniel's mum, had read some depressing article about bone metastases (cancer spread), which supported the argument for extra radiotherapy.

On 3rd October 2008, the journal records that Daniel played table-tennis with his sister Sasha. I was nervously awaiting some results from Barcelona following a diagnostic operation there and sought to reassure him about the delay (he told me he was not concerned and, typically, didn't want to know the results). There was discussion at a conference in Berlin about how doctors should break bad news. Nikki, a teenager with Ewing's sarcoma, Daniel's cancer, was in terrible and worsening pain, as a result of radiotherapy.

On 3rd October 2009 - just two years to go now - there was, it seems, discussion with Petra about prognosis. She wondered what cure rate Daniel's consultant achieved. Daniel was moving really well and wanted to try out for his college tennis team. I read about an eleven year-old boy patient who was fundraising for research after noticing that he was surrounded by pink ribbons for breast cancer but nothing for Ewing's. I did a telephone session as a Samaritan, a long one. A teenager in the US with another type of bone cancer was going to Mexico to try Coley's toxins, an alternative treatment I was particularly interested in.

The 3rd October 2010 had a long entry. This was two days after we were told that the chemotherapy Daniel had begun after a second serious relapse was not working. I met my sister Sian in Reading to choose presents for Daniel's birthday three days hence and pulled out of a Samaritan session that evening because my emotions were in turmoil. There is a lot of information about symptoms, including head pain: Daniel was anxious the cancer might have spread to his brain. My internet search was not reassuring but I sought to reassure him nevertheless. Daniel's cousin JJ, then a final year medical student, tried to reassure me in turn. Cancer spreading to his brain was always Daniel's greatest fear.

Despite the symptoms, he wanted to play table-tennis before going to A&E at his hospital in London. He insisted I first made wheatgrass juice - part of his diet. On the way we listened to coverage of the Ryder Cup from Wales. Thorough neurological tests proved negative but Daniel was nevertheless admitted. A kind nurse called Natasha remembered us from eight months earlier, when I had slept on the floor next to Daniel – she even remembered the bed! This time I stayed with my friends Djuna and Chris, thankfully oblivious to the fact that we had now entered the last year of Daniel's life.

So many memories, all from one date, and in many ways a microcosm of the whole journey. And then the 3rd October that really mattered. The entry for 3rd October 2011, my final entry, simply reads: 'My precious Daniel died at 00.50, peacefully in his sleep, surrounded by the people he loves the most. Certified a couple of hours later by Dr Zarif of Thamesdoc.'

MRI

But October 2011 and what has followed can wait. So much happened in the previous five and a half years, so much that was good and positive and inspirational, as well, of course, as much that was difficult and sad and wearing on the soul. We wish, naturally, that the gap between diagnosis and death could have been longer, indeed that the natural order of parent dying before child would have been maintained, but if the oft-repeated cliché that a life should be measured by its richness not its length holds true – and it does – it's right to celebrate and learn from those amazing years.

Petra, Daniel's mother, and I had separated before he was two. He lived mainly with her but I had always played a big part in his upbringing and lived just a mile away. Daniel's problems had started a few months earlier. We were playing tennis just before Christmas 2005: he was as competitive, and as much fun to play with, as ever. Suddenly he pulled up. There was a problem with his left leg, but he could not explain what. I jokingly said that I would move him around the court, to take advantage. We played on.

Tennis was always Daniel's first love.

A few months earlier, he had suffered an injury in the same general area playing hockey. He had physiotherapy and the problem resolved, or so we thought.

Another hockey injury early in January and, on the advice of the physio, Petra took him to A&E at our local hospital, St Peter's in Chertsey, Surrey. They took an x-ray, diagnosed a haematoma (blood clot) resulting from sporting trauma and said it would improve over time. It didn't. A swelling developed on his left hip and got bigger and bigger. On successive visits to the hospital, the diagnosis of haematoma was confirmed. But the pain got worse and so did Daniel's walking. He developed a highly pronounced limp, indeed he had to twist his whole body to get from A to B. It looked awful. In February 2006, Daniel, obviously popular as he was cheered on by his friends, struggled on crutches onto the stage at his old school to collect some prizes. At the same ceremony, the parents of a teenager who had died of cystic fibrosis a few years earlier gave out an annual prize. I wondered, barely comprehending, what it must be like for them losing a child, and marvelled at how they kept it together. But I didn't make the connection.

Eventually, Petra took Daniel to his GP, Paul Carty, who strongly advised an MRI scan, privately if necessary. I took Daniel for the MRI, in the Runnymede Hospital, a private institution attached to St Peter's, on Monday 10th April 2006. Petra had health insurance. I knew nothing then about MRIs, or any other scan, but it all seemed pretty routine. Two days later, Daniel and I were both lying on his bed in my house, reading. We were due to get the MRI result later that day. He was reading *1984* by George Orwell and, as always, was firing all sorts of questions at me. He had been really inquisitive since he could talk.

I was reading *In True Blood* by Truman Capote, a true story about the depravity and violence to which human beings can descend, in such contrast to this gentle soul who was sharing my reading time and who would literally not hurt a fly. I remember wondering whether I would look back on this reading session with nostalgia, as the calm before the storm. I was developing a foreboding that there might be something seriously wrong, though I still thought that the biggest decision we might have to take after the doctor's appointment was whether Daniel would have to forego his AS levels in a couple of months because of the need to operate.

We met Petra at the hospital. The orthopaedic consultant, Mr Sinnerton, immediately told us that the MRI showed up something serious, probably cancer. Daniel was in the room. We were completely thrown. Mr Sinnerton, wisely I think, suggested that it might be better if Daniel waited a few minutes in the waiting-room, even though he was of age in medical capacity terms.

Mr Sinnerton made it clear to me and Petra that this was

indeed serious. The MRI report, he said, referred to a huge swelling on Daniel's left hip, or maybe he used the word 'pelvis'. I knew instinctively that radiologists didn't throw words like 'huge' around without good reason. Petra and I never had the chance of getting used to the fact that Daniel 'just' had cancer – from the outset we were always dealing with an extremely serious cancer. Life-decimating rather than mere life-threatening or even life-limiting.

I asked Mr Sinnerton why the St Peter's doctors had not ordered an MRI in January. 'I can't explain it', was his frank reply. He used to work in the department. As shoulders, not hips, were his thing, he suggested we urgently contact an orthopaedic surgeon with the appropriate expertise. He gave us three names. I don't remember him using the term 'Ewing's sarcoma' but he must have done, because I googled it later that evening.

I do remember breaking down and Mr Sinnerton saying to Petra and me, a little insensitively I thought, that one of us was going to have to be strong for Daniel. He seemed uncomfortable faced with a display of emotion. Some doctors are.

When we left the room, Daniel could see that we had been crying, but seemed ok. This was the first sign of his amazing capacity to cope with bad news. I suggested we went for a coffee. Although it was by now after 6pm, I tried to call the numbers which Mr Sinnerton had given us, to no avail. There was an unspoken, almost symbolic handing over of the main responsibility for dealing with doctors from Petra to me. She had always taken the lead with regard to Daniel's health and done it well, but she seemed to recognise that we now needed to be more pushy and that I was better suited to that task.

Petra didn't want to be alone that night – she had tragically lost Mike, her second husband, in a skiing accident in 1999 – and so decided she would travel to her family in Bridgend, south Wales, with her two daughters, Sasha and Florence. Daniel stayed with her until she was ready to leave. I wanted some space to start researching the internet and speak to family. I didn't want to worry my mum, just a few weeks shy of her eightieth birthday, until we knew more. Mum was a widow of seventeen years and just about the most compassionate person I have known. Indeed, she is compassionate in a literal sense: the Latin root of the word means 'suffering with'. Hence my desire to protect her.

Early research

I then rang my good friends Norbert and Michaele in Germany. Norbert is a knowledgeable scientist and I wanted to talk to someone with scientific insight. The phone was answered by their son Tobias, then only twenty but a mature twenty. I broke down once more. They had friends visiting but Norbert promised to google immediately they went. He sent an email in the early hours, as ever putting as positive a take on things as the evidence would allow.

So, my research had started, within two hours of diagnosis. There was to be a cruel symmetry to this.

I learnt quickly that sarcomas are cancers of connective tissues – bone, cartilage, muscle. They make up around 1 per cent of all cancers. Most cases of Ewing's are in the bone, though some are in the soft tissue. The cancer is characterised by abnormal positioning (translocation) of particular chromosomes within cells. In that sense it's congenital. It almost always strikes during the first two decades of life.

After my telephone calls I went back to Petra's to collect Daniel. 'I am absolutely determined to get Daniel through this', I said. 'I will sell the house to finance treatment if necessary', she replied. We both knew there was bravado in what we said – how could we expect, like a couple of latter-day Canutes, to stem the tide of a serious cancer? In truth, it was a tsunami of malignancy we were facing. But it was always important to give each other hope, as much as giving it to Daniel. We had to find ways of coping too.

I had to be strong for Daniel, as Mr Sinnerton had said but inside I was churning. I slept only fitfully and was up early. I knew I was facing the likelihood of losing my precious son. He had such a wonderful personality: funny, self-deprecating. He was seventeen but in some ways so much younger. Daniel's innocence, his trusting nature, had always been part of his charm. He still believed in Father Christmas when he was twelve. That sense of wonder had never left him: Petra noticed it when she took him to Times Square in New York well into his teens. He embraced all that life had to offer. He was ambitious, but would not, I think, trample over others to achieve his goals. As a young child, he had simply been delightful, so easy and such good company, a real character and laughing readily. Later he donned the mien of teenage grumpiness only rarely.

That Thursday morning in April 2006 I had to put comforting memories to one side. I had some telephone calls to make. We knew we had to get to see a specialist

Daniel, aged seven, 'interviewed' by Peter White at the BBC. My favourite photograph of him.

doctor quickly. This was complicated by the next day being Good Friday. Hospitals would shut down for out-patients for the long weekend.

It took several calls but I eventually got through to Tim Briggs' private secretary. Tim is an orthopaedic surgeon at the Royal National Orthopaedic Hospital in Stanmore, just outside London. I puzzled why Mr Sinnerton had given us the names of orthopaedic surgeons – surely, we needed an oncologist, a cancer specialist? It eventually made sense – Tim and the other doctors specialise in operating on bone cancers. Even so, it probably would have been better had we gone straight to an oncologist. Janet said we should come to see him the next day – Tim was operating on Good Friday.

I made the calls on my mobile from outside the house because I didn't want Daniel to hear the urgency I knew I had to express. Incredibly, he was working, studying the Roman poet Horace for his Latin AS. This was the second early indication of his remarkable capacity to block out bad things and just get on with his life. Unfortunately for me, he wanted my help in studying Horace's *Odes*. On this morning, there was nothing I felt less like doing. I felt physically and metaphorically sick to the stomach. But ever since he was a little boy, imploring me to allow him to do something 'for the very last time, Daddy', I was hopeless at resisting his pleas. I hated disappointing him and he could find my weak spot with unerring accuracy. So we did some Horace.

I had reason to escape as I needed to pick up the MRI results from Mr Sinnerton. His secretary gave me a letter for Daniel's GP, Dr Carty. The envelope was open so I read the letter. I will never forget one sentence: 'This is probably extremely bad news for this young man.'

I asked to see Dr Carty, still in a state of shock but looking for some reassurance. He was kind but candid about his own lack of expertise with sarcomas. Ewing's sarcoma is one of around fifty subtypes of sarcoma. I later read that GPs might only see one sarcoma in their career. There are only some thirty new cases of Ewing's in the UK every year. So Dr Carty was right to defer to the experts.

I had some emails to write, to friends and work contacts. I guess in part I wanted support. I also told various people at the RSPCA, where I was vice-chair. I knew that I would have to give up voluntary work and perhaps paid work for the foreseeable future. My emails were emotional - probably a surprise to some people, who I suspect regarded me as quite self-contained and perhaps psychologically strong. I saw myself as an emotional person who didn't usually show his emotions; determined but not strong. But in relation to Daniel's illness, I was open about my emotions. It was as if my love for him and my worry about him transcended the boundaries I normally set. Some may have found it difficult to make the same adjustment and I could understand that.

I had another telephone call to make. I had recently started a relationship with Gill, literally just a few weeks earlier. As luck would have it, she had just left to spend a year travelling. Gill had met Daniel and, as was usually the case, immediately took to him. He had a winning way about him and kind eyes. I think people liked his natural modesty and the fact that when he got to know you a bit, he took a real interest in everything you did.

I had taken Gill to Heathrow just a week earlier and she had given me an emergency number for her first destination, a conservation project in Madagascar. After checking with her mother that I should make the call, I rang the number but heard nothing.

That evening, my sister Sian came over. As she left, I said: 'I cannot bear to think of life without Daniel.' I realised from the outset that my fight to help Daniel was not just about him. Yes I would do absolutely anything for him and would have given my life for him at the drop of a hat. There is nothing heroic or unusual in that: one hears many cancer parents say the same thing. I would gladly have made a Faustian pact under which Daniel got better but I would not be allowed to see him again. If Daniel had decided to make his life in some remote Pacific island, without access to the internet or Skype, I could have handled that if I knew he was well and happy. But for all this apparent altruism I also acknowledged my desire to protect myself from the coruscating pain of losing Daniel. Avoiding that was motivation enough to dedicate my life to helping him.

Diagnosis confirmed

In April 2006 there were more immediate things to consider. The appointment with Tim Briggs was at 9am. I again slept badly but was encouraged by an email from Kristin, a friend in Oslo, relating the story of someone with cancer who had taken a mushroom supplement called Agaricus blazei, from the Amazonian rainforest, and had done well. This was my first encounter with alternative or complementary remedies for Daniel. I knew even then that one had to treat such stories with great care and view the evidence critically. I was not about to give Agaricus to Daniel just because it may have helped one patient with a different cancer. However, nor should one underestimate the importance of the injection of hope which positive stories give. I was grateful to Kristin for giving me a little hope at a time when I felt precious little.

Daniel and I were about to leave when Gill called on the satellite phone. It was around 7.30am. Again, I had to take the call outside so that Daniel wouldn't hear. It was an emotional call but I was very glad to hear from her. It was difficult for Gill stuck in the jungle, and she soon came back for two weeks to be with me which was a remarkable act of love in a new relationship.

Daniel and I were now running late. A short way into our journey we noticed a huge plume of smoke rising into the sky. Daniel thought he saw a car on fire by Fairoak Airport, a private airport near my house. Important appointment or not, we had to turn back. A Land Rover was indeed ablaze. We could not get anywhere near it to see if there was someone inside but called the fire brigade before getting on our way once again. To compound things, I took some wrong turnings and we were late getting to the hospital (Petra got there before us from South Wales). Not a good start, although I should have realised that consultants work to only the most approximate schedules.

Stupidly, I had left a copy of the letter from Mr Sinnerton on the back seat. Daniel picked it up and I had to grab it from him - I didn't want him to see the comment about 'extremely bad news.' We were already doing our best to protect him. Petra wanted me to see Tim Briggs first, to say that we would prefer to tell Daniel about the cancer ourselves, if that was indeed the diagnosis.

Tim was bright and breezy. He looked at the scan - Daniel did indeed have Ewing's sarcoma. 'Could Daniel get better?' I asked hesitatingly, dreading the answer. Tim assured me that he could. He told me about another Ewing's patient of his who had just got married. It's always important, I came to appreciate, for doctors to tell patients with a serious illness about success stories if they are comparable. It gives such hope. Tim put Daniel at his ease. He explained he would need some more scans before starting treatment. These would determine the extent of the disease. Chemotherapy would then be given at University College Hospital in central London.

'What should Daniel do about his AS levels in a few weeks' time?' we asked. 'I would forget about them for this year', Tim advised. Daniel had other ideas. Over coffee in the hospital canteen, he was planning what work to do that weekend. Although it was a terrible blow for him to be told that he did indeed have cancer, we assured him that the news was not as bad as we had been expecting. I genuinely felt more upbeat.

Petra was going back to her sister in Wales. I suggested that she take Daniel with her. I thought he needed to be with lots of people who were close to him.

That afternoon, I went to a Good Friday service in Woking. I'd always thought deeply about religion and was brought up as a three times a Sunday attender. These days, religion for me is more personal contemplation than public ritual and I wouldn't normally go to church on Good Friday. I don't respect people turning to the Church only in bad times, but here I was falling into the same trap. In my defence, answers to the eternal questions had suddenly become more pressing and I badly needed solace.

I also travelled down to Wales that day, breaking my journey at my sister Sian's in Newbury. My general mood was one of qualified relief, that things might not be as bad as we feared. I remarked that the previous two days had been the worst in my life, as if the nightmare was over. It's strange how things not being as bad as one expected can give almost as much of a morale boost as unalloyed good news, even though the overall picture remains dangerous. This was an emotion I was to experience many times over the following years.

I spoke to Daniel on the phone later and said: 'Dan, I just want you to know that, whatever lies ahead, Mum and I will be with you every single step of the way.' The response was pure Daniel: 'Dad, I'm playing cards; I'll speak to you later.' Petra and I were the ones in need of reassurance.

Daniel came to my Mum's in Cardiff that weekend. On Easter Saturday we went to see Jonah Lomu play for Cardiff rugby team. Normal things were hard to do but I sensed that normality would be important for Daniel. On the Monday, back home in Chobham, I tried to get tickets for a Chelsea match. This was a mistake (not only because Daniel was a big Manchester United fan) since this was not a normal thing for me to do and Daniel picked up on it. The last thing I wanted him to think was that we were packing in as many good experiences as possible because his time was short. That was probably the reality but Daniel didn't need that message rammed down his throat.

Daniel was due a biopsy that week. This was to confirm the diagnosis. We told the anaesthetist, a kind woman with teenagers of her own, that Daniel had a bit of a cold, in case he should not have a general anaesthetic. Her response was that we needed to get on with the biopsy, which reaffirmed the message that we were dealing with something serious.

Daniel had a general anaesthetic when he was four but, not surprisingly, could not remember it. We explained that he would fall asleep just a few seconds after the injection. When we got to the operation anteroom, Daniel was first given a pre-med injection. After perhaps a minute, he whispered anxiously: 'I'm not feeling tired at all.' thinking he'd been given the anaesthetic! Petra and I were tearful in that anteroom.

That afternoon, Chris Henry, the CLIC Sargent nurse at the hospital, came to find us. CLIC Sargent is a wonderful charity which provides support for families of children with cancer. I had already spoken to Chris on the telephone. She's knowledgeable and with a reassuring manner, but straightforward. That first meeting was the only occasion during those early weeks when, in retrospect, I felt that she gave a bit of gloss, no doubt out of kind motives. The MRI report had referred to an 'aggressive neoplasm.' 'Neoplasm', I learnt, was another word for cancer. I nervously asked what 'aggressive' signified. Chris said that all cancers were aggressive. I don't think this is what the radiologist meant, but Chris's explanation at least provided some transient relief.

The next day, Daniel had a chest CT and bone scans, at separate clinics in London. With the bone scan he was first given a radioactive dye – a contrast – to help them read the scan. Petra took Daniel on an open bus tour of London to take his mind off things while the contrast took effect. The scan itself lasted longer than anticipated. That immediately worried Petra and me – had they seen something untoward? We were to learn that scans taking longer than normal didn't necessarily portend bad news. But as cancer novices we were naturally worried and Petra thought she picked up something in the demeanour of the radiographers. Radiographers, the technicians, aren't allowed to discuss what they see with patients – that is the role of radiologists, who are doctors. Cancer parents and patients are forever looking for signals in what medical professionals say or don't say, in how they react. It's something of a mug's game.

On that journey home Daniel suddenly became really sick – this was before chemo had started – and I had to weave across six lanes of the M25 at one of the Heathrow junctions to get him to the relative sanctuary of the hard shoulder. The nightmare was getting ever worse.

Scanxiety

I was due to speak to Tim Briggs on the Friday afternoon

to get the results of the two scans. I was so nervous – I knew the importance of the cancer remaining localised. As I said to friends, I so wanted some hope when Daniel began chemotherapy which we knew would be tough. Already I was getting paranoid about symptoms Daniel was reporting. The GP of friends in Nottingham kindly tried to put my mind at rest about chest pain Daniel was experiencing.

I couldn't stay in the house. I needed to be out in the open. I'd been expecting the call from Tim early in the afternoon but in the event it was after 5pm that he rang. The waiting game was something else we were going to get used to. Talk to any cancer parent or patient and they'll tell you about the awfulness of waiting for scan results. Indeed, someone has coined the apt word 'scanxiety.'

Tim told me: 'There's something abnormal showing on Daniel's lungs.' That was a big blow. However, seeking to be positive as usual, he added that whilst this would complicate treatment, it need not affect the outcome. I pressed him whether Daniel still had a reasonable chance and he assured me that he did. I later sought the same assurance from Chris Henry, the CLIC Sargent nurse. She was more careful in her choice of words. It must be extraordinarily difficult for doctors relaying bad news and so tempting for them to allay anxiety by massaging the message. The importance of doctors giving hope – realistic hope – is one of the themes of Daniel's story. (I later read about a surgeon who explained to a young girl with Ewing's that he'd deliberately placed a device where it wouldn't show with the evening gown she wore to her school prom, many years in the future. What a message of hope that must have conveyed.)

So upset was I about the CT scan that I forgot to ask Tim about the bone scan. I was to learn shortly that whether the cancer was in Daniel's bones (away from his primary site) was of even greater importance prognostically than whether it was in his lungs. I rang Tim back. 'There are some spots, but people with no cancer in their bones also have spots.' he said. I was less reassured this time. Even with the positive spin, things were clearly getting worse. We didn't tell Daniel at this stage.

Tim in fact can't have been in the least surprised that Daniel's cancer had spread to his lungs and elsewhere in his skeleton given the enormous size of his primary tumour. We didn't know at that stage just how big it was. I kept telling people that Daniel had cancer in his hip, not realising, so bad was my knowledge of anatomy, that the hip forms but a small part of the pelvis.

UCH

It was at that point that the main focus of Daniel's care shifted to University College Hospital in central London. I'd driven past its gleaming new tower block on innumerable occasions, without really noticing it. Treatment would be on the NHS, which as a staunch supporter I was happy about.

Tim had suggested we see Colin McMaster. Our appointment, for Friday 28th April, was already more than two weeks since the MRI scan, which seemed an age to us. I googled Colin to find out what I could about him. I didn't find out much but enough to confirm that he seemed to be an expert in Ewing's sarcoma. UCH was a specialist centre for this and other teenage cancers. We knew we had to have the best that the UK could provide and would go abroad if need be.

I recall Chris Henry telling me that surgeons, such as Tim Briggs, were temperamentally more upbeat than oncologists, such as Colin McMaster. I interpreted this as a gentle warning to be prepared for a bleaker picture than Tim had conveyed. So we were braced for even worse news that Friday. I prepared Daniel gently in the car journey, in the same terms as Chris.

We were to have so many meetings with Colin, in clinic and elsewhere, that many merge into each other. However, this first meeting remains crystal clear in the memory. It was in the Rosenheim Building, just south of the main hospital. Great work was done in the Rosenheim but it's fair to describe it as antediluvian by modern hospital standards. It's a red-bricked Victorian building, unsuited to the needs of today's cancer medicine. Facilities for chemotherapy outpatients were overcrowded and unsatisfactory.

Our appointment was around 10.30am. We were very nervous. The waiting-room was already full. Nobody talked much. On future visits I would look round and wonder who was going to get good news that day and who bad news. Cancer is like that. A patient may think he or she is doing well but then have a bad scan result, even without symptoms. Someone else may be expecting bad news because of some new pain but be pleasantly surprised. We became regular travellers on that rollercoaster.

It was to be over two hours before we got to see Colin. That was not to be untypical. All the sarcoma consultants ran late, but Colin was a particularly bad timekeeper. If it meant he was thorough, that didn't matter. Cases develop unexpected complications and there often has to be liaison with other departments for patients undergoing treatment. A doctor may need to deal with patients who are not actually in clinic. On that first visit, however, when we were so worried, it would have been nice to be seen quicker. Bryony, who was to be our specialist oncology nurse, thoughtfully came to apologise for the delay.

When the time came, we were summoned to Room 13. This was the room Colin always used. I am not superstitious in this way but I noticed later that there was no bed 13 on the Teenage Cancer Ward in the main hospital. Christopher Hitchens, the polemicist and essayist, noted in his book *Mortality*, published after his death, that the skyscraper hospital he attended had no 13th floor, a clever trick of construction.

Room 13 at the Rosenheim is right down the corridor and the walk takes long enough for nerves to jangle even more. The corridor of uncertainty, as Geoff Boycott might call it. How I dreaded hearing, on possible bad news days, the tannoy announcement by Colin: 'Daniel Thomas to room 13 please.'

Tall and with angular features and, I guessed, in his mid-forties, my initial impression of Colin McMaster was that he was super-charged, friendly and a bit chaotic. Colin asked Petra and me what we did - I imagine he was trying to get some impression of his patient's family. I told him I was a solicitor. Petra, an investment fund manager, hadn't worked while bringing up the children.

Colin confirmed the diagnosis of Ewing's sarcoma, and confirmed that there was cancer in the lungs and skeleton, in addition to the primary tumour in his pelvis. I had read somewhere that Ewing's was considered less serious than osteosarcoma, the other main type of primary bone cancer. Osteosarcoma too, mainly affects children. I had told Daniel what I'd read, unwisely because the information turned out to be wrong. Colin's reply was that there are bad and worse bone cancers. 'Only a minority of patients survive with your condition', he told Daniel. I could see tears welling up in Daniel's eyes, which haunts me even as I write this. I had the presence of mind to ask Colin to confirm that treatment wouldn't simply be on a palliative basis – the objective was to cure. Colin did confirm that. He also told Daniel that sometimes those at the back of the queue came to the front. A straw, at least, for Daniel (and us) to clutch at and I appreciated Colin providing it, the more so when I came to realise over the next weeks just how bad Daniel's cancer was.

Colin also used the word 'treatable.' I knew instinctively that treatable isn't the same as curable. It can be misleading when doctors say an illness is treatable because it sounds positive to the uninitiated. Chemotherapy and radiotherapy often kill cancer cells but fail to kill them all. The cancer then comes back, often in mutated and more virulent form. In fact, when doctors talk about cancer 'coming back' they really mean that some never went away but couldn't be detected. This is what Colin expected to happen in Daniel's case. There was a reasonable chance that Daniel would respond to chemotherapy – which we knew would take nine to twelve months – but just a few months later the cancer would be back, and then there would be little one could do.

Daniel asked, I recall, whether the cancer was stage 4. I don't know how he knew about the stages of cancer, which isn't an exact science but Stage 1 is the least serious. Christopher Hitchens wrote that all one needed to know about stage 4 is that there is no stage 5. Daniel's cancer would have been 4.9 if they had such a thing.

Out of the blue, Colin suggested a clinical trial for Daniel. The trial involved giving a drug called irinotecan for two cycles before moving on to the standard chemo regime for Ewing's. In fact, the standard treatment was also a trial, a large one across a number of European countries called Euro Ewing 99. I felt in no position to make a judgement about irinotecan and said we'd think about it.

Colin didn't make eye contact as I thanked him for his time, an early example of his discomfort in communicating when news was bad. But he'd dealt with us patiently.

The news had been even worse than I feared. When Daniel went to the loo, Petra said 'It's really bad, isn't it?' I said it was but not hopeless. Petra had correctly picked up the signals. I, with my literal lawyer's mind, tried to focus on the fact that Colin had indicated that a minority did survive. I knew that he didn't mean 49 per cent but hoped that perhaps he meant 20-30 per cent. I would have grabbed that. We determined that we would be positive for Daniel's sake.

Daniel, as was becoming the pattern, was his usual resilient self. His response, again, was to discuss what schoolwork he was going to do that weekend.

Colin's note of the meeting, which I got later, made sobering reading:

'*Seventeen year-old with relatively short history but extensive Ewings sarcoma … Aware that condition is treatable but recurrence frequent and that the disease chances for survival are low.*'

All he would say when I discussed prognosis with him a bit later was that it was 'possible' that Daniel would live for two years. Possible, but clearly not the expectation.

As soon as we got home after that first meeting, I got on to Gill Langley, whom I knew well through work. Gill worked for the Dr Hadwen Trust for Humane Research, which funds and promotes the use of alternatives to animal experiments. Gill is an excellent and well-respected scientist. I wanted to ask her about irinotecan. I knew something about clinical trials and the ethical issues which surround them and was concerned to make sure as best I could that this was the right option for Daniel. I was aware that clinicians, however ethical they are, may face conflicts of interest when considering a clinical trial for one of their patients. This is in two ways. Their legal duty is to the particular patient but they inevitably have an eye on the needs of their other patients with the same condition and perhaps other sufferers who are not their patients. The more data on a particular new treatment that is gathered, the more people with that condition stand to benefit. Doctors, quite understandably, want to push the boundaries, to test hypotheses. But what is in the best interests of patients generally may not be in the best interests of the individual patient.

The potential conflict is then heightened when the clinician is also a researcher. I knew Colin was in receipt of a Cancer Research UK grant. I had no reason to think that his advice that Daniel should have irinotecan was in any way tainted and, when I got to know him better, I realised that he was a man of integrity. But I didn't know that then.

Trusting the professionals

I was particularly concerned by the fact that we had already suffered a potentially crucial delay through St Peter's failure to carry out an MRI and the various bank holidays around this time were not helping either. What if the irinotecan had no impact? Colin later acknowledged that this was a legitimate concern but he didn't think that the additional delay would make any difference.

I sent Colin an email with my questions and copied Tim Briggs. It's interesting now to look back on Tim's reply:

> 'Whilst I appreciate that you need to be able to make the most informed judgement for Daniel, it's imperative that we start treatment and everybody will do their utmost for him. Sometimes you just have to put yourself in the hands of professionals who deal with this sort of problem all the time and let them get on with the job. Whilst I appreciate you must educate yourselves, I think that we as a team will always do our best for Daniel and I would urge you to take Colin McMaster's advice.'

Sound advice, no doubt, but I was never able to just 'trust the professionals.' I sometimes wished that I could – it would have made life easier and taken away much of the pressure. But Daniel's condition was just too serious for me to take a back seat and I realised that I had to test and challenge everything for his benefit. The motto of the Royal Society is 'nullius in verba' – take no one's word for it. It became my motto too. I knew from my own work that the more I am challenged, the more refined my judgements become and the better the decisions I make. With Daniel's cancer, I was acutely aware of my own severe limitations as a non-scientist delving into a highly technical and complicated area but as a litigation lawyer I was well used to dealing with subject matter of which I was largely ignorant – disputes can be about anything. I have dealt with many cases involving complicated science. The trick is to grasp enough to understand the broad issues, identify the right experts and work out the questions to ask. Similarly, with Ewing's I backed myself to learn enough to ask probing questions (to know, indeed, that there were questions to ask), to assess whom to trust amongst the many claiming they were the ones to trust and to make sure that Daniel got optimum treatment regardless of any NHS budgetary limitations.

I knew this had to be a joint effort between the doctors and Petra and me. Some parents prefer to leave everything to the doctors. I remember one father at UCH being exercised about the hospital food. I asked him what type of bone cancer his son had. 'I don't know and don't care', he replied. He was at the opposite end of the spectrum to me. I wanted to know everything. I do not criticise parents like him but temperamentally I had no choice but to get fully involved.

The weekend after the meeting with Colin, Daniel's

cousin JJ came to stay with me to help with research. At that time he was a second year medical student at Nottingham University. He, his sisters Katie and Annabel, Daniel and I had spent countless hours playing various sports together, at home and on holiday. JJ's dad, Julian, told me around this time that in light of my close relationship with JJ, I should regard him also as my son should Daniel not make it. It was a really kind gesture and it seemed superfluous to say that nothing could ever replace Daniel.

Trawling the internet trying to get more information on prognosis, JJ had come across an article by a nurse in Toronto. The article was a literature review of Ewing's – in other words, it didn't impart new information but brought together the consensus on treatment options and prognosis of leading practitioners. JJ suggested, apologetically, that I read it. The reason for his hesitation soon became apparent. The section on prognosis said that Ewing's patients with bone and lung metastases, like Daniel, had less than a 10 per cent chance of surviving for four years. It's not clear why four years' survival was taken as the marker – five years is usually the benchmark for 'successful' treatment with cancer. I knew that it was a fair assumption that the Ewing's figure would be even lower at five years. (One article I later read suggested that survival at five years for lung/bone met cases was just 2 per cent).

Worse than this, the Toronto article showed that Daniel ticked all the wrong boxes even within the dire bone/lung mets category. This was because his primary tumour was in his pelvis, it was (well) over a certain size, he was male and over fifteen.

The situation was obviously dire. With ultra low

expectations, I was actually excited to be told by a leading Italian Ewing's doctor shortly afterwards that, in their experience, 'only' 20 per cent with bone and lung mets survived for two years. Could Dan be one of the 20 per cent, despite all his additional bad signs?

I didn't discuss the article with Petra. She knew that the situation was desperately serious, but didn't want to hear statistics. It was important that, as the primary carer, she was able to stay as positive as possible because Daniel would pick up signals from her. She had her two girls, then aged twelve and eleven to think of as well. In addition, I wanted to protect her as much as possible, not least because she had already lost her husband in tragic circumstances. Some commented that this put more pressure on me but I felt able to handle it. I decided I would only need to share with Petra quite how bad things were if it was relevant to treatment decisions – if she was reluctant to do something which I felt needed doing. I'm not sure whether my approach was right but it felt right.

Chemotherapy

We had still not decided what to do about the irinotecan trial. The following Wednesday, Daniel had to have various tests - to his heart, kidney and so on - to make sure that he was fit for chemotherapy. Chemotherapy is not kind to the body. An aggressive cancer needed aggressive treatment. The tests were conducted in the Nuclear Medicine Department - the name itself was frightening. The tests were distressing for Daniel because he had to have a radioactive substance injected into his veins. He hated injections though sadly he got used to them. It seems relatively minor but it all added to the distress which he was feeling and to our distress having to watch his distress.

We were told to stay there after the tests to await the call to see Colin in the Teenage Cancer Unit. We waited and waited. Eventually Petra and Daniel left for home – Daniel had had enough and Petra needed to get back to Sasha and Florence. The waiting room in Nuclear Medicine became deserted and I suddenly felt emotional, as reality again struck. The sister there was as kind to me as she had been to Daniel.

I had another emotional hit when I first saw the sign 'Teenage Cancer Unit.' I recall Gavin Esler, the *Newsnight* presenter, saying he felt the same thing when he first visited the ward with his daughter Charlotte who had Hodgkin's lymphoma. Our paths didn't cross but Charlotte would have been on the TCU the same time as Daniel. She later did a film for *Newsnight* about her experience.

Colin eventually came in, accompanied by no fewer than six or seven colleagues: Sarah Rudman, his registrar, Vikky Riley, another of the specialist oncology nurses, probably an SHO (junior doctor) or two and various nurses. A consultant's retinue is a common feature on ward rounds – it's not surprising that some develop an inflated opinion of themselves, with patients hanging on their every word and their minions faithfully jotting them down – but the sheer number once again seemed to underline just how serious Daniel's condition was.

Irinotecan would not get rid of the cancer by itself and Daniel would soon have to move onto VIDE, the standard frontline chemotherapy combination for Ewing's, but it might help, was Colin's main message. He then left with most of the others, leaving Sarah and Vikky. Sarah said it was impossible to know whether irinotecan would help. It was like flipping a coin. On this basis, I was inclined not to choose the trial - why risk the delay of getting onto VIDE? - but Vikky chipped in that there was evidence suggesting that irinotecan could help. This made sense – there had to be some rationale for giving the drug first. Irinotecan was a long-established chemotherapy drug and Ewing's specialists were extrapolating from the experience with other cancers. I was to learn that no treatment had been developed specifically for Ewing's: it's just too rare for the drug companies to invest R&D in it. Sufferers of rare cancers get a raw deal for this reason. They nearly always have to piggy-back the experience with more common cancers, to which their cancer is inevitably biologically different.

I remember Vikky saying: 'Miracles do happen.' Her intentions were kindly, as they always were, but it was not reassuring to be told by a paediatric cancer specialist of seventeen years' standing that Daniel needed a miracle.

Another of the pre-chemo procedures was a bone marrow biopsy. This was on 5th May 2006, the day Daniel was due to start irinotecan. The point was to find out if his cancer was in his bone marrow as well as his bones. Sarah had explained that if cancer was detectable in the bone marrow, the chances were even less, though that hardly seemed possible. This time the operation took place at UCH.

When Daniel was being wheeled back to the ward, he suddenly started declining Latin nouns. This was anaesthesia-induced delirium but he was in fits of laughter and it was great to see. There was not to be much laughter later that day.

There was some uncertainty about the results when we eventually got them, but it appeared that the marrow was clear. This was a pleasant surprise given the fact that with Ewing's there is close correlation between bone metastases, which Daniel had in abundance, and bone marrow mets. In an expanding desert of bleak news we welcomed a small oasis of hope.

Sarah Rudman, the registrar, was surprised that we had no further questions about irinotecan. She had clocked me as someone with loads of questions and assumed there would be more that day. But I was happy it was the right thing to do, balancing the hoped-for benefits, albeit probably not great, against the risk of delaying VIDE. Bryony then explained about neutropaenia, where Daniel's white blood cells would take a real hit and he would be at risk of serious infections.

Daniel was due to have the irinotecan during the evening. Things dragged on, as they do in hospitals. It was around 9pm that the SHO, a serious young woman, came to insert the cannula in his vein. For some reason, she could not get the cannula in and another doctor had to come to help. This caused Daniel much distress. When finally, the irinotecan started to flow, he was in quite a state and became worse. In fact, he had a full-blown panic attack which lasted most of the night. With a reasonably sheltered life – my generation never saw conscripted war –this was the most distressing thing I had directly witnessed.

The idea had been that I would stay the night with Daniel. Because of his distress, Petra stayed as well. We had continuously to stroke his arm and constantly reassure him. Daniel regressed into childhood that night. He asked me to hold him and, a sure sign that he was frightened, told me that he loved me. As a child he used to say this all the time, but not as a teenager. He said it to Petra and his sisters but I guess it was different for a teenager with his dad. (As a child the expression of affection was sometimes tactical. Once, when he was three, he came into the kitchen and said 'Dad, I love you', followed immediately by 'I have just spilt some ink'... .)

We were told that these panic attacks do sometimes happen when chemo starts. My interpretation was that Daniel had been suppressing his fears over the past few weeks and that the powder keg exploded when he was finally confronted with the reality of treatment. Perhaps the operation earlier that day and the discussions about neutropaenia and the clinical trial had exacerbated things. Daniel's explanation was more prosaic: the cannula incident had been painful and the chemo felt strange going into this body. Thankfully, he was calmer when we went home the next morning. The experience was horrible for him and really upset Petra and me. More tears for the parents.

Welcome to the world of cancer

Welcome to the world of cancer. We were now well and truly part of it. The past few weeks had been horrendous and there was no sign of the horror letting up. My hope that we could enter chemo with all it entailed with realistic hope had been dashed. We barely had time to draw breath because already Daniel was having to deal with the side-effects of irinotecan.

Nevertheless the first chemo was a landmark and I tried to take stock. It was clear that Daniel was seriously ill. The chances of his surviving for even a few years were very slim. What was going through his mind? It's difficult to know. He had approached each stage up to now with acceptance and stoicism but the panic attack seemed to show what was going on deep in his psyche. He must have been really scared. How can anyone cope with devastating news like this, let alone when just seventeen?

Around this time, Daniel told us that he didn't want any more discussions with his doctors about prognosis, treatment options or scan results. The news had kept getting worse and he couldn't cope with any more. His refusal to engage became a major source of friction with his consultant, Colin McMaster.

As for me, to say that this was the greatest challenge I had ever faced was an understatement. Like most people, I had had lots of ups and downs in my life. Some I coped with better than others. But this was of a completely different order. The thought of losing Daniel was just too painful to contemplate. And he had all the side-effects and dangers of treatment to face and therefore so did we, by proxy. Nothing in life prepares you for the serious illness of your child. There's no manual to turn to and one has to fall back on instinct honed imperfectly by life's cumulative experiences.

I cried easily and often in those early months. Harvey, my new neighbour, remembers me breaking down when I told him the diagnosis and his not really knowing how to react (he and his partner Constance were to become good friends). I would sleep fitfully and wake up feeling sick and not rested. I couldn't help picturing Daniel's funeral in my mind's eye and thinking about what I would say in the eulogy. I would tell myself that if Daniel was going to die, I would prefer him to go quickly. We couldn't bear the thought of his suffering, especially if it was to no effect. Sometimes I half-wished that he'd be killed in an accident. Strangely, I found refuge in car journeys. I'd sometime just drive around aimlessly. When on my own, I didn't want the journey back from London, previously a nuisance, to end. In the era of mobile phones I knew it was illogical but, cocooned in the car, I felt safe from more bad news. I also found myself pining for Chicago, my faithful old dog who'd died fifteen years earlier. Perhaps like Daniel I was regressing to a more secure world.

Previous brushes with cancer

What had I known about cancer before this? No one escapes its clutches so I knew something. I remember the tube ads in the 1980s telling us that one in three got the disease and one in four died from it. The incidence is increasing, largely the product of a rising ageing population; people who get cancer in their later years would in ages past often have already died from something else. But this doesn't explain why growing numbers of children and young adults are getting the disease. Surely that can only really be attributable to the environment, lifestyle and diet?

When I was a child, cancer was the disease that dare not speak its name. People skirted round it. Even more than today, it was viewed with dread and talked of in hushed tones. Patients sometimes weren't told that they had cancer.

I remember the wife of the vicar of our church in Cardiff, informed she had just six months to live, drinking water containing live woodlice. Mrs Rosser lived for several years. That was one alternative remedy I didn't look at for Daniel (although a doctor in Bridgend hypothesised that live maggots might eat cancer based on their acknowledged usefulness in wound-healing).

I remember Ray Price, the mother of a friend, instead of asking 'Why me?' the plaintive cry of so many cancer patients, asking 'Why not me?' Daniel never asked 'Why me?'

I remember Mike Hannell, my German teacher at Marlborough College. Mike was a Welshman but had gone on an England rugby tour (which is sacrilege where I come from). As a fourteen year-old I wrote him an awkward letter when I learnt his arm was to be amputated. My family has always been strong on writing to people going through a bad time. My father wrote a much better letter. But I'm pleased I wrote. Mike died in his early thirties.

I remember Michael, one of Daniel's class-mates in primary school, dying of leukaemia in his early teens after missing so much schooling. His illness upset Petra and me, but we didn't begin to understand.

Fast forward some decades and my friend Jim died of a brain tumour. His illness was painful to witness. Intelligent and articulate, at times he could hardly string a sentence together. There were other times of relative lucidity but in a way they were worse for Jim because they highlighted his limitations. Marilyn, Jim's partner, once related how his consultant shouted at him when he didn't understand something. It beggared belief.

Jim would normally have been interested in complementary and dietary approaches to cancer. A long-time vegan on animal cruelty grounds, his lifestyle was healthy (a reminder that lifestyle, while it undoubtedly helps, is not necessarily a defence against cancer). But his illness meant that he could barely comprehend the chemotherapy and radiotherapy he underwent, let alone look for other solutions.

While in New York one weekend I picked up a copy of Hulda Regehr Clark's *A Cure For All Cancers*, which claims to do what it says on the tin if readers follow its detailed prescription. I was naïve about complementary approaches to cancer then and was to learn that anything which claims to be able to cure all cancers is, almost by definition, misguided and, worse, a cruel predation on the vulnerable.

Dad with my Grandmother on her ninetieth birthday.

There are some 200 cancers with thousands of subtypes, all of them biologically different. There's no magic bullet. This isn't to say that some complementary approaches can't be valuable. I gave the book it to Marilyn, Jim's partner, but I think she wisely kept it to herself. Dr Clark died in 2009, of cancer.

In late March 2006 I took Gill to meet Jim and Marilyn in his nursing home. She was bowled over. Jim even managed to strum a few chords on his guitar. Less than three weeks later Daniel was diagnosed. I think that Marilyn spared Jim the distress of knowing this, although she had to explain why my visits dried up. I did visit one last time, in July 2006, about ten days before Jim died. He was in a deep sleep and emaciated. I found the visit upsetting, because I knew I was seeing a dear friend for the last time but also because, inevitably, I projected into the future Daniel was likely to have.

Jim's funeral was upsetting for similar reasons but I wanted to go, for his sake and for Marilyn's. I've learnt that showing support by attending funerals is so important.

I also remember Gwenno, a teenager who died of leukaemia not long before Daniel was diagnosed. I followed Gwenno's story from afar and noticed how good news mysteriously quickly turned to bad to good again. It was a pattern I was to get used to.

But my closest encounter with cancer before Daniel's diagnosis was with my father. Dad was sixty-four when he was diagnosed with bowel cancer in 1988. He had an operation to remove the tumour and for a few months all seemed to be well. His surgeon, a former Welsh rugby international, was confident he'd got all the cancer out, as surgeons usually are. Dad travelled to the US for a holiday. Then one day in July 1989, I got a panicky call from him. The cancer was back, in his liver. Worse, there was nothing they could do about it. There was no treatment. He was going to die. In the event, Dad lived for less than six weeks.

What do I remember about that time? I remember going straight down to Foyles, the famous book shop in Charing Cross Road in London to see if I could find out more. In those pre-internet days, researching as a layman was a real challenge.

I remember with my sisters managing, with some pressing, to get Dad into the Bristol Cancer Centre (now the Penny Brohn Centre). The centre which was relatively new then, adopted a holistic, diet-based, complementary approach to cancer and had gained publicity and sparked controversy when it was endorsed by Prince Charles. I remember how touched Dad was that we were trying to find solutions for him. In the event, he was too ill to be at the centre, lasting just one day. He went there on the day of the Marchioness disaster on the Thames.

I remember he'd earlier gone to see a faith healer in Devon – Dad always had a strong faith. Faith didn't heal him but the session gave him comfort.

I remember that we spent the last ten days of Dad's life together as a family. It was pitiful to see a strong, vibrant man metamorphosing into a weak imitation in no time at all. Cancer can do that to you. I remember sleeping those ten nights in his room and thinking about the reversal in roles – when I was a little boy I would go into his bed for comfort and now here was I providing comfort to him. It meant I could take him to the toilet in the night. I remember being fearful of waking up with Dad dead next to me but he confided to a friend that it meant a lot having me stay with him and I was glad to.

I remember Dad, who had sailed through life despite a poor upbringing in a Welsh mining valley, becoming more empathic as his own suffering gave him a greater insight into the weaknesses of others.

I remember Daniel being baptised in my parents' house by Rev Saunders Davies, a compassionate vicar, a little earlier than planned, because Dad was dying. That was one emotional service.

I remember the GP increasing Dad's morphine to keep him comfortable but in the knowledge that it would probably hasten death – a grey area of medical ethics which philosophers categorise as a 'principle of double effect' (pain relief and hastened death). I understand why doctors do this. I remember bed sores developing in no time at all.

I remember the importance of hope to Dad, even in his desperate circumstances. A classicist like Daniel, he used to say 'dum spiro spero' - 'while I breathe, I hope' – a saying generally attributed to Cicero. I later thanked the Bristol Cancer Centre for the hope they'd given, if only for a short time and suggesting that even false hope was worthwhile. I would phrase the last bit differently now, but my passion about hope remains. Dad, a Francophile steeped in French literature, may have agreed with Albert Camus: 'Where there is no hope, it's incumbent on us to invent it.'

I remember handing Daniel, then nearly eleven months-old, to Dad on his death-bed and breaking down in tears. How Dad would have loved to see Daniel grow up and how proud he would have been of him. Daniel crawled for the first time literally one hour before Dad died.

I remember that thankfully we were all gathered round his bed when Dad died, late in the evening.

I remember, finally, the wave of emotion that hit me when I saw how full the church was at the funeral. The service opened with that great Welsh hymn of hope, *Mi Glywaf Dyner Lais (I Hear Your Gentle Voice),* sung to *Gwahoddiad (Invitation),* a melody to stir the coldest of hearts.

Ignorant

So cancer was not a new experience for me. But I was still overwhelmingly ignorant when Daniel was diagnosed. I knew that chemotherapy caused hair to fall out and made one sick but I didn't even know the difference between chemotherapy and radiotherapy. It sounds amazing to say that now. I would have struggled to tell you the difference between white and red blood cells, never having studied biology. Bone cancer sounded painful but I knew nothing about sarcomas.

I didn't know then just how common paediatric cancer is. In the US it kills more children than asthma, diabetes, cystic fibrosis and AIDS combined. Forty-six children are diagnosed there every day and seven die. One more statistic: cancer hits between 1:300 and 1:500 children. So, for a family of three children, the odds that one will get cancer are not far below 1 per cent. That surprised me.

I was familiar with some cancer language. I had something of a head start because I had been involved in a long-running and ground-breaking European case about the patenting of the oncogene, which predisposes mice to cancer. I knew that an oncologist was a cancer specialist. Over the next few years I was to become fluent in cancer-speak. Like all professionals, oncologists develop their own language which adds to the mystique and can inadvertently serve to create a barrier for patients. I also knew that cancer invaded any organs it could find. This perhaps, is why discussion of cancer is full of military imagery. One 'fights' cancer in a way one doesn't fight multiple sclerosis or heart failure. Someone wins or loses the 'battle' with cancer. Patients are nearly always 'brave.' In 1971, President Nixon declared 'war' on cancer and his legislation was subtitled *'An Act to Conquer Cancer.'*

But, overall, I was starting from a low base of knowledge. I knew I had to get up-to-speed as quickly as possible.

Getting used to cancer

Dad (after Daniel declined to do something): Sometimes
you have to do what the other person wants
Daniel (aged four): I know
Dad: Right, well let's start now
Daniel: No, let's start another day

Now that Daniel had received his first chemotherapy at UCH, the focus was about to shift back to St Peter's, our local hospital. Daniel had treatment or diagnostic procedures at no fewer than eight hospitals, five in this country and three abroad. Co-operation between the UK hospitals was essential and I became convinced that the then Government was right to want to make patients' information centrally available (with appropriate safeguards) so that any doctor can access it. The current situation leads to confusion and waste and, inevitably, to mistakes.

St Peter's had a particularly important role. Amongst many other nasty side effects, chemotherapy depresses the white blood cells and in particular the neutrophils, which fight infections. If Daniel's neutrophil count went below one (as it would) and he developed a temperature of 38°C (the combination is called febrile neutropaenia), we would have to get him to the local hospital quickly so that he could have life-saving antibiotics intravenously. The neutropaenic period – when his neutrophils would fall below one – would be between days seven and fourteen post-chemo. So he would need frequent blood tests.

Before the first neutropaenic period Bryony and Vikky, the two specialist teenage oncology nurses, came down to Chobham to see Daniel. They were concerned about his panic attack. Specialists nurses act as much as social workers as nurses, providing much-needed psychological support and liaising with medical staff in the community. Good ones are worth their weight in gold. Vikky spoke to Daniel by herself; whether she got much out of him I'm not sure. Like many others, she commented how much Daniel looked like me. I couldn't see it. My stock reply during the cancer years was 'As if Daniel doesn't have enough to put up with already.' Daniel would smile while inwardly sighing, no doubt. Secretly, I always liked people noting the resemblance. Illogical, but for me it cemented the bond between us.

Daniel was pretty vulnerable during this time. For a while, we didn't leave him by himself, even for a minute. There was much daytime TV viewing. More punishment. We became fans of *Deal or No Deal*, with its strangely alluring combination of greed, mutual competitor support and Noel Edmonds. Daniel loved *Frasier* and *The Simpsons*, too and knew every episode. He gradually became more self-sufficient.

Petra and I took the risk of infection seriously. We'd been told of the importance of hygiene in the home and scrupulously cleaned areas Daniel had contact with. I don't think my house had ever been so clean. Gill was good at helping with that. At UCH too, we were assiduous in following the detailed instructions for cleaning the bathroom after use. Not only did various items – door handle, wash basin taps, etc – have to be cleaned with disinfectant wipes but it had to be done in a certain order.

Colin McMaster's view was that most infections are self-generated. When Daniel's defences were low - when he was neutropaenic - the infection would probably come from within the body. We could create a hygienic paradise and it might make no difference. But we still felt it important to reduce the risk of infection as much as possible. Chemotherapy is dangerous. Quite often cancer patients die not of cancer but of complications caused by treatment. I read a study showing that, out of 350 patients with Ewing's, seven had died from chemo complications. That was a frightening statistic. In fact, it has been estimated that up to 10 per cent of cancer patients die as a result of their treatment. The list of potential side-effects with chemotherapy drugs is long. This is in part pharmaceutical companies covering themselves – if something goes wrong they can say 'We did warn you that this was possible.' But the risks are real too. For example, doxorubicin – one of the types of chemo Daniel was soon to get – is cardiotoxic: it damages the heart.

Daniel was given a drug called mesna to counteract the nephrotoxic – kidney-damaging – effect of ifosfamide, which he received with doxorubicin. That is the problem with cancer treatment – the drugs are so powerful that you need other drugs to deal with the side-effects and those drugs themselves cause side-effects. One day there will be a better way, perhaps with the much-vaunted but so far largely disappointing targeted treatments. Patients of Daniel's generation have to put up with the blunderbuss approach, where the drugs attack the cancer if you are lucky, but cause a lot of collateral damage in the process. Cancer treatment has been aptly described as medieval – it poisons (chemotherapy), burns (radiotherapy) or mutilates (surgery) – and the cocktail of torture for Ewing's is particularly sadistic. Plus chemo and radiotherapy can themselves cause cancer.

Medical negligence

I'd already been in touch with St Peter's to prepare the ground for febrile neutropaenia episodes. I'd wanted to write anyway about their failure to do an MRI between January and April 2006. Had the doctors been negligent? Petra felt particularly strongly about this. I wrote a letter to the orthopaedic consultant, Mr Constant Busch. According to the hospital website, one of his specialities is hip pain in young people. He'd diagnosed a haematoma (blood clot) in Daniel's hip. I didn't say in the letter that I was a lawyer and didn't threaten legal action. However, the letter was carefully constructed. I regretted afterwards saying was that I didn't want to hear platitudes. That was not necessary even if it was true. I also said that if it transpired that the three months we had lost could have made a significant contribution to the spread of the cancer, we would be extremely angry. I asked that Daniel be treated as a priority patient from now on, with the very best care.

I delivered the letter by hand and had a call the same day from Mr Busch. He expressed concern, both about what had happened and about Daniel. He would look into things as soon as possible. I appreciated the call, even if it was no doubt inspired in part by fear of legal action.

I received a written reply a few days later. Mr Busch admitted that Daniel should have had an MRI, if not when he first presented then certainly at some point before we did eventually have one (privately). That was a candid admission. He denied that cost had been a factor. I was not convinced. MRIs cost around £800. Unlike other scans, they don't carry any risk. It's difficult to understand why Daniel shouldn't have had one if cost wasn't a factor. At the first appointment, the registrar had asked two consultants whether Daniel should have an MRI, based on the x-ray result. They advised it wasn't necessary, but it was clearly on the agenda. On such seemingly small medical decisions so much can rest.

Mr Busch went on to say that he didn't know whether an earlier MRI would have made any difference to Daniel's chances. In legal terms this issue would have been crucial. To win a case for medical negligence, one has to show two things. First, that the standard of care fell below a reasonable standard – the doctor did something which no reasonable doctor would have done, or, more relevantly here, failed to do what every reasonable doctor would have done. Mr Busch admitted that they had breached this duty of care by failing to do an MRI.

The second hurdle is then to show that that negligence has made a difference. Lawyers call this causation – has the negligence caused 'loss?' In Daniel's case, his main loss would consist of delayed diagnosis making cure less likely. There was no doubt that an earlier MRI would have revealed the cancer, but would earlier treatment have improved his chances? It would certainly have reduced his period of pain and the law would compensate for that. But that was a secondary consideration.

Causation is frequently difficult to prove in medicine. Often, even if everything had been done perfectly, the outcome would have been the same. However, the crucial thing with cancer is to keep it localised. The chances of survival drop dramatically if it spreads. These days, children with Ewing's have a 65-70 per cent chance of living for five years if it remains localised, but only a 30 per cent chance if it has spread to the lungs (lungs are usually the first site of metastasis) and as I mentioned earlier, a less than 10 per cent chance if it has gone to the bones.

Highly complicated though the process of metastasation is there must, logically, be a point in time when it becomes unstoppable. The longer the delay in diagnosis, the greater the chance of metastasation. In Daniel's case could it have taken place during the months after Petra first took him to St Peter's? If so, the delay would have drastically reduced his chances. Even if metastasation had already happened, his primary tumour, in his pelvis, was clearly growing during this period. A large primary tumour with Ewing's is prognostically worse than a small one (though this may be linked to the metastasis issue – a large tumour is more likely to have metastasised, by simple dint of the fact that it has existed for longer). The massive size of Daniel's pelvic tumour also meant that it was probably inoperable, which itself reduced his chances.

These were imponderable questions. But for me they were irrelevant. I wasn't interested in bringing a legal case against St Peter's. My focus was always on getting the best treatment for Daniel, whatever situation we found ourselves in. I didn't want to waste energy in recrimination. I feel ambivalent about suing the NHS anyway. There are times, no doubt, when it can have a salutary effect in improving standards and for some patients compensation can be really important for quality of life. But because trusts self-insure, medical negligence cases take money away from patient care (in 2014, the NHS Litigation Authority put aside £25.6bn for known and future claims). I didn't want to do that. So I didn't pursue the question of causation.

In fact, a good deal of my anger is directed not at St Peter's doctors – though they were certainly at fault – but at myself. I simply have no explanation why I meekly accepted the doctors' assurances given to Petra, that Daniel had a haematoma which would get better in time. I should have questioned the diagnosis, especially when the swelling didn't disappear and Daniel's pain and walking got worse.

People say to me, kindly, that I shouldn't blame myself for accepting what we were told, that we do accept what doctors tell us. But this doesn't reassure me. I knew that doctors get things wrong. I'd done some medical negligence cases years ago. I'd also acted in several negligence cases against other professionals, such as solicitors, barristers and surveyors. I'm not starry-eyed about professionals. There are many lawyers, including eminent QCs who I don't particularly rate. I don't mistrust professionals as a class, either - there are any number, doctors included, who do a fantastic job - but everyone gets things wrong, no matter how qualified or talented. And I knew that NHS doctors often work under pressure and face resource shortages. So my failure to push on Daniel's behalf during those three months is inexcusable and I deeply regret it, whether or not it affected the eventual outcome.

Perhaps in mitigation is the fact that I didn't know that bone cancer was a children's cancer. When one thinks of childhood cancer, one thinks of leukaemia, perhaps lymphoma, and Daniel's symptoms were not ones I associated with those blood cancers. GPs frequently misdiagnose sarcomas, sometimes over a period of months. But none of this exonerates me. I let Daniel down.

I knew at any rate that I wouldn't be repeating my mistake. From now on I would be on top of everything. For the moment my priority was to make sure that Daniel got the best treatment from St Peter's. I wanted to use the unspoken threat of legal action to make sure that they upped their game. We could have used Frimley Park as our shared care hospital. It's only a little further away from Chobham and though similar in size, probably has a better local reputation. But I wanted to use St Peter's defensiveness to Daniel's advantage. It doesn't feel particularly comfortable to write that but we were dealing with an extremely serious, life-threatening illness and needed everything in our favour. So I made sure that the key people at St Peter's knew about Daniel's cancer prior to any admission for febrile neutropaenia. This included the haematologist who would be responsible for his care, Dr Laurie. I didn't want to rely simply on who happened to be on duty on admission. I heard that Daniel's case was discussed at a meeting. So things were set up in advance.

Neutropaenia

From day seven of that first cycle of irinotecan we took Daniel's temperature frequently. On day eight, I was out having a pizza with Gill when Petra rang to say that Daniel had a temperature of 38°C. I came home straightaway. The guideline was that, if temperature remained at 38 or 38.5 for thirty minutes, one should take the patient to hospital immediately. Daniel didn't quite meet this criterion but we decided to take no chances. I felt quite panicky, knowing time was of the essence. Daniel was calm and told me to calm down. When we got to A&E, the receptionist didn't know what neutropaenia was. Perhaps my expectations were too high but surely Daniel couldn't have been the first patient with chemo-induced neutropaenia presenting at A&E? I had to push to get Daniel a separate room – the whole point of neutropaenia is that one doesn't have sufficient neutrophils to fight infections and the waiting-room was full of people.

I rang the teenage cancer ward at UCH because I wanted them to be involved in Daniel's emergency care. 'St Peter's don't seem to know what they're doing', I said. This was probably unfair and it also served to transmit my anxiety to Daniel at a time when I should have been reassuring him. As I became more experienced, I learnt to deal with even difficult situations more calmly and to hide my anxiety from Daniel. But I was genuinely scared on this first febrile neutropaenia.

Daniel was admitted and put on intravenous antibiotics, though not as quickly as I would have liked (but, again with the benefit of hindsight, probably quickly enough). His neutrophils were 0.5, which I thought was very low but was in fact manageable. I was learning the hard way, at the cost of much stress. The staff gave Daniel paracetamol too early. Paracetamol brings down temperature, a good thing, but by the same token masks the underlying fever. So it's better to hold off until the patient's condition is clear.

Because he was neutropaenic, Daniel was given his own room on the ward. He was subject to reverse barrier nursing. Sometimes patients have to be isolated to protect staff; in Daniel's case it was to protect him from infection by staff. He was very ill that night and at one point his temperature rose to 39.5°C (I can still see Petra's look of shock the next morning). 39.5 - 103.1 in old money - isn't dangerously high but Daniel's temperature seemed to be rising inexorably. The nurses didn't seem to be concerned but I felt desolate and feared at one point that I might be losing him. No doubt another overreaction but my feelings of isolation were heightened by the fact that I couldn't get a mobile signal in the room and wasn't prepared to leave Daniel even for a few seconds to get a better signal. I've never felt so lonely.

He was on hourly obs – observations of his vital signs – through the night and I would sometimes ask the nurses to do them even more frequently. One nurse kindly mopped his brow to get the temperature down. I didn't get much sleep. I set my alarm for just before the next scheduled obs to make sure that it took place. Sleep was also at a premium because Daniel was having frequent diarrhoea. I would accompany him to the toilet, helping him to manoeuvre the drip trolleys attached to both his arms, one for the i/v antibiotics, the other for fluids. I would wipe his bottom – not great for a seventeen year-old to have his dad do that but Daniel didn't seem to mind. I would then manoeuvre him back to his bed and then start the cleaning-up process. As at UCH and at home, I was scrupulous about doing this properly, frequently changing the plastic pinafore and gloves I had to wear and making full use of the antiseptic wipes. More than once, just as the process was complete, Daniel would announce that he needed to go again. Broken sleep became a feature of hospital stays.

Things had calmed down by the morning and so had I. After a while, Daniel's temperature returned to normal. The antibiotics – broad-spectrum antibiotics, as they called them – were kicking in, thankfully.

Daniel was in hospital for a few days. Afterwards I wrote to Dr Laurie, thanking him for the care Daniel had received. He indicated that they were still learning about how to deal with febrile neutropaenia. Perhaps it wasn't as common as I'd imagined. I learnt later that many chemotherapy patients don't become neutropaenic, whether because their chemo wasn't as strong as Daniel's or because it wasn't especially damaging to neutrophils. Dr Laurie finished his reply with interesting advice: 'It remains helpful for both Daniel and you to emphasise the need for urgency with respect to suspected neutropaenic sepsis and not allow staff to make you feel you're making a fuss ...'

Daniel had a few days at home before he was due in hospital again for his second irinotecan. We'd got through the first cycle. It had been anything but easy. There was the awful panic attack, nausea, diarrhoea, the febrile neutropaenia. Daniel was weak and still in considerable pain, though they'd upped his pain relief. As Colin pithily put it, this was all normal for them but horrid for Daniel. The pain relief is something else I chide myself about. The analgesia Daniel had been given by his GP was proving inadequate. The pain was waking him at night, though he was accepting as usual. I assumed that there was nothing else that could be given and that we would have to wait for the swelling to go. I am again, looking back, astonished at my naïveté. Chris Henry took control of his pain relief and articulated the mantra that no patient need be in pain. Not quite true, sadly.

Second opinion

During our time at home I wrote to Colin McMaster about getting a second opinion from St Jude's Children's Cancer Hospital in the US, which I'd come across in my research. St Jude's is a centre of excellence. Funnily enough, its founder, in 1962, was called Danny Thomas. According to *Wikipedia* he was a Lebanese American nightclub comedian. So that's what Lebanese American nightclub comedians do in their spare time. St Jude Thaddeus is the patron saint of hopeless causes. That seemed pretty apt for our situation.

When Colin came to see Daniel with Sarah Rudman, his registrar, during Daniel's second chemo admission at UCH, I again raised the issue of a second opinion. I explained that we wanted to make absolutely sure that Daniel was getting the best treatment and said that I knew from my own work, test cases against the Government and so on, that with difficult problems, discussion with other experts helped to refine judgement. Colin brushed aside the suggestion, saying that much thought had gone into the Euro Ewing's protocol (which Daniel would soon be on). The time for discussion with other doctors would be if Daniel relapsed.

I felt I had handled the discussion ineptly with my analogy of test cases. I knew what I was getting it but the reference to legal cases might have put Colin on the defensive and it broke my informal rule not to refer to the fact that I was a lawyer. I heard about a lawyer in Bristol who at the first meeting with his child's oncologist warned him: 'I am a lawyer and if you make any mistakes I will sue you.' Not only was this crass and inappropriate, it could also be counter-productive. It could make the doctor defensive in treatment choices, when creativity might be needed despite the risk which accompanies it.

Because of the side-effects Daniel had experienced on the first cycle, Colin reduced the dose of irinotecan by 20 per cent. I could see the logic but it worried me. Surely a reduced dose would be less effective and we needed maximum effectiveness. I raised this with Sarah. She assured me that the reduction would not influence efficacy, which didn't really make sense – why give Daniel more than he needed on the first cycle, with the increased risk of nasty and dangerous side-effects? I am sure Sarah, out of kind motives, was trying to allay my concern.

Colin also said that Daniel would have G-CSF injections for ten days. This was the first we had heard of these injections. They boost the white cell count and therefore help to stave off infection. They are pretty standard with Ewing's care and I don't know why Daniel hadn't had them with his first cycle, except that they are very expensive (in the US, insurance companies sometimes kick up a fuss about sanctioning them). They're a burden to the patient – they have to be injected into the stomach, thigh etc – and perhaps Colin was waiting to see if they were needed in Daniel's case. The district nurse had to come every day to administer the injections, until several cycles in when Daniel trusted Petra to give them. He never trusted me to give them, which was fine by me.

Before he was due to have the second irinotecan, Daniel had a PICC line put in. This is a line inserted into an arm and through to near the heart. It carries chemo and other fluids. Blood can also be drawn from it. The idea is to save cannulas having to be put in all the time, or injections straight into the vein. PICC lines make life easier for everyone but it's an extra thing to attend to. The dressing needed to be changed every few days and there's a risk of infection or even of thrombosis. Showering is difficult and Daniel couldn't go swimming.

One of our major concerns was avoiding a recurrence of the panic attack during the second chemo infusion. I got in touch with a couple of people who I knew suffered from panic attacks. One sent a relaxation tape. Daniel seemed confident that it wouldn't happen again; we were less confident. Whether because of the earlier panic attack or by luck, we were given a side-room at UCH for the second irinotecan, complete with flat-screen TV. Usually side-rooms were reserved for teenagers who needed to be isolated. Daniel was happy with his new accommodation.

Annika, from Sweden, was a play co-ordinator on the ward. She always tried to involve Daniel in various events outside the hospital. She sat with Daniel during the chemo infusion, using visualisation techniques. What would he like to imagine doing? Playing tennis with his sister Sasha, he replied. Tennis was Daniel's first love. At one point he opened his left eye as Annika was visualising yet another rally with him, and looked at me as if to say 'What's this all about?' I knew then that, if he was able to laugh at the visualisation, he was going to be ok, and so it proved. Perhaps the distraction helped.

Daniel was weak immediately after the second infusion of irinotecan and I had to help him to the toilet. He was sick several times. The extraordinary thing is that that was the last time he vomited for 495 days. People associate chemotherapy with nausea and it can indeed be a major problem, but anti-emetic drugs are so much better these days. (It's pretty sad that I know the exact number of days between vomiting episodes. But I kept a record of everything. I wanted to celebrate the 500-day landmark but it was not to be).

On that Saturday morning after chemo 2, Daniel was in much better spirits. We watched a programme about the deaf percussionist Evelyn Glennie. That afternoon, I went to my sister's fiftieth birthday party in Newbury. I broke down talking to people but managed to hold it together with Mum who was still oblivious to what was going on.

Back home that evening Daniel was in a grouchy mood as we watched the Unicef pro-am football match from Old Trafford. This was to prove unusual for him – he was remarkably even-tempered during most of his cancer journey – but it made me worry about how he would cope with dying. I knew that could soon be on the agenda. On those rare occasions when Daniel was in a bad mood, Petra and I were tolerant with him. Perhaps too much so. Vikky explained that children with cancer still needed boundaries.

The second cycle was in fact much better than the first. The nausea was under control and amazingly so it seemed to us, Daniel was not admitted to hospital with febrile neutropaenia. It's impossible to underestimate the importance of this to him (or us). When his life was dominated by hospitals, tests and unpleasant side effects, those extra days of relative normality at home, before the next cycle, were priceless.

We still kept a close eye on his blood counts, sometimes every day. The district nurse would come to take the blood. Sometimes, if there was urgency, Petra or I would take the sample to St Peter's. Either way there then followed a routine by which I tried to get the results. Unlike UCH, St Peter's would not give them direct to us. They had to go via the GP. So I would ring the GP. The reception staff were always helpful. Sometimes they said they couldn't give me the results because Daniel was seventeen. I would patiently reply that this is the way he wanted things – even when considerably older – and that would do the trick (I also got Daniel to give them a letter of authority). The results should have been on the GPs' system immediately but never were. Sometimes the receptionist would chase, sometimes I would. Eventually the results would arrive. Sometimes the receptionist would give me the results, sometimes I would have to wait to speak to one of the doctors, all unfailingly helpful in explaining their significance.

I went through this rigmarole countless times. It may seem minor in the scheme of things and it was, but the amount of chasing Petra and I had to do over the years, for one reason or another, was enormous and could add to the stress, on top of everything else. Being a cancer parent is extremely time-consuming, particularly if one adopts the hands-on approach that we did.

Daniel's hair began to fall out during this second irinotecan cycle. Tufts of hair appeared on his pillow. We had been told to expect this precipitated moulting but that didn't make it any easier for Daniel. He decided to shave it all off. Many cancer patients prefer baldness to ugly strands of hair sticking out. It's not only hair on the top of the head which one loses, but also eyebrows and eyelashes. If anything this is worse because they define a face. Baldness is a fashion choice for some young men, but no one shaves off their eyebrows and eyelashes. Many assume that losing hair is worse for female patients and it probably is, but it was a real issue for Daniel too. He was thin and gaunt and pale and now truly looked like a cancer patient. It's an awful comparison but the image which kept coming to mind was of concentration camp inmates.

Needless to say, none of this had the slightest impact on our love for Daniel. Even if other people saw him differently, he was still the same Daniel and his wonderful personality remained. But it was still hard to see him looking like this. It was a constant reminder of what he and we were facing. I think it was especially hard for Petra and the girls because they saw Daniel like this all the time. At least when I was away from him I had some emotional respite.

Daniel made it to the Queen's tennis tournament

during the course of cycle 2. This was, I think, his first outing since treatment started. When we arrived in west London, we were faced with a long queue. It was already a hot day. Daniel was too weak to stand around so I offered to explain the position. Daniel was embarrassed but let me do it. He stood some distance away as I spoke to the steward. He always hated drawing attention to his illness. We had a memorable day and stayed until 9.30 at night. Too long really and I worried but Daniel wanted to watch Andy Murray in a late evening doubles match. I didn't know how many opportunities we would get like this.

Results

Daniel was due to have some scans during cycle 2 to see whether he was responding to irinotecan. The literature we'd been given at the outset indicated that, if it worked really well, he might continue on the drug. He had MRI and CT scans in June 2006. We were promised the results the following Monday. When I rang that day, Sarah the registrar said we wouldn't have the results for a week. I asked why, politely. Like her successor Charlotte Moss, Sarah had the priceless gift of conveying that she had more time than I imagine she did. Daniel liked her. However, on this occasion Sarah annoyed me. She said I had to understand that Daniel was not their only patient. This was uncalled for. I simply wanted to know the reason for the delay. We were naturally anxious about the results.

I decided early on what my approach in dealing with hospital staff would be and nearly always kept to it. I would always be polite and acknowledge, to myself and when appropriate to them, the pressures they were facing and the fact that they were dealing with several seriously ill children. Every child with cancer was as important as Daniel. I would periodically apologise to Colin and the other doctors that my proactive approach caused them additional work. I made a point of expressing gratitude, to staff at all levels and at all times, even when half-asleep in the middle of the night. Daniel learnt to do the same. (Saying thank you is so important. When Daniel banged his head in a playground as a toddler, I thanked Lambeth Council for their foresight in installing cushioned flooring and received a grateful reply - I expect they were used to getting just brickbats).

But the bottom line for me was that my son was facing an incredibly difficult challenge and our job as his parents was to make sure that he got the very best. I wanted to avoid confrontation, not least for my own sanity, but ultimately this was not a popularity contest. If some members of staff regarded me as pushy and someone who irritatingly challenged advice, well that was just too bad. Daniel had been dealt a spiteful hand and we were determined to give him every chance of beating the terrible odds.

The delay in getting scan results was to become a bugbear, especially when I discovered that other countries were often far quicker in giving results. When the MRI result was available, it showed that Daniel had responded to the irinotecan. We had dared to hope as much, because his pain had decreased. Chemotherapy is actually an effective, if brutal, analgesia. In broad terms, tumours cause pain by pressing on nerves. So as the tumour shrinks so does the pressure and the pain. The response was not spectacular but it was still heartening.

Despite this, the report of the MRI scan of Daniel's pelvis when I eventually got it was the most depressing document I had ever read. If I needed any reminder of the seriousness of Daniel's condition, this provided it. The crucial passage read (with my translation of medical terms in brackets):

'There is a huge tumour involving and rising from the left ilium [upper part of the hip]. The entire ilium is involved by tumour and the disease is extending to involve the left ischium [lower part of the hip bone] and the proximal left superior [uppermost] pubic ramus [another part of the pelvis]. There is tumour involving all the margins of the left acetabulum [deep socket into which the head of the thigh bone fits at the hip joints]. There is a large extraosseous mass [growth outside the bone] arising from the left ilium and this measures 13.2 x 12.7 cm [5¼ x 5 inches] in its greatest transverse dimensions. The mass is predominantly extending into the pelvis where there is displacement of the iliopsoas muscle [composite muscle made up of the iliacus and psoas muscles found in the groin]. The gluteals [muscles making up the buttocks] are displaced at the more superficial [close to the surface] margins of the mass. At the posterior [back] margin of the tumour, disease is seen to extend anterior [front] to the sacroiliac joint [joint between the ilium and sacrum, the curved triangular section of the spine]. There is further probably metastatic tumour involvement of both sacral ala [wings of the sacrum]. There are further metastases seen in the L4 and L5 vertebral bodies [part of the lumbar section of the spine], the right hemi [half] pelvis and the right proximal femur [thigh bone].'

It was always so difficult knowing what to tell Mum.

This was after two cycles of irinotecan. The position had been even worse at diagnosis. The MRI was only of Daniel's pelvis and lumbar spine. He had a separate, serious problem in his lungs. This was covered by a chest CT, which showed 'multiple intrapulmonary [lung] nodules [cancer] involving all the lobes [parts of the lung] which are typical of pulmonary metastases.' There was not much improvement there, although the largest nodule was now 1cm rather than 1.5cm. There was indication of cancer in the thoracic spine (the bit behind the chest). This was news to us. Daniel also had suspected mets in his skull but these were not scanned on this occasion.

The MRI was done on my Mum's eightieth birthday. We had still not told her about Daniel's cancer. There was to be a family celebration a few days later and we wanted her to enjoy this. That was reasonable but there was also an element of procrastination (Daniel loved that word as a small child). We all wanted to protect her. I had to make an excuse for Daniel's absence at the meal. Mum thought nothing of it and enjoyed her evening. Gill and I went to Cardiff a couple of weeks later and I broke the news to her. There were tears and she was deeply shocked, but not for the last time demonstrated her resilience. Sensitive soul though she is, she coped better than we imagined. I didn't tell her that the cancer had spread – cancer in the lungs just sounded too bad. Perhaps we overprotected her.

Sarah Rudman, incidentally, is now a consultant at St Thomas's Hospital in London, where Daniel was born: the overlapping circles of life (my father was born the day before Lenin died - they never met.)

VIDE

So that was irinotecan. Daniel's response was not good enough for him to continue on the drug. For the moment, he would move onto VIDE, the standard combination given to newly-diagnosed Ewing's patients. VIDE stands for vincristine, ifosfamide, doxorubicin and etoposide. These are all used for other cancers.

Daniel had to stay in hospital for three nights, usually from Friday to Monday when he had VIDE. This suited us because Daniel could then go to school some of the time. On the first cycle, there was a mix-up and the hospital called us in on the Thursday. Petra and Daniel were not too happy but I wanted to get on with VIDE. One day was highly unlikely to make any difference but small margins, if we could accumulate enough of them, might just have a beneficial effect.

VIDE meant several chemo infusions over the four days. We soon got into the routine. Daniel sometimes felt nauseous and lacking in appetite and slept a lot. But there were innumerable card games too. Petra or I would stay the night, usually me because of her need to look after the girls. The ward provided a Z-bed so it wasn't too bad, although night-time disturbances were frequent as the intravenous machines had an annoying beep and often malfunctioned.

There are wonderful facilities on the Teenage Cancer Ward at UCH – a pool table and all kinds of electronic gadgetry, which defeated me – but Daniel would only venture out of his cubicle if he thought there was no one in the lounge. He had become private and didn't want to talk to other patients. We did watch the World Cup Final with other families and witnessed Zinedine Zidane's infamous head butt.

Daniel also visited the lounge when Jermaine Defoe, the Spurs' striker came to visit Michael, a leukaemia patient. Daniel, ever star struck, wanted to be part of the conversation. The footballer told us that Sven Goran-Eriksson, until recently the England manager, contributed little – but then he had left Defoe out of the World Cup squad ...

Michael died a couple of days later. Children dying is not surprisingly, a feature of children's cancer wards. It's deeply upsetting, for the obvious reasons but also because it reinforces to other children and their families what they're dealing with. The staff are discreet about deaths, but other parents not always so. Daniel and I were in the kitchen one day when a father came in with his daughter. He informed us that an African boy had just died on the ward. Petra and

I, protective as ever, tried to keep news like this from Daniel, but who is to say that this other father was wrong in his openness, treating death as a fact of life, even of young life, rather than a taboo? Daniel said nothing to me afterwards, but somewhere in his psyche this kind of thing must have had an effect.

Daniel had febrile neutropaenia again during VIDE 1. I noticed a small chest rash one morning early in the neutropaenic period but didn't think too much of it. He developed a temperature later that day, so off we went to A&E at St Peter's. I was more relaxed this time. But we were soon in for a rude awakening. Daniel told the pleasant young doctor that he had a headache and struggled to look at light. When the doctor returned he announced that Daniel probably had meningitis. Petra and I looked at each other, and Daniel uttered 'Oh no!' He knew that meningitis was serious. It wasn't a great moment: as if having a life-threatening cancer was not enough. The doctor told us that Daniel should have a lumbar puncture to confirm the diagnosis. Lumbar punctures aren't pleasant.

Daniel was admitted. It was around midnight. The hospital was short of side rooms so we were given a small room in the medical assessment unit. It hadn't been prepared. There was a bucket with dirty standing water on the floor – and this for a patient who'd just been told he had a life-threatening infection. I made it clear that we were unhappy with the room and a move was promised early the following morning. Petra and I weren't willing to leave Daniel that night so we both slept – I use the word loosely – on chairs in the room.

A chest rash is one of the symptoms of meningitis. So

is photophobia – inability to look at light. Another of the doctors wasn't convinced it was meningitis, because the rash didn't blanche – turn white – when pressed. But over the next few days meningitis was high on the agenda. The doctors would ask Daniel if he had a stiff neck, another of the tell-tale signs. The problem is that if doctors keep asking you if you have a stiff neck, you convince yourself that you do. There can be a significant psychosomatic element with all pain. As the days went by, meningitis receded as a diagnosis but it was never ruled out.

I was worried when Daniel complained about pain in his left side (the site of his primary tumour). His pain had eased considerably but now it was back. Did this mean the cancer was growing again? It really brought my mood down and I felt guilty about Gill when I went home one night. It was difficult for her, removed physically and emotionally from the epicentre of what was going on but still worried about Daniel and about me. She'd been looking forward to seeing me; she didn't need me to be on another downer. It must have been tough for her more generally. We did as much as possible unconnected to cancer – badminton, cinema, friends – and I did my best to support her with her own problems. But Daniel's cancer dominated my life and my thoughts in the way that nothing else had ever done. The relationship didn't last beyond a few more months, though the parting was amicable.

Summer and autumn of 2006

Daniel (aged three, to my sister Sian): I'm very well, thank you, before you ask

Daniel's pain in fact, soon improved and he pressed to be discharged ahead of schedule so that he could go with Petra and Sasha to Wimbledon. He had line-judged there as a sixteen year-old the previous year, perhaps the youngest line-judge ever.

Daniel actually had a pretty good summer, all things considered. He went to school whenever he could. During the neutropaenic period of VIDE 2 my inclination had been to keep him at home, to reduce the risk of infection. Petra, however, wanted him to go to school, for as much normality as possible. She was right. So off to Godalming 6th Form College he went, with strict instructions to take his temperature regularly and report any symptoms to us immediately. The school was forty to sixty minutes' drive away from Chobham so I would stay in the locality in case of emergency. I was moved by the warmth of one of the receptionists, concerned about how he was doing and forever saying what a nice boy he was.

Pretty astonishingly, Daniel took his full complement of AS Levels that year, just a few weeks after diagnosis and in the middle of chemo. This was entirely his decision. Petra and I couldn't have cared less whether he took the exams, except that it gave him a focus and a sense of achievement. Daniel had always been incredibly self-motivated, even with homework. As a fourteen year-old, he'd voluntarily done past papers for SATS tests. Many children, especially boys, need to be chivvied and encouraged; with Daniel, it was the opposite. We had to help him to take the pressure off himself.

He took the ASs at home, with an invigilator. He was allowed a little extra time. Daniel got straight As. The results were a fantastic achievement in the circumstances but somehow one expected it with Daniel, unfairly diminishing his performance. He was naturally bright – that message had been hammered home by so many teachers – but, more than that, he performed well under pressure (Petra would notice how he would straighten his back when called in for a music exam and banish his nerves). He was later awarded the economics prize, out of around thirty-five students I think.

Despite the high expectations, we didn't hold back on the praise. I was with a friend when Daniel rang with his results. I told him how proud I was of him. This was a poignant moment for my friend because her father had never conveyed pride, despite her going to Oxford. I struggle to understand why parents don't praise their kids. For Alex

Ferguson, the two most important words in management are 'Well done' and he's right.

I took Daniel to see a county cricket match in Southampton one day in August 2006. He wanted to see Shane Warne bowl. As it happened, all we saw him do was drop a catch in the slips. But it was still a great day. I noticed Daniel was walking without a hint of a limp. It was a real thrill: just a few months earlier he could barely walk at all. In fact, I could no longer see any swelling on his pelvis. The chemo was obviously having an effect.

Scans at the end of July 2006 confirmed the good progress. There was a 73 per cent reduction in the mass growing from Daniel's pelvic bone. That might not be that significant prognostically – it's the cancer cells which are left which matter – but Sarah Rudman was so excited that she asked to speak to Daniel. By this time he'd announced he didn't want to know the results of scans, even when they were good. He knew that if we relayed good results, silence on another occasion would signify bad news. However, I understood that it must be important for oncologists who have to give out so much bad news, to be able to relay good news and so asked Daniel if he'd be willing to speak to her. He was reluctant but agreed.

To complete the sporting summer, we planned to go to the European Athletics Championships in Gothenburg towards the end of August. This was with Daniel's Cardiff cousins, Katie, JJ and Annabel, all huge sporting fans like us. We'd all been to the World Athletic Championships in Paris in 2003 and had a fantastic time and Daniel and I had also gone to the championships two years later in Helsinki. We all loved going to the athletics. There is a special atmosphere

Daniel, second from left, with his Cardiff cousins Katie, JJ and Annabel and Olympic gold medallist Allen Johnson at Crystal Palace.

at big events, cosmopolitan, family-orientated and not at all threatening like football matches – the contrast between the Paris championships and watching Wales play Italy at football at the San Siro in Milan a couple of weeks later was stark.

I'd been in touch with the children's cancer hospital in Gothenburg. When I told Bryony, Daniel's specialist nurse, she remarked 'We expected as much'– I was already getting a reputation at UCH. The problem was Daniel's platelets. Platelets are a type of blood cell. They're the clotting agent, to stop bleeding. Chemotherapy hits them hard. Daniel's were to become a real issue later on. For the moment, depletion was just temporary, at the nadir of the cycle. During the cycle in question – around VIDE 4 – they were hovering around the thirty mark, not dangerous but still of concern with flying. I had daily conversations with Sarah as we monitored the platelet count. She wanted Daniel to be able to go but felt constrained to advise against flying.

As it happened we couldn't have gone on the scheduled

day because Heathrow was shut after a major terrorist plot was foiled. This was the one which led to all those restrictions on taking fluid onto planes. Gill spent the afternoon speaking to SAS, the airline, to persuade them to give us a later flight, when hopefully the platelets would have recovered. Her persistence paid off. But logistics proved against us. The cousins went anyway themselves – their punishment was an emergency on take-off from Amsterdam. I lost the best part of a thousand pounds. I explained Daniel's situation to the landlord of our cottage. I didn't ask for a discount but left it to him to be generous if he wished. He didn't.

Daniel's mood was pretty good that first cancer summer. He did say to Petra on one occasion: 'I know this could be my last Wimbledon.' Petra brushed aside his comment. At the same time, he was talking excitedly about the Olympics coming to London in 2012, then six years away. The human mind works at different levels: sometimes hope and optimism are to the fore, sometimes despair and pessimism. We worked to maximise the former and minimise the latter.

As well as exams and sport, Daniel did a week's work experience at a barrister's chambers. This was with a friend of mine, Nathalie Lieven, now a leading QC. He was keen to do it even in the midst of treatment and we wanted him to absorb the message that we thought he would have a career. He had no hair and must have looked ill, but coped with the travel to London every day and I think quite enjoyed the experience, going to court a couple of times. I was impressed with how quickly he picked up some quite complicated legal concepts. Nathalie said he asked loads of questions, though not always the right ones.

New normal

'The new normal' is a phrase often used by cancer patients. A major part of my new normal involved research, desperately trying to find anything which would help Daniel. This was not because I didn't trust Colin and his colleagues. It soon became clear that he enjoyed a strong reputation in the Ewing's and osteosarcoma worlds. But he'd left us in no doubt that Daniel's chances were extremely slim. As a parent, if that's the message from the doctor, the natural reaction is to look for solutions elsewhere. I couldn't develop coherent hypotheses like research scientists, but I hoped that if I kept banging away at enough doors, one would open somewhere and lead me to my Ewing's eureka, or more prosaically and realistically to something which might just give Daniel an edge. I told myself that the harder I worked on research, the more chance there was of finding solutions, if only I could recognise them. I effectively gave up work for the remainder of 2006.

One shouldn't underestimate the emotional impact of spending hour after hour reading depressing and intellectually challenging material. If I had a pound for every article telling me that someone with Daniel's symptoms had a dismal prognosis, it would have defrayed quite a bit of the cost of the cancer journey. But for all that, researching was my therapy. I felt, perhaps misguidedly, that I could do something to help. I realised that I was experiencing emotional trauma but didn't think I needed formal therapy. Nevertheless, I was persuaded to visit Jane Elfer, a wonderfully empathic counsellor at UCH. Jane had evidently been told about my hands-on approach. I was surprised at one question: 'All this research you are doing, David – do you think that Daniel will die if you don't do it?' I replied: 'No, I'm fully aware of my limitations. But if all my research might throw up something which might just help Daniel a little, that's reason enough to do it.'

The problem was where to look and how to make sense of what one found. The internet is a wonderful thing but it generates a totally unmanageable amount of information. When I first googled Ewing's sarcoma, it came up with over 600,000 entries. Many of those were articles, themselves containing several references to other articles, which themselves contained several references to other articles and so on. How could I possibly read more than a tiny fraction of all this? And these were just the entries directly referring to Ewing's. I learnt quickly that information about other cancers, particularly cancers with biological similarities to Ewing's, could also be relevant.

And, more than this, I wanted to delve into complementary therapies, including diets. Anything to give Daniel an edge. Searching down one avenue would usually lead to others, potentially a good thing but adding to the already overwhelming complexity. People would sometimes say to me: 'You can't leave any stone unturned.' The problem was that there were thousands of stones, and to uncover them all would have been several lifetimes' work. The list of things which someone, somewhere recommended for a patient such as Daniel was extremely long. Somehow I had to try to discriminate between those which might have some value and those (the vast majority) which were unlikely to. It often took considerable research before I felt confident in rejecting something and more often I would put options on the back burner, to be revisited if appropriate.

And, as a non-scientist, let alone a non-oncologist, I didn't understand much of what I read. Articles about preclinical research were a particular mystery. Sometimes I would barely understand more than a few sentences in an article. Doctors quite often complimented me on my knowledge, and asked me if I was a doctor (which amused Daniel), but I knew how rudimentary my understanding was. It struck me later that it would have been better if I had taken a crash course in A level biology before reading about Ewing's. But time was not on our side, or so I thought.

Newton used the analogy of the seashore to describe the skimpiness of even his scientific understanding:

> *'I seem to have been only like a boy playing on the seashore, and diverting myself in now and then finding a smoother pebble or a prettier shell than ordinary, whilst the great ocean of truth lay undiscovered before me.'*

It wasn't surprising that my ocean of ignorance was vast but I came to appreciate that it wasn't that much smaller for Ewing's researchers and clinicians.

In those early months, Gill was a tremendous help with research. Not a formally trained scientist, she'd done science A levels in her twenties and had a natural aptitude. Plus she was more emotionally distanced from it all.

Surgery?

Two of the areas of conventional medicine I researched in the summer of 2006 related to surgery and stem cells. Colin had tantalisingly left open the possibility of surgery at our first meeting, unlikely though it was. From my reading, I knew that removing Daniel's primary tumour was the best solution, if it were achievable. Around this time I discovered, somewhat to my surprise, that cancer specialists would usually reply to emails. I knew they'd be busy with their own patients and (often) their research but more than this, I assumed they wouldn't be willing to commit themselves, certainly in writing, without knowing a patient's full history, or indeed to tread on the toes of the patient's own doctor. I thought that US doctors, in particular, would be reluctant to give their views given the litigation culture there and the pressure to make money. I couldn't have been more mistaken.

So many doctors were only too willing to help. Some would begin their replies with 'As a parent myself ...' Hitting an empathic chord undoubtedly paid dividends. It's obvious, but easy to forget, that doctors are human beings first and doctors only second (a message driven home when I heard about a Ewing's doctor who lost two children in an accident). I found that authors would send me their articles, thereby saving me the £25-35 cost of accessing most articles online. I discuss more about how to research in Annex A.

In the summer of 2006 I canvassed opinion, in necessarily general terms, about surgery in the US, Europe and India. Replies were understandably guarded, but there was a general feeling that we should look closely at the option. A theoretical possibility was a hemipelvectomy – removal of one half of the pelvis. It would be the left half in Daniel's case. It's a major operation by any standards, often involving amputation. Nick Clarke, the Radio 4 World at One presenter (I was once interviewed by him) and the father of young twins, had a hemipelvectomy at the Royal National Orthopaedic Hospital in Stanmore. He had a soft-tissue sarcoma and was a patient of Colin's. I corresponded with Nick. Sadly he died in late 2006. I recall his widow saying that serious though they knew things were, they had hope and at times believed in the hope. I thought that was a nice way of putting it.

One of the difficulties in Daniel's case was that his primary tumour was massive, nestling against several important organs – bladder, bowel etc – and nerve centres. It's a cardinal principle that one should operate only if one can remove all the visible cancer, plus sufficient margins to catch cancer cells lurking nearby. One American surgeon had written a chapter for a text book about hemipelvectomies and had operated on Ewing's patients, so I assumed he knew what he was talking about. He told me that, if one could get x per cent of the tumour through the surgery, one would reduce the chance of recurrence by a similar percentage. This surprised me but I passed on the thought to Colin and Tim Briggs. Colin had an apoplectic fit. The suggestion was oncologically ridiculous, he said, and showed the danger of not leaving things to the experts. Fair enough, but it's a mantra of cancer support groups that one should not be afraid to ask 'silly' questions. The wise saying, attributed to sages from Confucius to Mark Twain, 'It's better to keep silent and be thought a fool than to speak and remove all doubt' should not apply to cancer parents.

But I did try after this to advance my research much further before bringing ideas to Colin. I would tell him that he shouldn't assume that the fact that I was asking about something meant we were about to do it.

Colin suggested we go to see Tim Briggs. I suspect this was to put us off the scent about surgery. Tim explained patiently why it wouldn't be possible to get clear margins in Daniel's case. There was another factor lurking not far beneath the surface, too. Cancer doctors are understandably reluctant to carry out major surgery such as a hemipelvectomy where the cancer has already spread, with poor prognosis for the patient. That makes sense – why put someone through major surgery which is not going to stop the advance of the disease? That was exactly Daniel's situation.

Reluctantly we drew a line under surgery. Feelings were mixed. We were relieved that Daniel wouldn't have to have a major operation with all the pain, risk of infection and recovery time. But surgery, if successful, might well have improved his chances by reducing the risk of relapse in the primary tumour area. As he had at the outset, Tim at least made us feel more optimistic overall. As we left, Petra and I told each other that the truth probably lay somewhere between Tim's cheery optimism and Colin's deathly pessimism. I knew, in fact, that it lay much closer to the latter and I suspect Petra did too. But hope was still welcome.

Stem cells

What was the issue with stem cells? This was another complicated question, which took up much of my time in late summer 2006. There is divided opinion in the Ewing's world about the value of high-dose chemotherapy (or HDC) for serious cases. As with so much else, the jury is out; there is just not enough evidence. HDC, as the name suggests, is very powerful chemotherapy, more powerful than even the strong chemo Daniel was getting. So powerful that it destroys the patient's bone marrow, such that he or she has to have a replacement: a transplant. It's the bone marrow which generates the life-sustaining blood cells – red cells for oxygen, white cells to fight infections and platelets for blood-clotting.

There are two main types of bone marrow transplants – allogeneic and autologous. Allogeneic means a transplant from a donor ('allo' is Greek for 'other') and autologous means getting one's own bone marrow back. A hybrid - haploidentical transplants - is where marrow is transplanted from a parent. Allogeneic transplants are used for leukaemia patients: leukaemia is a disease of the bone marrow and so there would be no point giving back the damaged marrow. They are sometimes used for Ewing's patients too, but this is even more experimental than autologous transplants.

Of the two main types, Daniel was in line for an autologous transplant. Even this, we were told at the beginning, was unlikely. HDC was of particularly questionable value where a Ewing's patient had bone metastases, as Daniel did. However, the doctors would keep options open by taking ('harvesting') Daniel's stem cells after six rounds of chemo.

He would get them back to replenish the supply destroyed by the HDC. It's all highly technical.

The stem cell specialist at UCH was Deirdre Driver. She came to see Daniel one day while he was an in-patient for chemo. Deirdre is Irish, nervy but ready with a joke and eager to help. She put Daniel at ease and he liked her, whilst finding her humour on the wacky side. I had already learnt of a theory that giving back stem cells to a Ewing's patient could just reintroduce the disease, if the stem cells were cancerous. Ewing's is now thought to originate in the mesenchyme, part of the marrow. I wasn't completely reassured by Daniel's negative bone marrow biopsy: I was learning about the imperfections of cancer diagnostic techniques and their inability to pick up cancer below a certain size.

I'd also learnt that there was a special technique to 'purge' stem cells. Normally, when stem cells are harvested they come with a lot of surrounding blood. However, it's possible to harvest a purer form by separating off the CD34+ cells. CD 34+ cells are immature blood cells. The hypothesis was that there was then less chance that the reinfused stem cells would contain cancer. That risk should have been reduced by the six cycles of chemo Daniel would have had by the time of harvesting but there was no way of knowing whether they would have killed all cancerous cells in the marrow. Presumably not, given his poor prognosis. Studies in France and the US suggested a better outcome with CD34+-separated stem cells.

Sadly, nothing comes risk-free with cancer treatment. When stem cells are given back to a patient, they take time to grow. During this time, the patient effectively has nothing with which to fight infection and a low supply of red blood cells and platelets too. The patient is therefore at high risk. The mortality rate is higher with allogeneic transplants, but patients die after autologous transplants too.

Purged stem cells take longer to grow on reinfusion. So the patient is at risk of dangerous infection for longer. Colin in fact, wasn't convinced that giving back non-purged stem cells added to the risk. He could see the logic of the argument he told me, but there was no data to support it. Data is extremely important, clearly. But the fact that there is inadequate data supporting a risk (or benefit) does not mean that the risk (or benefit) does not exist: absence of evidence is not the same as evidence of absence. Where there was a dearth of data, I thought one should use principle, and instinct derived from experience, to fill the gaps. I don't suppose that Colin would disagree with this, but discussions usually centred on data. Unfortunately, with serious cancers one does not have time for enough to be generated.

I had an idea. What if we took two lots of stem cells from Daniel, one purged of CD34+ cells but the other not? We could then leave the final decision until Daniel had the HDC, if he did. I put the proposal to Colin.

There were two problems. The first was that there was no guarantee that we could harvest enough stem cells for one reinfusion, let alone two. The second problem was financial. The purging technique is expensive. There was a preliminary test required, an RT-PCR of circulating blood cells. Plus Daniel would have extra harvesting and so would use the equipment for longer. The figure of £2,400 was mentioned. Colin and I came up with a compromise.

We would pay for the preliminary test and the NHS would pay for the purging. I wasn't sure that the deal would stand up to legal scrutiny and in the event we weren't asked for the £2,400.

The RT-PCR test came back negative, which was encouraging – it didn't detect any cancer in Daniel's blood. It's blood which carries Ewing's cells around the body.

Daniel had his stem cells harvested over two days in August 2006. A massive needle was unpleasant for him, but otherwise everything went well. The good news was that they were able to collect two lots of stem cells, one purged and one not – in fact, Deirdre told me later than they had enough for three infusions. That was potentially important, in case we needed a transplant to support chemotherapy or radiotherapy in future. Most patients only have enough stem cells for a single transplant, if that. I was happy that we were covering the bases. I planned to do more research if the prospects of HDC increased.

Overall strategy

I was learning that Colin, though generous with his time, wasn't always that forthcoming and could be defensive. Meetings about one's child's serious illness can be extremely emotional and the subject-matter often highly complicated. It's so easy to think that one understands what is being said but then realise that one has forgotten key details almost immediately. So from early on, I kept detailed notes of meetings and telephone conversations. When I asked Colin in the summer of 2006 about prognosis, he was reluctant to be drawn and made a dismissive reference to 'whatever you're writing down there.' Perhaps he thought I might later drag up a prediction which didn't come true. If so, he was wrong.

At the same meeting, Colin was reluctant to share his treatment strategy for Daniel. 'It all depends how things pan out', he said. I understood that but want to have an idea of his plans. What were the broad options in different scenarios? 'We're developing our own strategy and wanted to make sure the two strategies, ours and yours, mesh', I explained. I'm sure he regarded this as absurd – how could we possibly know enough to develop a strategy? I couldn't hope to match his knowledge or experience, but I was finding out what other Ewing's specialists were doing around the world (quite apart from all the complementary options we were looking at). I would listen closely to Colin's advice about treatment but I wasn't necessarily going to accept it.

In that context, it didn't seem unreasonable to have a sense of Colin's plans for Daniel beyond initial chemotherapy and radiotherapy, always assuming he lived that long. The fact that plans might have to be shelved or adjusted didn't mean that they needn't be shared. Above all, I wanted a proactive approach, not one that simply reacted to relapse.

I did respect Colin for turning down my suggestion that we pay him on a private basis – he did some private work – for all the extra questions I had. I'm not sure this arrangement, either, would have been lawful, given that Daniel was an NHS patient (though I could not find anything saying it was not), but Colin's discomfiture may well have been primarily ethical.

Complementary approach

I didn't trouble Colin with my complementary therapy research. Since conventional medicine didn't, it seem, offer Daniel lasting hope, we had to look elsewhere, to add value to what conventional medicine could achieve. The term 'alternative remedies' is a misnomer. Many who look beyond the sort of treatment available in hospitals prefer the term 'complementary' or 'integrative' medicine – the remedies are not designed to replace the conventional but to complement or to integrate with them. That was certainly my approach. Despite chemotherapy's many drawbacks and questionable efficacy (beyond a short time), there was never any question of Daniel not getting it. Similarly with radiotherapy, which has a better track record than most forms of chemotherapy. Some do reject the standard cancer treatments, except perhaps surgery, and some 'alternative' practitioners are virulent in the criticism of chemotherapy, but for the most part other treatments are about adding value, not substitution.

In fact, I think it's misleading even to use the terms 'conventional' (or 'orthodox'), 'complementary', 'integrative' and 'alternative.' I came to realise that there is but one type of medicine worthy of the name and that is evidence-based medicine. Treatment either works or it does not. How one assesses the evidence is a complicated topic to which I will return in Annex A. One of the doctors who coined the term 'evidence-based medicine', David Sackett, defined it as 'the conscientious, explicit and judicious use of current best evidence in making decisions about the care of individual patients.' That definition applies as much to complementary remedies as conventional ones.

Some approaches in any event straddle the supposed divide. Many complementary therapies are aimed, in a general sense, at coaxing the immune system into attacking the cancer. One such therapy, Coley's toxins, was on my radar from early on. Immunotherapy can involve serious, extremely complicated science. Some see it as the fourth modality after surgery, chemotherapy and, radiotherapy. I came to believe that in immunotherapy, allied to surgery, lies the key to controlling cancer. Cancer, after all, represents a failure of the immune system to do what it's supposed to do. It seems logical that there lies the answer.

A major problem with chemo and radiotherapy is that they severely damage the immune system, making it even less likely that it will be strong enough to fight the cancer (strength, it's true, is not the only issue: cancer has a terrifying ability to hide from the key immune system protagonists). One has to hope, therefore, that these treatments can be effective without causing too much damage - one of the countless difficult balancing acts to be performed with cancer.

With the possible exception of Coley's toxins, I knew that there was no complementary therapy which would provide a magic cure for Daniel. However, my strategy – perhaps logical, perhaps naïve – was to try to support those parts of the immune system which could be supported and which were either needed to attack the cancer or to facilitate other cells in doing so, all to help make chemo and radiotherapy more effective. The strategy was also to make the body's environment as hostile as possible for the residual cancer we knew Daniel would almost certainly have after initial treatment.

As a minimum, I hoped that this would slow down the cancer's progress, buying us time. Time for Daniel was important in itself, provided there was quality of life. It also gave a greater chance for research to come to fruition, even though I knew that the timeline was depressingly long. That is true of all cancers but particularly of difficult cancers like sarcomas.

I visited quite a few complementary practitioners that first summer. There are some sharks out there, preying on the vulnerable. Oncologists of the more traditional kind are anxious to warn patients and their families of this, no doubt from kindly motives. I had a bad experience with two leading complementary cancer practitioners. The first, based in idyllic countryside in Hampshire, wanted to pretend Daniel was eighteen so that he could prescribe remedies for him (his Health Commission licence was for adults only). I didn't take up his offer. He was unenthusiastic in answering my questions and seemed uninterested in Daniel's plight.

Another practitioner, in the West Country, I found no warmer. Despite stressing in her book and promotional literature that each cancer and each patient was different, thereby pointing to individualised treatment, she proceeded to print off a letter which had all the hallmarks of standard-form advice. She was heavily promoting a particular remedy which seemed to be supported by precious little evidence. I broke down at one stage during the meeting. She appeared uncomfortable at this and was anxious to bring the meeting to a close when I still had questions.

But this kind of experience should not blind one to the fact that there are many genuine practitioners who really want to help. I met many of them as well. Their primary motivation was anything but money. I received so much help from all over the world, for free. Caroline Galloway, for example, a medical herbalist in Guildford, Surrey, went the extra mile to help, though she never met Daniel. I had constructive advice, often free, from Chris Etheridge of Cancer Options. He struck me as a knowledgeable scientist who was up-to-speed with both the conventional and complementary worlds.

In fact, it's not only the occasional complementary practitioner who is motivated primarily by money. Some conventional oncologists are too. One well-known oncologist Petra and I saw in London charged us £330 for less than an hour's consultation and he hadn't even bothered to read the letter I had carefully crafted.

During those early months I invested much time in looking into Daniel's diet. Diet can be seen as a form of immunotherapy. It's estimated that 30 per cent of cancers are related to diets. There are large-scale studies showing for example, that vegetarians are less prone to certain sorts of cancer. Many oncologists, whilst recognising the role of diet in prevention, nevertheless pooh-pooh the idea that diet can help once someone gets cancer. I never really understood the logic of this, but perhaps the thinking is that once cancer has been through sufficient stages to be detectable, it's just too strong for the chemicals in food and drink to have any effect. An increasing number of other cancer practitioners, including hospital oncologists, take a different view but they're still in a minority.

At any rate, UCH, Daniel's hospital, placed no emphasis on diet as a curative aid. The nutritionists there acknowledged the importance of fruit and vegetables, but only as part of a normal healthy diet. They also recognised the need for underweight patients to keep their weight up (obesity presents its own problems and is a risk factor for many cancers). At one point in the summer of 2006, Daniel was down to 6st 13lbs, skeletal for someone of his height, around 5ft 10½in. Colin admitted to some concern.

We asked to see a nutritionist on one visit. She recommended dairy-based fortifying drinks. The problem was that, by this time, I'd read so much about dairy being bad for cancer. This is particularly so with the hormonal and oestrogen-based cancers, but there was a consensus – not unanimity, to be sure – in the complementary therapy world that dairy was best avoided. This message had been reinforced in Lance Armstrong's book about his testicular cancer. He was advised to give up dairy, except cheese (it's not clear why cheese was excepted). His cancer had spread to the brain and carried a chance of cure of only 3 per cent. Daniel absorbed the message about dairy, helped no doubt that it was conveyed by a superstar who at that time still shone brightly in the sporting firmament – and that he'd survived. Daniel, long a vegetarian, gave up dairy and became a near-vegan.

It took me longer than I wanted to work out exactly what diet Daniel should be on – perhaps a couple of months. He got impatient with me, because he'd taken on board the message that diet mattered. The problem was that there was so much information out there and so much of it contradictory. There are as many diets for cancer as there are cancers. I knew the answer was to search for a consensus, but that meant extensive reading. I also needed to develop an instinct as to who could be trusted and who might be concerned only with promoting their own method.

One of the people I met was Max Tuck. A few years earlier, she had a chronic illness (not cancer). Nothing had worked until she turned to a raw food diet and juicing, with vitamin supplementation. She was convinced that this had done the trick and she now went for long runs and climbed mountains. Part of what attracted me was that she was a practising vet – and therefore trained in the ways of science. I always took particular note when scientists embraced the dietary and other complementary approaches to cancer. They couldn't be dismissed as wishful thinkers or quacks.

Max kindly came to the house to meet Daniel and Petra. This was unusual. In the vast majority of cases, practitioners never met Daniel because I did the research and wanted him to have to think about his cancer as little as possible. Daniel liked Max and listened closely to her advice.

Max was an advocate of the approach taken by the Hippocrates Centre in Florida. We considered taking Daniel there. A raw food diet lies at the centre of what they do, along with coffee enemas. It has some overlap with the Gerson therapy, which some claim has had remarkable results with cancer. Amazingly, a colleague and my former next-door neighbour had each recently been there (not for cancer in either case).

I was cautious about the Centre. It had an evangelising feel to it and that always rang alarm bells. A former patient, a scientist at Columbia University in New York, had reached the preliminary view that there was demonstrable efficacy from the Hippocrates approach. But the director was too upbeat when I spoke to him. I had more respect for practitioners who were guarded in their advice, because that reflects the real state of science.

I eventually came up with a dietary approach, after discussion with Petra. One of the best books was by Professor Jane Plant, a scientist at Imperial College London and survivor of multiple breast cancer relapses. She attributed the turnaround in her fortunes to changing her diet radically.

Soon after, Daniel started on wheatgrass juice. Full of nutrients, many think it's beneficial to health. Ann Wigmore, the founder of the Hippocrates Centre, extolled its 'anti-cancer properties.' That was a phrase I came to distrust, because cancers vary so much. With wheatgrass, however, if nothing else, there seemed reason to think it might help Daniel cope with the nasty side-effects of chemo.

So just about every day for the next five years I made the juice. This wasn't a straightforward process. I first had to grow it. I have never been a gardener – I love flowers but not enough to put in the work to grow them; I have never kept plants. So this was a new venture for me. I was amazed when seeds I planted actually developed into real grass; the miracle of nature, able to overcome the least green of fingers. I managed to grow broccoli and other seeds too. Daniel had these seeds raw most days too. Broccoli and other cruciferous vegetables are thought to be particularly good for cancer patients. I reckon that, averaged out, the whole wheatgrass process – planting, tending, juicing, washing up the juicer parts and taking to Daniel – took not far short of an hour a day. Often I would come home from work at around 9pm, hungry and exhausted, but the first thing I had to do was to make Daniel's wheatgrass. I'd never really understood the concept of cooking for love before; I did now. This was a real labour of love.

Daniel hated wheatgrass, but he was such a trouper taking it, along with other green juices. He would sometimes take it even when he didn't feel great. I had such admiration for him. Indeed, Daniel stuck to the whole dietary regime with complete rigour, more so than Petra and I encouraged. We would say that having x occasionally wouldn't do any harm, but Daniel would have none of it. On his eighteenth birthday in October 2006, I took him to an organic pizza restaurant and said he should have whatever he wanted. He used to love cheese but refused to have any. (There was never any dilemma, by the way, as to whether we should make the eighteenth or the twenty-first Daniel's special coming-of-age birthday. We didn't expect him to see his twenty-first birthday.)

Did his rigorous dietary self-discipline help the fight against the cancer? It's hard to know, but the fact that he felt that he was doing something to help himself shouldn't be underestimated. Psychologically, it was important that he wasn't merely a passive victim, having huge amounts of poison poured into his body. There was something he could do for himself, even if the advice came from us. A feeling of some control over an illness like cancer is so important. He believed that the wheatgrass and the rest were helping him.

Continuing treatment and scans

All the while I was researching, Daniel was undergoing treatment. He had six cycles of VIDE chemo and, apart from the first, coped well. Colin indicated at the outset that the chemo timetable would be interrupted and I read about many Ewing's patients whose chemo had to be delayed because of low blood counts or other reasons. Daniel had sixteen cycles of chemo in total as part of his frontline treatment and not a single one was delayed. Only three times did he have to go to hospital mid-cycle with febrile neutropaenia – some patients had to go virtually every cycle. I like to think that this was in part because of his diet; perhaps it was just luck.

As soon as VIDE finished, Daniel was to move onto a different chemo regime, concurrently with radiotherapy. The acronym this time was VAI. There were to be eight cycles of VAI, although actinomycin was not given while Daniel was having radiotherapy for toxicity reasons. As we drove in for the first VAI, Daniel told me: 'I like VIDE and wish I was staying on it.' I realised he meant that he knew he could handle VIDE and didn't know what to expect with VAI. He no doubt remembered that he'd reacted badly to each new chemo regime, irinotecan and VIDE. But it still struck me as sad that a seventeen year-old should say he 'liked' being on a vicious poisoning regime. How his horizons had narrowed.

Daniel's radiotherapist was Anna Cassoni. Anna's manner at the first meeting was brisk. Over the years we had lively exchanges of view. Sometimes I felt she was overdefensive about second opinions. But I came to really like her. Behind the brisk manner was a warm personality. I recall at that end of that first meeting her grabbing my hand with her two hands. At the time, it didn't seem to fit with the efficient directness which had preceded it. Anna cared about Daniel's welfare and would go to talk to him if she saw him in the corridor. When he complained of pains, she would examine him more thoroughly than any other doctor I have seen.

At that first meeting, she asked Daniel: 'Do you want to look at your scans so that I can explain where the radiotherapy will be directed?' 'No', Daniel replied. 'That's unusual for teenage boys', Anna remarked. In a way I was glad at Daniel's response because it fitted with what I'd told Anna before the meeting. I knew that the radiotherapy created a risk of secondary cancers – leukaemia or osteosarcoma. There was also a risk of a blood disorder known as myelodysplasia syndrome, which shares some features with cancer. In statistical terms the risk was significant – as usual I came across different figures, but something of the order of 15-25 per cent from around five to eight years after treatment, probably increasing later (no one was sure because only comparatively recently had there been long-term survivors of Ewing's).

Daniel would have to consent to radiotherapy. Petra and I didn't want him to know about the risk of secondary cancers. It would be a long time before the risk kicked in and we knew there was precious little chance of Daniel living that long. Why add to his worries by talking about a risk which would probably remain hypothetical? But I also knew that doctors had to warn patients about significant risks. I'm not an expert in medical law but I felt instinctively that a patient with capacity to make decisions (as Daniel had) must have the right to delegate discussion about risks to someone else, his parents in this case. Indeed, I thought that a patient had the right to delegate decisions, not just discussion; I never pushed that particular argument because it could raise a hornet's nest. I talked about discussion about risk with a barrister friend of mine, Paula Sparks, who practises health law. She confirmed my thinking. In the event, Anna dealt with consenting sensitively and sensibly, as she always did.

The radiotherapy would be to Daniel's left pelvis and sacrum – broadly, his primary tumour. Radiotherapy is local treatment, directed to one part of the body only. Chemotherapy, by contrast, is systemic – the idea is that it kills cancer cells wherever they lurk in the body. Anna was pretty confident that she could prevent a recurrence in the parts she was irradiating, despite the massive area. She had no control of cancer elsewhere in Daniel's body (there is a strange phenomenon, called the abfocal effect, where radiotherapy to one part of the body seems to cause regression of cancer in another distinct part, but that's rare). However, she offered some pretty upbeat statistics about recurrence elsewhere. This was much more optimistic than Colin's assessment and much more optimistic than I'd gleaned from the literature, but Petra and I gratefully accepted the offering of hope.

I'd asked Anna whether Daniel should have radiotherapy, not just to his primary site but also to other bone mets sites, in his right pelvis, spine and skull. An article by German doctors extolled the benefits of irradiating all known bone met sites with Ewing's. As ever, there was uncertainty about the advantages – another article rubbished the hypothesis. Linked to this issue was whether Daniel should have a combined PET/CT scan of his whole body. I'd vaguely heard of PET scans before Daniel became ill. PET stands for positron emission tomography. I gathered from my reading that the richer countries, like Germany and the US, were increasingly using a PET scan, in conjunction with a

CT scan, with Ewing's patients. Daniel hadn't had a PET scan, though he'd had separate CT scans of his chest. The machines are expensive – several million pounds. At that time only around eight hospitals in England had them. One of these was UCH, but they didn't use them for Ewing's.

Once again, the jury was out about the importance of PET/CT scans with Ewing's. I read any number of articles and communicated with several doctors who used them. No type of scan is perfect: they're not completely accurate even in relation to cancer which is big enough for detection. The human body is difficult to image. There are often false negatives and false positives. A false negative is where the scan (or other diagnostic technique) says that everything is fine when it's not. A false positive is where the scan shows an apparent problem which doesn't, in fact, exist. False negatives are dangerous because the patient is then not treated when they need to be, particularly relevant with cancer, when the best chance of success is when it's at its weakest. But false positives are also bad because, apart from unnecessary worry, a patient may then receive unpleasant and risky treatment which they don't need. One can get false positives, for example, from mammograms with breast cancer and PSA readings with the prostate.

From what I could make out, PET/CT scans give fewer false negatives. Two radiotherapists in Germany, Margo Rominger and Ludwig Strauss, guided me through the maze. Ludwig had a son around Daniel's age and his wife was also a radiologist at the centre. He would often give detailed explanations by return email. He later developed cancer himself and it was interesting to note how our relationship changed then, less doctor-parent and more one of friendship. He seemed open to more radical treatment options for his cancer. Many German doctors are less stuck in the orthodox v alternatives dichotomy than British oncologists.

I thought that a PET/CT scan would give us a better picture of Daniel's bone metastases at this point and therefore guide the decision whether he should have radiotherapy to those mets as well. Colin had told me that bone scans (which Daniel had had), though they cover the whole body were not much good with Ewing's, with too many false negatives. Ideally, we would have had a whole-body PET/CT scan at diagnosis – for a proper 'baseline' – but one now would still give us a clearer picture of where we had got to and a baseline for the future. We were happy to pay for a PET/CT if necessary.

Colin had also explained that it would always be difficult to read Daniel's MRI scans, to differentiate between the effects of treatment and the damage caused by the original cancer, on the one hand, and any remaining cancer, on the other. MRIs use strong magnetic fields and radio images to show anatomical structure. PET scans work on a different basis. They show metabolic activity. A type of glucose – a sugar – is given to the patient. Cancer absorbs sugar and the glucose therefore lights up if there is cancer in the body.

At that first meeting, Anna was dismissive about the need for radiotherapy to the bone mets. Better to leave this to chemotherapy. There were disadvantages in extra radiotherapy, particularly damage to Daniel's bone marrow reserve. So there was no point, she felt, in having a PET/CT scan. I accepted Anna's explanation at first but thought more about it and remained unhappy. Even if Daniel wouldn't have radiotherapy to his bone mets now, I wanted him to have the best scanning, because this could inform future treatment decisions. So I made my case and Anna and Colin relented.

Daniel had his first PET/CT scan in October 2006. The results weren't clear-cut but they were encouraging. I discussed them with Dr Jamshed Bomanji, the PET expert at UCH. Radiologists are often reluctant to have direct contact with patients but Jamshed was communicative. He'd just come back from a sabbatical at MD Anderson Cancer Centre in Houston, one of the leading US cancer hospitals. PET/CT scans were regularly used for Ewing's there and he wanted them at UCH.

Having spoken to many other radiologists too, I felt reasonably reassured that we were moving in the right direction. For the time being Daniel would only have radiotherapy to his primary tumour and sacrum. Detailed preparation goes into radiotherapy. Physicists are involved to map the precise targeting of the radiation rays. Daniel had to have a scan and rehearse the position in which he would lie in the radiotherapy machine: millimetres matter. He also had to have an operation, at Stanmore, to insert a 'spacer' to protect his bladder from radiation and thereby allow a higher dose (I believe spacers were developed at Stanmore). Spacers are made of the same silicon material as breast implants.

Daniel had just passed his eighteenth birthday and so had to go on the adult ward at Stanmore. This had two disadvantages. First, Daniel was inevitably placed with older patients. He never complained but it can't have been easy for him, psychologically, to be with generally much older patients with cancer. The second disadvantage was that Petra and I wouldn't be able to stay. Petra tried to on the first night but was kicked out at 2am by a sister. The fear, I think, was of visitors stealing other patients' belongings. Common sense should always be allowed to temper strict application of policies, whatever their rationale. Staff at UCH did on occasion allow me to stay when Daniel was on an adult ward.

Daniel's operation was on a Monday in October 2006. The Friday before, Petra and I had been to see Professor Gus Dalgleish at St George's Hospital in London. Prof Dalgleish is on the cusp of the orthodox and the unorthodox in his approach and some regard him as maverick. He has a particular interest in immunotherapy such as vaccines, including Coley's toxins and worked with complementary practitioners. As a result of our discussion we arranged, hurriedly, that Daniel, when having the spacer inserted should have a biopsy of his cancer, for possible vaccine therapy in the future. Colin wasn't persuaded but didn't object. Liaising between three hospitals in such a short period of time was quite a headache. In the event, Tim Briggs wasn't able to get enough tumour, disappointing for the vaccine option but a good sign of the progress Daniel was making.

After his operation, Daniel had morphine. His eyes became puffy and he developed a facial rash. These could have been signs of allergy to morphine. This became a running joke over the years. Whenever Daniel was asked if he had any allergies he would say 'possibly morphine', then look at me and smile.

Spacer in situ, radiotherapy got under way. It was a big unknown to us but in fact went as smoothly as chemotherapy had. Daniel would want Petra or me in the room with him until the machine started. When I first saw him in this monster of a machine, I was hit by a wave of emotion, just as on seeing the words 'Teenage Cancer Unit.' He looked so thin and vulnerable. But the radiotherapy staff were always great with him.

Daniel didn't get the degree of burning that we'd feared. We did all we could, conventional and complementary, to lessen the impact. He was tired, but not overtired. He had thirty-five sessions of radiotherapy, often twice a day. The original plan was that it would straddle Christmas and New Year but he did so well that they decided to bring forward the later sessions. I was pleased about this – we wanted treatment to be as concentrated as possible, if Daniel could tolerate it. He had chemotherapy at the same time. So this was a period of heavy treatment, but he coped well.

Debate

Daniel continued to go to school whenever he could. His ambition had long been to go to Oxford or Cambridge. In the autumn of 2006 his school, Godalming Sixth Form College, was taking part in a national debating competition. Daniel had no particular interest in debating but thought this would be good for his CV. So he put himself forward for the auditions and was selected. Whether this was because the teacher wanted to give him a boost, or he detected a talent, wasn't clear.

Participating schools were given two motions to debate. One team would debate one motion and another team the other. The two motions allocated to Godalming were tourism to human rights blackspots and animal experiments.

Daniel was chosen to discuss animal experiments. This was a strange coincidence because I've always been opposed to animal experiments and have done considerable legal work for Cruelty Free International, a leading anti-vivisection organisation. As luck would have it, Godalming was given the 'against' side to argue. Daniel would deal with the moral issues and his colleague the scientific arguments.

Daniel discussed the arguments with me. I was concerned that as an obvious cancer patient, he might come under attack, not in a nasty way but because via his treatment, he appeared to be benefiting from animal experiments. All cancer drugs are tested on animals and animals are also routinely irradiated. Was it therefore not hypocritical, the line of attack could be, for him to use such treatment if he was opposed to animal experiments? Daniel's answer, if it came up, would be:

'None of us can change the past. All we can do is shape a more humane future. The fact that cancer drugs have been tested in a way which I don't support shouldn't mean that I have to boycott them, any more than people should not live in Liverpool or Bristol because the prosperity of those cities was built on the slave trade. The LD50, a poisoning test in which a substance is given to animals in sufficient quantity to kill half of them, has been used for water. Should people opposed to animal experiments therefore boycott water as well, which would clearly be an act of suicide? It's literally impossible to live free from animal experiments.'

In the event, the issue didn't come up. Daniel had a more

Daniel was in remission here but still looks pretty ill (with cousins Annabel, Holly, Katie and JJ).

prosaic dilemma: whether to wear his beanie hat, as he did for school, or to go bald-headed. He was sensitive about his appearance. I'm not sure how he resolved the dilemma. Godalming lost the judges' vote 2:1, but Daniel was commended for his performance, which was encouraging for him. His team won the (small) audience vote convincingly.

One summer's evening in 2006, Daniel had a car accident. He dropped a bottle of water and lost control of the steering as, unthinkingly, he bent down to pick it up. He veered across the road, mounted a pavement and demolished a small wall. Thankfully he was unhurt. It could have been much worse, not just for him – he might have hit a child on the pavement. I mused whether, just as stress can trigger cancer (so some people think), this sharp jolt might send Daniel's cancer into remission. Completely unscientific, but one searches for any succour.

A few months later, there was excitement at UCH when Daniel and I were staying. Alexander Litvinenko had been poisoned by radioactive polonium in London, most people assume by Putin's thugs. He was a patient at UCH and the photo of him lying in bed there, bald and ill, became iconic. Early one morning, I took a stroll to clear a headache. When I returned the place was swarming with police and I had a job getting back in. It struck me as strange that far more police were required to protect him now that he was dead. Perhaps they were afraid someone would steal the evidence. I think Daniel enjoyed the proximity to a worldwide news story.

Reflection

And so we approached Christmas 2006. It had been an extraordinary few months. Christmas was spent in South Wales. One day we went to sand dunes with his cousins Holly and JJ and threw a ball around, always one of Daniel's favourite activities. He played with his old gusto, even diving around. It was wonderful to see. I wrapped his daily wheatgrass juice as one of his presents. He was not amused. Julian, my brother-in-law, said that it gave him great joy to see Daniel looking well – much better than he'd expected. I always passed such remarks onto Daniel and they gave him a visible lift. Sometimes, when people said that Daniel was looking so much better than, say, three months earlier, I felt like saying: 'But you said he was looking well then!' But you take what you can in the hope stakes.

I spent most of the holiday reading articles about Ewing's and putting together a table of clinical trials - a massive task since there was were so many Daniel might in principle qualify for. Sometimes trials would specifically be for patients with Ewing's, or Ewing's and linked sarcomas. Sometimes they might be for sarcomas generally. Weighed down by information overload, I wanted an easy reference point.

On Christmas Day, my thoughts inevitably drifted to next Christmas. Would Daniel still be with us? Would we be granted one more Christmas? The odds weren't that good, despite the encouraging start. Wholly irrational, because cancer pays no attention to the calendar, but I felt some degree of protection while it was still 2006. I knew 2007 would be a big year.

2006 had been the worst year of my life by a distance. So far.

Decisions, decisions

Dad (playing snap with Daniel): You have to be a good loser
Daniel (aged four): No, I want to be a good winner

I did indeed feel scared entering the New Year. I wrote this in my journal:

> 'Thoughts wandered to the horror of Daniel not making it, looking at him in bed, where he inevitably looks frail.'

Unexpected things got me down. I made enquiries about travel insurance. I was planning to take Daniel to Japan for the world athletics championships in August 2007. I learnt what many cancer families learn – that it's very difficult to get insurance at a reasonable premium, especially if the patient is still on treatment. If the cancer had spread, it's even harder. This reinforced the message about how bleak things were. I knew that insurance actuaries pore over statistics and that insurance inaccessibility was a metaphor for prognosis.

Charlotte Moss, Daniel's registrar by this time, described his situation at diagnosis as 'grave.' That was a new word for me on Daniel's journey. One can lay too much store by the words doctors use – they don't have time to choose their words as carefully as a lawyer drafting a contract – but 'grave' carried a certain resonance. At an earlier meeting, Charlotte had advised us to 'enjoy the time you have', advice no parent wants to hear.

Some days I felt more optimistic. This was usually because I had come across something vaguely encouraging in my research. Days producing some reason for hope underscored why I regarded research as my therapy, albeit an aversive form of peculiar brutality. But how Daniel felt was the key. If he was feeling well, that lifted my spirits, even though I realised that temporary wellness bore no necessary relationship to what was happening with his disease. Cancer loves to confound.

I encouraged Daniel to take as much exercise as he could. Many people think that exercise is important with cancer. It helps morale, too. One day in January 2007, he ran part of the way over to my house, a mile away. I think this was to prove to himself that he could do it.

Looking abroad

Around this time I made the first of my sixteen trips abroad for Daniel. Hyperthermia, which involves heating the tumour, is considered off-the-wall in the UK but used by several oncologists in Germany and it has a reasonable record with soft-tissue sarcomas.

Rudiger Wessalowski, a world-renown hypertherapist in Düsseldorf, couldn't have been kinder when I visited. Sadly, hyperthermia wasn't for Daniel but I did pick up other useful information, always the advantage of a face-to-face meeting.

It was also early in 2007 that I came across Enrique de Alava in Salamanca, Spain. Enrique is a research pathologist, committed to finding answers to Ewing's. He was incredibly supportive. I wanted to find out as much as possible about Daniel's particular tumour. What were the prognostic pointers? Patients with superficially the same cancer respond so differently to the same treatment that there must be differences in their cancers (or perhaps elsewhere in the body). In understanding those differences lay the key to finding cures, I thought. I'd already discovered, almost by accident, that Daniel had a rare form of Ewing's: something called the EWS/ERG type of chromosomal translocation. That put him in the 5-10 per cent category. He had a rare form of a rare cancer. That might complicate things yet further.

I had a long chat with Enrique, who said he was impressed by my knowledge (another scientist fooled). 'It's gratifying to see a father take such interest', he added. He recommended that we analyse Daniel's tumour for four markers which might be significant. Tumour markers are found in the body (usually in the blood or urine) when cancer is present.

As the tests couldn't be done in London, Enrique

agreed to do them, for free. The plan was that Colin's then secretary, Christine (not her real name), would leave the tumour sample on the ward when we came in for chemo. An envelope was left by Daniel's bed. Inside was a scan report I'd also asked for. There was no sign of the sample and it was too late by the time I arrived at the hospital to chase.

Back home, I realised there was also a small piece of cotton wool, held together by sellotape. I rang Christine: this was the tumour sample, she said. There was no label, nothing. It was so unprofessional. The sample could easily have got lost and we would then have been left with nothing for diagnostic tests, except the 'slides' which Stanmore retained. I'm not particularly squeamish, but it did feel odd holding Daniel's tumour.

After checking Spanish customs regulations, I couriered the sample to Enrique. When the results came, they showed that Daniel's cancer had a high reading for vascular endothelial growth factor (VEGF) and insulin growth factor 1 receptor (IGF1R). These are part of the biology of the tumour. The reading for IGF1R was to prove of particular interest. VEGF seems to be relevant to angiogenesis, the process by which tumours acquire the blood supply they need to grow. I read much about angiogenesis. There was considerable excitement in the 1980s when an American doctor called Judah Folkman identified its role. The history of cancer, sadly, is littered with false dawns and anti-angiogenic drugs have so far proved relatively disappointing.

At the time, I didn't know whether the results from Spain would be useful. But I was glad to have them in the bag. The more we knew, the more sophisticated I hoped judgements could be, though information would need to be treated with caution in the current state of knowledge. This was the approach of a dedicated amateur, but I still feel it was right. There was an important caveat: the risks or burden for Daniel of getting the information mustn't be too great. But that wasn't an issue with a tumour sample already biopsied.

I passed the Spanish results to Colin. He didn't comment. Perhaps he thought I was wasting my time. I probably worried too much about what he and others thought of my approach. Doctors do sometimes have to protect paediatric patients from their parents. There have been court cases in the UK where doctors and parents have been at loggerheads, most famously in recent times over whether a seven year-old boy with a brain tumour, Neon, should have radiotherapy contrary to his mother's wishes. We were never in that territory and I hope that over time Daniel's doctors came to realise that my approach was rational and evidence-based, even if inevitably based on limited understanding.

I wanted more prognostic clues. Lymphocyte recovery was another marker which some Ewing's doctors thought was significant. Lymphocytes are a type of white blood cell and have a key role in fighting infection and cancer. Chemo decimates them. One study found a correlation in serious Ewing's patients between lymphocyte recovery during the first chemo cycle and prognosis. Prognosis was still poor, but survival time improved if lymphocytes recovered to a certain level by a particular point. The same correlation had been found with other cancers.

Different measurement scales are used in the UK and the US, but I worked out that Daniel's lymphocyte recovery was excellent, not only on his first but subsequent cycles too. That seemed to be consistent with his response to chemo. I didn't know if there was a connection but Dr Hiroyuki Tsuchiya, a wonderfully kind sarcoma doctor in Japan, had given lymphocyte transfusions to a Ewing's patient with stubborn metastases in his lungs. The patient had then done really well.

Watford scare

In February 2007, Daniel and I watched Watford play Bolton in the Premiership with my good friend Dominic and his son Miles. This was Daniel's first Premiership match – strangely, given that he had been to a Bundesliga match in Germany, the Euro 96 final and a Champions' League final (we had a perfect view of Zidane's famous volleyed goal). On the morning he said he had pain in his left knee and hip overnight. The pain in his left knee was similar, he thought, to pre-diagnosis pain. Pain, I knew, was usually the first sign of relapse.

It upset me that Daniel wanted to bring his crutches with him. It had been a symbolic moment a few months earlier when he no longer needed them and this seemed symbolism of the opposite kind. I tried to reassure him, but a blight was put on the day. He was clearly worried. The football didn't help – one of the worst matches I have seen. Dominic, a Watford season-ticket holder, was embarrassed about the fare his team dished up. Their stay in the Premiership was suitably short.

The negative experience was capped by a speeding ticket. I explained to the police why it had been a tough day (I wasn't talking about the football). I said, candidly, that I couldn't claim that the stress had caused the offence but threw myself on their mercy. There was the risk of a response: 'Well, you shouldn't have been driving, should you?' But they generously withdrew the ticket.

Daniel's pain subsided and with it my anxiety levels. We had so many of these scares that I've forgotten most of them.

Preparing for the end of frontline chemo

Daniel finished his frontline chemotherapy in March 2007. That was cause for joy, but it also brought anxiety. While he was on chemo I felt reasonably confident that the cancer was being kept in check. No chemo, or radiotherapy, and the cancer could get up to its evil tricks once more. Other Ewing's parents, I learnt, were just as scared at the prospect of chemo ending. Wanting one's child to have a nasty and dangerous poison is just another way in which cancer pollutes normal thinking.

The first post-radiotherapy scans were in April 2007. I'd spent weeks putting together a table of options for future treatment, from my reading and discussions with doctors around the world. The conventional approach with most cancers is to give frontline treatment and then react to a relapse if it happens. This is the so-called 'wait and watch' approach. I hated wait and watch, because it was almost inevitable that Daniel's cancer would return, when it would be extremely difficult to deal with. So I favoured preemptive treatment, if there was something with a reasonable chance of working and Daniel could handle it. I therefore researched like mad to see if there was a likely candidate.

I prepared a table setting out the options and pros and cons. It didn't include everything - no complementary medicine and omitting some more speculative conventional options - but still ran to several closely-typed pages. The list of options, all used by Ewing's doctors somewhere, was long and bewilderingly complicated.

This is a short extract:

Treatment option	Rationale/ Objectives	Efficacy	Disadvantages (other than psychological/QoL [quality of life])	Timing	Comments/ Questions
High-dose chemo with autologous stem cell rescue	• attack cancer/ reduce risk of relapse from MRD	• tandem ME: JCO Vol 21, 16 (August) 2003: 3072-3078: Burdach et al: 9 out of 28 in CR at 5 years (maybe bit lower for Dan's age group?); 11/28 alive. Better results now according to SB • experience mirrored at Düsseldorf • treosulfan: reasonable results at Münster post-relapse; about 30 cases pre-relapse there (following amendment to Euro Ewing protocol) – comparable results so far as with BuMel. 15 months (so far) EFS with pelvic post-RT local recurrence patient (i.e. worst case) in Düsseldorf .Also used in Poland: Pediatric Transplantation 2005:9; 618-621 (Drabko et al) • generally: opinion divided about efficacy for bone mets. E.g. MSKCC NY say not for bone mets. St Jude do it, though not sure about efficacy. Many major centres seem to use it for bone mets	• ME: risk of serious blood toxicity/ mucositis/ diarrhoea. One death in 50 cases in Düsseldorf; one in 28 in SB JCO article. High-dose etoposide associated with treatment-related AML/MDS (8% at 40 months for survivors): Expert opinion in pharmacotherapy (2004) 5(5) (Rodriguez-Galindo) • treosulfan: lower toxicity, though Uta Dirksen presentation at Stuttgart Dec 06 unclear. St Jude: 'toxicity profile is very appealing, and if we could acquire the drug we would certainly be evaluating it here.'	Asap provided Daniel in 'remission', including no BM involvement/ able to tolerate? Maybe after RT to bone mets	BuMel not possible for Dan. Some places (e.g. St Jude) use carboplatin with ME (see also pt 24 in Bone marrow transplantation (2007), 1-6 (Yamada et al) (Japan) – v bad bone mets with pelvic primary). Thiotepa also used, and Ecteinascidin-743 (activity in ES pts in US phase 1 trials, though unspectacular results in Milan trial) SB uses ME with treosulfan/topotecan (similar to irinotecan?) **Q:** is there a biological reason why HDC would work for primary/lung mets but not bone/BM mets? **Q:** Daniel has 2 lots of SCs, one CD34+-separated, one not (though RT-PCR of blood after VIDE 4 negative). Use non-separated first if having tandem HDC?

Looking back, I'm surprised how much I had learnt in a year.

The first option I listed, however, was 'Do nothing.' This was a serious option, as was 'Do nothing for a time', second in my list. Naturally, the last thing Daniel wanted was more unpleasant treatment. He would have loved to put the whole experience behind him. I would have loved that for him, for all of us. He was doing so much around this time – a trip to Brussels with his school, winning a prize with a string quartet at the Godalming Music Festival, playing with a baroque ensemble at a school concert and then accompanying the jazz band for his own composition. We wanted him to enjoy life.

But we also knew that Daniel was desperate to get better. The single entry in the 'Disadvantages' column for the doing nothing option referred to minimal residual disease (MRD). This is the cancer a patient may still have after treatment but which is currently undetectable. It only becomes detectable when it grows into a tumour. Hitting the cancer when it's at its weakest, before it has had a chance to mutate further and grow, is a basic oncology principle.

When I sent my paper to Colin and some of the other doctors, I acknowledged how extraordinarily difficult these decisions were and how they must have to make them on a daily basis. I didn't know what reaction my table would elicit from Colin. Whichever way one looked at it, the subliminal message was that I wasn't willing simply to accept his judgement. I hoped that he would welcome a parent getting so deeply involved but the opposite reaction would have been understandable.

To his credit, Colin thanked me for setting everything

out. It had been hugely laborious and emotionally taxing work. I was really feeling the pressure of making the right decision.

Everything would be blown out of the water if the scan results weren't good. I was tense the weekend before meeting Colin on 16th April 2007. But we had some light relief. Daniel and I went to watch Man Utd play Watford in the FA Cup semi-final in Birmingham, courtesy once again of Dominic. Unlike our previous Watford experience, it was a magical day. Man Utd won 4:1 with all their stars playing – Giggs, Ronaldo, Rooney et al. Daniel talked non-stop in the car both ways. He asked me to give him sentences to translate into Latin. And we played fizz buzz and other games. That was Daniel – he loved serious things and frivolous things in equal measure. He told me about his plans for his twenties. He wanted to line-judge at Wimbledon again and play tennis. 'Will I be able to go abroad after my A levels in June?' he asked. 'A few weeks in France might be possible but perhaps not further afield for the time being', I replied, secretly thinking that even France might be pushing it. He was considering, he said, starting to learn Greek and going back to school for a third year sixth to do French and philosophy. It was wonderful to hear him talk so positively.

Daniel also touched on the meeting with Colin, suggesting he might want to discuss treatment options with him since I had said I was expecting good results. It made me anxious, because he didn't really understand about microscopic disease. It's difficult to discuss treatment options without prognosis slipping into the conversation. I knew that prognosis was still extremely bad. The truth was that Daniel was happy to discuss things with Colin provided he heard only good things, but we couldn't fix that. Petra agreed we didn't want Daniel's hopes to be crushed when he was feeling so positive. Managing these things was always so difficult.

The day before the meeting, I went to a park to prepare and watched *Amazing Grace*, the brilliant film about Wilberforce's fight to end the slave trade.

The next morning Daniel was in high spirits, and was writing a commentary about his two compositions for Music A level. He had to go off for a bone scan, a relief because he wouldn't be there for the PET scan result. It was actually excellent. 'Overall, Daniel has done very well to date', Colin said, 'better than average for his admittedly extremely poor prognosis group, although a good response might only postpone relapse by, say, three months.' The overwhelming likelihood was still that Daniel would relapse.

Colin favoured high-dose chemo (HDC), with a transplant of Daniel's own stem cells. I was surprised, given that he had always said HDC was unlikely. It was back in the frame because of Daniel's excellent response to treatment. I wondered silently if the PET/CT scans had helped persuade Colin. They gave a clearer picture than MRIs. I admit that it comforted me to think that all the research I was doing might have helped to identify the correct course. I'd really fought to get Daniel these scans (I believe they are now routinely used for Ewing's patients at UCH).

The next step was for Colin to meet Daniel to discuss HDC. This was a few days later on the ward. I appreciated his making time out of clinic. Vikky the specialist oncology nurse was also there. Colin gave a positive message to Daniel: 'You've done very well and so I'm suggesting high-dose chemo to reduce the chance of the cancer coming back. You started at the back of the race but have now come forward quite a bit.' That was an encouraging message for Daniel to hear and I later thanked Colin. The side-effects from HDC, however, would be horrible. Vikky chipped in: 'You will feel more wretched than you have ever felt, Daniel.'

Colin wanted Daniel to have HDC as soon as possible, because relapse could happen at any time. So it was fixed for early May; various tests were needed first. Daniel still wanted to do his A levels in June. It seemed a long shot but we encouraged the thought. I used the intervening time to research more about the side-effects. Was there anything which we could do to limit them? They fell into two categories: those which were life-threatening and those which were 'merely' unpleasant. Each arose from the fact that Daniel would have a seriously deficient immune system. He didn't know about the life-threatening risks and we were happy to keep it that way. His cancer was extremely life-threatening, so we were trading one kind of life-threatening risk, which the HDC might just reduce, against another, which was fairly remote. So the balance of risks pointed to Daniel having the treatment, even if the chances of long-term success were low.

One of the main risks was a liver disease called veno-occlusive disease, which can be fatal. I came across a Ewing's teenager in the US who died a lingering and nasty death from VOD post-HDC. There was also increased risk of secondary cancer.

Mucositis leads to a sore mouth or throat. I'd come across traumeel s, a homeopathic remedy. Unusually for homeopathy, it was going through a clinical trial, in the US. The lead researcher couldn't tell me the preliminary results but I got the impression that they were good. The pharmacists at UCH didn't know about it, but the risks seemed minute so we gave it a go. As luck would have there was a homeopathic pharmacy – an old-style apothecary from a bygone age – not far from the hospital.

Another technique some advocated was simply sucking ice cubes during the infusion of the HDC. However, an article suggested that this could reduce the effectiveness of the chemo, depending where the cancer was. Nothing – but nothing – is straightforward with cancer, not even sucking ice cubes. Early one morning, I rang the main author of the article, Takehiko Mori, in Japan. He reassured me and seemed really chuffed I was taking an interest in his research. Colin had no objections to the ice-cubes so when the day came, Petra and I kept up the supply of ice-cubes. Whether because of the traumeel s, the ice-cubes or plain luck, Daniel's mouth sores and sore throat were not nearly as bad as they might have been.

My worries the night before HDC were many and varied: the risks of treatment, whether it would work, how Daniel would cope, the effect on his morale, his willingness to keep going with the diet. As ever, perspective helped. It was the evening Madeleine McCann was kidnapped in Portugal. It was a salutary reminder that some parents were having to deal with something even more serious. Millions of people around the world were facing the most dreadful tragedies or hardships. We were by no means alone and we were luckier than many. Whenever I heard on the news that a child had died in an accident or a soldier had been killed in Afghanistan, it struck me that those families had, in an instant, completely lost hope, perhaps without realising that they'd needed it. We at least had some hope. Even in the darkest times we had hope to cling onto.

Indeed, there were children and families worse off at UCH. That same week, two children died of cancer. Another child, Peter (not his real name), was autistic; he once had general anaesthetic on the ward, after refusing to cooperate in the unfamiliar surroundings of the operating theatre. His mother had died and his father was a transsexual, now called Angie, and an agoraphobic. Peter hadn't seen Angie, whom he still called 'Dad', for eight years. There's always someone with bigger problems.

On the morning of his admission to UCH, Daniel went to school for his Economics A level mock exam. He continued to amaze. I'd been in touch with the school examination officer about arrangements for his A levels, in case Daniel took them. I asked her provisionally to arrange home invigilators, as with his AS levels. Her reply was sharp. She complained about the late notice and the fact that we couldn't be more definitive, not understanding, it seems, the unpredictability of cancer and its treatment. There was no hint of compassion or flexibility in any of her communications. She was also abrupt with the hospital education officer. I noted in my diary that she was in the wrong job. Daniel's comment was: 'She has a lot to deal with.' He was more tolerant of her intolerance than I was.

Daniel was allowed home for the weekend after various tests. We came back in on the Sunday and read some Tacitus together. It was a happy and special time with several games of Black Jack, a hospital regular.

That evening, Daniel said he was willing to stay by himself because I would be with him in hospital for up to three weeks. This was quite an unusual gesture from him.

I'm sure that he appreciated the support we gave him. But he took it for granted as well and I'm glad that he did. It showed that he didn't doubt that we'd do whatever we had to for him.

There was still the issue of which stem cells to give back – the ones purged of CD34+ or the unpurged ones. Daniel knew nothing about this. I rang, in Philadelphia, one of the main advocates of using purged stem cells. To my surprise, he thought that Daniel should have the unpurged ones, Colin's view too. Was it the right decision, particularly since as it happened Daniel only had relatively minor infections? Had we given him his cancer back via diseased stem cells? As with so much else on this journey, there is no way of knowing.

Daniel had his usual pains, nausea and several bouts of diarrhoea and some mucositis. But really it could have been so much worse. He did some work for his A levels, despite feeling decidedly below par. One evening we went for a lovely walk in Regent's Park.

Another evening, I left Daniel to go to an event about clinical trials. I was keen to go because Ian Judson, a leading sarcoma specialist at the Royal Marsden was speaking and I wanted to find out more about a particular trial. Ticketless, I had to blag my way in. I didn't get back to the ward until 10pm. 'Why have you been so long?' Daniel wanted to know. It was easy to forget how vulnerable he was. On another occasion, he didn't want me to go to the kitchen because I'd already had my permitted parole for the evening, a trip to Sainsbury's. He found upsetting the movie *Philadelphia* in which the Tom Hanks character dies of AIDS. Did it resonate with him, I wondered? He watched an episode of *Friends* as an antidote!

Daniel was discharged ahead of schedule. The next day

he went to school – astonishing again. He was a bit nervous about bumping into the examination officer who'd been so unhelpful.

We were getting through the HDC experience. Many of the kids on the teenage cancer ward had leukaemia and needed donor stem cells. It inspired me to become a bone marrow donor. I remembered the offer of a bone marrow donation by a colleague, Sean, when Daniel was diagnosed. To become a donor, one has first to give blood in the normal way so that they can check if you are suitable. I went along to a clinic in early June 2007 but was turned away, because the prophylactic antibiotics I'm supposed to have before a procedure (due to a minor heart condition) would contaminate the blood. I was genuinely disappointed.

Daniel took his first A level on 8th June, less than five weeks after HDC. He was so determined to get on with his life.

Barcelona

Throughout this time, I was continuing to research. One day in June 2007 I got up at 4am to go to Barcelona to see Jaume Mora, a paediatric sarcoma doctor and colleague of Enrique de Alava, the research pathologist who had analysed Daniel's tumour. Dr Mora – unlike most other practitioners I communicated with, he preferred to use surnames – is another hero of Daniel's cancer journey.

Visiting children's cancer wards was always poignant: I can still picture one poor child screaming in the waiting room in Barcelona. Everything at the Hospital de Sant Joan de Deu is in Catalan but Dr Mora's English was good, having done part of his training in New York.

He gave me over two hours of his time. He talked quickly and technically, so note-taking was frantic. He shared ideas but most importantly, he gave me hope. One of the easiest ways doctors can transmit hope is by talking (anonymously) about other patients with the same serious disease who have done well, if only for a period. I did wonder on this first visit whether Dr Mora was perhaps too definite in some of his views, but I came to appreciate that he's a knowledgeable and conscientious doctor, hugely committed to his patients (and those like Daniel who were not really his patients).

Dr Mora's big diagnostic thing was RT-PCR, which helps to detect microscopic cancer in the bone marrow (different to the RT-PCR of his blood Daniel had in 2006). RT-PCR turned into something of battle-ground between Colin McMaster and me. There was a difficult meeting at the end of June 2007. This was the day of the foiled Haymarket car bomb; Gordon Brown's statesmanlike response was probably the high point of his premiership. Colin seemed not in a good mood. He told Daniel that he might relapse and he might not (it was hard to fault that logic). 'Relapse could happen at any time - even tomorrow - and in any part of the body', he added. 'There is no further treatment which could reduce the risk. There are some interesting new developments with Ewing's but many developments fail.'

Colin thereby pre-empted the discussion he knew I wanted. He also knew that Daniel didn't want to discuss prognosis or treatment options. After Daniel left, Colin was still more pessimistic. 'There is a high likelihood of relapse and it will probably happen over the next six to nine months', he said. He wasn't in favour of maintenance chemo (low-dose chemo to keep residual cancer in check), which Dr Mora used, though he was not as averse to it as he'd once been. I had in fact heard about a Ewing's patient, aged seventeen who'd done really well on low-dose chemo as frontline treatment. The family were Jehovah's Witnesses, so the patient couldn't have normal-dose chemo because of the risk of a low red cell count and the consequent need for a transfusion.

Colin was also against Daniel having an RT-PCR of his bone marrow. The information gained wouldn't help – there was no treatment at this point. He added: 'It would be unethical for me to sanction the procedure.' Maybe I was oversensitive, but the implication seemed to be that it was unethical for me to want him to have it. 'The fact that other Ewing's clinicians take a different view is simply because there are always different views', he added.

Colin also gave the impression that he was handing day-to-day responsibility for Daniel's care over to his new registrar, Nick Turner, who was at the meeting. Dr Turner didn't make eye contact when I shook his hand at the end. I sensed that he was embarrassed at Colin's dismissive manner.

I felt deflated afterwards but strangely inured to it all. Petra was reluctant to put Daniel through anything else – understandably, given the fatalism we'd just been fed. In light of all my conversations with other doctors, I wasn't prepared to be fatalistic and pointed out that relapse would be horrible physically and psychologically for Daniel. I was determined to try to prevent relapse, or at least to put it off for as long as possible.

Daniel and I had mooted going to South Africa for the inaugural Twenty20 cricket World Cup in September. Petra had been reluctant but now conceded: 'You might as well go.'

One good outcome from the meeting.

We kept our despondency from Daniel. It all seemed to pass him by. He was upbeat about his prospects, which Petra found heartbreaking. He went to Wimbledon that afternoon. He was in such good spirits and it made me all the more determined to fight for him. He lifted my mood, as so often he did.

The following day he saw *42nd Street*. Daniel loved musicals. He was continuing to live life. We also watched *Goodbye Bafana*, a film about apartheid. His hair was beginning to grow back. We played a lot of table-tennis around this time and he was moving so well. He had a natural talent and could do all the spins, with a majestic backhand. He was inconsistent - probably the result of a raw, uncoached technique - but when he was on song he could be sensational. We spent countless hours playing together, as he did with Sasha and Florence. Daniel was a talented all-round games player, not at the top level certainly, but he was chosen to play tennis for Surrey at his age group a couple of times and also played representative football and cricket (I didn't think he was good enough for the football team, skilful but lacking physicality, but the coach seemed to like him). When we played tennis on public courts, people would stop and watch him.

In early July, he went to Cambridge to have a look at the university and was impressed, particularly by King's College. He also went to a Latin summer school at University College London, next door to the hospital. He told me of another student who missed a day because he was queuing for the Proms: 'That's the definition of a geek', pronounced Daniel. He didn't see himself as a geek and indeed many of his interests were ungeekish. But he began to learn Greek and enjoyed it.

This was a tough time for me. Some days I felt tired, low and listless. I had a chat with Chris Henry, the CLIC Sargent nurse who'd been so helpful at the outset. It wasn't her fault but the chat made me feel worse. I wanted her to say that Colin had a reputation for being overly pessimistic but in fact she said: 'He would think he's being realistic and wants to convey the message about quality of life for whatever time Daniel had, avoiding unnecessary procedures.' She added, a little more encouragingly, that Colin was happy to be surprised about pessimistic predictions.

My general demeanour wasn't helped by the fact that I was handling a major court case, a complicated judicial review, which was proving a nightmare. The trial was due towards the end of July. For a variety of reasons, things were happening very late which added to the pressure, with much work still to be done. I wasn't in the best frame of mind to handle such a difficult case.

However, my main focus was on Daniel having an RT-PCR. It involved a minor operation, probably under general anaesthetic (though it could be done under a local), so this wasn't something I was pursuing lightly. Any operation carries risks and naturally the last thing I wanted was to put Daniel through something unnecessarily. But there were studies in Israel and France showing a correlation between bone marrow RT-PCR positivity and survival from Ewing's. The number of patients involved was small but we also had Jaume Mora's experience in Barcelona. Anecdotal evidence, especially from a specialist doctor, shouldn't be disregarded – it just needs to be handled with care.

I sent Colin an email on 13th July 2007. As usual, I put much thought into composing it. As well as content, I tried to get the tone right. This was never a relationship of equals: we needed Colin much more than he needed us. In truth, I doubt that he cared how I expressed myself. His own emails were short, no doubt reflecting how busy he was. The brevity could camouflage meaning, such that I had to seek clarification, further trying his patience. (Oscar Wilde once apologised to a friend that he didn't have time to write a short letter. I doubt that Colin's emails were the result of Wildean crafting.)

On this occasion, my politeness camouflaged my anger at Colin's attitude during the meeting in June. I was determined that, tiptoe around sensitivities though I might, Daniel was going to get what I thought he needed – the RT-PCR test. I never allowed my gaze to be diverted from goals.

In the email, I set out the limited nature of our objectives - it was important that Colin understood I was a realist, on the same prognosis wavelength. I then wrote:

'... *we have given very careful thought to Daniel having an RT-PCR of his bone marrow. As you said, there's no point obtaining diagnostic information, particularly where there will be some price for the patient in obtaining it, unless there's something one can do with it. However, since there are treatment possibilities (to put it no higher), knowing whether Daniel has [microscopic metastases] is very important to us in making judgements about risk-taking. You will know that there is a highly significant correlation between presence of Ewing's micromets post-treatment as determined by RT-PCR of the BM and relapse and everyone seems to agree that the best time to hit microscopic ES cells, if possible, is when they are microscopic.'*

And then to the solution. Confrontation was not the answer. Daniel and I liked the definition of diplomacy by the Italian Daniele Vare: 'The art of letting someone else have your way.' I wanted to let Colin have my way, so I continued:

> 'The children's cancer hospital in Barcelona is willing to do the RT-PCR for us. They work closely with Memorial Sloan-Kettering, where as you probably know researchers believe that using STEAP 1 and cyclin D1 as markers provides even more sensitivity than using just the fusion transcript (see [ref]). Obviously, it would be much better for Daniel to have the procedure done at UCH and we would be grateful if you would re-consider. Subject to any technical considerations, we're keen to have it done as soon as possible. Ideally, it would be done at the same time as taking out the spacer, which Daniel would like to have out asap, but I think that would depend on whether the latter could be done at UCH (since the RT-PCR would have to be).'

So the solution was Daniel having the RT-PCR at the same time as removal of his spacer (inserted to protect his bladder from radiotherapy). It was now proving uncomfortable. If he was having an operation anyway, he might as well have the RT-PCR at the same time. I hoped that Colin could see that I'd done my research and that my desire for an RT-PCR was rational. He might disagree, but the message was: we will have it done in Barcelona if need be. Did he really want his patient to travel to Spain? Everything was such a battle, as I noted in my diary.

We were asked to see Colin on 20th July. Petra was dreading

the meeting because she felt he conveyed no hope. She wanted to be in and out as quickly as possible. We were worried about the pain Daniel was having. On the way in to London, the mood was nervous but light. Petra related how, when Daniel was four, she'd found a chocolate bar down his trousers in a shop. He denied taking it, naturally. Someone must have put it there. They are like that in Chobham.

There was in fact, a joint meeting with Colin and Anna Cassoni – two for the price of one, as I lamely joked as we went in. There was a doctor from Addenbrooke's in Cambridge present too: there were often visiting doctors, testimony to UCH's expertise in sarcomas. Colin was in a much better mood. He apologised for being so negative at the previous meeting. 'Daniel has had a really tremendous response to treatment and that's prognostically important', he said. 'He might make it or at least have a lengthy period in remission.' He cautioned against relying on advice from doctors who didn't know Daniel's detailed case – he'd fallen into this trap himself – and I assured him we were fully aware of this.

Colin agreed to Daniel having an RT-PCR. He acknowledged that there was some benefit of having more information about Daniel's bone marrow now, although interpreting it would depend on the context. He didn't want to discuss treatment options until he saw the result, which we said was fine.

As I left, I turned to Colin and said: 'I'm sorry for being a pest.' He replied jokingly 'Yes, you are!' The meeting was more positive than we'd anticipated and so much more pleasant than the previous one. There was, as so often, a sting in the tail: Colin said the pain which Daniel was experiencing could be the start of a relapse. But he didn't seem too concerned. Petra and I felt so much better afterwards and bounced back down the corridor. When I told Daniel that the meeting had been really positive, he replied with a smile: 'Is that because you got your way on the RT-PCR?'

My uplifted mood meant that I was better able to continue my preparation for the court case. That evening I went to the leaving party of Stewart, a good friend of mine. Stewart was my successor as legal officer at Child Poverty Action Group and we'd taught judicial review and human rights together. He's now a relatively senior judge. It was his wife Nathalie with whom Daniel had done work experience in 2006. It was great to be able to relax and catch up with old friends. While I was at the party, Daniel rang to tell me that Chobham was flooded, so I stayed with Stewart and Nathalie in Hampstead. I spent the weekend preparing for the case.

Pain

Daniel continued to have pain in his hip. He mentioned using crutches. He'd played football for twenty minutes with Sasha and Florence but the pain continued to increase. So concerned was I that I asked Nick Turner, Colin's registrar, if we could have a PET/CT scan. I felt pessimistic. Daniel began to take paracetamol, a mild form of pain relief but still pain relief.

As we fretted about the scan results, Daniel rang with his A level results. Had I forgotten they were coming, he asked. I hadn't, but in truth they mattered so much less to me than what was happening with his cancer. He truly surpassed himself, with 99 per cent overall in Latin, 97.5 per cent in Economics and 96 per cent in Music. His Economics marks were the best in the school's living memory. It was an astonishing achievement and I again told Daniel how proud I was of him. He knew it was another record year for A levels – the media was full of allegations of dumbing-down – but I assured him he would have been in the top echelon, no matter what the system of marking.

His cousin JJ wanted to know what had gone wrong in Music – only 96 per cent. 'Daniel is truly inspiring', he said. Mum commented how proud Dad would have been. He would indeed.

The day after the A level results, Nick Turner rang to say the PET/CT was clear. They took a particularly close look at the pelvis. I knew how worried Daniel was so I ignored his stricture about not wanting to know scan results. Pride and pleasure one day, huge relief the next. A magical couple of days. I knew the relief might be short-lived but on this journey we had to enjoy the moment. Mum wanted to know if Daniel was cured, so I had to explain gently about microscopic cancer.

While we were having good news, someone else was having bad news. That was always the pattern. Someone was up, someone was down. I felt a bit guilty during the good times knowing that others were having a terrible time, but it would send one mad thinking like this all the time. Daniel and I had a wonderful day watching England play India in a one-day international in Southampton.

Some light relief

Dad: *Sometimes you have to wash your hair, Daniel*
Daniel (aged two): *Well, sometimes I don't*

The US Tennis Open was, as Daniel put it, the third leg of a personal Grand Slam – he'd been to Paris with his tennis club and Wimbledon several times. He was always useless at keeping in touch with me when he was away, but that was fine. It gave me a partial break from cancer as well. Petra and I had discussed her getting a second opinion at Memorial Sloan Kettering Hospital in New York. A number of doctors there had given me informal second opinions. However, a meeting would cost $3,000 (for surgery, a foreign patient had to pay a deposit of $300,000, which inevitably excluded the vast majority). A formal second opinion wasn't essential and we decided to give it a miss.

Hot on the heels of New York was another magical

experience. As a seriously ill teenager Daniel was entitled to 'make a wish.' I'd read about these charities before Daniel's journey but never imagined that one day he would be in line for a wish. This was something for other families.

UCH had links with a leading make-a-wish charity, Starlight. Daniel, ever indecisive, had ummed and ahhed about what to ask for. It didn't have to be a day out – one could request a laptop or something similar (Andrew, a nineteen year-old American dying of Ewing's and brought up in the Christian tradition of giving, donated to a homeless charity). Eventually, Daniel decided to ask for tickets to the *Last Night of the Proms*. He'd always enjoyed watching it on TV and a couple of times we'd been to the spillover concert in Hyde Park.

We heard nothing for ages and I'd nearly forgotten about it. Then, just a few days before the concert – Daniel was in New York – I had a call from Starlight. Five members of the BBC Symphony Orchestra had given up their personal ticket allocation so that we could go. Such kindness. In addition, Daniel would be allowed to attend the final rehearsal in the Royal Albert Hall on the morning. The orchestra then wanted to know where Daniel's interest came from – they'd never had a request like this before. Daniel explained that he played the clarinet and piano. So they said: 'Bring your clarinet along and you may be able to join us for one piece.'

Daniel was thrilled. But he was worried about what to talk about with the clarinettists. So we suggested he take along the score for the piano and clarinet sonata he'd composed for his Music A level. Daniel was reluctant to take the piece, a mixture, I think, of modesty and not wanting to draw attention to himself. But we said he could ask for advice about improving his composition skills. He reluctantly agreed.

Saturday 8th September 2007 was one of those special days that come along infrequently in life. Many people, for whom life is a never-ending struggle for survival, never experience them. The magic of this day was accentuated by all the horrible days which had preceded it.

Daniel rehearsing for a school concert just before he was diagnosed.

Starlight sent a car for us early on the Saturday. The BBC Symphony couldn't have been more accommodating. I was ushered to one of the boxes from which to film with Petra's camcorder. I sat next to the BBC cameraman, who was desperately trying to keep track of the Russian soprano Anna Netrebko as she diva'd all over the stage. Daniel later left me in no doubt how inadequate my filming had been.

I felt emotional, as a Welshman, listening to the beautiful melody that is *Ar Hyd y Nos (All Through the Night)*, and as Daniel's father, *Danny Boy*. And then I spotted Daniel sitting in the orchestra. He took part in the rehearsal for the whole of the second half of the concert, *Land of Hope and Glory*, *Rule Britannia*, *Jerusalem* and the rest. He was sight-reading, but seemed to keep up.

When rehearsal was over, Richard Hosford, the principal clarinettist and Elizabeth Burley, the pianist, asked if they could play Daniel's sonata in one of the side-rooms downstairs. So down we trotted. The conductor, Jiri Belohlavek, joined us – he'd noticed that there was a stray clarinettist in his orchestra. Richard and Elizabeth played the sonata and played it beautifully. They were sight-reading, inevitably, but how they brought the piece to life. I fought back the tears, by no means the only time during the day. And when they had finished they asked Daniel if he would like the orchestra to record the piece next time they were in the studio. Bit of a no brainer really.

Starlight had thoughtfully organised a hotel for us for the afternoon, conscious that Daniel would be tired. We watched England play Israel on TV. And then back to the Albert Hall for the concert. As we waited to go in, Margaret Thatcher arrived to a chorus of shouted praise from admirers. I didn't join in. I was not a fan. The most important thing a political leader can do, in my view, is to impart values, to set the tone for the nation. Policies come and go. Lady Thatcher's policies are for historians to debate. I couldn't hold a serious conversation about monetarism and supply-side economics with someone who knew what they were talking about. Some unions, vital work for their members though they do, no doubt needed reining in. But what mattered for me were the values she espoused. Many were the opposite of those I wanted Daniel to absorb. This was the age when individualism transcended into selfishness, when compassion was sneered at, when certain forms of bigotry were given a cloak of respectability. Greed was not invented in the 1980s, but it was legitimised –

'Greed is Good', Gordon Gekko's mantra in *Wall Street* – and we are all paying the price now. It has become the vice of our age. So I didn't join in the cheering.

We had great seats, behind the choir. The concert was unbelievably good. I particularly enjoyed Monti's bohemian *Czardas*, a favourite of Daniel's too. I'd been a bit ambivalent about *Last Night,* loving the music but feeling uneasy about the jingoism inherent in the patriotic songs. But my misgivings melted away. I came to realise what a cosmopolitan event it is. We counted flags from about thirty-five different countries. There is patriotic pride, certainly, but of the benign sort, not the in-your-face sort of English football fans or the arrogance of cultural supremacists. This is a celebration, above all, of music.

So many happy memories. No day during this journey was free of worry. Daniel told me that he'd been having pain over the past couple of days above the left pelvis and in his lower left leg, which was outside the PET scan field. And the day was pregnant with poignancy because I knew the overwhelming likelihood was that we would lose Daniel. The happier he was, the more poignant I felt.

But let none of this detract from a special day. Starlight and the BBC Symphony were so kind. Richard, Elizabeth and Susanna, the orchestra director, later sent Daniel a Christmas card, which really touched him. They seemed to take him to their hearts and said he could go to any of their concerts. Richard later told me he'd not expected Daniel to live long.

And the orchestra were true to their word about recording the piece. A CD arrived a few days later. I cannot separate out parental bias but I love it as a piece of music. My friend Tobias played it to some of his music student friends at Humboldt University in Berlin, without telling them the composer. Who did they think? Mozart and Schubert were amongst the suggestions. Of course, it's not at that level but nor is it what I would expect from an eighteen year-old A level student. I wanted, in a fit of irrational pride, to send it to Classic FM, explaining the context in which it was composed, but Daniel, modestly and probably wisely, would have none of it. It was nowhere near good enough, he said.

However, Paul Meelor, who composed the motet *Ubi Caritas* for the Royal Wedding in 2011 and also the Military Wives Christmas Number 1 *Wherever You Are* suggested that the piece had great musical worth and was 'a powerful expression of someone [with] obviously a great deal to give'. Praise indeed. Daniel composed the piece when he was on chemotherapy. Perhaps adversity stoked his creativity, as it has with so many other artists down the ages.

Mum was tearful when I told her about our day at the Albert Hall. She understood that Daniel wasn't out of the woods but strongly believed in the power of prayer. So many people were praying for Daniel, she said. Daniel was tired after the concert but still officiated at a tennis tournament in Aldershot the following day.

South Africa

South Africa soon followed. This was our first time to Africa. Daniel did ok on the long overnight flight, although the airline hadn't been helpful about legroom. We got in at around 7am but he still wanted to go to a cricket match later that day.

Newlands is a wonderfully-appointed cricket ground, with the majestic Table Mountain as a backdrop. We saw Zimbabwe beat Australia, a major upset. This was one of the few international competitions Zimbabwe were allowed into at the time, thanks to Mugabe's tyranny. The Zimbabwean cricket team, the Zimbabwean nation, needed all the glory they could get.

The apartheid legacy interested me and I think Daniel. There were contrasting experiences in the first couple of days. The Cape Coloured taxi driver who took us back from the match displayed the first 'pure' form of racism I'd really encountered. Nowadays racism in Britain is usually of the nasty sort, often perpetrated by people struggling with their own inadequacies and resentments, rather than borne of a view about intrinsic superiority and inferiority or attributes distributed on a racial basis. But this taxi driver pronounced: 'The white man knows how to rule.' In his world, coloureds came next in the pecking order and then the black population at the bottom of the pile. He was nostalgic for apartheid. Unemployment had not been a problem then, apparently.

By contrast, Arlene, one of the waitresses at the hotel (and white), was of a modern outlook. She didn't understand racism. She had empathy for suffering animals too - oppression is oppression, no matter who the victim. Her philosophy was: every day is magical so make the most of it.

The top of Table Mountain had recently had a spate of muggings. Is nowhere sacred? Cape Town, like many cities with wide disparity in wealth, has a real violent crime problem. I felt uneasy at the thought of the cable car up the mountain - one of many phobias - but Daniel was determined to ride it and didn't care whether I came or not. He wasn't sympathetic about my vertigo (I didn't remind him of the time he clung to me going up the Eiffel Tower). My protective instincts overcame my wussiness. The driver on the way down remembered me from the way up and offered me a seat next to him. I deserved that act of humiliating kindness. The views from the top were just stunning.

The taxi driver back to the Cape Town Waterfront was an economic migrant from Malawi. 'Why do you talk to everyone?' Daniel wanted to know. In the airport on the way home, when Daniel had gone to the loo, I was approached by a tourist board official with a questionnaire. Daniel's comment on his return: 'I can't leave you for two minutes without finding you talking to someone, can I?!' He preferred simply to observe.

We did all the usual touristy things. On Robben Island, Nelson Mandela's home for twenty-seven years, the guides are former political prisoners. We listened to the stories and stood in Mandela's tiny cell and saw where the prisoners had to cut stone day after day of back-breaking, mind-numbing tedium. It was still difficult to imagine it all as a prison, as a symbol of a system of evil perversion. I had struggled in the same way at Dachau concentration camp years previously.

I wanted Daniel to come on a township tour too. But TB was rampant there so we decided not to take the risk. It was a shame. I'd always wanted Daniel to have a rounded view of the places we went to, to understand history and its cultural glories but also to know something of the injustices which humankind inflicts. Cancer apart, so much of his life was privileged and he was surrounded by love and for the most part by people being nice to one another. That was the side of life to accentuate but there was another side. I would bore Daniel with my favourite sporting aphorism, by the West Indian writer CLR James, particularly apt on this cricketing holiday: 'What do they know of cricket who only cricket know?' It's in fact, an adaptation of Rudyard Kipling's 'And what should they know of England who only England know?' from his poem *English Flag*. Daniel was fortunate in being acquainted with a world far beyond England and I wanted that world to extend beyond normal tourist exposure.

He was able to go on a safari. There was only time for a day trip. We watched at close quarters two male springboks fighting for supremacy, with the loser knowing when it was time to depart with tail metaphorically between legs and saw all the major representatives from the African jungle, including lions (not at such close quarters). We were able to stroke amazingly tame cheetahs just like one would stroke a dog or a cat. This was perhaps Daniel's favourite memory of the whole trip. Our guide had a real feel for nature and empathy for the animals. I couldn't resist making a critical comment in the visitors' book, however. In the wild we saw ostriches and outside the restaurant was a large pool with crocodiles swimming freely; in the shop were luxury ostrich and crocodile products. It seemed incongruous and didn't live up to the stated ethos of the park of respect for nature.

So that was South Africa. I wondered, inevitably, if it would be my last holiday with Daniel. He complained periodically of pain in his hips and his jaw when he returned, but was pretty well. I loved our time together. The cricket was only average, a stunning reverse sweep 6 by Kevin Pietersen aside. But that, as CLR James might have said, was incidental.

When we landed at Heathrow at 6.15am, Daniel announced that he wanted to go to school, despite barely sleeping.

It was back to reality for me. When I switched on my computer there was an email from Colin's secretary saying that he wanted to see us. I worried that this was about the scans Daniel had just before we went to Africa. I rang his registrar, Sandra Strauss, who was initially reluctant to give me the results which upped anxiety levels. But the scans were fine.

Yet more decisions

There were two main medical issues on the horizon that autumn. First, was the RT-PCR, with the operation due in a few days' time. The second was whether Daniel should have extra radiotherapy. This had been rumbling on for a few months.

Daniel's radiotherapy had been to his primary tumour, in his left pelvis and also to his sacrum which adjoins the pelvis. But that left several metastatic sites. I was concerned that we were leaving these to chemo. I knew that bone relapses were common with bone metastatic disease. Earlier in the year, I had been to see Stefan Burdach, a leading Ewing's clinician and researcher in Munich and ever helpful. He was a proselytiser for irradiating all known met sites, whenever possible. He explained that there was a correlation between bone met sites at diagnosis and relapse sites in around two-thirds of cases.

Colin's reservations were twofold. First, he thought it inevitable that Daniel had bone mets at diagnosis beyond those shown on the scans. We knew that the bone scan – the only systemic scan he'd had at diagnosis – had missed mets in Daniel's skeleton. It was fair to assume from this and the extensive nature of Daniel's skeletal disease, Colin said, that it would have missed others too. His logic was pretty unassailable: there was little point using radiation for some bone mets (the known ones) if one missed others (the unknown ones).

Colin's other concern was bone marrow depletion. Radiotherapy, even more than chemo, depletes bone marrow reserve, if it's to areas where there is reserve, like the pelvis and spine. Daniel's left pelvis had already been denuded of marrow. A low marrow stock would make recovery from future chemo more difficult, and could lead to several other problems. Ultimately, there was the risk of catastrophic bone marrow failure, which would be fatal.

I went away to do some more research. Round 2 – and it did feel like that sometimes – was at the joint meeting with Anna Cassoni, the radiotherapist, in July 2007. This was the meeting at which I had been expecting a battle about the RT-PCR. Anna was against having extra radiotherapy, unless we'd decided not to have further chemo. This was because of the bone marrow issue. There were no studies, she said, showing that Ewing's was more likely to come back in previous sites, simply anecdotal evidence.

As ever, it was an impossible balance. I said that we'd like to get a second opinion. Colin asked an astute question as we left: 'Do you want a second opinion or a different one, David?' I assured him it was the former and for that reason I wouldn't go to Prof Burdach: I already knew what he would say.

So I set about finding the best person and spoke to several Ewing's specialists and radiotherapists. Normally second opinions are obtained on a doctor-to-doctor basis, but I wanted to ask questions direct and hear the answers, with all their nuances. I thought the opinion needed to be from outside the UK because UK Ewing's doctors tend to follow the same approach. I eventually decided on Jürgen Dunst in Lübeck in northern Germany. Lübeck is a smallish town, not the sort of place you would expect to find a specialist centre, but Prof Dunst came strongly recommended and was part of the hierarchy for the large-scale Euro Ewing's clinical trial. He agreed to see me.

My visit was planned for the beginning of October 2007. Just before I went, Daniel finally had his RT-PCR biopsy, at the Royal National Orthopaedic Hospital. On admission, Daniel and I threw a ball around in the car park for an hour, joking that this was probably unique for patients about to have an operation at an orthopaedic hospital! Later, around 10.30 after Petra and I had left, a patient asked him and another patient to stop talking. It was highly unusual for Daniel to talk to other patients.

I got to the hospital at 7.45 the next morning but still missed the doctors' ward round: the day starts early in surgery. Dr Mora in Barcelona had advised that we take as many samples as possible, to increase the chance of locating any cancer. That confirmed my own research. However, an Italian doctor who came to see Daniel said their clear instruction from Colin was to take only two samples, one trephine (bone marrow tissue) and one aspirate (liquid), from the right pelvis. I wasn't happy with this. I got hold of Sandra Strauss, Colin's registrar. She said she would check. Daniel was just about to leave for theatre – the one time I wanted there to be a delay, surgery was running to time.

Extraordinarily, part of the route to the theatre at the RNOH is outside, with a plastic sheeting for a ceiling on the footpath. I was getting increasingly anxious as the porters wheeled Daniel in, with the number of samples issue still unresolved. As he went into the preparation room, I asked to see Tim Briggs, who would be operating. Tim came in with one of those 'What is it this time, David?' looks (I'd also pulled him out of theatre the previous year). Tim said they would take a few samples and Sandra rang with the same message.

Where had the confusion come from? It was another reminder of the importance of checking everything. If that made me unpopular, so be it. Nevertheless, I noted in my diary that day: 'I hate all this challenging. They must think I'm a real pain.'

The following day, I flew early in the morning to see Prof Dunst. What Ryanair call Hamburg Airport is actually in Lübeck, so for once their geographical elasticity worked to my advantage. Lübeck, for several centuries the capital of the Hanseatic League, is a beautiful town, a UNESCO heritage site because of its Gothic architecture. Less happily, a number of migrants, including children, were killed or seriously injured in a fire in 1996, thought by some to be deliberate and motivated by racism.

The hospital is on the university's site, a short bus ride

from the airport. I liked Prof Dunst. With this kind of Ewing's, he said, one had one good shot. It was much better to frontload treatment as much as possible rather than try to deal with relapse. Precisely my instincts.

He'd done his homework and had prepared a table of Daniel's scan results. He's one of those doctors who hone in on hopeful signs. What most impressed him, he said, was the improvement between Daniel's June 2006 MRI – that horrible scan done on my Mum's birthday – and the October 2006 PET scan. The speed of response was important. 'There is evidence that good chemo responders – like Daniel – are also good radiotherapy responders', he told me. He also said that if Daniel survived for three to four years, one could assume that he was cured.

Prof Dunst advised that we irradiate all known bone metastatic sites. He wasn't concerned about bone marrow depletion. There was some risk of treatment-related osteosarcoma – the other main type of primary bone cancer. He also advised strongly that Daniel had radiotherapy to his lungs too – whole lung irradiation.

I came out of the meeting in a buoyant mood, even though I knew I would have a struggle to get the additional radiotherapy back in London.

However at the airport, empty at this time, I was suddenly overcome by a feeling of desolation. When I discussed with the Italian doctor the samples issue the previous day, Daniel had piped up: 'Will more samples mean more pain?' His concern, understandably, was whether the operation was going to hurt. Daniel's comfort was always a top priority for Petra and me. But he was desperate to get better and so in his extremely serious situation some risks had to be taken.

As it happened, Daniel experienced little discomfort from the operation. Typically, he was back at school within two days and back on wheatgrass juice. But that night at Lübeck Airport, when I was tired and lonely, it really hit home what he was going through and the impact our decisions had on him.

It was Daniel's nineteenth birthday a couple of days later. When Petra asked him what he wanted, he replied: 'Good health.' The reply was light-hearted but no doubt deeply meant. We had a knock of tennis on his birthday, the first since his illness, but he didn't enjoy it – he couldn't move freely.

Prof Dunst had told me they used whole-body MRIs, which could help to recreate the situation at diagnosis. UCH didn't use them then. I contacted radiologists who were experts in the scans. Stefan Burdach was a big fan. Others, too, advised in favour. One, Nadir Ghanem, invited me to call him at home in the evening and went out of his way to stress the importance of not giving up hope, even if things got really bad.

I was persuaded about the value of a whole-body MRI. Colin wasn't. He didn't think it would recreate the picture at diagnosis and so wouldn't help with the radiotherapy decision. Different medical views yet again.

I broached the subject of going to Lübeck with Daniel on the way home from a tennis tournament he'd been line-judging in Bath. Whole-body MRIs are unpleasant if, like Daniel, you are claustrophobic, because you're inside a small tunnel. I thought I should tell him that Colin wasn't in favour. As soon as I started to explain the rationale, he interrupted: 'Do I need to know this?' He agreed to go. I was touched how much he trusted me: he was willing to do something unpleasant even though he knew that Colin, whom he respected, thought it was a waste of time.

Ryanair were up to their usual tricks at Stansted – making us (along with other passengers) join a long queue, and paying extra, because I hadn't done something quite right online. We could have missed the flight and the appointment. Daniel, anxious to avoid confrontation as usual, urged me not to complain (I couldn't resist the temptation).

At the hospital, we met Beate Stöckelhuber, a radiologist who was to be very supportive. The MRI took much longer than anticipated. With a couple of short breaks Daniel was in this cramped space for an hour and three quarters. Fortunately the machine was open-ended both sides. He was sedated and took pain relief but it was still a challenge for him, especially when he got hot at one point. He coped really well and yet again, I was so proud of him. They let me sit in with him, close to the opening of the machine. I noticed that the hands of my watch went haywire. This was from the strong magnetic field. They returned to normal when I went out of field.

And then the anxious wait for the results. The report from Dr Stöckelhuber arrived on 24th October, two days before we were due to meet Colin and Anna. The report was lengthy. Long reports were always a worry and this one contained some worrying aspects. There was a reference to three 'highly suspicious areas', where we already knew about the cancer. I emailed Dr Stöckelhuber for clarification. She rang the next day and I felt reassured. The take-home message was that, although there were one or two question-marks, there was no evidence of cancer in any places that we didn't know about. Nothing showed in the skull, which the diagnosis bone scan had flagged up.

So if the result was reliable, it strengthened the case for further radiotherapy, which Dr Stöckelhuber (originally a radiotherapist) strongly favoured. The MRI scan, she said, indicated that Daniel had reasonable bone marrow reserve. We could also have a bone marrow scan; I hadn't heard of BM scans.

We still hadn't had the result of the RT-PCR, nearly four weeks on. I had the usual frustrating time chasing this. I knew it was being done in Leeds, under Prof Susan Burchill with whom I'd been in touch about something else. It transpired that RT-PCRs with Ewing's patients were only supposed to be done on a double-blind basis as part of the Euro Ewing 99 trial – in other words, neither the patient nor his doctor would get the results. The tests were done simply for research purposes. That was no good to us, obviously. We needed the result to guide decision-making. Colin, knowing this, must have made a special arrangement with Prof Burchill.

Daniel was worried about the various results – as well as Lübeck, he had a pelvic MRI at UCH. The meeting with Colin and Anna and Vikky Riley, the specialist nurse, started off well enough: the UCH MRI was clear. Colin then told Daniel that no further treatment was needed at this stage. He thereby, once again, pre-empted the discussion he knew we wanted to have.

Rather in contradiction, he added: 'Daniel, there are some other options I want to discuss with you.' Daniel replied that he didn't want to be part of the discussion.

'Daniel, you have to', came Colin's riposte. Daniel asked quietly: 'Can't you just tell Mum and Dad first?' Colin was having none of it: 'I can't just talk to your father. You need to make decisions.' I intervened by saying that Daniel understood that he had ultimately to make decisions but I thought he was saying that he wanted us to filter things. I turned to Daniel and said: 'It's entirely up to you if you stay or leave, or you can leave and come back, or take time to think what you want to do.'

Daniel turned to Colin: 'I don't want to hear bad news.' It was pitiful. Still Colin tried to engage him in discussion and again I had to intervene. Daniel left and Vikky went to speak to him.

It was all really unacceptable. It's for patients to decide what they want to discuss, not for doctors to decide what they need to hear. Some teenagers want to know everything. I came across some who planned their own funerals. Others, like Stephen Sutton, the remarkable teenager who inspired so many to donate to the Teenage Cancer Trust, choose to play out their final days in public. But that wasn't Daniel. If Colin had any concerns about what Daniel really wanted – though I can't imagine how he could have – he could have spoken to him separately about that issue, without Petra or me present. Or he could have asked Daniel to confirm his wishes in writing. It was all so unnecessary. Vikky in fact sent me an email after the meeting, acknowledging that Daniel had made his position about involvement in discussions clear. She suggested that he appreciated that I was taking the burden for him through taking the lead with the doctors. I didn't care about that: it was our job as parents to take as much of the pressure from him as possible.

Daniel, fortunately, wasn't in the room to hear Colin tell us that the RT-PCR was positive. This was the first bad diagnostic news in over a year. Colin didn't know how much cancer was shown up or what the result meant. He seemed to be making the point that this confirmed his view that the test was unnecessary. There were, he explained, indications from the Euro Ewing's trial that the prognostic significance of RT-PCR positivity was not as clearcut as first assumed. More encouragingly, he said the cancerous cells were not necessarily viable and might not grow.

Anna then took over on radiotherapy. She had a letter from Prof Dunst. She seemed defensive and repeated all the risks from more radiotherapy, on top of bone marrow depletion. Stem cell rescue wouldn't help this, she said (disagreeing with Prof Burdach in Munich). The risk ranged from short-term to medium to long-term. The medium risk, at around five years, was that his femur head – at the top of his leg – could collapse, perhaps necessitating a hip replacement. The long-term risk, from around eight years' time, could be serious toxicity problems leading to secondary malignancies. We knew about that.

Anna wasn't prepared to discuss the benefits of more radiotherapy. This made for an unbalanced discussion. All medical decisions are a balance between harm and benefit, so one can't make a sensible decision without considering both sides of the equation. Anna said she'd raised some questions with Prof Dunst and gave me the copy of the letter. She was clearly exploring the issues in a conscientious way. Anna, Petra and I retired to another room to continue the discussion, so that Colin could see other patients.

'I find the whole issue very difficult', I said to Anna.

Having apparently been so set against further radiotherapy, she surprised me by saying that she did too. We discussed irradiating various sites. She was willing to irradiate the bone mets sites in Daniel's right pelvis and lumbar spine. It felt as though I was negotiating with an experienced radiotherapist who knew immeasurably more than I did. It was all a bit surreal.

Anna was against giving Daniel radiotherapy to his lungs. A UCH patient had died after a combination of high-dose busulphan (part of the same family of drugs as treosulfan, which Daniel had) and lung radiation. We agreed to leave this for the time being, despite Prof Dunst's strong advice. I felt there was only so much risk I could ask Daniel to assume. His bone mets seemed to be much the bigger problem.

We left the meeting to think some more. It had been exhausting, and we had the disappointing news about the RT-PCT to contend with. I failed to keep my upset about that result from Mum. Daniel came over in the evening to do some Virgil. As he got out of the car, he asked: 'Were you happy with the meeting?' This was Daniel code for 'Were the results ok?' I said I was happy, sidestepping the code. He then felt emboldened to ask if the UCH and German MRIs were ok and I said they were. He didn't ask about the RT-PCR so I didn't tell him.

I had a frustrating few weeks trying to get hold of the RT-PCR report. At one point Christine, Colin's then secretary told me she had higher priorities than sending the report. I wasn't sorry when she returned to Australia, not least since one day, amidst all the inefficiency and poor attitude, she gave me the Aussie 'mate' treatment.

Her replacement, Joni, was so much more helpful.

The RT-PCR report didn't mean much to me. I discussed it with Gill Langley, who had helped me at the outset with the irinotecan trial, and Enrique de Alava in Spain. Enrique's response didn't cheer me up. He thought the cancer it showed probably was viable.

Petra, based on Anna's advice, was initially reluctant for Daniel to have more radiotherapy; we had long conversations and she eventually came round to the idea. My view was that if there was residual cancer (as the RT-PCR and all the statistics showed was overwhelmingly likely), now was the time to hit it, if there was a reasonably safe way of doing so. But the issue of Daniel's depleting bone marrow worried me (there were two aspects: functionality and reserve). I spoke to various doctors about a bone marrow scan. The evidence about the usefulness of the scan was confusing - nothing new there. In the end, Anna said she felt comfortable about bone marrow depletion.

I had written to Anna and Colin a few days after our meeting. I acknowledged that they were anxious to protect Daniel and promote his quality of life and continued:

> 'Against that, Daniel has such incredible zest for life and such determination to get better that we feel we have to explore all reasonable options. He is doing more at the moment than most healthy kids. ... Simply waiting to see if he relapses, as would be very likely, worries us a great deal.'

I thanked them for pointing out the medium and long-term risks from more radiotherapy but said that they seemed pretty hypothetical given Daniel's prognosis.

Shortly afterwards, it suddenly occurred to me that perhaps we should also irradiate the site of his RT-PCR biopsy, since we knew that there were suspicious cells in that area. I thought I was pushing my luck but Anna agreed.

Daniel's eyes filled up when Petra told him we thought he should have more radiotherapy. He knew only vaguely about the bone mets in his right pelvis. He was momentarily quiet when I took him to see Anna for consenting and she told him about the small risk of needing a hip replacement. But he soon recovered. He always did. Daniel didn't want to tell Sasha and Florence about the extra radiotherapy. We were protecting him; he was protecting his sisters.

Radiotherapy took place over Christmas again. It went well and Daniel had few symptoms. Was it the right decision? I believe it was. I later read some research from Münster, presented at a conference in London. It was small-scale but indicated that 27 per cent of patients with serious Ewing's who had all known bone mets sites irradiated survived without relapsing for at least three years, against only 17 per cent who didn't have extra radiotherapy. The figures were not dramatic, but if you were in that extra 10 per cent it would be everything. And it meant that we weren't simply dealing with anecdote.

Magdalen College, Oxford

The Autumn of 2007 was a really busy time. So much going on medically. So many excruciatingly difficult decisions. So much worry about symptoms Daniel reported. So much reassurance we needed to give Daniel. So much reassurance we needed ourselves. So difficult to know how much to tell Daniel, to gauge how much he really wanted to know. I noted in my diary one day: 'Reminded me again of the difference between the truth and the whole truth.' Sometimes we were economical with the truth. But everything was geared to protecting Daniel and giving him hope.

Daniel was unaware of most of the medical angst. This was a rich period for him. He qualified as a tennis umpire, scoring maximum marks at the National Tennis Centre at Roehampton. He umpired his first tournament, a competition for players in wheelchairs, in Cardiff and typical Daniel, was able to laugh at himself when he called 'Game, set and match' prematurely. He had quiet authority though I'm not sure he would have dealt with McEnroe in his brattish prime.

His primary focus that autumn was getting into Oxford. He'd finally decided on Oxford rather than Cambridge, after the usual months of indecision. We were glad because it was nearer and we knew we would need to scuttle back and forth. If, that is, he survived that long. And if he was accepted. Cathy, one of his teachers, thought he would walk into either university. Daniel was far less confident.

Daniel decided to go for Magdalen College, Oxford. Magdalen is one of the oldest Oxford colleges and is also one of the best. Daniel liked the feel of Magdalen when he visited.

I lost count of the drafts his UCAS personal statements went through. They had to be just right. He was offered a place at University College London – just next door to

UCH – Bristol, Warwick and Royal Holloway. The latter, with its breathtaking architecture, is just a few miles from Chobham. Daniel thought he might need to go there because of his health. But Oxford was his goal.

One of the dilemmas with the personal statements was how much to say about his illness. There was no question of going for the sympathy vote but the universities would need to know because of his special needs.

In truth, Daniel's preparations had started months earlier. We drew up a reading list, ranging from Cicero to Melvyn Bragg's *12 Books that Changed the World*. Current affairs weren't his strong point so he asked me to cut out articles from newspapers for him. Danny Finkelstein and Ben Macintyre in the *Times* were favourites.

Whatever Daniel read he made me read, so we could discuss it. That was his rule. We read a book of essays about history – the link between history and geography, the place of personality in history, why do empires rise and fall, that sort of thing. We read Virgil and some Plato, even stuff on Greek theatre and architecture. I learnt a lot. If he ran out of time, he made me prepare a summary of what I'd read. After I'd done something, Daniel sent me an email: 'I'm not happy. We need to talk … urgently. This isn't what I was expecting. I'm very disappointed right now. I want you to know that you've let yourself down, you've let me down …'

The truth is that Daniel could have sailed into Oxford without my help, but he was so keen. He had begun doing philosophy AS level at school. One day he told me he now knew more than I did (no doubt correctly). Ever since he was a little boy, he was competitive with me. Whatever we were doing, he had to beat me. He would ask Petra 'When

Forever competitive.

will I be able to beat Dad at tennis?' or whatever it was. Once or twice he let things get out of proportion but otherwise it was healthy competitiveness, full of fun and laughter. We used to tease each other relentlessly. He loved playing Twenty Questions on car trips, though he had difficulty grasping the concept that he had to guess the answer within twenty questions.

Daniel had to write a couple of essays for Magdalen. These, too, became Herculean labours of love for him. He could never be accused of just dashing something off. In the things that mattered to him, he was a perfectionist.

He had mock interviews and spoke to my friend Georgina, who had been to Magdalen (as well as my old school), and to a barrister friend Zoe, who'd studied Classics at Cambridge. Zoe later wrote to me:

'He was so self-effacing and charming when I spoke to him on the phone about Horace and Cicero and the

Aeneid and all sorts of things – I was impressed by
his poise but also his complete openness – a very rare
combination for a young man of his ... age.'

Everyone was willing him to do well. His illness no doubt reinforced the good wishes.

After the reading and the essays, the interview questions. We dreamt up likely questions (and some not so likely, knowing Oxbridge interviewers' predilection for off-the-wall questions). Over and over his answers Daniel went. The idea was to give him a degree of fluency because he was afraid of seizing up in the stress of the moment.

Daniel was called for an interview, by no means a given in his mind. The college put special arrangements in place. The interview took place on 5th December 2007. He sounded disappointed afterwards. None of our questions came up. The next day he was even more down. He hadn't been asked for a second interview by another college. The way the interview system works at Oxford is that the chosen college gets first crack but then other colleges can interview in case the chosen college decides not to offer a place. If the first college is certain that they want to offer the student a place, there may be no point the student going for further interviews, but that was relatively rare.

I felt low, too. I knew how much Oxford meant to Daniel but, more than that, how important it could be for his illness that he kept positive and focussed on his future. It didn't make sense that he'd been rejected out of hand. He couldn't have gone from a strong position to zero in the course of one interview, surely? I worried that he'd perhaps dried up or appeared formulaic, overprepared.

We wouldn't know for a couple of weeks. Daniel started radiotherapy and I got on with my research and work.

Daniel rang me at 8pm on 16th December. Magdalen had offered him a place. Everyone, family and friends, were thrilled. Mum said it was her best Christmas present. Getting into Oxford is an achievement for anyone and Classics is one of *the* subjects at Oxford and Magdalen one of *the* colleges. But Daniel's achievement was extra special. He had an exceptionally serious illness and hadn't long finished a year of really tough treatment. He was still getting worrying symptoms and wasn't physically strong. And he was carrying a terrible psychological burden, however upbeat he appeared on the surface.

It transpired that Magdalen had been certain they wanted Daniel. He was proud that, of his intake of seven classicists at the college, he was the only one from a state school. In truth this was somewhat illusory. Because his schools didn't teach Latin and Greek, for years he'd had one-on-one teaching by two excellent tutors, Cathy and Caroline. He wasn't fighting his way out of a blackboard jungle into the dreaming spires. But I didn't point this out.

Magdalen were kind to offer Daniel a place. My guess is that, in years gone by, they might not have done so. Not only would Daniel's illness mean that he would be higher maintenance than 'normal' students, but they must have realised that there was a good chance that he wouldn't graduate. In that sense, I suppose, he was blocking another student, but no one knew for certain what would happen and it was right that he be given his chance.

At his school concert a couple of days later, they played his composition. Petra had to drive home for the score only for Daniel to discover that it was at school all along ... This was typical Daniel. He played clarinet in a string quartet, the wind band and the orchestra and accompanied the orchestra on piano. He really enjoyed himself and it was wonderful to witness.

Daniel told me that it would be five years before he was through university. All I cared about was that he was thinking about getting through university. He gave me a list of books, pre-reading for Oxford, he wanted for Christmas.

There was still so much to worry about. We were forever teetering on the cusp of relapse, peering into the abyss. Some worry was avoidable. In March, Daniel had an MRI scan of his pelvis. When I got the report, it said there was little change – a good thing – but referred to an abnormality in the right ileum (part of the pelvis). This would be a new abnormality, a very bad thing. I was puzzled, so emailed the radiologist. She refused to answer my query, hiding behind the fact that Daniel was now eighteen. This angered me. I contacted Colin, who eventually discovered that the radiologist had mixed up her right and her left, something she was apparently prone to do. I suggested, only half in jest, that this seemed something of an occupational hazard for a radiologist. My relief overcame any desire to complain to the radiologist but she'd still given me three days of needless worry. It would have been so much kinder and more professional to have fronted up and admitted her mistake. I spared Petra the worry and of course Daniel.

That incident took its place in a cancer memory bank already threatening to explode. But it was history and I could semi-enjoy Christmas. For my presents Daniel gave me the BBC Symphony Orchestra recording of his composition, *Imperium* by Robert Harris and two measuring jugs (for his wheatgrass). The measuring jugs were appreciated but were just shaded in sentimental worth by the recording. His taste in presents was often eclectic. For Father's Day earlier in the year, he gave me a bar of Toblerone and some Tupperware. One year he gave me a paper shredder.

And so a second cancer year drew to a close. Daniel was still with us – by no means a given at the start of the year and certainly not when he was diagnosed. The RT-PCR was hugely disappointing but technically he'd not relapsed. And he had experienced so much and achieved so much. We had a lot to be thankful for.

As the New Year dawned, Daniel asked me: 'Is 2008 going to be a good year for us, do you think?' 'We have to make it so, Dan', I replied.

The battle for IGF

Daniel (playing hide and seek, aged three): Come and find me Daddy. I'm going to hide under the dining room table
Dad: Don't tell me where you're going to hide, because I'll know where to find you
Daniel: But I want you to find me!

We didn't know it then, but when Daniel finished his radiotherapy early in 2008, there was to be no more treatment for two years. If I could have glimpsed into the future, how would I have reacted? With relief and gratitude that Daniel would live for at least two more years, naturally; with some lessening of angst but also with the re-doubling of effort, to do my best to ensure that the eventual treatment would be the right one. But we can't look into the future other than through the cloudiest of spectacles. Our emotions and our actions are framed by what we know of the past and the present and it takes time even for those temporal guides to mould their lessons into proper perspective.

Daniel's perspective in the early months of 2008 with Oxford to look forward to, was to hope that there would be no more treatment and that he was cured. At times he appeared even to believe this. We didn't lie to him but did nothing to strip away his comfort blanket. Our perspective was different to Daniel's: we expected relapse, probably imminently, and expected it to be fatal. But we clung onto the hope that it might not be so and that some time, quality time, could be bought for Daniel.

As ever, I was pursuing a number of research avenues, conventional and complementary. But my primary focus in the early months of 2008 was insulin growth factor 1 receptor inhibition. I put a really big effort into getting an inhibitor for Daniel. It resulted in a dispute with Hoffmann La Roche (Roche), one of the world's largest drug companies and the Medicines & Healthcare products Regulatory Agency (MHRA), the government agency responsible for licensing drugs and clinical trials in the UK. It also sadly led to a straining of relations with Colin McMaster, something I'd been keen to avoid.

The take-home message from my reading was that blocking the IGF1R cancer pathway was potentially important. IGF1R is a type of protein. Cancer patients, including Ewing's patients, often have too much of it ('overexpression'). We knew from Enrique de Alava's analysis that Daniel's tumour heavily overexpressed IGF1R (I will from now on generally use the umbrella abbreviation IGF). IGF inhibition had been on the research agenda for quite some time, but it was moving forward with some alacrity just at this time. Could that be propitious timing for Daniel, or might it be too late? Or would this turn out to be yet another disappointment in cancer research, something which worked well in the lab but not in patients?

I'd first raised the question of IGF inhibitors with Colin just before Christmas 2007. I knew the Ewing's research community was excited about them, though I also knew that Ewing's scientists were more easily excited than patients. Researchers into difficult cancers salivate when a new drug, or an old drug used in a new setting, produces any response in a patient. The benefit in terms of overall survival time might be miniscule or non-existent, but to get any response with intractable cancers is a biological achievement. Patients and families, needless to say, are only interested in cures or at least buying more time with symptoms under control.

Over the course of Daniel's cancer journey, I read masses about IGF inhibitors and communicated with innumerable clinicians and researchers. As early as September 2006 I read an article by Uto Kontny, a doctor in Freiberg, Germany who was always ready to share information by email or telephone. Once, after no contact for several months, he remembered Daniel's name.

The inhibitors really came on my radar in March 2007. Lia Gore, a paediatric sarcoma doctor in Denver, told me excitedly about promising results in some of her patients with Roche's IGF inhibitor, codenamed R1507. Inevitably, patient numbers were small but early results in Ewing's patients were good, especially those with lung metastases. Daniel had lung mets at diagnosis. Almost as important, the drug seemed to be well-tolerated – medico-speak for few side-effects. This was indeed a rarity with cancer treatment. All her patients were able to work or study, with no neutropaenia (low white blood count).

Clinical trials

Dr Gore's patients were on a phase 1 trial for R1507. A word about the complicated world of clinical trials. In brief summary, after exhaustive laboratory tests a new drug which works sufficiently well in animals and in vitro (test-tube) and is not too toxic moves to clinical trials. Two types of permission have to be obtained, one from a regulator and the other from an ethics committee. In the UK, the regulator is the MHRA, although approval for certain types of drugs is obtained on an EU-wide basis from the European Medicines Agency, which happens to be based in London.

Trials undergo a number of phases. Phase 1 trials are normally with healthy volunteers – students or others who want to earn some extra cash. Doses are normally small and the volunteers don't normally suffer serious side –effects. An exception was the trial a few years ago of a particular drug (like IGF inhibitors, a monoclonal antibody) at Northwick Park Hospital in London, which went horribly wrong.

Phase 1 trials aim to find out whether a new drug is safe and to learn more about how it behaves in the human body. Patients aren't normally involved in phase 1 trials. However, because of the dearth of treatment options with many cancers, once chemotherapy has failed (as it usually does), patients are often allowed onto phase 1 trials. There is a centre at the Royal Marsden Hospital in Surrey which is dedicated to these. Patients know that there's little chance of the trial bringing a cure, but a small chance is better than no chance. Phase 1 patients usually say, laudably, that they also want to contribute to medical research generally, to help others.

Phase 2 trials again focus on safety but also on efficacy – whether the drug actually works. All phase 2 trials have detailed eligibility criteria, setting out the type of disease which a patient must have to qualify and also various medical conditions which will exclude him or her. Age is often a criterion, too, with children frequently excluded, putting them at a real disadvantage. Often there is an upper age limit too. This is because older people typically have conditions other than the one of interest, which may confound the results. They may die before the trial is complete, as well. The world of clinical trials can be ruthless, as I was to find out.

The number of patients on phase 2 trials is relatively small, though larger than phase 1. In fact, phase 2 is often divided into two subphases. As a trial moves from phase 1 to phase 2a, the inclusion criteria are likely to be restrictive. This is because little is still known about the safety of the drug. If the phase 2a results are sufficiently promising to merit moving to phase 2b, the eligibility criteria may be relaxed somewhat. The MHRA told me that between a half and two thirds of new drugs which have passed phase 1 fail to get past phase 2. Around 85-90 per cent of new drugs which enter clinical trials fail even to reach phase 3, and many of those that do subsequently drop off. Phase 3 involves much larger numbers of patients. Here, under a process of randomisation, patients are divided into two groups. Half will receive the new drug (or other type of therapy). The other half will receive either a placebo, if the type of treatment is new, or an existing drug for that condition. It's pot luck which group one falls into – hence the randomisation. Patients are not told whether they are getting the new drug (the study is 'blind'). Nor, usually, is your doctor (the trial is then 'double-blind').

The rationale for only giving half the patients the trial drug is that one can tell how good a remedy is and how safe only by comparing those who get it with those, in a control group, who don't. Randomisation is thought important to remove clinician bias in choosing who goes into what group. Bias doesn't mean that doctors prefer some patients to others, but that, for good reason, they'd be more likely to enter into the new drug group patients whose disease profile suggests they're more likely to benefit and that would skew the results. For a similar reason, prospective trials, where no one knows what will happen, are thought more valuable than retrospective studies which look back at what has happened to a patient population who were simply given what their doctors thought best.

Randomisation makes sense but I worried about Daniel being randomised out of a new drug at phase 3. By the time it was discovered that the results were sufficiently good to merit a full licence from the MHRA – a 'market authorisation' as it's called – it might be too late for him. But in fact there appeared to be hardly any phase 3 trials with Ewing's; they're nearly all phase 1 and phase 2, probably a reflection of how rare the cancer is.

Clinical trials are mired in ethical issues. There are international guidelines setting out basic principles. One of the earliest arose out of the Nuremberg trials, prompted by the appalling experiments conducted by the perverted Josef Mengele and his fellow Nazis (sadly by no means the only example from the last century of experiments on people). The main treaty, however, is the Declaration of Helsinki. The declaration sets out the basic principles, most notably that of informed consent. I was surprised to learn that experiments were sometimes permitted on people with severe learning difficulties who couldn't give consent, if other people with the same condition – not the patient – might stand to benefit. The potential side-effects could only be mild, but it's still unethical, I believe. In no other circumstance is it permitted to experiment on people who neither consent nor stand to benefit from a treatment and yet society allowed it for a highly vulnerable group.

IGF inhibitors were at the cusp of phase 1 and phase 2. I discovered that it's common for a new drug to be at different phases at the same time, with different eligibility criteria. This makes it problematical to find out what is going on, especially where the trial is multinational. Colin was well across what was happening in the Ewing's world. UCH is a leading centre for Ewing's trials and he or one of his colleagues are often the principal investigator in the UK for a trial drug. But even his information was sometimes incomplete or out-of-date, understandably given the complicated and ever-moving picture.

A further complication is that drug companies sometimes don't publish their full trial protocols, just a summary. So one may not know all the eligibility criteria. This proved a real problem with my attempts to get R1507, the Roche IGF inhibitor, for Daniel. On one occasion, Colin said he couldn't let me have the uptodate protocol without

Roche's permission. Roche refused. I can see that Colin was caught in the middle, but there's something seriously amiss if a doctor feels he has to withhold important information from his patient.

Despite all the difficulties, my early research made me cautiously optimistic about IGF inhibitors. Many doctors agreed with my strategy of attacking the microscopic cancer Daniel was overwhelmingly likely to have.

I first made contact with Roche just before Christmas 2007. I quickly had a reply from Dr Stanley Frankel. He was in charge of R1507 trials and was upbeat about getting Daniel on a trial, depending on eligibility. Those three words were to prove crucial. Not unreasonably, he wanted to speak to Daniel's doctor.

I wanted to find out the status of R1507 in the UK: did it have a clinical trials licence, for phase 2? I wrote to the MHRA, the government regulator. The reply was quick but disappointing: the information was confidential. Why, I asked. It was a legal requirement of the European clinical trials directive, came the response. I read the directive and thought the MHRA was wrong but left it for the moment.

My MHRA correspondent also said that patients don't become involved in trials until phase 3. This was clearly incorrect and an astonishing misapprehension for someone working for the body in charge of clinical trials. This was another lesson from Daniel's cancer journey: never take at face value what you're told. If it's important, check it.

The fundamental problem was that Roche required patients to have 'measurable disease' before they would qualify for a trial for R1507. This is a standard requirement with cancer trials. It means that cancer must be visible, and measurable, on a scan. Daniel didn't have any cancer visible by scan. That, of course, was really good. But it was bad as far as eligibility for the trial was concerned. The rationale for the criterion was plain to see. Drug companies and doctors need to know whether a trial drug works, by comparing the before and after. The easiest way to do this is to measure whether a tumour shrinks on a trial. Daniel's RT-PCR test had been positive for bone marrow disease but RT-PCR positivity doesn't constitute measureable disease, because one can't see the disease on a scan.

However, I'd noticed that the R1507 eligibility criteria – or at least those I had access to – referred to 'measurable or evaluable disease.' What did 'evaluable' mean in this context? Clearly, it had to mean something different to 'measurable.' Could we argue that although Daniel didn't have 'measurable' disease, he had 'evaluable' disease because of the RT-PCR result? I came across a useful definition of 'evaluable disease': 'A tumour or tumours which you can tell are present but the size of which cannot be measured accurately.' RT-PCR positivity could fit that.

I was already devising my legal strategy, whilst being reluctant to use legal arguments openly. That might encourage Roche to bring in their own lawyers, unlikely to be a positive development.

I decided to write to Stanley Frankel, in as friendly and constructive way as possible. I aimed to engage him with Daniel's plight on a human level: whatever financial and regulatory pressures pharma executives are working under, they might well have children of their own (Dr Frankel had three). I would tell him something about Daniel and his dreams.

I sent my email on 8th January 2008, after numerous drafts. I gave Roche the chance of saying that Daniel qualified under their existing criteria. This would be much easier than persuading them to change the criteria, particularly since the trial was already under way in some countries. They wouldn't have accepted that their criteria were unlawful, so I didn't raise this at this stage.

When copying Colin, I explained that Petra and I saw our role 'as helping to ensure that treatment (however experimental) which is indicated for Daniel in his desperate situation is available to him and that he's not prejudiced by any technical or resource obstacles.' I was, I said, happy to engage with the MHRA if necessary. We looked to him to guide us what treatment was right for Daniel, no matter what obstacles there might be to getting it.

I'm not sure that Colin would have agreed with this division of labour. I imagine that he saw it as his role, not parents', to access treatment a patient needed. It would be understandable if he resented my intervention. But I had already gained the impression that he wouldn't rock the boat with drug companies.

Dr Frankel again replied promptly. Though based in the US, he was meeting Colin the next day to discuss the R1507 trial – some coincidence. Was this a good omen? I was frustrated that I wouldn't be there to influence the discussion, but at least Dr Frankel would have Daniel's case in mind.

Colin's feedback was disappointing. Yes, there would be a trial opening at UCH in two to four months' time. Daniel would be offered a place 'providing he fulfils the eligibility criteria as described in the protocol which will by then have been approved by MHRA and ethics committees.' That told me precisely nothing: my argument was that Daniel already met the criteria. I pointed this out. Drug companies give doctors some leeway in deciding whether a patient meets eligibility criteria, although, for reasons of professional ethics and credibility, doctors can only stretch a point so far.

Colin's reply again missed the point: neither the MHRA nor an ethics committee, he said, could alter eligibility criteria and certainly not for an individual patient. We should put things on hold until the trial started. He did acknowledge that Roche's IGF was clinically the right thing for Daniel. But I felt I was banging my head against a brick wall. Why did Colin not understand what I was saying? I wrote again, suggesting that he was perhaps equating possible clinical benefit from participation in a trial with meeting the eligibility criteria. They couldn't be the same thing if the criteria were drawn, or interpreted, too restrictively so as to exclude those who might benefit. I hadn't, I said, suggested that the MHRA and ethics committee should tailor regulatory approval to the needs of one patient. However, they couldn't, in assessing an application for a clinical trial, simply rubber-stamp criteria devised by the sponsoring company.

I felt uncomfortable raising legal issues with Colin and said so. Legal arguments by a lawyer, however gently put and whoever the immediate target, have the knack of creating barriers, the opposite of what I wanted. We had a reasonably good relationship and I wanted to keep it this way. But I had to do my best for Daniel. It's easy in life to remain on good terms with everyone but achieve nothing.

I hate personal confrontation but hating is not the same as avoiding. My politely-expressed messages were being batted away. We needed to know whether Roche and Colin agreed that Daniel already qualified. Otherwise I would have to up the legal stakes with the MHRA. I felt strongly that, though there was no guarantee that an IGF inhibitor would work, now was the time to try, not wait for Daniel to have measurable disease again (i.e. relapse).

There was another factor. Under the protocol, R1507 had to be given by itself. Again, this was perfectly understandable. If a patient's condition improves on a trial, the drug company needs to know that it's due to their drug and not some other treatment. But this would mean that, on relapse, we would have to choose between the standard treatment and R1507. Even worse: it emerged that R1507 could only be given on second relapse – when it would be even less likely to work.

I got increasingly frustrated. There was an impenetrable wall. Colin did at one point float the idea of Daniel having the drug 'off trial', if Roche agreed. There are a couple of ways a new drug can be given off trial, including via compassionate use, where a drug company gives a trial drug to a patient who doesn't meet eligibility criteria (see Annex B). But Colin added that he wouldn't advise Roche to give Daniel the drug off-trial, which told me that he wouldn't try to persuade them. I asked Dr Frankel, but never received a reply, despite chasing.

It was a stressful period. Time was marching on. I assumed that the MHRA would shortly be making a decision whether to grant a clinical trials licence for R1507, by which time the eligibility criteria would be set in stone.

In fact, I had even less time than I realised. I thought from reading the UK clinical trial regulations that the ethics committee would decide its position first. But this was wrong: the two types of permission can run in parallel, although nowhere does this seem to be written down. I would need to move quickly to persuade the MHRA not to approve the eligibility criteria in their current form.

I was acutely aware that my putting a fly into the regulatory ointment could, if I was at all successful, delay other patients, every bit as deserving as Daniel and perhaps in greater immediate need, getting the inhibitor. That was the last thing I wanted. What is one to do in this situation? The intransigence I was facing wasn't my fault. I was giving Roche and Colin an easy way through, by interpreting the criteria flexibly and sensibly or giving Daniel the drug off-trial. We were still well within the two-four months' timescale for the start of the trial. But the worry that I might be making things worse for other patients, if only in the short term, added to the pressure I was feeling.

My biggest worry was that Daniel's cancer could explode into life at any time. We knew from the RT-PCR he still had cancer. Time mattered.

Legal arguments

It looked as though I would have to deploy legal arguments. The target had to be the MHRA, as part of the machinery of government. Its decisions come under what lawyers call public law. The agency can be judicially reviewed if it makes legal mistakes. As someone affected by its decision, Daniel could in principle bring a case. The irony was that he knew nothing about what was going on.

Daniel had no right to sue Roche. They owed him no duty in law as far as trial eligibility was concerned (it would be different if he suffered as a result of their negligently failing to ensure the safety of their drug). Similarly, there would be no legal case against UCH. Although UCH is a public body and therefore in principle can be judicially reviewed, it wasn't making any regulatory decision. And the ethics committee was simply making a recommendation.

I had to get myself up to speed about clinical trials regulation. I needed to explain how I thought the MHRA should approach approval of clinical trials, in a way advantageous to Daniel. For a while I struggled. The argument I eventually came up with was that, under the UK clinical trials regulations implementing the EU directive, the MHRA had a legal duty to ensure that trials generated as much useful information as possible. Its duty was not simply to ensure that a trial drug was sufficiently safe, in the context of the benefit which it might bring. In the letter I drafted, I drew on a paragraph in a schedule to the regulations:

'Before the trial is initiated, foreseeable risk and inconveniences [must] have been weighed against the anticipated benefit for the individual trial subject and other present and future patients. A trial should be initiated and continued only if the anticipated benefits justify the risks' (my emphasis).

I argued that the ethics committee, in giving its opinion and the MHRA, in deciding whether to grant authorisation, 'must ensure that eligibility criteria are appropriately drawn, neither too broad so as to include those who should be excluded nor too narrow as to exclude those who should be included.' It was the latter category with which I was concerned. The reason why avoiding inappropriate exclusion was important, I suggested:

'The amount of useful data to be obtained from the trial would [in that event] be unnecessarily reduced and with it the scientific validity of the trial. This is particularly important with extremely rare cancers such as Ewing's, especially where the rarity is exacerbated by metastasation. It must be of overriding importance with rare diseases, particularly where they are life-threatening, to include all those whose participation could contribute to the research. Otherwise non-participating current patients and future patients – to whose interests the MHRA and the ethics committee are statutorily obliged to have regard – may lose out because less research insight will be gained than should have been the case.'

Participation of patients in Daniel's situation could benefit the efficacy objectives of the R1507 trial, I suggested: it had to be of value to Roche to know whether the inhibitor could prevent or delay microscopic disease (detected by a RT-PCR) becoming macroscopic (visible by scan); and the data would be particularly valuable where the patient's cancer heavily overexpressed IGF1R, the pathway under investigation, as did Daniel's.

The argument in part relied on the dependability of RT-PCR in predicting what would happen with a patient's cancer. I thought the study evidence, from Israel and France, was pretty good. Importantly, using RT-PCR positivity as a yardstick for entry into a cancer clinical trial wasn't a new idea. I had learnt that eligibility into a planned trial for a novel agent for high-risk Ewing's patients could be via RT-PCR positivity. Similarly, Schering Plough, a large drugs company, was not going to insist on measurable disease for their IGF inhibitor. It was important to get the point over to the MHRA that I wasn't, as a mere layman, asking them or Roche to enter unchartered or scientifically irrational territory.

It was true that RT-PCR positivity wasn't as clear a prognostic indicator as measurable disease and patients with only RT-PCR positivity would have to be assessed separately and with greater circumspection, but the data would still be useful, I argued. It's common to have multiple entry points to a trial, with the consequent need to assess results differently for different groups.

I had a back-up argument, involving the Human Rights Act. Sadly, human rights have become a term of abuse in this country. You would never believe it from some media coverage, with its obsession about a handful of foreign criminals avoiding deportation for family reasons or because of possible torture, but the HRA has in fact been a real force for good for all sorts of vulnerable people, for protecting vital freedoms such as freedom of expression and for ensuring the accountability of the state for deaths occurring on its watch.

I used the HRA in this way:

'The MHRA is, of course, a public authority for the purposes of the Human Rights Act 1998 ('HRA'). Under section 6(1), it is unlawful for a public authority to act in a way which is incompatible with rights under the European Convention on Human Rights. One of those rights is the right to life under Article 2. Signatory states have a positive duty in certain circumstances to ensure that that right is protected. In my view, the MHRA has such a duty where it is deciding whether to approve the eligibility criteria for a clinical trial for a life-threatening disease, particularly where (i) the disease is very rare such that there is a desperate need for useful data; (ii) there is a dearth of alternative therapeutic solutions; and (iii) the disease overwhelmingly affects children. A regulatory decision which excluded patients with extremely poor prognosis who might benefit from participation and whose participation would contribute to the research objectives would, I believe, breach Article 2.'

Sadly death was what we were facing: without appropriate intervention, Colin expected Daniel to die in the near future. A decision by an arm of the state – the MHRA – which might just make a difference to whether Daniel lived could therefore, in principle, engage Article 2 of the convention.

The HRA argument was speculative but, I thought, cogent. Like my main argument, it would be breaking new ground. I have spent a good deal of my career running novel arguments in test cases against public bodies. So novelty was not a deterrent. The arguments were the sort that, as a lawyer, I would have loved to run, even though I knew success wouldn't be easy. But my sole focus was on getting R1507 for Daniel. Legal arguments had to take their place in my overall strategy.

The final part of my letter challenged the MHRA's refusal to tell me where Roche's application had reached. I made a freedom of information request. In my experience, public authorities rely too readily on confidentiality exemptions where third parties have a stake in the information in question. I pointed out that Roche had published their phase 1 protocol on the internet and had openly discussed the phase 1 results and their plans for the phase 2 at conferences and elsewhere. There was no risk of their commercial interests being prejudiced by release of the information I had requested. The agency relented on this point.

My letter was potentially the most important I'd ever written. I wanted to add credibility. So I explained that I was a consultant to Bindmans, a leading human rights law firm. I also asked two well respected barristers, Daniel Alexander QC and David Wolfe, whether they agreed with the arguments. If so, I would say so in the letter. However good the arguments I was conscious that, at the end of the day, I was a parent trying to secure a particular objective for his son. Daniel Alexander is an intellectual property lawyer. As luck would have it, he'd been involved in the patenting of the RT-PCR. He often acted for and against pharmaceutical companies so knew his way around this area. He was also a deputy High Court judge (at a young age). David, a leading human rights barrister and now also a QC, was born in South Africa where his father was the only white anti-apartheid activist to be executed.

Daniel and David made helpful comments on my draft. They recognised the counter-arguments but gave the letter their approval. I realised that one of the counter-arguments was that, with multinational clinical trials, a drug company was entitled to keep the same eligibility criteria everywhere. I was only attacking regulatory approval in the UK.

I also sent the draft to Colin, partly as a courtesy and partly because I wanted him to know that I was serious. UCH wasn't directly involved in the legal issues but I suggested that he might want to share the draft with the hospital's lawyers. Since I was a lawyer and he wasn't, I felt that this was the right thing to say. UCH's lawyers might be able to bring some pressure to bear too, to help us all out of the impasse.

I took my letter to the MHRA office in Vauxhall, London late in the afternoon of 4th February 2008. The MHRA's headquarters overlook the River Thames but I felt I had crossed the Rubicon. I told Colin that I regretted going down this path, but, now that I had, I asked for a formal decision from the Trust as to whether Daniel in his present condition would qualify for the phase 2. I didn't receive a reply.

I asked the MHRA for a reply within seven days but knew it would probably be longer. There was no time to relax, however. The MHRA was only one of my targets. The other was the ethics committee which would need to support the trial. I put essentially the same arguments to the committee. There was one additional argument. A Department of Health document advised that committees needed to ensure that the benefits and burdens of research needed to be distributed fairly amongst all groups and classes in society. One of the relevant factors was age. As noted earlier, there are significantly fewer opportunities for paediatric patients, including paediatric cancer patients, to access trials. There was therefore, I argued, a particular responsibility on ethics committees to ensure that eligibility criteria for paediatric cancer trials, such as that for R1507, are not drawn too restrictively. Ewing's is overwhelmingly a paediatric disease.

I asked to be allowed to attend the ethics committee meeting. It's always best to present arguments orally where possible. With some clever acting the committee would, I hoped, be able to see that I was a reasonable person, conscious of the various pressures facing the different parties; a parent simply trying to do the best for his seriously ill son but in a way which would also benefit other patients.

Dr Michael Pegg, the chair of the committee, replied. He was sympathetic to Daniel's plight but we wouldn't be able to attend (because we had a vested interest in the trial under discussion). However, he suggested that Petra and I meet with Sir John Lilleyman, advisor to the National Research Ethics Service. There seemed to be appreciation that the issues went far beyond this particular trial. Sir John is a former President of the Royal Society of Pathology which was relevant as RT-PCR is a pathology technique. He had specialised in childhood leukaemia. He was later to be a non-executive medical director of the MHRA. He was as establishment as it was possible to get.

We readily agreed to a meeting. I had by this time received a letter from Dr Martyn Ward, head of the clinical trials unit at the MHRA. He, too, was personally sympathetic. But predictably, the MHRA didn't accept my legal arguments. The job of the agency, Dr Ward said, was to 'ensure the protection of public health whilst supporting effective drug development.' The development process was owned by the developer and the MHRA didn't mould a trial for reasons other than safety or scientific validity. In fact, my whole argument was that scientific validity would be enhanced by allowing RT-PCR positive patients to be included, because this would give additional useful data.

But the overall message was clear: apart from safety considerations, it was up to drug companies to decide who qualified and who didn't. This was a disappointingly conservative view of its role by the MHRA. I put their letter to one side while we pursued the ethics committee, because that seemed more promising.

The meeting with Sir John Lilleyman was cordial and constructive. He tried to steer me away from litigation, in the manner of a practised politician. I assured him that this was the last thing I wanted; there was quite enough stress in dealing with Daniel's illness as it was. However, the bottom line was that we would do whatever was necessary for Daniel, including litigation.

Sir John sent us a copy of his follow-up letter to Michael Pegg. To my surprise, he said that a 'pretty good case' could be made for Daniel's inclusion in the Roche trial. It was quite a coup to get his support.

In the meantime, Dr Pegg told us that his committee had written to Roche asking why RT-PCR positive patients like Daniel were excluded. It's common for ethics committees to ask questions of drug companies. But we were making progress.

Around the same time, Jaume Mora in Barcelona told me that there was to be a meeting of principal investigators for R1507 in Paris on 25th April 2008. I decided to open up a political front. I asked our MP, Michael Gove, if he could make representation to the minister responsible for clinical trials, Dawn Primarola, and took initial soundings of contacts in the Labour Party, then in government.

Sir John had advised us to get the RT-PCR test done again, as had others. This had always been my intention, in case the first result was a false positive. It had been such a problem getting the test done in the UK and then getting the results, that this time we would go to Barcelona. Dr Mora would take quantitative samples, which were thought to be more reliable than the qualitative approach in the UK. A quantitative test measures how much of the thing in question is present; a qualitative test simply asks whether any is present.

But before Barcelona I wanted to make sure that Daniel didn't have macroscopic disease – disease visible by scan. If he did, most of the legal arguments would be irrelevant. Ludwig Strauss, of the German National Cancer Centre (GNCC), had offered to do a PET/CT scan for Daniel for nothing. We were in the heart of the IGF struggle and I was fed up fighting with Colin. It hadn't been easy getting the first PET/CT at UCH and each subsequent one had felt like a concession to my special pleading. I was tired. It may seem odd that it was easier to take Daniel to Germany to have a scan than try to get it done at his own hospital. But that's how it felt.

So I took up Ludwig's offer. I would make it a pleasurable trip for Daniel. The GNCC is in the beautiful city of

Heidelberg with its majestic castle. But I was conscious it was one more thing for Daniel to do. We stayed with my friends Norbert and Michaele near Mainz. Norbert, generous as ever, told me what an impressive young man Daniel was. At the Centre, a radiologist asked about suspicious lesions shown on the Lübeck whole-body MRI a few months earlier. Daniel left the room, upset, before I was able to reassure him that they were benign. Ludwig took an interest in what Daniel was doing. Daniel later told me off for having told him that he was going to Oxford – 'that's bragging.'

Ludwig mentioned, privately, that he'd seen a small nodule on the scan. This might be an infection, but it kick-started the usual worry. Daniel, however, was buoyant on leaving the hospital. He'd heard about the five-year benchmark with cancer survivorship but had the wrong end of the stick – he thought that if you survived for five years, you were cured, whereas the yardstick is a simply measure of 'successful' treatment. I let him remain in ignorance.

We got home from Germany at 1.45am. Daniel rang me at 9am to take him to school.

My worst fears were realised when Ludwig emailed on 3rd March 2008: the scan showed cancer in the chest, he said. I found it hard to concentrate at work that day. I made wheatgrass later that evening as usual, with little enthusiasm. But I had to keep up normality for Daniel.

When I rang Ludwig, his secretary was rude – this was the last time I could speak to him, she said. This was just about my only bad experience with the German medical system. Ludwig himself was patient and said I could email any time.

It was a worrying week: we were due some UCH scan results, too. I knew how serious relapse within the first two years was. I felt better after another email from Ludwig tempering some of his earlier pessimism. Daniel's pains had lessened. I approached wheatgrass preparation with renewed enthusiasm.

I felt strangely calm before the meeting with Colin. Daniel was laughing and joking in the waiting-room. The meeting went far better than I expected. The UCH scans were good. Colin didn't think Daniel was relapsing. How he was feeling was an important part of the assessment and he seemed and looked well, Colin explained.

After Daniel left, we discussed the IGF issue briefly. I concluded: 'I'm sorry for being high maintenance and would love to say I will not continue to be but …' I let my voice trail off. Colin said he understood what we were trying to do. He promised to get UCH radiologists to look at the Heidelberg scan. When they did, they weren't impressed with the quality. It proved to be a false alarm, though the worry lingered for several months. The episode was a lesson that it's always best to have scans done at the same hospital, on the same machines: calibration varies from machine to machine. I acknowledged to Colin that I'd made a mistake.

IGF again

Now that we were reasonably confident that Daniel didn't have measurable disease, the IGF issue was back on. Daniel and I set off for Barcelona, on 15th April 2008. I was confident that the hospital would be good– Spain in fact had better cancer results than the UK – but I still worried about taking

Daniel to a foreign hospital where there might be language issues. If anything went wrong I would feel responsible, because this was a risk we were assuming voluntarily. My anxiety increased on the morning of our flight when Jaume Mora emailed that they proposed using deep sedation. I had no idea what this was. I googled and came across an article by Michael Sury, an anaesthetist at Great Ormond Street Hospital. On a quick scan it seemed concerning but I couldn't get hold of Dr Sury.

I did manage to track down Mary Self, whose husband Richard is a consultant anaesthetist. Mary and I had exchanged emails about her book documenting her astonishing recovery from chondrosarcoma (cancer of the cartilage), after being at death's door. Mary is deeply religious and put her recovery down to the power of prayer: elders in her church followed the healing protocol in St James's letter.

Richard kindly came out of a meeting and was reassuring. So off Daniel and I went to Barcelona. The hotel in the middle of the city was plush and comfortable – just sixty-eight euros for the two of us. Plus we got to watch the Italian version of *Deal or No Deal*. Soon after we arrived, Dr Sury kindly rang and also put my mind at rest.

We were at the hospital, perched high over the city, by eight the next morning. Daniel's teeth were chattering, his nervousness increased by the fact that Petra wasn't with him. In the event, he was given the option of a general anaesthetic so all the worry about deep sedation was for nothing. They took four bone marrow samples, in his anterior and posterior iliac crest (part of the pelvis) on each side. The UCH samples had just been from his right pelvis.

The operation was in the paediatric unit. A couple of clowns were there to entertain the children. Daniel stood out as the British boy, so they made a beeline for him. He was suitably embarrassed. The clowns became a running joke between us every time we went back to the hospital. The more Daniel tried to melt into the background, the more they picked on him.

Astonishingly, within one and a half hours of his coming out of the recovery room, Daniel and I were at the Nou Camp, FC Barcelona's magnificent stadium, not far from the hospital. Ever the starry-eyed sports fan, he had his picture taken with lifesize cut-outs of Thierry Henri and Ronaldinho.

I later told him about the girl with spinal Ewing's whom Dr Mora had wanted him to meet: she'd been paraplegic but could now walk. Like Dr Mora, I was trying to convey hope that there could be a positive outcome from a bad start. But Daniel was shaken by the thought of paraplegia, though reassured, I think, by my explanation that spinal primary cancer was different to spinal metastases (which he had). I wished I'd kept my counsel.

Daniel and I played multiple games of Black Jack that day. Daniel eventually won 16:15, having been 15:9 down. We would have continued playing until he got in the lead. When we got home, Daniel complained of worsening pain in his right hip, away from the biopsy site. So more worry there. But it had been a good trip.

It was six days later, on 21st April, that I opened an email from Dr Mora, with the usual trepidation. To my surprise and immense relief the news was good. Daniel's samples, he wrote, were 'rigorously negative for the EWS-

ERG fusion transcript' – in other words, there was no sign of cancer. Petra and I had been expecting bad news. We were also expecting to have to make difficult decisions about low-dose chemotherapy which might have to be in Barcelona every couple of weeks if Colin wasn't willing to give treatment here. Given the result Dr Mora advised against more treatment at the moment. We should have the test done again in six months.

I knew there was a possibility of a false negative – that the test had failed to pick up cancer which was there. The samples were hypocellular (fewer cells than ideal). But Dr Mora still thought the result was prognostically significant. It was encouraging news. Daniel's hip pain had eased and he was exercising. What's more, a few days later he was accepted to line-judge at Wimbledon, so things were on the up.

The test result destroyed my main legal argument about the Roche trial. There was now no evidence that Daniel had residual cancer, by scan or RT-PCR. There was therefore no diagnostic benchmark by which one could measure whether the R1507 inhibitor was working. The cost and effort involved in bringing a major legal case wouldn't have deterred me had I felt it might help secure treatment which Daniel needed. But for sure, I could do without the additional anxiety.

* * *

Looking back now, what were the lessons from those difficult early months of 2008 and the battle for the R1507 inhibitor? I was disappointed by a number of people and institutions. First I was disappointed by Roche, though not surprised. They were acting in what they saw as their narrow financial interests. Companies have to look to the interests of their shareholders; that's their legal duty.

However, even if Roche were not willing to change their eligibility criteria, or allow Colin McMaster to interpret them flexibly, they could easily have allowed Daniel the inhibitor off-trial. I would willingly have signed a waiver of legal liability, not that Roche would have had liability. This too, they weren't prepared to do.

I was forced to conclude that desperately ill youngsters like Daniel count for little in the calculations of drug multinationals. The companies are institutionally geared to sacrificing individuals on the altar of shareholder satisfaction, executive pay and voracious appetite for market share, where necessary. That may seem harsh, but I believe it's true. The irony is that including RT-PCR-positive patients like Daniel in their trial would, in my view, have given Roche valuable additional information and therefore ultimately served their financial interests. But their outlook was myopic and they wouldn't look beyond traditional ways of running cancer trials.

Let me present the credit side of the balance-sheet. There are unquestionably any number of drug company employees who are dedicated to finding cures for serious diseases and helping individuals in difficult situations where they can. I spoke to quite a few such people during Daniel's journey. The problem is not individuals but the system: history teaches that institutional pressures encourage people to behave in ways they wouldn't in other contexts.

I also learnt that drug companies channel cancer drugs

to the developing world, at a fraction of the normal cost. They don't publicise this. One may wonder, cynically, whether the reason for this unusual coyness is that they don't want to highlight the huge mark-up on drugs sold in affluent countries, but even so many benefit from this act of charity. I'm sure some companies try to plot as ethical a way through the jungle that is cancer research and treatment as they can. The picture, as ever, is more nuanced than sloganised soundbites would suggest.

But the charge-sheet is nevertheless long and serious. Anyone reading Ben Goldacre's recent book *Bad Pharma* would take prescription medicines only if they had no choice. Many of the themes weren't new to me but I was shocked by the scale and breadth of corruption and unethical behaviour Dr Goldacre described and the examples he gives. He's a medical doctor who has studied in detail how the pharmaceutical industry works and how it interacts with his own profession. His approach is careful, evidence-based. He's no radical when it comes to medical treatment and has been vocal in his criticism of homeopathy and other remedies he considers 'quackery.' He acknowledges that many drugs are beneficial. He's on the side of good science. So his litany of criticisms should be taken seriously.

Dr Goldacre argues that huge numbers suffer and die unnecessarily because of the behaviour of pharmaceutical companies. Indeed if his criticisms are merited it must, logically, be millions. I wish I'd known more about this at the time. I would have read articles with an even closer eye. But even then, I would have struggled to distinguish between the genuine and the tainted. Ben Goldacre's point is that doctors usually cannot either. The recent exposure of Roche withholding data about Tamiflu, the influenza drug, is but one of many examples.

To put the charge at its most mercenary: society isn't getting nearly enough out of the billions of pounds invested in medical research. While there's so much money to be made out of illness, behaviour will be corrupted. That, I believe, is a truism. I discuss more about the issues, the sometimes inglorious behaviour of academics and journal editors and possible solutions on my website.

All the sins of omission and commission of drug companies are exacerbated by weak regulation by bodies such as the MHRA and the European Medicines Agency. Conflicts of interest have been plentiful in both agencies and no doubt others around the world. With Daniel's case, I felt the MHRA's attitude was supine, far too deferential to the wishes of Roche. The agency chose to emphasise that drug companies own the development of drugs. There is a resonant phrase, 'regulatory capture', which describes what can happen when the regulated are more powerful than those regulating them. This seems to have happened all too often with medicines regulators. As a society, we remain obsessed with the secrecy of information, even where there's no good reason for it.

I recognise that it wouldn't have been easy to show in a legal case that the MHRA's approach was unlawful. But that doesn't mean that the MHRA couldn't have adopted the approach I suggested. That's how public law works. Public bodies have to keep within the law. So for example, they have to interpret legislation correctly. But the legislation often gives them a wide discretion. Provided the chosen course falls within the bounds of that discretion, it's lawful. I believe that had the MHRA adopted my argument - that the more information one has about the potential efficacy of a new treatment, the more refined the judgements about whether safety risks are worth taking, and the wider the pool of patients, present and future, who stand to benefit - it would have been perfectly lawful.

But the MHRA opted for the bureaucratically easy way out. Seriously ill children had to take second place. The ethics committee was at least willing to look at the issue, after our representations, and Sir John Lilleyman understood what we were trying to do.

That leaves Colin McMaster. Doctors have a central role in clinical trials. I found my dealings with Colin over this issue really frustrating. It's right to acknowledge that much goes on behind the scenes which patients and their families never get to know about, because they don't need to. I'm sure that parents like me who want to know everything can be tiresome. I was acutely conscious that Colin was busy. Sometimes no doubt I got things wrong, such that a query (and the chasing which followed) was misplaced and frustrating for Colin to have to deal with. But communication wasn't good. I should certainly not have been denied information which Colin had.

The message seemed to be: this is how the system works and there's nothing anyone can do about it - Roche set the eligibility criteria, Daniel needed measurable disease, he didn't have it, end of story. I was therefore left to challenge the system by myself. I was perhaps better able to do so than many, as someone experienced in using the law in a campaigning context against public bodies and powerful corporations and challenging received wisdom. But I resented the fact that I was left to do so without the person who could have helped the most.

I should also acknowledge that Colin campaigns to improve the lot of teenage cancer patients and their access to experimental drugs. Indeed, he was chair of a national committee trying to get more clinical trial opportunities for paediatric patients (I offered to provide *pro bono* legal advice). I have no doubt that he did his utmost for Daniel within the constraints of the system as he saw them. But we needed a doctor who was prepared, if necessary, to challenge the system, to push the boundaries for his seriously ill patient.

It's worth noting that the vast majority of cancer parents, indeed patients more generally, never know when they're denied access to trials which could help them. If a doctor concludes that a patient doesn't fit the eligibility criteria or perhaps doesn't even know about the trial, the patient remains in none-too-blissful ignorance. It was only because I did my own research that I discovered there was even a problem.

There was, I suppose, one other key actor in this play and that was me. It was a demanding role. And yet, although I certainly wasn't looking for a fight with the medical establishment, in a strange way it was quite therapeutic. I was doing something for Daniel which might just tip the scales in his favour. I had no illusions about the rockiness of the terrain I was traversing but it gave me some control over what was happening to Daniel. For all my research, I was way outside my comfort zone with the science of Ewing's. Battling to get Daniel an IGF inhibitor, I felt more within my zone.

I'm pleased, at any rate, that I did challenge the system. It used to surprise me how meekly people seemed to accept trial eligibility criteria. Articulate, resourceful parents, who would otherwise stop at nothing for their desperately ill child, would simply report that their doctor had explained that, unfortunately, their child didn't qualify for a given trial. Parents and doctors alike appeared to treat eligibility criteria as if handed down on tablets of stone to Moses on Mount Sinai. I couldn't understand why no one would challenge the criteria or argue for a liberal interpretation.

The irony is the result from the Barcelona RT-PCR in April 2008 which filled us with such joy at the time, may have been counterproductive by undermining my legal argument. Had the test proved positive, I would have done everything possible to get Daniel an inhibitor, anywhere in the world. Amazingly, there were doctors - in Spain, France and the US - willing to try to access it for Daniel. It wouldn't have been easy, I recognise.

At any rate, in April 2008 I was glad to put the IGF issue to bed, for the time being at least.

More opportunities and more worry

Dad: Daniel, it was very rude what you did earlier, wasn't it?
Daniel (aged four): Right, was there something else you wanted to say or was that it?

The early summer of 2008 was relatively free of worry and crisis. Daniel line-judged once more at Wimbledon. It was wonderful to see him back there. He rang after his first session on court to say that the umpire had overruled him on the first point and again on the last! Daniel didn't like getting things wrong, especially in front of hundreds of people and TV cameras, but he treated it all with his usual equanimity and self-deprecation. Work colleagues said my eyes lit up when I related the story. They always did, apparently, when

Full of concentration at Wimbledon.

I talked about Daniel. His cousin Holly, visiting Wimbledon one day, was full of admiration for him line-judging when still not well.

On the medical front, we weren't allowed to bask in the mellow glow of reassurance for long.

We were due to get a PET/CT result on Friday 18th July. On the Monday of that week, Petra rang me early in the morning. She sounded panicky: 'Last night, Daniel showed me a hard swelling in his left testicle. It's been there for a few days.' Petra had been up half the night researching on the internet, something she normally left to me. She had convinced herself that this was cancer.

I did my own quick bit of researching. I knew that Ewing's could spread to any part of the body, but had never come across metastases in the testes. Could this be a new cancer, possibly caused by treatment? Testicular cancer often appears around Daniel's age. Google identified a Ewing's case where treatment might have caused testicular cancer.

I was aware that testicular cancer has a cure rate of around 98 per cent if it hasn't spread. But I also knew from reading Lance Armstrong's book that the platinum-based chemotherapy can be brutal. Daniel would surely not be able to have this, because his immune system was already severely compromised. I would still have settled for testicular cancer, in preference to relapsed Ewing's.

I had a freedom of information case in the Court of Appeal the following day but had to put preparation on hold as we got an urgent appointment with the GP. Dr Sekhon, thorough and sympathetic as ever, was reasonably reassuring. It could be a cyst but with Daniel's history we should get it checked. He would speak to UCH. Petra looked drawn and worried. Daniel, typically, seemed superficially normal. I noted in my journal that I felt oddly distant from it all. Just one more crisis to deal with.

Dr Sekhon wasn't sure the swelling emanated from the testicle. Did that make it worse? I wondered. Ewing's sometimes goes to the lymph nodes in the groin. Cancer in the lymphatic system isn't good because it can easily spread.

The following day, I came out of the court hearing to speak to Joni, Colin's secretary. She said Colin wanted a recent PET scan reviewed. That worried me. Daniel would need an ultrasound scan on Friday. As I was having a post-case dinner with my colleagues Becky and Katy, Petra said Daniel was now complaining about pain in his right testicle, later extending to his groin: something else to worry about.

I had several chats with Katie and JJ, Daniel's medic cousins.

And so the week went on. The Friday arrived. Daniel was scared in the night but still had a Greek lesson before we drove to London: yet another example of his ability to operate at two levels. I picked up a speeding ticket, driving through roadworks on the A40 into London.

I knew straightaway when we walked into Colin's room that the news was good. He was in an upbeat mood and told Daniel that he'd watched Wimbledon for the first time in years to see if he could see him line-judging. The PET was clear. We'd been so worried and yet the testicle issue had, it seemed, barely registered with him, no doubt because the chances of cancer there were pretty remote. The ultrasound turned out to be clear too, after a thorough analysis.

Becky sent me a text: 'My heart & my stomach just turned as your txt arr – I'm so, so glad!' Katy said she could cry.

It's difficult to capture the relief which, if one is lucky, follows this kind of anxiety. It could lift one's mood like nothing else. Petra had been so convinced the news would be bad that she hadn't prepared for Daniel's forthcoming week at a Greek summer school, at Bryanston in Dorset.

The morning after the meeting, I woke at 4.30, my mind racing. I sent emails to various doctors about treatment options, because I knew the relief would probably be short-lived. But it was most welcome for all that.

It had been a difficult week. My focus, naturally, was on this latest drama. But so much else happened too. The day the crisis blew up Daniel heard he'd earned a distinction in his Grade 8 saxophone exam, though he forgot to mention it initially. He'd only been playing five minutes. He came to the court hearing. Everyone in our team made a fuss of him and Kate Olley, the junior barrister, wrote to me later:

'I liked him instantly. I always "judge" people on their energy and his seemed to be intelligent, unusual, friendly, fair-minded, and yet somehow his sense of humour was very obvious too.'

Daniel could have this sort of effect, even without saying much. People seemed to feel they could connect with him. He said little to me about the hearing but told Annabel, his cousin, that he'd really enjoyed it and could see himself as Judge Thomas one day!

What else happened that week, according to my journal? George Noakes, the former Archbishop of Wales, died. He'd been our vicar as kids and we used to play tennis and table-tennis with him. I had a letter from World Vision that Mugabe had ordered aid agencies to stop working in Zimbabwe but Camelia, my sponsee, was thought to be ok. It was another reminder of how lucky we were to live in this country. I came across a distressed bird; someone took it to a wildlife rescue centre before I could. A friend of my sister's had received an admission of negligence from the hospital about the death of her seventeen year-old son, who had muscular dystrophy. A leading neurologist had discharged his own son from the same hospital because the oncologists, wrongly as it transpired, wouldn't accept he had a particular cancer. My sister Sian commented to her daughter Holly: 'Now you understand why Uncle David challenges everything.' I was cheered by a recent article about the fate of Ewing's patients who didn't relapse during the first two years.

So as usual, all life was there in that week, the good and the bad, some of it affecting us as a family, much of it not.

Immediate crisis averted, I was able to enjoy my friend Dominic's fiftieth birthday party. Daniel, too, had another lease of life. A few days later, we had our second knock of tennis since he was diagnosed. This time he enjoyed it much more.

The testicle issue didn't go away. Over the next few months, there were periodic scares and several ultrasound scans. Colin later admitted to being puzzled by the swelling. Radiotherapy was thought perhaps to be the culprit. Eventually the problem fell off the radar.

Making more memories

We were lucky that, amidst the emotional mayhem, we had times of partial respite. In February Daniel and I had a holiday to Classical Italy. He was serious about preparing for Oxford – we'd already seen the Greek tragedy *Agamemnon* by Aeschylus at University College London near the hospital.

Italy was great. Daniel wasn't really into archaeology but all the same loved Herculaneum, Pompeii and Rome, as well as the trip up Mount Vesuvius; we had both read Robert Harris's historic novel *Pompeii* before going. We thought the Colosseum would be good when they finished it. We went to the Keats museum at the bottom of the Spanish Steps, which inspired Daniel to want to improve his reading. We saw a rubbish game between Roma and Fiorentina in a three-quarter empty Olympic Stadium. A friend, Gianluca, organised a typical Roman apartment for us. On one occasion a restaurant happily cooked Daniel a meal with the organic pasta and tomato sauce we brought – a case of taking coals to Newcastle. So many happy memories.

The day we went to the Sistine Chapel Daniel related, for the umpteenth time, that his leg was hurting. 'Nothing bad is going to happen, is it?' he asked plaintively. But if I couldn't persuade Anxiety to stay at home, at least I managed to keep her out of sight most of the time and I hope that Daniel did.

* * *

A child's cancer, any serious illness, dominates one's life. But it doesn't insulate one from other aspects of life, from the highs and lows, though it may sketch them in a different hue. It may also accentuate difficulties.

The summer of 2008 was an especially difficult time for me, because it heralded the break-up of a relationship which meant a huge amount. It's not fair to go into detail about Sophie (not her real name). We are all prisoners of our personalities and circumstances and each feeds off the other. I mention the break-up simply because it affected me deeply and made an already treacherous journey even harder to navigate. We were as close as two people could be, or so I thought, and for a time the laughter which had been on strict ration since Daniel's diagnosis swelled to banquet servings. It made such a difference. Our journey together gave me strength for my journey with Daniel.

So, when the relationship suddenly took an unexpected

turn, first into the sidings and then the buffers, I felt let down. The passage of time has eased the pain and I never questioned Sophie's myriad qualities. She was confronting her own difficulties and I believed, with changing degrees of confidence, that she wanted the relationship to continue, had she been able to pilot a way around them. But the hurt was real and persisted for some time. I wish I had kept it from Sophie, but I didn't.

The double-blow fed on itself: the pain of the break-up made the pain of Daniel's cancer more acute; his illness meant that I coped worse with the break-up than I otherwise might have done – at the very time I needed the particular brand of support which a close relationship gives, it was removed. There was nothing unique about the double-blow. I came across so many cancer parents who faced multiple problems, some related to their child's cancer, some not. Fate doesn't dole out her largesse and her brickbats in equal measure. Many were going through much tougher times than I was, with financial and job worries, family trauma, anxiety about accessing treatment for their child, feeling let down by certain friends, other illnesses to contend with in the family, and so much more (so many couples split after the death of a child). I think of the family of Hannah, a delightful girl with Ewing's in Michigan diagnosed the same month as Daniel. Hannah's sister had a serious brain tumour as a child and her parents lost multiple close family members to cancer during her journey, including Hannah. I think of a sarcoma patient whose son was diagnosed with Ewing's; they had treatment side-by-side in hospital.

But Fate is too ephemeral to be a useful object of frustration. Human behaviour is a more visible target. One morning, in early September 2008, I received a package through the post. It contained a book I hadn't ordered, *The Emotional Incest Syndrome: What to Do When a Parent's Love Rules Your Life* by Patricia Love. I have read only the blurb on the back but the title says it all. It was accompanied by an anonymous typed message:

> *'It's about time that you relinquished your role as an "over-involved" parent. At twenty your son deserves to possess his own life while at fifty it's high time that you dealt with your long outstanding life issues and stopped living in denial. Academic intelligence aplenty but a paucity of emotional intelligence!'*

Wow. I guessed who'd sent it (not Sophie), someone whose feelings towards me were unrequited, someone who had caused me considerable problems. People are entitled to their judgements but I didn't take the barbed comment seriously. I value emotional intelligence much higher than whatever academic intelligence I possess. More importantly, this person, herself generally compassionate, wouldn't have been interested in me if she truly believed I was at the psychopathic end of the empathy scale. My interpretation, perhaps generous to myself, was that she regarded my lack of interest in her as symptomatic of emotional deficiency, which must be a comforting way of looking at the world.

I brushed it off but was still shocked that anyone would choose to attack my relationship with Daniel (about which she knew little and understood less) when he was seriously ill and I felt under great pressure. And that she would do so anonymously, which was presumably calculated to create doubt about who in my circle thought this of me.

There was never any chance that I would allow any of this to distract me from doing my best for Daniel. My focus at no point wavered.

The break-up with Sophie, meanwhile, did have a silver lining. It was part of the reason I became a Samaritan. Self-pity may provide short-term comfort but it's corrosive of the spirit, and I didn't want my spirit to be corroded. 'Self-pity is our worst enemy and if we yield to it, we can never do anything wise in this world', Helen Keller, who had more reason than most for self-pity, once remarked. So I lifted myself out of self-indulgent despondency and did the Samaritans training, just when Daniel was starting at Oxford.

* * *

One of Daniel's concerns was his loss of hair. Trivial in the scheme of things, but it mattered to him. Normally hair

Daniel became quite self-conscious about his loss of hair.

ravaged by chemotherapy grows back within six months, but occasionally it doesn't. Daniel was one of those cases. He was keen to have a hair transplant. We were worried that, if he had more chemo – as was likely – it would all be a waste. Daniel and I visited a trichologist (a new word to me), Barry Stevens, in

Essex. He didn't offer a magic cure which I respected him for. Putting on weight was important, he thought. Through his parents, also trichologists, he'd seen the hair of emaciated concentration camp survivors grow as they gained weight. Otherwise Barry advised Daniel to be philosophical.

Barry's clinic was at the polar opposite of the M25 to us. We thought it would be a good idea to complete the ring in one trip. It wasn't. The holiday traffic led to a journey of little more than an hour taking three and a half hours. But Daniel was in high spirits. He would like to live to a hundred he said and was planning to travel after Oxford. He was pleased that Colin thought he was looking better each time. More wistfully, when I remarked it was bad luck about his hair he replied: 'Again!' This was the first time he had articulated even a hint of self-pity.

The next day Daniel went to Bryanston for the Greek summer school. Petra, who was away with the girls, had put stickers on his car: 'Ur the best', 'Join in', 'Eat lots.' She was worried the cancer was making him insular and lowering his social confidence. But he seemed to have a good week: he played in an orchestra, shot pool and went to a fancy dress party as an Egyptian mummy (unlike his dad he enjoyed fancy dress parties). Best of all, he met a girl. When I learnt this I was so happy that he'd experienced love, I hope without heartache, its handmaiden. I'd assumed that cancer, and the self-esteem damage and introversion it spawned, would cause love to pass him by.

There was one more medical staging-post before Daniel was due to start in Oxford. I wanted to have another RT-PCR, as Dr Mora had recommended. Petra wasn't convinced but agreed. So off to Barcelona Daniel and I went, in late

September 2008. Daniel had line-judged in Maidenhead in the morning and I'd been to a lunch party in London so it was a bit of a mad day. Dr Mora told Daniel he was doing well and although his disease was high-risk, RT-PCRs were predictive of survival.

Daniel later asked me why his operations were in the paediatric wing. I explained that Ewing's is largely a disease of the first two decades of life. 'Does that mean it doesn't come back in the third decade?' was the follow-up question. I knew why he was asking: it was his twentieth birthday the following week. He was searching for straws to clutch.

We had a look round Barcelona, including Gaudi's Sagrada Familia. On the steps of Barcelona Cathedral, conscious that Daniel would soon be moving away from the shelter of home life I decided the time was right for a father-son chat. Daniel politely humoured me, probably thinking 'What an idiot.'

In the evening we were in a restaurant when we had two calls from Petra. In the first she said that her father was seriously ill with pneumonia and wasn't expected to last the night. Daniel asked me, hopefully: 'But Bampy might not die?' In the second, soon after the first, Petra said her father had died. He had celebrated his ninetieth birthday earlier in the year. Daniel was quiet for the rest of the evening but we played cards on the plane to take his mind off things.

Undergraduate

The first day of Fresher's Week, 6th October 2008, was Daniel's birthday. Two days earlier he queried why it was only then that I was asking what he wanted for his birthday.

I joked: 'It's a low priority for me.' He replied: 'Well, it's a high priority for me.' Daniel never lost the child's joy in getting presents. Petra got him a suit, a mark that he was nevertheless entering the adult world. I think he liked the Oxford Dictionary of Quotations I got him, too. Daniel devoured quotations.

At 4pm on his birthday I got the RT-PCR result. Everything was clear. Huge relief, although Daniel didn't want to know the result. He had chest pain but embraced Fresher's Week. He told me he felt comfortable at Oxford and was already working on his first essay. He attended Freshers' Fair and when pressurised into joining societies he wasn't really interested in, did so in a false name so he wouldn't subsequently be hassled! Typically he burnt some toast, setting off the smoke alarm: everyone had to pile out of the house. I was so happy to see him at university and yet the usual parental excitement was dimmed: I knew he would probably not graduate.

The week was interrupted for Bampy's funeral. I was to pick Daniel up, after dinner at the College. Daniel suggested I come at 10pm when everyone would have gone to a quiz. For years, whether because of the cancer or otherwise, he'd suffered the teenager's embarrassment of parents, understandable in my case but it extended to Petra and even the girls. It diminished over time but he never completely shed it.

It's well-known that students take their washing home. On this evening, Daniel brought his washing-up with him as well! He wouldn't listen to my pleas that we just do it there. This became a regular feature of his time at Oxford, aided by our visits being frequent, because of his diet and hospital visits and assorted panics. We were too indulgent, no doubt, but we wanted to ease things for him as much as possible. His diet, wheatgrassing and other juicing meant that he spent longer on food than other students and he was often unwell. Plus, he could twist us round his little finger and frequently did.

I must have paid a small fortune to get Daniel and Annabel to clean my car.

As the autumn drew on, there were the usual health scares: chest and other pain, numbness, a problem with his eye. I noted everything and worried, though I learnt to discriminate to some degree between symptoms of concern and those which in other times wouldn't have merited mention. I felt sad when Daniel commented one day that he'd forgotten what it was to feel normal.

For the first few weeks at Oxford, Daniel wouldn't tell his friends and housemates about his cancer. We cajoled him softly. We knew they would be supportive and wouldn't look at him any differently, which is probably what he was worried about. He seemed reluctant to go into the house kitchen and lost a fair amount of weight. I talked to him sternly about that: he didn't have weight to lose. His appetite diminished, though he regained the weight by the end of term. He became a bit slapdash about juicing, eating vegetables and so forth. Maybe this was because he thought he was over the worst with the cancer. Psychologically that would be good for him, but we had to get the message over, gently, that he couldn't take his eye off the ball. I so wish we hadn't had to mention the word 'cancer.'

He did eventually tell people about his cancer. He discussed with me what he should tell Felix, his tutor. Felix comes from Munich and Daniel really liked him. Felix's reply was kind and acknowledged that the cancer must be an immensely difficult thing to live with.

For all the minor crises and dilemmas, Daniel loved his first term in Oxford. He joined the swing band and the table-tennis club. He wasn't able to make as much of Oxford as had he been well, but he was still living his dream.

We played tennis with my sister Charlotte and Daniel's cousin Annabel just after Christmas 2008. His mobility still restricted, Daniel played at the net for one and a half hours, anticipating well and hitting the ball beautifully. It made me so happy.

The death of Petra's father was a real sadness but, that apart, 2008 was a positive year for Daniel. There had been a surfeit of scares but over two and a half years since diagnosis, he had lived longer than expected. Colin had said that Daniel would do extremely well not to relapse during 2008. Well, he hadn't, as far as we knew.

Was it even conceivable that Daniel was going to be ok? I barely allowed myself to think the thought.

A year without treatment

Dad: That plane is going to Heathrow
Daniel (aged four): How do you know?
Dad: Well, Heathrow is very close to here
Daniel: Well, why are they going by plane if it's so close?

Daniel had no hospital treatment in 2009. There were still endless scares from assorted pains. Looking back over my journal, I'd forgotten how many illnesses – normal, everyday illnesses – Daniel used to have: fever, headaches, nausea. A consequence of his depleted immune system, I assume. He would get very tired. Fatigue is a common symptom of cancer and its brutal treatment; there have been several studies about it. It tends to get brushed aside because we all suffer from tiredness in our communication-heavy and opportunity-rich lives. But cancer tiredness is different: it's debilitating and causes a downturn in mood and morale and it sometimes affected Daniel's. Always late going to bed, he would sleep in late unless he had a tutorial or hospital appointment. Then it would take him a while to come to, before his sparkling personality would shine through once more.

Quite how he managed to keep up with his coursework I don't know. One of his tutors said Daniel never used his illness as an excuse for not doing an essay, unlike other students who would hide behind everyday ailments. More than once, he did all-night sessions.

'How are you feeling Dan?' I used to ask him. 'Really tired', would come the reply. 'But apart from that?' as if the tiredness didn't matter. It mattered to him. Sometimes I corrected myself, conscious of how my dismissiveness must have appeared. I skated over the tiredness because I knew it wouldn't kill him, whereas the things my question was really aimed at - pain, fever - could portend something serious.

But for all this, in relative terms 2009 was a good year. Daniel began really to enjoy Oxford. He joined the university tennis club, though didn't play much. He managed a game of badminton and even a short bike ride. He went to fancy-dress parties and some union debates and talks. There were swing band practices and concerts and the Magdalen Orchestra. He had his football with him. Whenever I visited, he greeted me with some new trick he'd learnt. One day he proudly told me that he'd done seventy-six keepy-uppies in his room. I was glad he had his priorities sorted. He seemed to be making friends and trampolined at his friend Anna's party in Birmingham. One day someone came into his room as we spoke on the phone. 'Can you ring back?' Daniel asked, before adding 'Actually, don't bother, bye!'

I was more than happy to be side-lined. Visits by Petra or me were nevertheless frequent, mainly to take Daniel food. One Sunday evening in early February 2009, I was taking some frozen wheatgrass juice to him. Petra and the girls were looking after Jess, my recently-acquired collie cross from Brighton RSPCA. Petra rang from Chobham Common, in a panic: Jess had gone missing. It was dark by this time. I turned back. The girls were upset. I donned my wellington boots, and assured them I would find her. I wasn't so sure. Chobham Common is massive – the M3 runs through the middle. Jess had got lost in a part she didn't know. There was snow on the ground, making it more difficult for her to find a familiar scent. I worried she might have fallen into an icy pond. Petra and the girls drove up and down the roads bisecting the common.

It was a filthy evening. I had visions of being out there all night, with all the wildlife - deer, foxes, rabbits and the rest. But I knew I had to find Jess. She was a rescue dog, originally from Ireland, with all manner of phobias. The thought of her feeling abandoned again drove me on. I called and whistled, called and whistled, in vain. Needles and haystacks came to mind. Normally I would give the common a wide berth at night. It was pretty spooky but I felt strangely serene. This may be stretching a point, but there was an analogy with how I dealt with Daniel's cancer. When you have to do something, you just do it and objections, rational objections, which would normally raise their voice realise they are wasting their time and that brings its own calmness.

Harvey, my next-door neighbour came to join the search. Daniel was worried and rang from Oxford. Unexpectedly, at 8.30 in the evening, Harvey's partner Constance rang:

Jess had appeared outside their front door. Massive relief all round. When I picked her up she was bloated, presumably after an extra Sunday lunch on the common. I drove to Oxford with a traumatised dog.

A few weeks later Daniel and I were in Barbados to watch England play the West Indies at cricket. I had casually mentioned going one day, not meaning it seriously. Daniel didn't let me forget. We played tennis there, despite the baking sun. Daniel's mobility was excellent – I told him I could tell no difference compared to pre-cancer days.

One evening he started to ask about different sorts of cancer but then stopped himself. This was typical – he was interested intellectually but emotionally could face thinking about cancer no more than he had to.

A tour of the island took us to Codrington College, now a theological college but once a slave plantation. Strangely the otherwise excellent tour guide didn't mention that. Perhaps he wanted to smooth over this dark episode in Barbados' past. Daniel haggled the price for an Amerindian mask, a sign perhaps of his growing confidence.

The cricket itself was a bit of a washout – you go all the way to see cricket in Barbados and then it rains – but we did see two fantastic innings by Chris Gayle, the West Indies captain. But the highlight was a trip in a submarine, with astonishing close-ups of the sealife.

While we were in Barbados, Colin emailed that the latest x-ray was clear. He was glad to see Daniel looking so well, he added. I asked Daniel if he wanted to know the result – code which he understood meant it was ok. 'I knew it would be', he said. Lucky him.

RT-PCR again

The third RT-PCR in Barcelona in April 2009 was again clear. Dr Mora noticed a skin haemorrhage around a biopsy site, plus the bone marrow was sticky (possibly caused by cancer). He later eased my concerns, but internet research when I got home after midnight, exacerbated them - so often the pattern. The old proverb 'A little knowledge is a dangerous thing', promulgated by Alexander Pope, should have been my companion on this journey.

The problem is, one has to possess a little knowledge as a staging-post to possessing a modicum of knowledge and I felt I needed at least a modicum, about everything related to Daniel's cancer. The journey along the knowledge spectrum could be painful because I would often read something which, without context, seemed more alarming than it was. In truth, it's not having a little knowledge which is dangerous but having a little knowledge thinking it's sufficient knowledge. I don't think I ever suffered from that particular self-delusion.

The irony was that the more I learnt, the more I realised that I knew less than when I thought I knew only a little.

I was mightily relieved to get Dr Mora's message two days later while stuck in a traffic jam in Richmond, that the RT-PCR was negative. Rarely have I felt so happy in a traffic jam. The skin haemorrhage persisted for several weeks and remained one of many unresolved problems.

Other Ewing's patients

By this time I was following the stories of many young cancer patients on two American hospital websites, CarePages and Caringbridge. Seriously ill patients and their families have their own webpage, on which they can post updates and photographs and other people can add messages. It's a brilliant concept because it means that families can let people know what's happening without having to take loads of telephone calls. And for people like me the websites were a godsend because I could keep in touch with what was happening with other Ewing's patients. I was following well over a hundred by the end.

I came across so many remarkable youngsters. Each story was a rainbow of human emotion, of hope and despair, of love and occasional rejection, of terrible injustice but of stoic acceptance, of pervasive anxiety with episodic relief, a story more vivid than any scriptwriter could have devised. So many inspirational children. Brittne in Texas had lost her mother to cancer shortly before she was diagnosed with Ewing's. Not long out of treatment, Brittne was helping in a homeless shelter. Children with cancer often led fundraising initiatives.

These individual websites and online support groups such as Sarcoma UK provide wonderful succour. Even recently bereaved parents or parents whose child was dying were there for other parents.

This was the human family at its best. Cynically, one may regret that it takes hard times to bring out the best in people - Dunkirk to instil the Dunkirk spirit, the Blitz to inculcate the Blitz spirit. The truth I suspect, is that many people are only too eager for the opportunity to demonstrate the 'better angels of their nature' (to borrow from Abraham Lincoln's Gettysburg Address) and to rise above the trivial concerns of everyday life. Empathy was the dominant emotion on these websites.

I found more puzzling how many Ewing's children in the US went recreational hunting. It's deeply embedded in the culture, at least away from the conurbations. One mother of a young man, diagnosed with pelvic Ewing's the same month as Daniel, described one day his breathless excitement at bagging 'gobblers' on a turkey shoot. The mother ended the blog: 'Disclaimer: some animals were seriously injured in the making of this Carepage update.' Maybe there was irony which I missed.

A teenage girl in Arizona went on a prong horned elk hunt armed with a crossbow. A crossbow? Apparently Arizona law allows crossbows for those with damaged arms. I'm sure the elk understand. Another Ewing's patient, an eleven year-old girl, shot an elk one day. Her mother described the priceless look on her daughter's face as she saw her 'smackdown.'

I would often wonder why no one seemed to make the connection between the suffering their children were enduring and the suffering they were needlessly inflicting on animals (kills are not always clean and animals too young to fend for themselves are orphaned). As far as I could tell, these were good kids from loving, God-fearing families, an illustration of how important culture is in shaping behaviour and how it enables ethical inconsistencies to be glossed over.

I didn't feel it appropriate to share my thoughts about this but, a few days after the elk hunt, I did tell the mother of the eleven year-old about IGF inhibitors. She posted this message:

'I have to share a blessing with you. I received an email from Dave Thomas, someone whom I have never met,

but like you has been praying for [us]. He was inquiring about a clinical trial that is available for Ewing's patients. He expressed that he knows there has been some success with it. So I forwarded it to Dr Cooper and he ... said that this is the trial that we are praying ... to get into! I believe God led this gentleman to send me this email, knowing that tomorrow we may have to make some tough decisions.'

God bringing people into the lives of cancer sufferers was a theme of many webpages. It did feel odd to be identified as an unwitting messenger, but who knows what part any of us may be called to play without realising it? Sadly, the inhibitor didn't work for this girl and she died a couple of months later.

Religion

Religion did indeed feature large in CarePages and Caringbridge updates. This was in contrast with British support networks, where religion barely got a mention. Occasionally someone might say that they were praying for someone, but that was all. No doubt many British patients had a faith; it's just not the British way to talk about it – 'We don't do God', as Alastair Campbell famously said of Tony Blair's Government. I recently read of a nurse in the US who clasped the hands of newly-diagnosed Ewing's patient as he waited for scan results and asked if they could pray together. Inconceivable in the UK and, many will think, inappropriate on a number of levels.

I thought about religion even more than normal during Daniel's journey, musing one day in my journal after watching *Songs of Praise* from Hereford Cathedral: 'Could so many people have been inspired to write such beautiful music on a false prospectus?'

Some parents in the US would regularly quote verses from the Bible, sometimes as part of long discussions about religion (one could even call them sermons). The themes included God's love, faith and hope. A favourite verse was from Romans chapter 8: 'And we know that in all things God works for the good of those who love him, who have been called according to his purpose.' I wondered whether this was to bolster confidence that their child would get better, a case of faith rewarded. Many parents were convinced that God had something special in store for their child and that this was the reason for the trial by ordeal, and why he or she would be spared. Sometimes they were, usually they were not, leading to parental reappraisal of God's plans but not to loss of faith, at least not openly.

Some children inspired others to faith. It was surprising how often parents professed that their faith had been strengthened, not diminished, by their experience. One might have expected the opposite, but I could identify with a stronger feeling of spirituality during Daniel's journey. There were exceptions. A young boy in North Carolina said plaintively to his mother one day: 'I think God hates me.' His mother posted: 'I said you know I think he hates me too ... God gave his only son by choice. I didn't choose to give mine. He is making that choice for me. That is HATE, not love!!!!! '. She later recovered her faith. Her son didn't make it.

The father of fifteen year-old Anna posted one day as she was slipping away:

'I really don't see the sense in all this suffering, I know God has a plan and I hope some day I understand it, but at this moment I truly can't see the glory in a young girl suffering like this. The words like "God will walk with you all the way," seem so hollow when I hear my baby screaming in pain for hours on end...'

For him too, this was just a blip on the journey of faith. He was sure, because of what happened in Anna's last moments that Jesus was there to take her away.

These were rare faltering steps in journeys of faith. Some parents were atheists and resented being told that God loved them and their child and that they were now in a better place if they died. But atheists and agnostics generally kept their views to themselves.

Many bereaved parents were convinced that their child was in the arms of Jesus and that they would meet again one day and were grateful that the child's earthly suffering was over. And yet the poisonous pangs of grief remained. This would puzzle me and I would inwardly muse, uncharitably: 'If you're convinced that your child is blissfully happy with Jesus, free of pain and that you will meet again one day, what exactly is the problem?' Perhaps the parents had less faith than they professed.

Sometimes the contradiction would manifest itself almost comically. One day in 2010, a nineteen year-old named Michael died from Ewing's. Loads of people expressed their condolences on his webpage, in the way you would expect – deepest sympathy, can't imagine what you're going through, and so on. One entry grabbed my attention. It began: 'What a wonderful day!' This was not a cruel troll, however. The message continued: 'Michael is pain free and with his Maker!' It made sense, if one is lucky enough to have that degree of faith. But the logic is that we should want our children to die the moment they are born. Some bereaved Ewing's parents were more nuanced, explaining that they had a bitter-sweet sensation at the moment of death: bereft at losing their child, happy that he or she was in Heaven with Jesus.

A common explanation was that God must have needed the child more than the parents. The atheist bereaved mother in AC Grayling and Max Gordon's recent play *On Religion* despaired at that argument but it helps some make sense of their loss. We have such incomplete understanding of life and of death.

Like Anna's dad, many parents of faith wondered why God permitted their children to suffer. The problem of suffering has really exercised me too. Why would God create Daniel with a susceptibility to cancer? My interest in the problem of suffering long predated his illness, in fact. My favourite A level was Religious Studies, which ranged into areas such as the arguments about the existence of God. We also studied the problem of suffering and I remember the Greek philosopher's Epicurus' succinct capturing of the paradox:

'Is God willing to prevent evil, but not able?
Then he is not omnipotent.
Is he able, but not willing?
Then he is malevolent.
Is he both able and willing?
Then whence cometh evil?

Is he neither able nor willing?
Then why call him God?'

There have been many attempts to square the circle of the existence of evil and a benevolent, omnipotent deity. There is a branch of theology devoted to the geometrical conundrum, called theodicy. I discuss theodicy and the role of prayer in relieving suffering on my website.

I couldn't explain all the suffering but in some ways it helped that we weren't alone in our anguish. As well as cancer there were, sadly, any number of serious illnesses from which children were suffering. Perhaps cancer has a unique combination of features – life-threatening, painful, brutal and dangerous treatment, unending diagnostic tests and hospital visits, scanxiety, troubling symptoms, the thought of something evil growing inside one's body. But families with other childhood conditions – autism, cystic fibrosis, brain damage and the rest – will have their own horror stories to tell.

World Child Cancer bike ride

That summer of 2009, I did a sponsored bike ride for World Child Cancer (WCC), an excellent charity which helps children with cancer in the developing world. I was conscious that I was devoting most of my energy – and quite a bit of money – to helping Daniel. I knew that he was just part of an avalanche of suffering. So I wanted to do something.

I met Geoff Thaxter, one of the main driving forces behind WCC one day at UCH in late 2007. Geoff's daughter

Lisa had died of osteosarcoma when she was twelve. I took to Geoff immediately. He was warm and grounded. He spoke highly of Colin McMaster – no one knew more about sarcoma, he told me.

Sadly Geoff himself died of cancer, a brain tumour, in 2009, not long before my bike ride. Daniel had been in remission for a couple of years by this time so I felt reasonably confident in planning it. I had decided to ride to various children's cancer hospitals in England, starting in Leeds and finishing at Daniel's two main hospitals, the Royal National Orthopaedic Hospital in Stanmore and UCH. Because I wanted to raise awareness as well as money, I sought statements of support for WCC's work from each of the NHS trusts and then media coverage on the back of that. Somewhat to my surprise, each of the trusts cooperated. I had expected bureaucracy to get in the way.

I worked hard on the fundraising too. I had left it too late for corporate fundraising, but still managed to raise £13,500, with help from family members who joined the ride. My friends Norbert and Michaele raised over a thousand euros at a concert in Germany. I'm not a natural fundraiser and in common with many, hate asking for money. But I did my pitch, stressing WCC's credentials and how much could be bought with so little in poorer countries. It seemed to strike a chord. Probably Daniel's illness helped because I could make the connection.

I was struck by the symmetry in the statistics: in the developed world, around 80 per cent of children with cancer are cured; in the developing world, it's only 20 per cent. Susan Picton, a consultant paediatric oncologist at

Leeds, told me that in the developed world, 99 per cent of patients with retinoblastoma (cancer of the eye) are cured; in the developing world, virtually no one is. All because they don't have access to chemo. It need hardly be said that the situation is completely unacceptable.

Inevitably there are several reasons for the disparity – socio-economic factors, most particularly; poverty of education and transport; perhaps some cultural aspects. But it's inescapable that tens of thousands of children are suffering and dying of cancer each year unnecessarily. WCC, trying to bridge the gap, is doing great work in a number of countries. But ultimately these issues have to be solved at governmental and transgovernmental level.

To exacerbate the unfairness, many children with cancer in the developing world don't have pain relief. Everyone will have a sense of what that means but particularly if you have been close to cancer. As I said in my pitch for sponsorship, the thought of children dying without pain relief is simply horrific. Watching your child die in agony must be unbearable; to know that the pain is avoidable must add feelings of despair, anger and hopelessness to the bitter cocktail of emotion.

Again, the reasons for the disparity in palliative care are complicated. It's not just a lack of resources. Some countries have strict narcotic laws, which unintentionally catch the opiates used for pain relief. But so much more could be done. Some years ago, I visited Casa Alianza, a charity for street children, in Nicaragua. The thought of any of these children having to cope with cancer, on top of all the other problems and dangers they face, as some inevitably do, is arresting.

I made a YouTube video to plug the bike ride, or rather my friend Evelina did. I had in mind a simple piece to camera. Evelina's concept was more artistic. I had scripted roughly what I was going to say. I also wanted Daniel in the video, because the theme was the disparity in treatment. He wasn't keen but agreed. Evelina is such an artistic perfectionist that there were numerous takes. The location, light and sound on Chobham Common had to be perfect and I fluffed my lines often enough. Daniel looked at a photo album, supposedly containing pictures of children with cancer in Africa, which were then interposed in the video. He and I were also filmed playing tennis: the message was that he was fortunate to have the chance of playing again. I wrote a line for him, upbeat for his ears but without saying that he was cured, which I knew he wasn't.

Daniel didn't enjoy the filming. I hadn't fully absorbed how much he wanted to relegate cancer to memory, to be tapped as infrequently as possible. It made me even more worried about how he would cope with relapse. Daniel didn't watch the video and didn't want to know about our filming at UCH either.

Prior to the ride, I attended a WCC dinner in the House of Commons. Ramon de Beneducci, another guest, expressed an interest in taking part in the Oxford leg. The conversation went something like this:

Ramon: *My son is a student at Oxford so that would fit in*
Me: *Oh is he? Is he at the university?*
Ramon: *Yes*

Me: *That's a coincidence. So is my son. What year is your son in?*
Ramon: *Chris is in the first year*
Me: *So is Daniel. Which college is Chris at?*
Ramon: *Magdalen*
Me: *That's incredible. So is Daniel! What is Chris studying?*
Ramon: *Classics*
Me: *You are joking! They must know each other*

There were only seven Classics students in the first year at Magdalen, so naturally they knew each other. When I told Daniel the story, he was initially amused, until it dawned on him that this meant that I knew the father of one of his friends. That wasn't good. Who knows what I might learn about what went on at Oxford? Daniel liked to keep certain things under wraps.

The ride covered nearly 400 miles. My sister Charlotte and her children Katie and Annabel joined me for large stretches. Charlotte later described it as the best week of her life; she needs to get out more. Some of the riding was quite tough, especially over the Pennines and Peak District (and when I gallantly but foolishly took over my friend Djuna's hopelessly inadequate hired bike one day). One day I took the party up a really steep hill, used for time trials by proper cyclists, someone mentioned. When we eventually got to the top we discovered that it was the wrong way: I cycled off with abuse ringing in my ears. We stayed with my good friends Mark and Nicki in Nottingham and with Annabel's friend Zara in Birmingham, having arrived at her parents' beautiful house thoroughly drenched, after a sodden battle with the city's rush hour. Otherwise it was cramped in the camper van, which JJ had secured at a cut-price rate from Lazee Days in Derby (these were anything but lazy days). We managed to find places to park where we didn't have to pay.

One evening, I recall, there was a stunning double rainbow near Barston Lakes south of Birmingham. I had never seen one of those before. Charlotte, Annabel and I were given a free meal at an Italian restaurant in Wakefield (we were wearing our WCC T-shirts). The problem was we came to expect it everywhere and would feign surprise whenever presented with a bill.

But visiting the hospitals was the highlight. We were given a warm welcome wherever we went. It was a privilege meeting the kids; some had done drawings for us. Katie (in her first year as a doctor), JJ and Annabel (both medical students) were used to seeing sick children but there is something different about children with cancer. The physical effects of chemo and the cancer itself are so visible. Charlotte was really moved. I occasionally wonder what has happened to these children and to others whose cancer journeys intersected with Daniel's. By the law of cancer averages, some will not have made it.

I picked up some media along the way, though not as much as I would have liked. I did a live interview from the camper van with BBC Radio Oxford one Saturday morning, with an audience of at least three (in the camper van). I got a story in the *Law Society Gazette*, the journal for solicitors. Prior to the ride I had sent them a worthy press release, with facts and figures and the personal background. Predictably, no take-up. Then one day Terry, my brother-in-law, suggested we ride along the Banbury-

Oxford canal. Picturesque, no doubt, but he had suitable tyres and I didn't. I was back-marking when my road tyres lost their grip and I ended up in the canal, with my bike on top of me. Everyone was highly amused, naturally, and photos were taken. I sent one of them to the *Gazette*, which this time did bite. They were often sent photos of solicitors doing sponsored bike rides or swims, they wrote, but this was the first time a solicitor had done both at the same time. The wit of lawyers knows no beginning. The piece got some publicity for the charity, which was the point.

There was quite a welcoming party at UCH, including some of Daniel's nurses. Colin, who was supportive of the venture throughout, made a generous speech. It must have been a poignant moment for Gill Thaxter, Geoff's widow. I had dedicated the ride to him.

Daniel sadly, couldn't be there. I had wanted him to cycle the final mile with me. He had recently cycled a couple of miles, to show he still could, I think. But he was on the Greek island of Naxos. One of his tutors, Andrew Hobson, had a villa there and each year hosted the first year classicists, part-work, part-fun. Petra and I worried about the long journeys and Daniel's diet, but it was important that he went. He slept longer than the others but seems to have enjoyed himself. Andrew's wife (who was once Marilyn Monroe's psychotherapist) made sure he had his food though one evening Daniel rang Angela, Petra's sister, to ask how to work the oven!

The bike ride was rounded off with WCC's official if belated launch in the House of Lords in November 2009. Daniel decided he had a better offer in Oxford, another example I suspect of not wanting to think about cancer, but my mum came along with other family and friends. She loved it and was starry-eyed meeting Chris Hollins, a WCC supporter. Chris was that year's winner of *Strictly Come Dancing*. Annabel later included the House of Lords reception in the little book about the ride she gave me at Christmas.

I began to think about doing another bike ride the following year. The idea was to visit hospitals where some of the doctors in Germany or Spain who had helped me were based. But it would need Daniel to remain in remission.

* * *

Bike ride over, Petra and I decided against another RT-PCR in Barcelona. Colin indicated that this far out Daniel's bone marrow was unlikely to be diseased. In addition, the biopsy would be from the sternum (the bone in the middle of the chest), because the marrow in Daniel's pelvis had deteriorated. I read of cases where the needle had slipped on the sternum and punctured the lungs or heart. As ever, we faced a cost:benefit assessment: the risk of something going wrong was negligible but then the benefit of the procedure wasn't clear-cut. Dr Mora supported our leaving things until Christmas.

On 5th October 2009, the day before Daniel's twenty-first birthday, Colin informed me the latest x-ray was clear. I thought it was a propitious moment to take stock: 'My feet are firmly on the ground but could there come a time when you think Daniel is cured?' I asked. I immediately regretted the question because I knew the answer before Colin uttered it. Daniel was only three and a half years from diagnosis, a fantastic result given where we started but still far too early to think about a cure.

Colin didn't mince his words: 'Yes, there could come a point but not for years and years. Only this morning I saw a patient who had relapsed after seven years.' He did add: 'But Daniel is in a much better place than he should be. The longer time goes on the better.' Despite my self-flagellation, I realised that what lay behind my question was, as ever, a desire for hope.

When I told Daniel Colin had said he was doing really well – I didn't relay the whole conversation – he asked, hopefully, 'Did he?' Naturally he liked hearing positive views from Colin, all the more so, I imagine, because Colin didn't sprinkle false optimism around. Daniel's need for hope was even more pressing than mine.

A couple of months later, I came across another of Colin's patients, a twenty-eight year-old solicitor in London. Alex had relapsed after ten years, shortly after getting married. We exchanged information about complementary therapies and diet. Alex died a few short months later, after the cancer had spread to his brain. I didn't need a wake-up call but, if I had, Alex's tragic story would have provided one.

In that autumn term of 2009, a first year Oxford student died of meningitis. Desperately sad in itself, news like this sounded alarm bells, given the state of Daniel's immune system. There was also swine flu around. It was not just cancer we were worrying about.

But still. My sister Sian and Maria from Nicaragua both used the word 'miracle' to describe Daniel reaching his twenty-first birthday. It did feel that way, and I was so thankful: this 'extra' time was precious. Daniel asked again whether the five-year benchmark ran from diagnosis or end of treatment. He was counting the months. By his reckoning, another eighteen months and he would be in the clear. But he was also unsure about a hair transplant, because he might need more chemo. 'Have I been lucky so far or have the diet and supplements helped?' he asked Petra. There was doubt jostling with hope.

Daniel was as strict about his diet on his twenty-first birthday as he had been on his eighteenth. No garlic bread, which he loved.

Worrying symptoms, again

In December, my friend Michaele in Germany was diagnosed with breast cancer. I was pleased at least to be able to help her and Norbert with research, repaying some of their fantastic support. At the Christmas service for the local Mencap, I learnt that the mother of one of the club users had died of leukaemia. Cancer seemed to be everywhere.

Daniel, meanwhile, had three episodes of acute pain under his left ribs. The episodes were only once a week, which didn't sound like cancer. He hadn't wanted to tell me because he thought I would be on the phone to UCH straightaway. I reminded him 'Mum and I have to know what's going on so that we can assess whether to speak to a doctor.' He understood but I detested having the conversation, when all he wanted was to live a normal student's life.

The pain reappeared. It seemed to be in his abdomen

as well. I wrote to Colin: should the field be extended in the MRI he was due to have? Daniel preferred to leave the MRI until after Christmas. Did he have a foreboding, I wondered? Petra, too, mused about postponement: a bad result would ruin Christmas for everyone. She felt we were living on borrowed time. I sympathised. There can be a real temptation to delay scans: sometimes the inclination to bury one's head in the yielding comfort of the sand can be strong. But we knew that not knowing bad news wouldn't help Daniel.

On results day, 21st December 2009, Petra wanted me to go in first. As so often when we feared bad news, it didn't materialise. Both a chest x-ray and the MRI were clear. The latter covered the areas where Daniel was having pain. Colin examined Daniel thoroughly. His platelets, the best indicator of the state of the bone marrow, were 102, below the normal range but standard for post-treatment. This seemed to vindicate the decision not to have an RT-PCR in September. We wished Colin a happy Christmas, relieved that yet another crisis had been averted.

Daniel was much bouncier when I rang him at home in the afternoon. It's awful to contemplate the burden which young cancer patients carry, all cancer patients but especially young ones. Later on there was heavy snow in London. I managed to ruin my clutch in crawling traffic on Highgate Hill. It was 2.30am by the time two cheerful Bangladeshis, no older than Daniel but with their own recovery business, got me home, exhausted and facing a large repair bill, I assumed. I couldn't have cared less.

The following couple of days, I was so happy to be able to tell my bike sponsors that Daniel was doing well.

As the year drew to a close, my thoughts began to turn to tentative plans for 2010. I hadn't previously allowed myself to project beyond cancer. We were still in the middle of the forest, a dense forest, but maybe there was the flickering of sunlight peering through a glade. Perhaps all the extra things we had done had increased Daniel's chances. The meeting with Colin had revitalised me, after yet further weeks of worry. I allowed myself to sketch out, ever so faintly, plans for my work, for the books I wanted to read, the books I wanted to write, the sport I wanted to play, the films and plays I wanted to see, the neglected friends I wanted to catch up with, the voluntary work I wanted to do, the places I wanted to visit. I even thought of going out to Malawi to see one of WCC's projects, as preparation for my next bike ride. Above all I wanted to make up for lost time.

Was I tempting fate?

Relapse

Dad: Who were Wales playing yesterday?
Daniel (aged four): I don't know
Dad: England
Daniel: I was going to say England, but I thought I might be wrong
Dad: Well, it doesn't matter if you might be wrong, you can still say it
Daniel: But I like being right

Fate was duly tempted and wreaked her terrible revenge. My counting of pre-hatch chickens ceased abruptly.

The first few months of 2010 were one of those times when it felt that the world was falling in. There was illness and worse, everywhere in our families.

My niece Annabel, Daniel's cousin, nearly died. She was on placement as a medical student in Swansea when she developed acute appendicitis. The operation seemed to go ok and she was discharged, only to be readmitted in agony a few days later.

This time she was in a different hospital, one of Europe's largest. As a medical student there, one might have expected the staff to go the extra mile for her. Not a bit of it. Despite increasing pain her consultant, too busy at a neighbouring hospital, didn't come to see her for days. His registrar, outwardly confident, couldn't get to the bottom of the problem. I suggested to Julian, Annabel's father, that he ruffle some feathers. He overcame the instinctive deference to doctors which so many share, and put in some calls as did Katie, Annabel's sister and then a doctor at the hospital.

At last things began to move. Annabel had an operation to remove a bowel obstruction, caused by a ruptured appendix. The surgeon later said he hadn't expected her to survive the night. Thankfully she has made a good recovery and, now that she's a doctor, has vowed to treat patients with the sensitivity she was denied.

There was one light moment during an awful week. Her brother JJ, also then a medical student, had tentatively suggested a possible way forward, something he'd read on the internet. The registrar reacted with disdain. Revisiting the article, JJ realised it was from 1909! A reminder that the internet, wonderful resource though it is, is to be handled with care.

While Annabel was in hospital, Katie was knocked off her bike. She refused to allow the paramedics to take her to A&E – because she had seen its workings from the inside … Then Charlotte, their Mum, broke her wrist badly on an icy school playground and was in pain for months. My Mum suffered from several bad bouts of irritable bowel syndrome, maybe stress-related. My brother-in-law Terry's Mum, Eve, became seriously ill. Amy, Terry's daughter, experienced multiple health problems too. Nothing new there, sadly. Amy is exceptionally disabled. She has congenital Rett's syndrome, a life-threatening condition with its origins in a rare chromosomal malfunction. Daniel's cancer also results from chromosomal abnormality. Strange that two cousins, from apparently healthy stock, should each be afflicted with chromosomal defects with such devastating consequences. Medical science may one day unravel these genomic mysteries.

Even the pets joined in. One Saturday evening, JJ and I were watching TV. Suddenly there was a crashing noise upstairs. My dog Jess came stumbling downstairs, barely able to walk and defecating and vomiting at will. She had found a bag of apricot kernels (an alternative cancer remedy I was considering for Daniel). Fortunately, I knew that they contained cyanide, apparently harmless to people in small quantities but highly toxic, it seems, to dogs. The emergency vet was able to administer the antidote in time. A few more minutes and she would have died. A few weeks later, perhaps related, Jess developed serious pancreatitis, another life-threatening disease. And Sweep, one of the children's cats, had advancing cancer. Petra gave experimental chemo a go, more because things were already tough for Daniel, Sasha and Florence than out of expectation of success. Daniel never knew about this crisis either. Sweep's chemo worked.

Saddest of all, Petra's Mum died in March 2010. Daniel was very fond of her. He lost both his maternal grandparents during his cancer journey. He played the piano at the funeral, as he had at his grandfather's and the girls sang. They too, have suffered grievous loss in their short lives, far more than any child should.

And then, in the midst of all this carnage, there was Daniel. The New Year was only a few days old when my hopes for a further extended period of remission evaporated into the snow-filled air. Daniel's chest pain, nearly omnipresent at the best of times, had become more intense and frequent and he could bring it on by breathing deeply. But he was still able to play table-tennis and the pain was not really bothering him at night. I was worried but not overly so.

On the Friday, we decided Petra would take him to the GP, just to check things out. I went to London. Around 12.30, when I saw Petra's name on the mobile, I assumed she'd been unable to get an appointment and wanted me to have a go; that had been the plan. If only. In fact Dr Watkinson had detected a pleural effusion and had urgently referred Daniel to St Peter's Hospital, given his medical history.

So that's when it all started again. If my life changed in April 2006, when Mr Sinnerton told us Daniel had cancer, the call from Petra, on 8th January 2010, marked the beginning of a new and deeply troubling phase.

We didn't know the seriousness of the situation for a few days. Hope lingered, at times quite strongly. A pleural effusion is commonly called water on the lungs. I had vaguely heard of the pleura because there had been a spate of court cases about asbestos, which causes mesothelioma, cancer of the pleura. But I was otherwise ignorant. Daniel's cancer journey reminded me of the macabre geography lesson we had in the 1990s, as civil war broke out and atrocities were committed successively in various places in Yugoslavia - Sarajevo, Srebrenica, Pristina. I had a similarly macabre anatomy lesson as Daniel's cancer successively brought various parts of his body into focus.

The pleura is the lining which surrounds the lungs. In fact there are two linings, the visceral next to the lung itself and the parietal next to the rib cage. Fluid lubricates the lungs to aid breathing. An effusion is where fluid gathers between the two linings. As with many medical conditions, there can be many causes. The main two are infection, including pneumonia, and cancer. As I understand it, cancer eats away at the linings, which then causes the fluid to seep through to the gap. Sometimes cancer is found in the fluid, a particularly bad sign.

We were hoping for an infection, naturally. The consultant at St Peter's wasn't sure, though he may have strongly suspected cancer. Daniel's C-reactive protein was sixty, high but not particularly so. An elevated CRP results from inflammation, which is consistent with an infection, but is also consistent with Ewing's sarcoma (and many other cancers).

Sasha was upset and wanted to be at the hospital with Daniel, despite a forthcoming A level. The staff drained 1.5 litres of fluid, a fair amount. It wasn't coloured, as it would have been with an infection. But a chest x-ray showed nothing sinister. The UCH doctors thought it unlikely that cancer would have come so quickly to cause this amount of fluid, given the clear x-ray on 21st December. Colin was away so we couldn't ask him.

Daniel was discharged that evening. He told me he loved me – a sure sign that he was anxious. He had a bad cough but not much shortness of breath, which is often associated with pleural effusions.

I was booked in to do a Samaritans session on the Sunday evening with my friend Rich. I thought I could handle it. It was a mistake. One of my first calls was an active suicide – where the caller has already done something before they call. The caller had simply given up hope and wouldn't let me call an ambulance.

On the Monday evening, I got concerned about Daniel's hacking cough. There was another effusion: the fluid had returned, quickly, a bad sign. The GP advised another x-ray in the morning. Later I told Daniel I didn't think this was cancer and almost believed it, an instance of when my instinct to reassure overcame rational assessment. It was a mistake to give Daniel false reassurance.

The following day was even tougher. Colin kindly rang me from a conference. From my description, cancer was top of the list. St Peter's had ruled out pneumonia. This was one of many occasions when we 'wanted' Daniel to have a serious condition like pneumonia - anything but cancer.

At one point that Tuesday, Petra thought Daniel was dying. I noted with concern that Dr Pilai, in his letter to the hospital, used the past tense: 'Daniel had been in remission.' However, a consultant thought infection was more likely the underlying cause than cancer. The x-ray was again clear apart from the fluid. Daniel was encouraged by talk of an infection – which made me feel even worse, because I wasn't convinced. I broke down when a fellow Samaritan asked if I was ok – people showing they cared always got to me.

I read somewhere that 65 per cent of patients with

malignant pleural effusions died within three months and 80 per cent within six months. I didn't sleep well.

The next day, after some chasing, a registrar disclosed there was nothing sinister in the lab analysis. That was good, but Colin had warned that the test was hit-or-miss. The latest x-ray showed more fluid, but no visible metastases. Good again, but not the same as no metastases. 'Is Colin worried?' Daniel asked. 'He's surprised at developments but will not commit himself until he has seen the planned CT scan', was the best I could do. Nevertheless, we were all mildly encouraged and had a game of knock-out whist.

It was a struggle for Daniel, nauseous and in pain, to get to UCH for the scan. I asked Colin if he could let me know if the results were bad, so that I could prepare for our meeting the following day, but didn't hear from him.

My journal entry for the following day, Friday 15th January begins: 'Awful, awful day.' And so it was.

On the way in I had to stop the car at one point, because of the pain Daniel was in. 'Whatever the news Dan', I told him, 'we will get you through this.' He didn't answer. Once at the hospital Petra again sent me in to see Colin first. Daniel had relapsed. The priority was to sort out the effusion, Colin explained, before we could think about treatment. He would need to go to the Royal Brompton Hospital in west London, a specialist heart and lung hospital.

Colin was pretty blunt at that meeting. He was not unkind to Daniel, but nor was he kind. There was no softening of what he must have realised was a devastating blow for Daniel (not to mention Petra and me), no expression of hope, no reassurance that there were a number of treatment options (as there were, even if none was likely to be successful for long). It was a reminder that, for all his many qualities as a doctor, Colin was not at his best when the news was bad. He retreated behind the mask of a technician, telling it as it was, as though he was giving the latest inflation figures.

Doctors must often feel like messengers there to be shot at. The reality is that, with serious illnesses, they usually have little influence over the outcome. But medicine is above all a profession of compassion. The intellectual challenge, the interesting and varied workload touching on a range of specialities, the opportunity to exercise judgement, the gratification of achievement, the money, the status even, may all go into the mix, but compassion must be king, in medicine as in life. And it's not enough to feel compassion, it must be communicated and a key part of communicating compassion is, wherever possible, communicating hope.

That morning, as we waited to go to the Brompton, I told Daniel that perverse as it seemed, his prospects were better now than at diagnosis because he hadn't relapsed within two years. Statistically this was correct. I had read a number of statistical analyses of Ewing's relapse, including one by Colin and his colleagues. The picture varied but I clung to one reasonably large-scale, multi-institution study in the US, showing that 30 per cent of patients who relapsed more than two years after diagnosis survived for a further five years. Still pretty dreadful but far better than Daniel's chances of surviving for five years at diagnosis. (Daniel hadn't relapsed for nearly four years, though there was no correlation between time beyond the two year marker and improved prospects, as one might have expected).

Much depended inevitably, on the nature and extent of

the relapse. I didn't tell that bit to Daniel. We didn't know much about the relapse at this stage. I reminded him how highly everyone thought of Colin and showed him a long list of emails I was planning to send other doctors. He urged me to get on with it.

We met Melanie (not her real name) for the first time. She was the specialist oncology nurse for young adults. She was helpful in sorting things out with the Brompton. Our later experience was to be less positive.

The texts started to come in as we waited. Sian: 'My heart goes out to you. It's so terribly cruel.' Charlotte simply: 'I'm so sorry.' JJ, upbeat and practical as ever: 'Right ok. We need to look at latest IGF criteria and anything else in case chemo is unsuccessful. Let me know when to start asap.' Annabel: 'Am praying all the time that he is going to be ok. Thinking of you both loads.' I was throughout so lucky with family support.

We really liked the Brompton. It's big enough to have top-class specialities but small enough to be homely. Even the food is good. I met Simon Jordan, the surgeon. I knew from the UK sarcoma website that Simon enjoyed a high reputation. All his patients seemed to like him – and quite a few of the women fancied him!

Simon later showed us where an effusion could be seen in the corner of the December x-ray. Colin had earlier, unprompted, said that he and a radiologist had looked again but could see nothing. I didn't pursue the contradictory information: as at diagnosis, my sole focus was on finding solutions for Daniel.

Daniel was in a lot of discomfort still. He asked me not to keep leaving him to make telephone calls. One of the calls was to his tutor Felix, who was understanding and said Magdalen would be as flexible as they could be. He would handle everything. I broke down during the call. Petra and I had resolved to pay for Daniel's room for the year, even though whether he would ever go back to Oxford was questionable. It was important to convey positive messages.

Later that day Mr Jordan's registrar, Mohammed, another doctor with an excellent bedside manner, inserted a chest drain, which was painful for Daniel. They drained five litres, a record, someone said, for the hospital. (Given that the Brompton is the national lung and heart hospital, dealing with pleural effusions all the time, that would be saying something). Jaume Mora had asked me to pass on that Daniel would get back into remission and this cheered him.

Daniel was to have a pleurodesis which sticks the two linings together, using talc. With no gap between the two pleural linings, there is nowhere for fluid to accumulate.

Back on the research treadmill

I was doing loads of research, in between hospital visits, including into photodynamic therapy. PDT uses light to attack cancer; UCH applied the technique for cancers close to the skin, but not for Ewing's. I knew of a Ewing's patient who had recently had the procedure in Philadelphia. Her doctor, Keith Cengel, offered to speak to Simon Jordan. The timing was important because the type of pleurodesis could affect whether PDT was possible. The pleurodesis was urgent and so the dilemma added to the pressure I was feeling.

The call from Dr Cengel was not the only one I took in the crowded ward waiting-room. I was also looking at immunotherapy options at the National Cancer Institute at Bethesda in the US. Sadly, the Brompton didn't preserve Daniel's tumour sample in nitrogen, a prerequisite for the trial Daniel would have entered; I had not thought about asking. In truth, we would probably have not gone down this path, though it remained on the agenda for a future relapse.

Daniel had the pleurodesis on 20th January. Sian came up to be with me. More supportive texts arrived from family and friends. One from Julian, my brother-in-law: '… what a fight he's been putting up these past four years … Dan's a magnificent example, role model and inspiration to us all especially how to live our lives … in the face of such adversity.' Charlotte hoped the fact that this was Dad's birthday was a good omen.

Petra and I were both in tears as we left Daniel outside the operating theatre. Petra said: 'He has no idea does he?' We agreed it was the best way. Simon Jordan later came out of theatre: 'It has all the hallmarks of Ewing's.'

The doctors had described a pleurodesis as a relatively minor procedure. Well, relativity is a relative concept. Daniel was put in the ITU ward, with 24/7 monitoring. There was a small risk of mortality. He had two chest drains and oxygen via his nose. I couldn't stay with him in ITU. My mind still in the hospital, I got on the wrong train and ended up in Basingstoke, clearly not something anyone would do on purpose.

Daniel was in considerable pain for some time. His eyes were hollow and his voice thin. Three days after the operation, however, he wanted his Latin vocab. He was deflated when the lab confirmed a relapse. I had already discounted any possibility that it wasn't. 'The fightback starts today, Dan – no skimping on juices etc', I said. 'Mum and I feel it's important you go back to Oxford whenever you can, even if it's only for a few days. I'm happy to take a flat in Oxford, to look after you.' Daniel wasn't keen on that idea; probably it was the thought of my cooking, or cramping his style. I added that I had spoken to doctors in India and Germany that day, to help give him confidence that a solution would be found.

We were due to meet Colin again on 25th January and Daniel was to have a PET/CT scan the same day, to see if he had cancer elsewhere. Petra was reluctant that he go to clinic; it was borderline whether he was up to travelling anyway. Daniel agreed that JJ, who was staying with me, could go instead. Colin had worked at Queens Medical Centre in Nottingham, where JJ was a student.

I had emailed Colin over the weekend about options. At the meeting, he said the time to relapse meant that chemo was more likely to have an effect (overall the statistics put that at less than 50 per cent) and for longer. But the take-home message was unequivocal: 'Daniel will not be cured.' I was puzzled why Colin felt the need to crush hope in this way. Prognosis was dismal, certainly. But the chances were not zero.

Oliver Wendell Holmes Sr, the 19th century doctor and poet, once cautioned: 'Beware how you take away hope from another human being.' Martin Spinelli reflects in his book *After the Crash* about his experience with doctors treating his son Lio, seriously brain-damaged in the accident which killed his wife:

> *'I was now well versed in the general language of the*
> *medical establishment. It was a language of pessimism,*
> *preparing families for the worst. This has the effect of*
> *lowering expectations (for recovery and for treatments)*
> *and can, if you are not very careful, lead to a deadly*
> *and self-fulfilling spiral of hopelessness (if something is*
> *hopeless, then there is little point in trying) …'*

By this time, I was used to Colin's negativity and to an extent let it wash over me. Even good news he tended to give in the minor key, whereas other doctors use the descant. But his fatalism did worry me, for this reason. When a doctor gives up hope that he can cure a patient, what does that do to his creativity? I desperately wanted thinking outside the box. Colin continued to be highly professional and conscientious, genuinely concerned about Daniel's welfare. But I felt from that time on that psychologically he had given up on him; that he was simply managing inevitable decline, that all he could hope to achieve was a few months here and there. Anything better would just be a matter of luck, which no one could influence. I worried that pessimism allied to a conservative approach to treatment was a self-fulfilling prophecy with serious cancer. One could not blame Colin for his deep pessimism, but pessimism is different to defeatism.

More than this, doctors, especially those treating young people, surely need hope themselves, at least until the terminal stages are reached. The need is less urgent than for patients and their families, but it must exist. In crushing my hope, Colin was also crushing his own. With so many seriously ill patients, surely he needed hope to sustain morale?

I determined that I would continue to search for creativity elsewhere, to ally to Colin's undoubted expertise and clinical judgement and the high standard of care at UCH. This had been my approach all along. Creativity does not equal recklessness, doing something for the sake of it.

Daniel came up for his PET/CT scan that afternoon. He looked tense and wanted me in the room. Still in pain, he made himself walk down five flights of stairs. He wanted to go to a concert in Oxford at the weekend; that was heartening.

Colin had warned that the scan was very likely to show cancer in Daniel's bones. I had arranged to pick up the report from Joni, his secretary, prior to the next meeting. I have never been so nervous opening an envelope. I knew that if the cancer was back in Daniel's bones, that was pretty much it. Imagine opening an envelope containing exam results, or an anticipated hostile letter from a solicitor – and then multiply the anxiety level by a hundred. That's how I was feeling. When I read the report, in a secluded spot, my heart lifted, even before I had taken in the contents. It was short. Short reports were usually better, because it meant little out of the ordinary was seen. I didn't understand a reference to a pericardial effusion but the great news was there was no evidence of cancer in the bone.

We went to see Colin. Petra latched onto his observation that there was little difference between the chemo options. One of those was low-dose etoposide. The etoposide would be in tablet form, which Daniel could take at home, which held obvious advantages. In addition, he would not go neutropaenic and so would not be at risk of infections necessitating hospital stays.

I had indeed read about low-dose etoposide with relapsed Ewing's. A girl in Germany, who had relapsed twice in her pleura, was then cancer-free for nine years (and continuing) on the regime. I was open-minded about low-dose chemo more generally.

But I also knew that low-dose chemo was not the favoured option on relapse. I didn't think that Colin could have meant that there was nothing to choose between low-dose etoposide and other chemo regimes at higher doses – why would doctors ever recommend the latter in that case? Apart from anything else, they are far more expensive for the health service, because of the hospital time involved.

As we deliberated, Daniel became impatient with me: he wanted to get on with chemo. He complained that I always made the treatment decisions. Strictly speaking that wasn't correct. We always stressed that decisions were his; all we could do was guide him. But I sympathised with the lack of control over his predicament which he felt. It must be so disempowering to have other people discuss which brand of horrible treatment one should have. However, Daniel was in no position to make informed judgements.

I had become convinced of the importance with a difficult cancer of getting as many opinions as possible, informal or formal, from reputable sources. Some Ewing's parents in the US were getting multiple opinions. Naturally, deliberation cannot be allowed to delay urgent treatment.

I emailed Colin, setting out all the arguments for low-dose chemo, as I had promised Petra I would do. He confirmed that his preference was for normal-dose chemo (the terms 'normal-dose' and 'low-dose' are not precise - there is gradation rather than clear demarcation - but they serve as a rule of thumb). The normal-dose regime used at UCH was cyclophosphamide and topotecan but I knew many doctors in the US were using a different regime, irinotecan and temozolomide. I had numerous email discussions, especially with Lars Wagner in Cincinnati, who was extremely helpful throughout Daniel's journey. He was one of the pioneers of irinotecan/temoz. Colin was sceptical: there was no proper comparative study between the two regimes, he pointed out, a legitimate concern.

What finally persuaded me to go with cyclo/topotecan was an email from Vivek Subbiah at MD Anderson, in Houston. Their experience, he explained, was that irinotecan/temoz could work after cyclo/topotecan had failed, but not the other way round.

It had been an exhausting few weeks of research.

Bureaucracy

Because of continuing symptoms, Colin ordered two MRI scans, of Daniel's spine and pelvis. He was a cautious orderer of scans so this concerned me (a friendly 'fingers crossed' simply added to my worry – had he felt something on examination?). That night, I woke up with a start remembering Colin's comment that the earlier CT scan seemed to show changes to the bone. The early hours are so good at building things out of proportion. In the event, both MRIs were clear.

Chemo had been projected for 8th February 2010.

However, Melanie said there could be a problem: 'Daycare have not had five days' notice.' This bureaucratic mentality was anathema to me. Daycare had many patients to manage, no doubt, but hospitals have to be responsive to patients' clinical needs. Daniel had an aggressive cancer and we had already lost seven weeks since the December x-ray. No one had mentioned a five-day rule while I agonised about the appropriate treatment option.

Many people, lawyers included, are good at identifying problems, far fewer at fashioning solutions. Margaret Thatcher's comment about one of her ministers, Lord (David) Young, resonates with me: 'All my other colleagues bring me problems, David brings me solutions.'

As a contingency, I spoke to the Churchill cancer hospital in Oxford. Having chemo there would mean Daniel could go back to the university. Colin explained transferring him wouldn't be straightforward – as a different NHS trust, there were funding issues – but he would do his best. In the event, chemo started at UCH without further delay. This was the usual pattern. If one objected to a bureaucratic obstacle with reasoned argument, the obstacle was dismantled, an illustration of the advantage held by families able to navigate the system (my sister Sian has lots of experience of this in accessing services for her daughter Amy). It really shouldn't be like this.

I hated being thought of as a forceful parent. But my job was to ensure as best I could that Daniel, in his desperate situation, got what he needed. We wanted every other cancer patient at UCH to get what they needed too, but we had no control over their care. I comforted myself that another patient was not bumped down because a slot was magically found for Daniel. That's not how it works; rather, additional capacity is identified.

These occasional skirmishes risked damaging relationships, but more importantly they caused Daniel anxiety. I tried to protect him – he didn't know about a quarter of my communications with the hospital – but inevitably he picked up on some things. He didn't have the experience to realise that, when the hospital said something wasn't possible, that was simply the first step in negotiations. Part of the trick was knowing which battles to fight and which to concede. If something simply caused inconvenience with no clinical implications, I would leave it. There were, inevitably, any number of inconveniences and so many long hours of hanging around but we just put up with them.

I should stress that UCH was normally excellent in accommodating Daniel's needs. Were I to list all the acts of kindness, of professionalism, of care shown by staff there – and the other hospitals – this would be a monotonously repetitive book. As is sadly the way of things, it's the times when things go wrong that stand out.

We were fortunate in any event, that we didn't have to worry about the cost of treatment. Goodness knows how much Daniel's care cost. It must have run into several hundred thousand pounds, perhaps more. We didn't have to battle with insurance companies, as US cancer parents did. At times, it seemed that insurance executives there were determining treatment, not doctors. One example horrified me. A teenage girl's cancer was growing and she needed treatment desperately but the insurance company wouldn't pay for it until the new financial year in a few weeks. Morgan died soon afterwards.

True, rationing is inevitable in any health system. Demand far outstrips resources. In the UK, treatment availability varies from area to area, the so-called postcode lottery (an inevitable consequence, it seems to me, of devolved decision-making, which everyone says they want). The US system is at least reasonably transparent. In the NHS, doctors may not tell patients about a given treatment because they know that it will not be sanctioned. This was one reason why I was determined to know what was going on in the Ewing's community around the world.

But we knew Daniel would get standard treatment and that removed a significant source of anxiety. And I didn't face the withdrawal of vital insurance if I were to lose my job – the fate of many cancer parents in the US, at a time when they faced precisely that risk because of having to spend so much time in hospital.

* * *

Daniel was really sick the night after the first chemo infusion. He pleadingly called out 'Dad' twice in the car to the hospital. He looked so ill walking into the Rosenheim. He was tachycardic (fast heart rate), with a low oxygen reading and had a temperature. He probably had an infection. Chemo had to be put on hold. Not good news.

Daniel was admitted, his first time on an adult ward at UCH, and was anxious I stayed with him. I slept on the floor and waited to be turfed out. Luckily we had a fantastic nurse, Natasha, who turned a blind eye. In the morning, she asked me to get into the chair so that she wouldn't get into trouble.

The next day was little better. Daniel had three bouts of diarrhoea in the night. Late in the afternoon, I noticed that his stomach was really swollen. Danny, Colin's registrar and the SHO, Sarah, went to look at scans. They looked concerned, or at least that's how I interpreted things. And then they disappeared. I had no idea what was going on. Perhaps they had an emergency. It was some time before another registrar said it could be an oedema (a swelling caused by excess fluid). She didn't think it was sinister. Daniel was oblivious to my anxiety, simply irritated by the fact that I couldn't leave to get his food.

JJ kindly picked me up from the hospital to save me getting a train home. Another exhausting day.

There were further concerns with the abdomen but in time they subsided with the swelling. Daniel's pain lessened and he started to do some work in hospital. One evening as we played pool on the teenage cancer ward, Daniel said he realised that testicular cancer was the 'best' to have but where did Ewing's come in the league table? I replied, somewhat disingenuously, that there was no league table as such. 'But is it highly treatable?' Daniel pressed me. 'Yes it is', I replied, more disingenuously. Should I have been straighter with Daniel? Perhaps, but he needed hope.

Still, I hated half-truths with him. In every other aspect of our lives, I tried to be straight with him and drummed into him the importance of being honest, even when playing assorted games in the garden. Cancer forces some uncomfortable compromises.

One Saturday in February I missed the amazing dénouement of Wales' Six Nations rugby match against

Scotland, when Daniel wanted me at the hospital earlier than planned. The result gave me a brief lift. Wales in sport is close to my heart, somewhat inconsistently because I strongly dislike nationalism, with its focus on what divides humankind rather than what unites.

Daniel was having so many scans that he took a Coldplay CD rather than the usual Beatles' No 1 hits for a further CT scan. Dr Seddon was on ward round duty when the result came. Consultants on ward rounds face a real difficulty discussing scan results when the patient is not theirs because they may not know much about the background.

The CT scan showed no change since the previous scan a few weeks earlier, Dr Seddon said. That was a massive relief. She gave me the CT report and I put it into my pocket to read later. I slipped out the report while Daniel's attention was elsewhere and this is when I began to panic. I couldn't match 'no change' with what I read. The report indicated cancer in the chest wall and left lung and a pleural effusion on the right. 'The conclusion was: 'There has been further progression of the extensive pleural infiltration …'

The liver, thankfully, was clear, but this wasn't a reassuring report. Quite the contrary. I had to hide my concern from Daniel. I rang Katie and felt bad about doing so, on her birthday. The line was too poor for sensible discussion. JJ was unable to reassure me. I barely slept that night.

Colin eventually confirmed that things had got worse since January. One comfort was that the cancer seemed to be confined to the left pleura, albeit covering all of it, a huge area. He didn't think that the cancer was in the lungs or probably the lymph nodes.

But the enforced delay while Daniel's pleura effusion was addressed had, after all, been a major problem. I wondered whether he should have had low-dose chemo in the interim, as I'd suggested to Colin. Daniel got back into remission pretty quickly, but I worried that the additional cancer, perhaps mutating and migrating to new areas (including the lungs), could precipitate second relapse and make rescue via radiotherapy harder. Whatever the truth, one thing is clear: it cannot be a good thing to leave a rampant cancer untreated for several weeks. With the benefit of hindsight (always a wonderful facility), I wish I'd challenged harder about interim treatment. We hadn't expected the gap to be so long and as ever I was labouring under a lack of experience, but perhaps I failed Daniel, not for the first time.

* * *

Daniel (2nd from right) with Katie, Annabel and JJ, who were to give me such help as medical students and doctors.

I had the same dilemma about what to tell Mum as at diagnosis. There was a difference of opinion within the family, with protective instincts again to the fore. I wanted to be able to give genuine hope, perhaps some mildly encouraging scan result. But I held off for too long. I felt uncomfortable when, oblivious to the relapse, she would ask how Daniel was and I felt constrained to answer 'Fine', when I knew he was lying in a hospital bed, very sick. But more important it wasn't fair on Daniel. He naturally wanted Grandma to know and needed as much familial support as possible. I tried to explain that she wasn't strong but I made the wrong call. It gave him a bad message. I should have focused on his needs. Another reminder for me that one cannot please all the people all the time: sometimes hard choices have to be made.

When I did tell Mum, in March 2010, she demonstrated remarkable resilience, not for the first or last time. Sure, there was a downside. I now had to deal with her anxiety on top of everything else. She would look to me for reassurance, when I needed reassurance myself. For all that, it felt far better being honest. And it was far better for Daniel.

Struggling…

Before chemo started Daniel struggled psychologically. That was hardly a surprise. His hope that cancer was history, a bad memory, had been cruelly dashed. He knew his future was uncertain, at best. At times he was in a significant pain and pain always depresses mood. Pain medication can do the same. One day he was in bed for nineteen hours – in part, I suspect, because he was losing hope.

Showing a relaxed style of playing keyboard in happier times.

I'm not sure that even the piano gave him much solace at this time and he simply loved playing the piano. My mind went back to when he played *The Entertainer* beautifully, as a ten year-old at a school concert, just days after Mike, the girls' father, was killed and drew applause far beyond the polite and encouraging, and to a later school concert, when the barbeque hubbub quietened as he played Debussy's *Arabesque* al fresco. These seemed distant memories.

Daniel rarely smiled during these weeks and Daniel always smiled. His temperament was wonderfully equable and he laughed easily. But not at this time.

Another day, he even talked about giving up on Oxford. That was almost blasphemy for Daniel and fortunately it didn't last. Petra and I tried to keep him as upbeat as possible, encouraging him to go into the garden, to do something constructive, however small, some light reading if he couldn't cope with his studies.

There was thankfully, a sea-change in his mood when chemo started. My journal read: 'The old Dan, which is fantastic.' He began to talk about careers advice, internships and accommodation for the next academic year. He was thinking of spending a year in France or Canada, perhaps as a tennis coach and planned to line-judge during the London Olympics. He'd been accepted for Wimbledon that summer. What language should he learn after French? (Daniel had always loved languages and the origins of words and would send me the 'word of the day' off some internet site. He would sometimes 'read' a dictionary!). He was going to travel to Australia and New Zealand and Argentina. We went to a Classic FM concert at the Royal Albert Hall, with Julian Lloyd Webber playing Elgar's cello concerto and Rhidian, the former *X Factor* contestant, singing the beautiful Welsh love song *Myfanwy* and the Welsh national anthem *Mae Hen Wlad Fy'n Hadau*, which surprisingly drew the loudest applause of the evening. Daniel struggled with fatigue but he made it through. Another day we kicked a football around, which was just great, even if Daniel's legs were weak.

Scan results began to improve. Rene, Colin's new registrar from South Africa, started to tell Daniel about one result. He stopped her: 'I don't want to hear.' So Renee turned and told me instead, in Daniel's hearing! But the good news cheered him. Colin told Daniel his response to cyclo/topotecan was excellent, with just a small area of concern at the bottom of the left thorax. Daniel's appetite picked up and with it his weight.

There were down periods after this, usually associated with pain, but fewer and less pronounced. My own mood mirrored Daniel's. JJ told me one day that he could tell how Daniel was from my demeanour. I was often exhausted arriving home from UCH late at night. Much of the feedback from Ewing's doctors was depressingly negative. Just occasionally, however, there was something positive. Stefan Burdach said one Saturday morning that they used cutting-edge radiotherapy techniques in Munich: that could be an option. A Ewing's researcher in Baltimore thought that Daniel's pleural cancer, if a leftover from the original cancer, could be eradicated. He didn't know Daniel's full history or condition, but his email really gave me a lift. I showed it to Petra to keep her spirits up. We both needed hope to sustain us. It really was a horrendous time.

I was sustained by friends as well. It's impossible to overestimate the effect which messages of support have in this kind of situation. They make you feel just that little bit less isolated. Some of the warmest support was from people I barely knew. I'd never met Robin, a close friend of my former colleague Jim who'd died of a brain tumour in 2006. That didn't stop Robin giving unstinting support. Every week, he lit a candle in Gloucester Cathedral for Daniel. Similarly Gillian, a friend of Sian's, texted after the PET scan result: 'You are so brave and the most wonderful father. A ray of hope is a small blessing but all the hopeful and positive energy surrounding you and Daniel from friends and loved ones will make all the difference. You are not alone but it may feel that way...'

Jo, a former RSPCA trustee colleague, was praying for Daniel all along; so many were. Maria, originally from Nicaragua but now living in Spain, regarded my family as her second family. I felt she was living the nightmare with me. My ever kind neighbours Kevin and Frances gave Daniel a digital camera and compiled a CD for him. Another friend Chris, gave Daniel the book on philosophy he'd just written. Unbeknown to me, the sister of my Italian friend Caterina, visited a Ewing's doctor in Milan, advice presumably she had to pay for. So many friends and colleagues were supportive, with offers to stay. Bruce relegated his own serious illness below Daniel's. Many were amazed by Daniel. Marilyn, Jim's partner, offered to help financially as she said Jim would have wanted. So did Mark. Marilyn wrote one day:

'You seem to be involved with many issues but I know one thing for sure: if I were to be in Daniel's position you are certainly the one I would want to be in my corner. I marvel at your energy and tenacity and much admire the way in which you meet each new challenge. Daniel must be a remarkable young man too and he is incredible in his determination to continue with his studies whilst coping with his setbacks ...'

Whether compliments like this were merited – Daniel certainly deserved his – wasn't the point. It gave such a lift that people were taking the trouble to say supportive things, even if they only had a hazy notion of what we were going through. I never doubted that I was right to fight so hard for Daniel – though I certainly had doubts about my ability to make the best decisions – but it was so reaffirming to hear this kind of thing. There were many, many times when I felt lonely and scared and many times when friendship helped.

Not everyone was so lucky with friends. It's common for cancer families to feel abandoned by erstwhile friends. One parent mused: 'Maybe they're tired of hearing about the things that we desperately need to talk about.' A teenager wished her stayaway friends could have chemo for a day, to gain insight into her ordeal. In most cases, I suspect, not knowing what to say (and so saying nothing) wrongly comes across as not caring. One or two of my friends seemed to find it difficult to talk about Daniel's illness, perhaps because they struggled with their own mortality or fear of serious illness.

Most, however, intuited that the important thing is to communicate empathy, however awkwardly. There was a rather pointless discussion on a support website about people saying 'I'm sure [child x] is going to be ok.' This annoyed some parents: 'How can they possibly know?' It didn't annoy me because I thought that people were just trying to be kind. A person's motives are what matters, not their articulacy.

The nightmare continues

Dad: Does Mummy get cross when you switch the tele off with your feet?
Daniel (aged four): Yes, but I can handle it

Remarkably, Daniel took some of his second year Classics exams. He'd made a point of telling me that the Classics Mods at Oxford were the hardest exams in the world. I would tease him about this: how could one compare Oxford Classics exams with, say, astrophysics exams at some American university? However, a colleague who'd gone to Oxford told me one day, unprompted, that the Classics Mods were the hardest exams in the world so the urban myth was well and truly established.

Just to sit the exams was extraordinary. My friend Dominic texted: 'Daniel's bravery and fortitude never cease to amaze.' Stewart and Ian, ever supportive, echoed the sentiment. Daniel was in the middle of chemo and had endured an appalling couple of months. Just a couple of weeks earlier, it seemed inconceivable that he would be able to take the exams. He was given some extra time and breaks in the middle, during which he wasn't allowed to refer to his books – fair enough – but also wasn't allowed to think about the exam. How can they stop you thinking about something, I asked? The trick, it seems, was that the invigilator, a research student, had to talk to him about all and sundry during the breaks!

Daniel did well – firsts in some papers and 2:1s in others. Not as well as he'd been expected to do but in the circumstances it was pretty special. I thanked Felix, his tutor, for all his support. Felix replied:

> 'We're all delighted that Daniel managed to get through his exams, which is a major achievement. He has been truly impressive in the way he's dealt with it all...'

If the first few months of 2010 were simply awful, the middle months were surprisingly upbeat. Daniel was back in full swing with his work. He would often talk to me about which options he should take for his Finals (or Greats). He took an interest in the General Election that summer.

He played rounders and frisbee and a bit of gentle tennis. Someone had written 'I ♥ Dan' in his room. With his wonderful capacity to block off bad memories, he seemed to have forgotten just how miserable things had been. He chided me for not thanking him straightaway for his Father's Day gift (a football book). He always kept me on my toes.

He even line-judged for ten days at Wimbledon. It meant having to postpone chemo for a week, which I felt uncomfortable about, knowing how important it is to hit cancer cells when they're at their weakest. But Petra was keen he have some pleasure and she was right.

Wimbledon line-judges are allocated two ground passes a day for family and friends. Daniel told me I was banned this year, because I hadn't shown enough enthusiasm the previous year. He was inviting his friends instead.

That was the Wimbledon of the astonishing match between John Isner and Nicolas Mahut, which Isner won 70:68 in the fifth set, far and away the longest match in tennis history. Daniel didn't get to line-judge that one but he was senior enough now to do the semi-show courts, with some big names, past and present (Leconte, Armitraj, the Woodies). On the middle Saturday, he lost his mobile phone in the grounds. Losing his mobile, losing anything, was a frequent occurrence for Daniel. He would just toss things down and forget about them (around this time, his bike was taken after he left it unlocked outside a shop). That evening, I drove him to New College Oxford where he was playing at the summer ball with the swing band. The arrangement was that I would pick him up at 2am. I whiled away the hours in a pub reading some articles about stem cell transplants, as one does. Daniel rang to blag some extra time. He was really enjoying himself.

* * *

I had a couple of trips abroad in the summer of 2010. The first was to Tel Aviv to see Simon Slavin, an immunotherapist recommended by a Ewing's mother in California.

It was the time of the General Election. I sent Daniel an email with the result of the Oxford East constituency last time and gave him my hotel in Tel Aviv, in case my mobile didn't work. There followed this exchange:

Daniel: *This email has told me nothing new nor interesting.*

Dad: *Maybe not interesting but unless you knew the Oxford East result in 2005 (possible) and where I'm staying in Tel Aviv (extremely unlikely), it was new. And I think grammatically it should be "nothing new or interesting." But then I'm not an Oxford student.*

Daniel: *The election info was not new, the hotel info not interesting. Clear?*

I had never been to Israel. On the plane, I sat next to a Palestinian human rights activist, Nadera Shalhoub Kevorkian, who'd recently won a prestigious international prize. Her mother-in-law, she told me, was the last survivor of the Turkish genocidal massacre in Armenia. Nadera had worked at a clinic with paediatric cancer patients. Scandalously, young Palestinian children with cancer were, she said, denied access to Jerusalem for chemotherapy because they were considered a security risk. I have enormous sympathy for the Jewish people, persecuted for centuries and still surrounded by enemies bent on their annihilation, but they shouldn't allow a siege mentality to justify indifference to the basic human rights of others.

Nadera, a Christian, said she would light a candle for Daniel at the Holy Sepulchre Church, the site believed to encompass Golgotha, where Jesus was crucified and the tomb where he was buried.

The meeting with Dr Slavin, in his beautifully appointed office, took place at the crack of dawn. It was a major disappointment. He didn't seem to have read the material I had sent him. In fact, he began by taking my medical history! Once home I read a blog complaint that he didn't read notes properly. But I was convinced that his overall message was right: the time to strike, whether with immunotherapy or anything else, was when a patient had only minimal residual disease.

Back at Ben Gurion airport, after a day reading about immunotherapy looking out over the Mediterranean, I was touched when a young immigration officer, enquiring why I was in Israel, said she was sorry to hear about Daniel's illness.

I got home at 1am. Daniel had voted in Oxford East. I had missed voting for the first time.

The trip to Germany was at the end of May 2010. A few days before I went, I was on my way to a dinner in London when Daniel rang to say he had a temperature. He was in his neutropaenic period so I diverted to Oxford.

When I got to Daniel's room, his temperature was normal, and he was helping Sasha with her Latin homework. I felt calm as I left him for the hotel. I had been asleep for only about an hour when Daniel rang. His temperature was spiking again and he was shivery. So off to hospital we went. It eventually transpired that Daniel had an infection, but not related to the chemo. I explained that Germany was just to gather information for options down the line – a stock phrase of reassurance we used.

In Germany, I met three doctors, two in Frankfurt and one in Bonn. All gave me plenty of time; none would take any money. Elke Jäger, in Frankfurt, was running a trial into Coley's toxins (or mixed bacterial vaccines), the only one I came across at a hospital. I was impressed with her general oncology knowledge. She was getting some good results with the trial, she told me.

I had been interested in Coley's toxins for some time. William Coley was a young surgeon in New York during the latter years of the 19th century. Frustrated at losing a nineteen year-old patient to bone cancer, he researched the records of all bone cancer patients in the city for the past fifteen years. He came across the case of an Italian immigrant who had made a miraculous recovery after two episodes of erysipelas, a severe skin infection caused by the bacterium *Streptococcus pyogenes*. He was still alive and well years later.

Coley hypothesised that the bacterium had cured the patient and began to inject streptococcus cultures into seriously ill patients, with some success. Significantly, when patients got better it was for the long term, unlike with so many cancer treatments. Initially, he used a live vaccine but when that proved too dangerous, used killed bacteria. He faced scepticism amongst the medical establishment. I got hold of an article he wrote in 1935, at the end of his career. What excited my interest was that some of his best results were with sarcomas, and specifically Ewing's sarcoma, then called endothelial myeloma. The success rate was well below 50 per cent but that was better than the standard. Chemotherapy was not yet a cancer treatment and many tumours were inoperable.

An interesting twist was that Coley's main antagonist was Dr James Ewing, the famous pathologist who gave his name to Daniel's sarcoma. Ewing was an evangeliser for radiotherapy, then in its infancy.

I read masses about Coley's toxins and spoke to several people interested in the remedy. I also came across a seventeen year-old boy with Ewing's in Japan, who at death's door had made an astonishing recovery after a skin bacterial infection and the high and fluctuating temperatures which followed. This was the principle on which Coley's toxins worked. The patient wrote to Daniel, twenty years on.

Dr Coley's methodology and reporting were not up to modern standards, but he was a serious and well-respected doctor. His toxins fell into disuse with the advent of chemo but there has been a resurgence of interest in recent

Daniel was a massive football fan.

decades, as chemo has proved disappointing as a cure. I found out that a Canadian company, MBVax, was running some trials. They put me in touch with an Irish doctor, who didn't impress me, but the trail eventually led to Henry Mannings, a GP and hospital cancer doctor in Norfolk and to Elke Jäger in Frankfurt. Hence my visit to her.

Dagmar Dilloo in Bonn was my next port of call on this trip. She used to work at University College London, next to Daniel's hospital. When I arrived she thought I looked tired so gave me a bar of chocolate! Her particular area of interest was dendritic cell vaccines. Daniel couldn't have these because his tumour biopsy sample hadn't been cryopreserved (in nitrogen), so the trip to Bonn was in preparation for a further relapse.

The final doctor was Peter Bader at Frankfurt University. His son was at Bath University. Peter carried out allogeneic stem cell transplants for sarcoma patients – in other words, bone marrow from donors. He couldn't quite believe that I had come over to Germany to see him and other doctors. A trip to Germany seemed like nothing (I was lucky I could afford these trips) - I would have gone to the moon if need be. There are in fact various types of allogeneic stem cell transplant. But the evidence to date wasn't that encouraging for Ewing's, and the risks and burden for the patient were not inconsiderable. I put in the box marked 'definitely seems to be something in it, but clinical research at too early a stage.' That box was getting quite full.

Daniel wanted to know whether the German doctors were nice. This was his way of asking whether the trip had been useful.

Deciding on the type of radiotherapy Daniel would eventually have was to prove a major headache. It took countless hours of my time, over seven months. There were three more trips to Germany and one to Cambridge, emails and telephone calls with doctors in the States, Canada and Europe and many hours poring over articles. Colin had made it clear that conventional radiotherapy - of the sort Daniel would have at UCH - was unlikely to work. So I explored other options.

One was tomotherapy. Conventional radiation beams - photon therapy – travel in straight lines. Many parts of the body diseased with cancer are funny shapes and so a straight trajectory doesn't really do the trick. The pleura is curvaceous. With tomotherapy, the radiation is delivered helically (think of a helter-skelter), such that treatment can be better targeted to diseased areas. Higher doses to the pleura are also possible, without exceeding the dose safe for the lungs as collateral damage. I was keen that Daniel should have higher dosage, if tolerably safe, because his left pleura was full of cancer. There's a rule of thumb with radiotherapy that higher dosage means greater efficacy. That wasn't proven for Ewing's, but nor did there seem reason to doubt it.

This, at least, was the theory with tomotherapy. It's still relatively new and there's much still to learn. At a meeting with Colin in early June 2010, I asked a question in passing, to help me with the research. For some reason, Colin then told Daniel that radiotherapy would permanently damage his left kidney. This wasn't a great thing for Daniel to hear, on top of everything else. I have no idea why Colin did this – risks and side-effects would be for Anna Cassoni, not him, and he knew Daniel wanted to know as little as possible. Daniel had a go at me afterwards for asking about radiotherapy. We were always on edge in these meetings, worrying what Colin might say. I needed to know things and we couldn't go through the performance of Daniel leaving every time, so I would take a calculated risk about the course conversation might take. Sometimes I got it wrong, as on this occasion.

When we met with Anna a few weeks later, she said the top of the kidney would be affected, but not for years, perhaps many years. I liked the fact that she was talking to Daniel about life years ahead.

In private, Anna told us Daniel had done extraordinarily well to get this far. She was less confident of preventing local recurrence – cancer coming back in the chest – than she had been with the left pelvis. Daniel's was an unusual case and she couldn't predict the outcome. That, in a strange way, I found encouraging – Colin had been all too clear he could predict the outcome. Anna saw no advantage in tomotherapy or other form of intensity-modulated radiation treatment (IMRT), because of the large area of Daniel's cancer. I was conscious, however, that UCH didn't have a tomotherapy machine and Anna therefore had no experience of using the technique. However much a doctor keeps uptodate, there's no substitute for personal experience.

I was surprised that Daniel was in bed, depressed, when I rang later that afternoon. He'd apparently told Petra he knew he wouldn't have a long life. When I asked Petra what lay behind this sudden pessimism, she had a real go at me: 'If I tell you, you will only speak to Daniel and who could he turn to then? You have broken other confidences.' It seemed terribly unfair to me – short of some extraordinary reason I would never break a confidence. Respecting confidences is second nature to me as a lawyer and Samaritan, but it's also my personal ethos because it's essential for trust in relationships; trust once lost is never fully recovered. There can be grey areas, admittedly, when a recipient of a confidence doesn't realise it's a confidence, where a simple misunderstanding can sour relations.

I realised that what underlay Petra's attack was upset about Daniel's fatalism. Needing someone to blame is a natural human reaction. It's indeed deeply upsetting to hear one's child say something like this - particularly when you know it's true. Daniel's comment gnawed deep into my bone, too. It showed that all our exhausting efforts to protect him emotionally were only partially successful. I knew Petra was under a huge amount of pressure. As well as Daniel, she had the girls to look out for. But the episode still upset me greatly.

It was as well that I had a tennis ball to take my frustration out on that evening. I decided to let the disagreement pass. I appreciated how important it was that Petra and I got on, mainly for Daniel but also for ourselves. I reminded myself of my oft-repeated mantra that I would absorb any amount of crap to help Daniel. This journey was all about him and my emotions were strictly secondary. I didn't doubt, either, that Petra would subsume her emotions to his. It's a wonder, in fact, that we had so few difficult conversations, so few disagreements and that we worked so well together.

The next day I made a point of telling Daniel that Anna thought his response to chemo was excellent. 'Doctors don't throw words like "excellent" around', I said. He seemed pleased and was back to his old self. We watched the World Cup Final with JJ. Thankfully Holland's brutal, anti-football tactics didn't prevail against Spain.

* * *

A few days later I was back in Germany, this time to discuss tomotherapy. Daniel was anxious that we should not delay treatment, but Anna had said there had to be a four to six-week gap between chemo and radiotherapy.

This first trip was to Münster, the leading centre in Germany for Ewing's. I was impressed with Münster with its parks and cycling culture, less impressed with the train fare from Brussels and the exchange rate with the Euro. The children's cancer hospital is part of the university complex. I met first with Professor Normand Willich, who struck me as a doctor of the old school, courteous and cautious. He declined to charge me, describing the case as 'interesting.'

Tomotherapy was an option, but he was concerned about the radiation the right lung would inevitably get (even with 'blocking' part of the radiation) and toxicity resulting from the high-dose treosulfan Daniel had received, the issue raised by Colin and Anna some time ago.

I then met Uta Dirksen, tall and striking. I was so pleased to meet her at last, after our many telephone calls. She invariably conveyed the impression that she had time, returning my calls quickly and not hurrying them to a close. She took an interest in Daniel and suggested he might want to come to Germany to see the forthcoming woman's football world cup. I felt she really cared about his progress.

Uta's feeling was that tomotherapy could well be right for Daniel, although they had only used the technique for a few months. Their experience, of around twelve cases, was that irradiating both lungs after high-dose treosulfan wasn't a problem, so safety wasn't a major issue. I left Münster with more information but still uncertain what to do.

After I got home Daniel was planned for the (conventional) radiotherapy he was due to have at UCH. He'd had a headache for three days. The planning took a long time and they had to start again at one point. Daniel was as patient as ever and didn't seem upset when one of the radiographers remarked that it was a very big area they had to irradiate.

My next port of call was to be Munich, to see Professor Michael Molls. Prof Molls worked closely with Stefan Burdach. There had been telephone calls and emails with Marciana Duma, a junior doctor at his hospital, from a family of doctors in Romania.

In one email to Dr Duma, at the end of July 2010, I outlined our objectives. We wanted to: irradiate all the left lung to the maximum safe dose of 18-20Gy (because of the likelihood of disease there); irradiate the whole of the left pleura, increasing the dose over the lung dose wherever possible; protect the right lung, without affecting what the left got; and spare other organs including the kidney as much as possible. These were challenging objectives.

Prior to my visit, the Munich team sent a PowerPoint presentation in time for a meeting with Anna. Petra, Daniel and the girls had gone on a week's holiday to Corfu so it was

Not sure what Daniel is doing to Annabel's arm…
Amy, JJ, Katie and Holly also in the photo.

just me at the meeting. Petra had woken me at 6am: she was worried about safety with a higher dose.

Anna was impressed with the Munich PowerPoint but her opinion differed. She'd come round to the idea of giving higher doses where possible, but had concerns about Daniel's lungs and heart and bone marrow depletion. She sketched out her own plan. She didn't think that a week's delay would make any difference. She added: 'You look tired and should look after yourself.' I said the decision was really weighing on me.

I went to the office afterwards but couldn't do much work. I really did feel weighed down, with the complexity of everything and the responsibility I felt towards Daniel. Twenty million people had been affected by dreadful floods in Pakistan. Not for the first time I felt guilty about all the money I was spending on Daniel. But it was good to catch up with old friends at Djuna and Chris's wedding party the following day.

Daniel, back from Corfu, told me he'd been having chest pains for the past week or so, perhaps hurting a bit more than previously. I barely slept - no more than an hour - and was at Gatwick by 4.30am on 11th August for the flight to Munich.

Prof Molls started our meeting by showing me photos of his two grandchildren, a nice human touch. He asked for some help with something in the UK. I was glad to reciprocate the help he was giving me. He chatted about their research projects. There followed a long discussion with Prof Molls, Dr Duma and another radiotherapist, Nicolaus Andratschke. Dr Andratschke, at a guess in his thirties, was more experienced with Ewing's. His English was excellent and he filled me with confidence. By the end of the meetings, three options had become eight, with further suboptions. They were trying really hard to come up with the best solution for Daniel, with a slide show to aid my understanding. My head was spinning. Dr Andratschke told me I negotiated like a lawyer! My approach was to push for the most efficacious solution and then rely on them to tell me what the safety risks were. Dr Andratschke was clear that the highest risk of a second relapse was to the pleura, so getting an effective dose there had to be the priority.

The main risk was pneumonitis which could lead to fibrosis, which in turn could cause lung collapse. That shouldn't be fatal, because one can live with one lung, but it was obviously a serious consideration. There was some risk of pneumonitis even with the UCH plan, as Anna had explained, but it increased with tomotherapy. Professor Molls said he'd come across only one or two cases of fatal pneumonitis in his career and he stressed that he ran a safe centre and wouldn't countenance unreasonable risks. We discussed the risks to the heart too. Dr Andratschke said he would speak to Anna.

After the meeting, I typed up my notes in the hospital garden. I was still uncertain what to do. The risks were really bothering me. But, as ever, we were dealing with two types of risk – the risks from treatment but also the extremely high risk of the cancer returning and the dire consequences that would hold. I wanted to have a detailed plan from Munich so that we could make an informed assessment. That would involve taking Daniel there.

The flight back was delayed and I didn't get home until 1am. I had been up for nearly twenty-four hours. Even so, I set my alarm for 7am to write to Anna. Time was of the essence. Anna was direct in her reply: a slot could not be kept open for Daniel indefinitely. I understood the point but was irritated by Anna's irritation. We were throughout acutely sensitive to other patients' needs. Daniel never missed a single appointment. If traffic meant we were going to be even ten minutes late, we rang ahead – even though we knew we would probably be hanging round much longer. Daniel was a model patient and never abused the service. I didn't want him to be prejudiced now because we were, quite reasonably, considering other options. There is inevitably flexibility in radiotherapy scheduling because patients are sometimes too ill, and I pointed this out. Anna said she would do her best to accommodate us.

I managed to arrange a planning CT scan at Munich for the next day. I was getting concerned about Daniel's pain, and I could tell he was. He blamed me for the delay. It was, as ever, impossible to have a sensible discussion with him without explaining my real concerns, which he didn't want to know. At one point, he asked for time to think about going to Munich. He rang back two minutes later and agreed! I never doubted he would take our advice.

We left early the following morning, a Friday, from Gatwick. It was another long day, with the return flight to Stansted. Yet Daniel was surprisingly perky, except for a short while in the afternoon. It was a special day together. After the hospital we visited Bayern Munich's impressive new stadium, and I bored Daniel by musing yet again why it was Bayern Munich (one German word, one English) and not Bayern München or Bavarian Munich. One of the great mysteries of our age. After that we saw the Glockenspiel at the Marianplatz.

The visit to the hospital itself was more mixed. Dr Andratschke had come up with a new plan. A colleague in Vienna agreed wholeheartedly that the pleura, rather than the lung, was the priority. If we failed to control microscopic cancer in the pleura, it could migrate to the lungs anyway. If cancer subsequently did come back in the lungs, one could then irradiate them, perhaps with stereotaxic radiotherapy. Dr Andratschke explained that his was an individualised plan for Daniel, based on principle rather than data.

I was leaning heavily towards tomotherapy. But a huge fly got stuck in the ointment. Dr Duma watched Daniel's planning CT live. When I asked her if it was ok, she seemed flustered and wouldn't discuss anything until she had spoken to Prof Molls and Dr Andratschke on the Monday.

A weekend of anxiety followed. I checked my journal

for early January, just before Daniel had relapsed, and found that the symptoms he was now describing were similar. By the Sunday, his chest pain was constant and had extended to his back. I spoke to NHS Direct in case this was a possible heart problem, a side-effect of doxorubicin or the battering his body had taken. Focusing on cancer, it's easy to miss other problems.

I slept badly, fearful what the next day would bring. I didn't hear from Dr Duma, which served to increase my anxiety. But Rene, Colin's registrar, thought the pain might be due to the pleurodesis, an infection or a pulmonary embolism. Cancer she would put lower down the list of possibilities, especially after the excellent chemo response. Daniel's pain was now actually better.

As so often, mild reassurance became harsh reality. Late afternoon, Anna Cassoni rang: Munich had informed her the cancer was back. Everyone agreed we would have to shelve radiotherapy for the time being. It was unlikely to be effective with the amount of cancer shown on the CT. I was deeply disappointed that we hadn't had a chance of trying tomotherapy.

I hated telling Petra. I briefly mentioned a surgery option and said: 'I'm not giving up hope.' We agreed the strategy should be to try to get the cancer under control with chemo and then hit it with high-dose radiotherapy

I pushed to have a CT done at UCH in time for a meeting with Colin at the end of the week and said I would get the images from Munich.

Sian came over in the evening. I knew from following other Ewing's cases that the end could now come quickly. I said: 'Even if Daniel makes his birthday [in October], he's very unlikely to see the next one.' Charlotte, my other sister, was also struggling.

Petra had given Daniel the news. I recorded in my journal:

> 'Felt very heavy-hearted making wheatgrass. Dan pretty upbeat which broke my heart. I said it was better to have a problem in one location. ... He accepts things so well. He has some back pain today – he said "I guess it doesn't matter now"...'

He knew that each time it became more difficult to control the cancer.

Had the delay made things worse? It's a legitimate question and one I have often asked myself. 'This time it was your fault', Daniel told me later. I was happy to be his punch-bag if it helped him, but, trying to be objective, I don't think the delay made any difference. Daniel had been due to start radiotherapy at UCH a week earlier, on 9th August. He clearly had already relapsed by then, even though we didn't know it, and if the cancer was too large for radiotherapy on 16th August, it was presumably too large on 9th August. In fact, Daniel wouldn't have had another CT at UCH and so would have started radiotherapy there without anyone realising its probable futility.

I was, however, annoyed with myself for not questioning why there had to be a gap between chemo and radiotherapy. I had simply assumed that Daniel needed recovery time. I resolved that, if we were lucky enough to get another response from chemo, there would be no gap, all things being equal.

Anyway, now wasn't the time for introspection. I had to get on with things. Lars Wagner in Cincinnati said he was praying for Daniel, which touched me. Jaume Mora in Barcelona was as prompt and helpful as ever. Daniel wanted me to bring more mushroom supplements. He wasn't giving up.

Waiting

The waiting for the meeting with Colin on the Friday was horrible. I found it difficult to concentrate in work and broke down speaking to my colleague Michelle. As ever she grasped the technicalities quickly and told me to forget about work if necessary. She and so many other colleagues were so supportive throughout.

Daniel was complaining about pain on his right side as well, around the liver. On the Thursday, Colin told me he was finding difficulty getting a slot for chemo – same old, same old. I called in UCH and went to the private ward, on floor 15, to see whether there were beds there.

I asked Colin if he could summarise the UCH CT in a sentence so that I could prepare for the meeting the following day. I was on edge, checking my emails every couple of minutes. Colin replied that the cancer was 'mostly' pleurally-based, and the right chest seemed ok. Some reassurance, then, but the 'mostly' bothered me. There was no time to clarify.

There were two work placement students, James and Emily, with Colin at the meeting. It started badly because Colin once again, started to tell Daniel about options. Once again Daniel told him he didn't want to know. Once again I had to intervene on his behalf.

When Daniel left, I apologised about the difficulties with communication (not that I felt I needed to): 'Daniel would have just stayed there feeling uncomfortable and probably not taking much in had I not intervened.' I added: 'If Daniel ever says he wants no more treatment, as I know often happens with cancer patients, we would respect that.' Colin added that he had the opposite concern that he might decide that more further treatment was pointless but Daniel wanted to continue. It must have been an interesting discussion for James and Emily.

The good news was that the relapse was not as bad as the first time and seemed to be confined to the left pleura (I never did get to the bottom of the 'mostly'). Colin said that the proportion of chemoresistant to chemosensitive cells would be getting worse – this is what happens as cancer progresses – but radiotherapy could kill chemoresistant cells. His recommendation, after discussion with colleagues, was oral (low-dose) etoposide (as had been on the agenda after the first relapse). Colin explained that it was a mild radiosensitiser – in other words, it should make subsequent radiotherapy more effective, albeit exacerbating the side-effects a bit.

The plan was to have radiotherapy concurrently with the chemo, if the latter worked. This is what I wanted to hear – no gap between chemo and radio.

All in all, it had been a much better meeting than we could have expected. I liked the fact that Colin told Daniel that he could be on etoposide for over a year. This would have given Daniel the message that he should still be around in a year's time. He did some work that afternoon.

The following day, Lars Wagner told me about dramatic responses being seen from oral etoposide with Ewing's relapses. That cheered me up. Dan told me: 'Dad, I don't want to feel nauseous like this for a year', but it was early days.

We only had a few days relative respite from worry. Daniel's pain was not abating and he wanted me to speak to Rene, Colin's registrar. I emailed Rene, copying in Colin. Colin himself replied just before 11pm saying we should bring Daniel to clinic if we were worried. That itself worried me and once more I slept badly.

An x-ray showed no deterioration from the previous week. Colin joked: 'We both have sad lives emailing each other at 11pm!'

Daniel perked up over the next few days. He cheered me up through sounding so cheerful. He wanted me to meet Barney, his aunt Angela's new puppy. Barney was lively – Jess, my dog, wasn't impressed – and the kids loved playing hide and seek with her. Daniel had never particularly been a dog lover, but he grew to love Jess and Barney. He wanted to look after Jess while I was out one day, 'so she won't have to be on her own.' He asked me: 'Who do you think is Jess's favourite, you or me?'

In early September, Daniel and I went to see England play Bulgaria at Wembley – the first time we'd been to the new Wembley. Jermaine Defoe, whom Daniel had met back in 2006 on T12, scored a hat-trick. Daniel was embarrassed about parking in the Blue Badge area, because he could walk well. (On another occasion, he blurted out 'I'm not disabled' during a general discussion about the Disability Discrimination Act and yet had no problem claiming disability living allowance for segments of his journey).

At the end of the first three-week cycle, Colin wasn't concerned about the pain in Daniel's neck, putting it down to the tennis umpiring he'd been doing. He remarked: 'I have learnt with Daniel that there are two sorts of pain, pain to worry about and pain to ignore.' In one sense he was undoubtedly right – there were so many false alarms over the journey – but Colin's willingness to dismiss some symptoms as a 'Daniel pain' became a source of increasing worry for Petra and me and also for Daniel. We reported everything, so that the doctors had the full picture. It was the right approach but it risked inviting scepticism when there were so many episodes of pain.

Petra wasn't convinced about the umpiring hypothesis. I was ready to grab hold of it. Daniel continued to umpire. We took him to the GP, who thought the problem lay in the trapezius muscle, consistent with umpiring.

Black Friday

The night before the next meeting with Colin, at the end of cycle 2, Daniel and I went to a concert in the Albert Hall. We saw the guitarist Craig Ogden playing *The Ashokun Farewell*, a personal favourite. Perhaps with a sense of foreboding, Daniel said: 'I won't see much of Oxford in the next two terms.' However, despite pain in his arms and hands affecting his piano-playing, neither Petra nor I were particularly worried before the meeting. We were to suffer a rude awakening. Friday 1st October 2010 wasn't a good day. Black Friday, to go along with all the other Black Days. It was pouring with rain, so much so that the Ryder Cup at

Celtic Manor near Newport had to be interrupted.

Colin said that the latest chest x-ray showed that the cancer was growing and seemed to be at the apex (the top of the lungs). So much for the umpiring hypothesis. Had Daniel not been umpiring, would Colin have taken the symptoms more seriously? Was it just bad luck that there was an alternative, plausible explanation?

Colin told Petra and me privately that he was concerned about the neck and arms. Although there was nothing obvious on the x-ray, even on their special machine enhancing the images, the natural explanation was of cancer in the spine. Daniel should have a spinal MRI, to be followed by radiotherapy if his fears were confirmed. He made it clear he didn't want to discuss radiotherapy: 'You probably know as much as me, David, about radiotherapy.' I just looked at him. We both knew that was nonsense.

The chemo regimen this time was to be irinotecan/temozolomide. It's tough because the patient has the chemo intravenously two weeks out of three, five days a week. So Daniel would have to come to UCH every day for those two weeks. This would seriously interfere with his plans to return to Oxford.

The morning then got even worse. The three of us met with Melanie to make arrangements for the MRI and chemo. The context is important: Daniel, a young man of nearly twenty-two, had just been given devastating news. His cancer was growing again. He knew he was approaching the last chance saloon, with last orders on tap. I cannot imagine what was going on inside his mind. I knew mine was scrambled. Naturally, we wanted to have the MRI as soon as possible and then get on with treatment. But Melanie said there were no

MRI slots available any time soon. Plus, chemo would not be able to start for ten days. I said that was unacceptable. 'I appreciate that Daycare have to juggle the needs of many patients but the timing of chemo has to be determined by Daniel's clinical needs and he needs chemo urgently', I said politely but firmly. Using the term 'clinical needs' to a medical professional - with the implication that she was unconcerned about meeting them - was no doubt a red rag to a bull.

Melanie's reply has stuck with me like a limpet: 'The policy is to give priority to patients who are having curative chemo.' I couldn't believe what I was hearing. Was she really telling Daniel, without authority from his doctor and knowing that he didn't want to hear anything about prognosis, that his cancer was incurable? She quickly changed 'curative' to 'newly-diagnosed' but the damage was done. I'm sure she was reacting to the pressure of the moment. None of us is word-perfect through a working day; life isn't scripted. But cancer professionals have to be able to deal with situations like this without saying something so obviously inappropriate. I was persistent, certainly, but calm; paediatric cancer practitioners have to deal with parents who are distraught and hysterical and still exude sympathetic authority. It's their job.

I didn't pick her up on her comment because I didn't wish to draw Daniel's attention to it. The discussion continued. We talked about Daniel being admitted. 'I know there's already a waiting-list for beds in oncology for Monday', was the reply. 'We'll take him to T15 [the private ward] if necessary', I said. Melanie said that beds cost £1200 a night – we no longer had insurance – and thought we would have to pay for the chemo as well.

When we came out of the meeting, Petra asked me, out

of Daniel's earshot: 'Did Melanie really say what I think she said?' Perhaps it helped Daniel that, sadly, he had little confidence in Melanie's medical judgement.

Colin later spoke to one of the radiologists in MRI who found a slot for Daniel for the Monday.

Daniel was keen to get started on chemo. Petra and I were as positive with him as possible. 'You know that x-rays are not that accurate', I said. He threw that back at me when I told him the x-ray hadn't shown anything on his right chest, where he'd been having a lot of pain. Daniel had started learning the accordion and was finding it quite heavy. I suggested this might explain the arm pain. Neither of us believed it.

As always, research was my antidote to bad news. I had, in fact, been corresponding with a French surgeon in London rejoicing in the name of Loic Lang-Luzdanski. He performed radical pleurectomies - in other words, he removed both linings of the pleura. I couldn't understand how that was possible: what would protect the lung? I had already arranged to meet him the following Tuesday. Loic told me that Colin was the best doctor in Europe for Ewing's. I passed this onto Daniel. I wanted Daniel to retain faith in Colin. His response, laughing: 'So why do you think you know so much?!' I didn't, of course.

I forgot to buy a ticket for the train going home, and was handed a £20 penalty. I told the train employee that it had been a really bad day with my son's cancer. It was true, but I should probably just have paid. He kindly let me off.

I made up three batches of wheatgrass, determined to maintain what had become normality for Daniel. That was becoming ever more difficult. The following day he complained about head pain, and his left eye was dilated. He wanted to go to A&E at UCH. We listened to the Ryder Cup on the way up. The young doctor, Taj, couldn't find anything neurologically amiss on a thorough examination but decided to admit Daniel. He was pleased to get a room to himself. Not for the first time I marvelled at his ability to recover psychologically.

But he was clearly masking deep-seated anxiety. He had a panic attack at MRI and asked to be brought out. We played cards but it was a stressful day waiting for the results. In the event, it showed no new sinister development. Massive relief once again.

Radical surgery?

On 5th October, I had my meeting with Mr Lang-Luzdanski, at the private London Bridge Hospital. He'd spoken to Colin on the Friday, without giving Daniel's name, but Colin had immediately guessed who he was talking about. Daniel laughed about that and told Petra. Colin had been sceptical about a pleurectomy when I had raised it with him initially, back in January. It was like peeling a grape, he said. I knew he was almost certainly right but as ever felt I owed it to Daniel to check everything.

I brought along colour diagrams of the thorax and above. Loic was open and friendly and a tennis player so he had that in common with Daniel. He had a teenage son.

Only two doctors in the UK did radical pleurectomies – I'd been in touch with the other one, in Leicester. Loic performed about one a week and hadn't had any peri-operative mortality. This surprised and impressed me in equal measure, given the pretty dire statistics I had read about 'ordinary' pleurectomies (where just one of the linings is removed).

Nonetheless, this was major surgery. It would take four to four and a half hours, Daniel's chest would need to be opened up (a thoracotomy) and he would lose two litres of blood. Loic would only do the surgery if it was designed to achieve long-term remission. Quality of life should nevertheless be good, he said and Daniel should be able to play tennis, with some retraining. One of his patients had just been surfing in Portugal.

To my surprise, Loic said that Daniel's pleurodesis would make the operation easier (doctors at the Brompton had said a pleurodesis would make surgery more difficult). Loic would want to work within Colin's overall plan – he was the maestro, he said. He admired Simon Jordan's work and would be happy for him to observe the operation. I liked the collaborative approach.

I came out of the meeting with a real spring in my step. Loic exuded confidence (I reminded myself that surgeons were often optimistic by nature). We would have to get Colin on board and we would need to get Daniel into remission again, a tough ask at this stage. Loic confirmed that the January relapse had been really bad, with some deposits in the lung and a tumour the size of a tennis ball in the fat around the heart.

Could a radical pleurectomy really solve all this? It all seemed a little too good to be true, but Loic had prepared for the meeting – as doctors don't always do – and discussed Daniel's scans with a radiologist. He had correctly surmised that Daniel's left pupil could be dilated. He clearly knew his way round the thoracic anatomy.

At any rate, his can-do attitude was just the boost I needed and I was keen to relay the conversation to Petra. We obviously had an extremely difficult problem in the pleura. Chemo wasn't going to solve it and radiotherapy was unlikely to do so. Might surgery just do the trick? Clearly, this wouldn't be a pleasant experience for Daniel but I knew he would embrace it if everyone was on board. It might just save his life.

I went straight to UCH after the meeting, with something positive to hold onto. My mood was brought down a few notches, so often the way, by a conversation with Helen, a registrar. She seemed straight-talking but competent. She said there were some spots in the soft tissue around Daniel's left lung. I replied that Colin had said the disease was confined to the pleura. Helen looked surprised, but didn't break rank.

Chemo eventually got underway. The following day, 6th October, was Daniel's birthday. He spent most of it in hospital. To my surprise, he told Colin it was his birthday. He was usually a closed book with the hospital staff. Colin examined his head – we'd almost forgotten the reason for his admission with everything else going on – and thought it was ok but couldn't rule anything out. More anxiety.

Daniel probed me for reassurance: 'Is it a good time to get cancer at my age?' 'In the sense that you're otherwise healthy', I replied, but as Ewing's is overwhelmingly a childhood cancer and teenagers fare worse than younger children, this was disingenuous.

Daniel was able to go home for the evening but overnight he became sick and shivery and worried he had a brain tumour. Petra had a migraine coming on so I took him to UCH, cancelling yet another work meeting. Kirsty, one of our favourite nurses at Daycare, looked after Daniel with her usual efficiency. His blood pressure was low, even for Daniel, so chemo was off, a big blow. He was re-admitted and Daniel wanted me to stay as long as possible, though pretended he was cool about it. I got home after midnight.

Daniel was concerned that he couldn't feel Colin touching his fingertips – but wasn't sure that Colin had actually touched them! Down at MRI for a brain scan, he was insistent that the contrast dye shouldn't be put through his PICC line – he had picked this up from somewhere – and rang Daycare to confirm. I was pleased to see him taking greater control. I managed to scald my arm with green tea for Daniel, as I tried to be too clever opening the heavy ward door.

Daniel was able to leave the hospital on occasion, for the internet café and Planet Organic, which was to become a favourite haunt. They even did wheatgrass juice there. He told me as we walked there one day that he was very competitive – as though I needed telling – and enjoyed racing unsuspecting fellow pedestrians to the next lamppost. I would say to him: 'Just remind me Dan, how old are you?' In truth, I loved the fact that he was still a child at heart.

Daniel was keen to re-start chemo. But the doctors were treading carefully, because he was the first patient on irinotecan/temoz at the hospital.

Late one evening, Antonio Shah, Colin's new registrar, phoned me to say that, provisionally, all looked well with the brain scan. I was so relieved, as was Daniel. I really appreciated the call from Antonio. We liked him. He was friendly and disarmingly frank when I asked him something about radiotherapy: 'Oh, don't talk to me about radiotherapy, it's so complicated!' That became a catch-phrase for Daniel and me. I told Colin about Antonio's kindness and thanked him, too, for facilitating the various scans and early start to chemo.

This wasn't quite the end of the brain scare. The following week, MRI rang Petra: they wanted to re-scan Daniel's head because some of the images weren't clear enough. Had they seen something, Petra naturally wanted to know. We'd been given only the provisional results to date. She didn't get a proper answer. I spent ages trying to get through to the radiologist. I was worried that, if there was a problem, the second scan might not show it because irinotecan and temozolomide, unusually for chemotherapy drugs, cross into the brain and therefore could have shrunk cancer there to microscopic size in the meantime.

The re-scanning would be on the Saturday, 23rd October. Daniel was back to Oxford. We decided not to tell him until the Friday. I loathed doing so, not least because he'd just been awarded a scholarship by Magdalen. He'd been to have his new gown fitted. Once again we had to bring him down from a high.

It proved another false alarm but Daniel nearly pressed the panic button during the re-scan, probably an indication of his general anxiety. My anxiety manifested itself in a dream that Daniel was dying.

Daniel's pains continued and at times he struggled psychologically, but he got on with his Oxford life. He took part in a pub quiz. He had to say a few words in Latin at a dinner in Magdalen going back centuries (he enjoyed the evening but the ritual less so). He went to see England play the All Blacks at Twickenham with Sasha and to an Oxford Union debate with the motion 'Is the English Channel wider than the Atlantic?' (not sponsored by the Geography Department), with Malcolm Rifkind and Nigel Farage among the speakers. I took part in a debate myself – not sure why or how, with everything that was going on.

Paul's House

We had begun to stay at Paul's House, a newly-opened Clic Sargent 'home-from-home' by UCH. Families of children with cancer are able to stay there free of charge, to save having to travel back and fro to the hospital. It's a wonderful place. We stayed there quite a bit while Daniel was having chemo.

One day he watched Philip Schofield, the presenter of ITV's *This Morning* do a piece to camera at Paul's House. Clic Sargent was the programme's Christmas charity (they raised £440,000). Philip later announced on air that a patient featured on the film had died a couple of weeks later, from leukaemia. Daniel didn't say anything, but it must have been a further reminder of how precarious was the thread holding his life together.

Another day, I left him at Paul's House when I went to some appointments. At 1.30 in the afternoon, the hospital called – was Daniel coming for his chemo? I rang his mobile. No answer. Nothing unusual about that, but with cancer you worry. Daniel was a pretty dopey crosser of roads, head in the clouds. He was discovered still fast asleep, well into the afternoon, an illustration of how tired he got.

Early in November 2010, I went to Addenbrooke's Hospital in Cambridge to see Drs Neil Burnet and Gail Horan about tomotherapy. I had been continuing with my research and had sent Colin and Anna a table setting out what I saw as the pros and cons of the main tomotherapy options as against external beam radiotherapy. It took me hours to compile.

Addenbrooke's, more famous for heart transplants, was one of a handful of hospitals in the UK with a tomotherapy machine. In fact, it had just acquired a second. I had been in touch with one of the sarcoma patients on the Sarcoma UK support list who'd been to see Neil and had spoken highly of him. Neil, it seemed, no longer treated sarcoma patients but Gail, who was from Ireland, did. They were both welcoming.

Neil is attached to Cambridge University so we had the predictable jousting about his advising a patient who was at Oxford. The Munich tomotherapy plan was good, they thought, but sadly things had moved on with Daniel's cancer. There were disadvantages with tomotherapy, including a technical one related to a patient's breathing patterns. They shared Anna's concern about Daniel's depleted bone marrow reserve and the need for a therapeutic dose to the left lung. Anna, it seems, had been one of Neil's lecturers.

Overall the message from Neil was depressing. It was 'not impossible' that local control could be achieved, no more than that. Daniel's best chance revolved around the fact that his original cancer had been radiosensitive, which was an indication that the relapse cancer might also be responsive to radiotherapy and the fact that Ewing's often produced one-off cases, not conforming to usual patterns. Daniel's was one of them. Because the history was unusual, the outcome might not be the expected one either. It didn't seem much to cling to.

I was more upbeat with Daniel when I got back. 'You're always positive after these meetings', he remarked – maybe I overdid it a bit. I was disappointed again that the prospect of tomotherapy appeared to be receding. Neil kindly expressed his follow-up letter to Anna in accessible terms, because he was copying it to me. He described the case as 'fascinating' and concluded:

'Gail and I were both moved by the courage of this young man … in dealing with this disease … we would certainly like to wish Daniel well for his ongoing treatment.'

Warm touches like this are so important in the forbiddingly cold world of cancer.

The next day I went to an Open Day at the Theology Faculty at Oxford with my friend Martyn. I was interested in perhaps doing a further degree. Daniel was surprisingly sanguine about the possibility of my being at Oxford the same time as him. I must have been in a lifelong learning phase because I also did a one-day course at the London Welsh Centre to revive my Welsh. It was important for Daniel to see me getting on with my life.

If ever I felt myself slacking in my efforts to find answers for Daniel, not driving myself as hard as I should, reading about a child's death would act as a spur. And not only the deaths themselves, but the suffering which preceded it. When would our turn come, I wondered? So the research continued. Not that Daniel was always impressed. I passed on a short article about the beneficial properties of rhubarb. His reply: 'Is that the quality of your research?!'

There were other lighter moments. During the England cricket tour to Australia, JJ copied Daniel and me into a text, not realising we were together: 'Reassuring to see the Ashes return to normal.' So – Daniel's idea – we sent identical replies, simultaneously: 'Personalised texts always make me feel special.' JJ replied: 'Haha! Ok this one has been individualised I promise.' To both of us.

On another occasion, Daniel noticed me limping. I explained I had a bad toe. 'How long have you had it? Does it keep you awake at night?' Daniel asked with a smile – the questions I had asked him a thousand times.

Daniel accompanied me to a reception at the House of Commons about the primate trade: he wanted to meet Brian May, the Queen guitarist. One freezing December evening we went to see *Question of Sport*, with a *Strictly Come Dancing* theme, at the BBC in London. And, just prior to Christmas, Daniel attended the live broadcast of BBC *Sports Personality of the Year* in Birmingham. There was snow-induced travel chaos and he wasn't well. But *Sports Personality* was his favourite programme and he was going, come what may. So off he went, with Sasha.

A magical day

But the unquestionable highlight of the autumn was our visit to the media day for the end-of-season Masters tennis tournament at the O2 in London. We were surprised that Daniel was eligible for another make-a-wish, through Dreams Come True (DCT). He settled on meeting Roger

Federer, his all-time hero. In fact, ambitiously, we would ask if he could knock-up with him.

DCT weren't optimistic about even a 'meet and greet', as they're called. 'A' listers like Federer are difficult to pin down and it would have to be when he was in this country (though in fact we would have travelled to him). I decided to try a more direct route. I rang his management company. A man answered the phone. I began my spiel but he cut me short to get Roger's Mum, who helps to look after his affairs. I'm pretty sure that I had been speaking to the man himself. Either that or he has a vocal doppelganger. Mrs Federer listened patiently. She, too, wasn't optimistic. 'Roger gets loads of these requests and it upsets him to see children with cancer', she said. I thought: 'Actually it's pretty upsetting for a child to have cancer too', but it wouldn't have been tactically astute to say that. Mrs Federer promised to see what they could do.

I didn't ask whether it might be possible for Daniel to have a hit with Roger. One step at a time. I broached that a bit later. The reply came that Roger didn't want anything interfering with preparation for the tournament. Daniel joked: 'Yes, I can understand he doesn't want to risk damaging his confidence by my exposing weaknesses in his forehand.' It had been worth a try. Daniel wasn't sure he was up to playing at the moment anyway.

DCT had by this time made great strides: Daniel could come to the pre-tournament media event and meet Roger. Just for a minute or two, but Daniel was thrilled. Would he, I wondered, be able to attend the press conference? Ok, came the answer, Daniel can sit in on a TV interview, but only Daniel. Barclays, the main sponsors, threw in four

Daniel weighing up whom to have as his doubles partner.

tickets for the tournament. It was getting better and better.

The media event was on 19th November 2010. The two days beforehand were tough. I had to cancel a drink with my friends Stewart and Richard to take Daniel to hospital in Oxford, because of increasing pain in his hip and elsewhere. He needed codeine, a bad sign and felt the cancer was back. Antonio, the UCH registrar, hypothesised a fracture. I hoped he was right, anything but cancer (naively, because a fracture would probably be caused by cancer). The examination was inconclusive.

I deliberately didn't ask about the pain the following day and Daniel didn't volunteer. I read that pain was a reasonably common side-effect of irinotecan. Something to hold onto. Daniel went to a union debate about China.

And so to the big day. It didn't start well. We had an appointment first thing with Prof Hassan in the Churchill Hospital in Oxford, to prepare for chemo there. Daniel noticed that the consent form described the objective of the chemo as 'controlling' the cancer – not eradicating it.

But his mood soon picked up. We focused on the day ahead. Daniel was worried about being tongue-tied in the presence of the great man, so we worked out some questions he could ask him. He was excited.

After lunch at Planet Organic, we made our way to the old County Hall, where the media event would take place. We met Fiona Taylor from DCT. There was a frisson of excitement as someone announced 'Roger's coming.' He was scheduled to do an interview with David Frost. Daniel was allowed in and Fiona and I slipped in as well. Roger was patient with Sir David's obsequiousness. He oozed professionalism and it was easy to understand why sponsors love him. At one point, he did three TV interviews on the reel - in English, French and German. He was good with Daniel and willingly did whatever we asked – Sasha and Florence wanted signed tennis balls.

Daniel also had his photo taken and sat in on interviews with other top players. Fiona, who organised things brilliantly, mentioned to Andy Roddick that Daniel was a line-judge at Wimbledon. 'Nobody's perfect', came the quickfire reply. Novak Djokovic was a comedian too. We were impressed not only by how nice everyone was to Daniel but how well they got on with each other. The PR was brilliant and we made the obvious contrast with the boorishness of so many footballers. At one point we were chatting with Rafael Nadal in the corridor. It was all a bit surreal. He was as unassuming as he comes over on TV.

Always interested in the media, Daniel was allowed to join the media pack at the photocall (with Big Ben as the backdrop) and press conference.

Daniel simply loved the day, though worried that when he showed his friends the photos, they would think he had been to Madame Tussaud's! He gave pride of place at home and college to a t-shirt signed by the players.

And the best bit of the day for me? The fact that Daniel had barely any pain. As I wrote in my journal: 'A magical day.' It really was.

Nicola Arazani from the Association of Tennis Professionals later offered Daniel more tickets. He offered yet more when I thanked him for everything! Daniel decided these were good tactics – I would have to think of further reasons to thank him!

Fiona described Daniel as 'such a lovely person.' I'm sure they're effusive about all the children they help, but it was still good to hear. Typically, he got me to draft the requested piece for DCT's newsletter. Daniel was worried about the LTA coming across the article – tennis officials aren't supposed to fraternise with the players.

Surgery rejected

Back in the real world, we were frustrated about the inconsistent information we were getting about whether Daniel had cancer in the soft-tissue in his chest and Petra made the point to Colin at a clinic appointment. His feeling now was that the cancer was outside the pleura. The discussion moved onto surgery. Colin was against the idea because Ewing's attacked soft tissue in an unfocused way: one couldn't therefore be sure of excising all the cancer in the left chest.

'The reason we're looking at surgery is because the radiotherapists aren't confident of radiotherapy working', I explained. Colin replied: 'I understand but equally Daniel has done much better than anyone thought likely at the outset and he responded well to radiotherapy before.' That was an unexpected glimmer of hope. It wasn't certain, he added, that Daniel had microscopic cancer in his lungs and the fat around his heart, where there had been a big tumour, could easily be taken out.

It was evident that Colin had been speaking to Loic Lang-Luzdanski when I went to see him again, just before Christmas. He was far less upbeat this time and was now against a radical pleurectomy. There had been a lot of soft-tissue cancer in October. He did say, however, that Daniel's response to the latest chemo was amazing and he was effectively back in remission.

I had no problem with Colin putting the dampeners on surgery. He knew far more about the pathology of Ewing's than Loic and it was his job to tell it as he saw it, to protect Daniel from highly invasive surgery he thought was pointless. Colin laughed once when I said I saw part of his role as restraining my wilder ideas. But it was true: I wanted to test the waters and encourage creativity.

I have no reason to think that ruling out a pleurectomy was the wrong decision. It would have been awful for Daniel to have major surgery only for the cancer to return quickly. But at the time I was so disappointed that an option which might just save Daniel's life had to be discarded.

Daniel continued on chemo until Christmas. One day the temozolomide spilt and ruined Daniel's trousers, a reminder of how toxic chemo is. I would always check that he was getting the right dose. I never saw anyone else do this, but I knew that mistakes occur in even the best run hospitals. Indeed, a twenty-seven year-old UCH patient died from a chemotherapy overdose – killed not by his cancer but because someone didn't care enough. A 2008 study in a leading cancer journal found chemo or other medication mistakes with 7 per cent of adults and 19 per cent of children. My job was to look out for Daniel (at St Peter's once, he said 'well done' when my checking prevented a nurse administering an antibiotic potentially damaging to his kidneys).

But there was fun during chemo, too. We played cards, usually, or Daniel would devour a philosophy magazine. He laughed at an American philosopher bracketing an argument I put in an article on ethics with Jeremy Bentham, the utilitarian philosopher. We joked that Bentham and Thomas were names not normally found in the same sentence – one a great philosopher, the other some nomark who died long ago. Bentham, incidentally, donated his body to University College London.

On Christmas Eve, I had a call from Anna Cassoni. Could I come to clinic that morning? I was taken aback and wasn't prepared for a radiotherapy discussion, but couldn't turn down the opportunity. Petra couldn't come and Daniel was having chemo.

We had a long, technical discussion about the radiotherapy Daniel should have. Anna advised a therapeutic dose to his left lung, with higher doses – boosting – to those areas in his left chest where the tumour had been particularly large. I was very happy with this – it was what I'd been trying to achieve all along. There was a 'fighting chance', she felt that radiotherapy could work. I was happy with that, too. There was nothing on the latest scan which one could definitely say was cancer. I was even happier with that.

Daniel continued to protect Sasha and Florence from anything related to his cancer. He had, however, told a friend studying biochemistry about his good scan result. The friend had, in turn, spoken to Sasha before her interview at Brasenose College Oxford (to study biochem) and had mentioned the scan result. So this is how Sasha got information about her brother! Sasha wanted Daniel to be the first to know she'd got into Brasenose.

* * *

On Christmas Day, Daniel and I took Jess for a walk. There was still snow on the ground. Suddenly, Jess took off after a deer. It resembled a cartoon – Daniel chasing me chasing Jess chasing the deer. Fortunately, the deer won. Daniel proudly showed me one of his presents, a digital album with photos of him with Federer et al.

On a trip to see *Meet the Little Fokkers*, he told Annabel that he realised he would probably have to resit the year. He seemed cool about that. He was still talking about travelling and he really wanted England to win the bid for the 2018 World Cup, which meant he thought he would be around to see it.

Would he, I wondered, as the year came to a close? It seemed extremely unlikely. But there was still hope.

2011: part one

Dad: *So, if there are 3,600 seconds in an hour and there are twenty-four hours in a day, how do we work out how many seconds there are in a day?*
Daniel (aged five): *Easy, use a calculator*

And so to 2011, that most momentous of years.

Actually, the year started off well enough. One hour in, Daniel rang to wish me a happy new year; normally, he would wait graciously to receive such greetings. We played tennis and he wasn't too tired or out of breath, so much better than in the summer.

This was all manna from Heaven to me. I knew it wouldn't last but Daniel talked about going to the next Ashes series, both here and in Australia. We studied the Roman poet Propertius together.

The picture became more nuanced as the year got

into its stride. Down times were related to pain. Daniel worried about what it signified. Cancer was now old hat to him. He was desperate not to relapse again. At times, he seemed demotivated with his college work, more interested in playing Wii with the girls for hours (to the extent that Petra had to confiscate it). Occasionally he talked about leaving Oxford. He was fed up with the constant comings and goings. Who could blame him? He must have felt like a semi-detached student, forced to miss so much of what the university had to offer and just normal socialising with friends.

However, one evening we went to see an NBA basketball match at the O2. Neither of us were particularly basketball fans – my standard, rather glib comment is that it's too easy to score – but we agreed that the Americans knew how to put on a show. It was great entertainment and we were fortunate to pick a really close match, unusually going to the third overtime period (the Americans don't do draws). I was worried about missing the last train home but Daniel was determined to stay to the end. We got home at 2am. He was on top form.

Around the same time we went to Old Trafford to see Manchester United play Liverpool in the third round of the FA Cup, courtesy of Clic Sargent. Petra and I didn't feel it right to apply for the various grants on offer because we didn't need them, but Daniel would have lynched us if we'd spurned Man Utd.

It was another special day, although neither of us liked the animosity between the fans, with the puerile references to the Munich and Hillsborough disasters. It took me back to when Daniel was about ten, when we saw Cardiff City play Exeter. The atmosphere then had been poisonous. Bad language never bothered me but I didn't want Daniel at his tender age to see just how nasty human beings can be to each other. Long before cancer, I was overprotective of Daniel, perhaps – even into his teenage years, I would check on him during the night.

Daniel had wanted me, rather than one of his friends, to come to Old Trafford, because he was worried about hooliganism. Such a gentle soul, though I'm not sure what he thought I could do faced by rampaging hordes.

Amidst the usual nonsense and banter, I succeeded in adding to his worries. I advised him to keep well away from the tube platform edge, having read an article about a well-known London solicitor, a transvestite leading a double life, who'd been pushed under a train by a friend. 'Oh, I'm going to be worried about that now', was Daniel's reply.

Alex, a fellow Samaritan with connections at Anfield, later offered to try for tickets for Liverpool's league match against Man Utd. 'Yes, give him the sob story!' Daniel joked.

Exam

The Tuesday after the FA Cup match, I took an exam, my first since university – just for some light relief. This was to be a part-time judge. I might not be able to sit immediately if appointed, given Daniel's prognosis, but felt I needed to plan for the future.

I prepared as diligently as I was able to amidst all the research and hospital visits, plus the work I was managing to do. I felt as ready as I could be. The night before, I stayed with Daniel at Paul's House, but didn't get a good night's sleep. Daniel had a comfortable double bed but mine was makeshift. The alarm went before 6, for an early start.

The exam was tough and there were lots of complaints. There was too much complicated material to assimilate in the allotted time, more than in practice as a judge. I panicked at one stage, and thought to myself: 'What the f… am I doing here taking this stupid exam, with Daniel seriously ill and in the middle of chemo?' Not the best frame of mind for a challenging exam.

I returned to Paul's House and got Daniel up (never an easy task) before we went for his chemo.

Later that day I learnt that Julian, my brother-in-law, had prostate cancer. Annabel his daughter was back in hospital following her bowel perforation and Eve, my sister's mother-in-law, was struggling after a major spinal operation. So we weren't alone in our anxiety.

It took me a few days to open the letter from the Judicial Appointments Commission: I wasn't feeling strong emotionally. Becoming a judge was not a particular ambition but I wanted Daniel to be just a little proud of his Dad. It wasn't to be on this occasion. I considered explaining the circumstances and even drafted a letter. My concentration hadn't been good, perhaps diminished by stress. But I couldn't be sure that Daniel's situation had affected my performance. I may simply have had a bad day. I admire the philosophy of the great Australian Davis Cup team of the 1960s – Laver, Rosewall, Newcombe et al: 'If you're injured, don't play; if you play, don't complain about being injured.' So I left it.

Soon after the exam, Anna Cassoni needed to consent Daniel for radiotherapy. In the waiting-room, a cancer parent said how much better Daniel was looking. That was thoughtful.

'How much do you want to know, Daniel?' Anna asked. 'Just the immediate side-effects', he replied.

After he left, Anna and I tied up the loose ends. I was content that we had, as far as I could tell, got the balance right between efficacy and risks and burden for Daniel. I thanked Anna for all her help and apologised it had been such a painful process. She laughed: 'I can cope with one of you, but couldn't cope with five!'

Radiotherapy started towards the end of January 2011. The first day was a long one for Daniel and Petra – they didn't get home until 6.30pm after an early start. The worry was whether Daniel's platelets would stand up to a further blast of radiation. I researched high and low to see if there was anything, conventional or complementary, which could be done to boost the level. A platelets expert at Harvard who had been to Magdalen, David Kuter, was keen to help but couldn't suggest anything. To my surprise, Mum joined in the discussion, recalling that, fifty years ago, her cousin's platelets increased after her spleen was removed. That seemed a bit drastic.

The most promising complementary remedy appeared to be papaya leaf extract, which could be given in the form of a tea. There didn't seem to be a downside so we gave it a go. Daniel wasn't thrilled to be taking yet another thing – he told me he was nearing his tolerance level – but as always went along with what we suggested. The taste was quite bitter.

Every day we were on a knife-edge as to whether Daniel could have radiotherapy. One day, his legs were shaking as he was waiting for his daily blood results (the staff knew him so well that he would get his bloods done without authorisation from a doctor). We still had some harvested stem cells which might in principle support the platelets, though there were technical uncertainties. Somehow or other Daniel's platelets got through the five-week radiation assault. He even thought that traumeel s, the homeopathic remedy, helped to minimise inflammation of the oesophagus. He had a couple of red cell blood transfusions.

Colin kindly told Daniel he could pop in to see him any time during radiotherapy. He was getting it in optimal circumstances, he added, given his response to chemo. One day I showed Daniel references to articles Colin had written. He seemed to like that, because it underlined that Colin was a real expert. Another day, after Petra and I couldn't feel the lump which Daniel had identified, he commented dismissively: 'We'll ask Colin I think!'

Although we completed radiotherapy, Daniel's platelets were still too low for chemotherapy. He needed time off treatment. That was a big concern, especially when his assorted pains continued. He began to have pain in his left ear, which I read could emanate from the cervical spine. As ever the picture was mixed and I learnt, or re-learnt, just how complicated pain is. This time, a doctor in Sweden helped with my education. Daniel was convinced the cancer was back.

We went to a concert at the Royal Albert Hall. In the car

coming back he mentioned the new pain. When I probed, he replied wearily: 'Oh I don't know, Dad.' He wanted reassurance but was fed up with all the questions. He looked at me with pleading eyes, as if to say 'Please help me, Dad.' It cut me in two. So I did some more research when I got home.

These proved false alarms, or perhaps more accurately alarms that didn't sound loud enough. Petra was in tears as Colin examined Daniel towards the end of March, after pain around the heart. 'One to add to Daniel's aches and pains', he remarked. 'It should go away.' A CT scan wouldn't help. If the pain persisted, they would do an ECG to check damage to the heart linings, a possible side-effect of radiotherapy.

More relief after more worry. But Daniel later remarked, to my surprise, 'If this doesn't cause Colin to take pain seriously, what would?' This was to become a recurring theme and I blame myself for not pressing harder. The trouble was we wanted to accept reassurance from doctors, because the alternative was so scary.

I had continued to research low-dose chemo and arranged to visit Jaume Mora in Barcelona and two doctors in Marseille, Jean-Claude Gentet and Nicolas André, who also used low-dose chemo for sarcoma patients in remission.

On 30th March, my alarm went at 3.45am. I was at the hospital in Barcelona soon after 11, my fifth visit. The injection of hope Dr Mora always administered was worth the air fare alone. Their experience, albeit with a small number of patients, was that those with Daniel's ERG chromosomal translocation did better, although one had died.

Dr Mora thought doing nothing would be a major mistake. Of five relapse Ewing's patients, none had relapsed on low-dose chemo. He also felt that a multifaceted approach was really important because the cancer finds different pathways. Colin's wait and watch approach was the classic one, he said. But cure rates for metastatic Ewing's patients hadn't improved for decades, so one had to try something new. This was precisely my philosophy.

I told Daniel the meeting had been really positive. 'Does he agree with you and not McMaster?' 'Basically yes', I replied. 'That doesn't sound very positive', was his riposte. He laughed when I told him I had seen the clowns.

At Marseille airport as I waited for a bus, a young Chinese man asked me to interpret for him and his wife. He was a photobiochemist at a Spanish university and was in Marseille for a conference. I explained why I was there. On the bus he gave me his email address. They were, he said, moved by what I was doing for Daniel. He knew some doctors in China. I was very touched.

A couple of days later, Quansong sent an email:

> 'It was also our pleasure to meet you, one of the greatest fathers, in Marseille! ... We are very sorry about Daniel! We will try to do something for him, which will be our new project. This project ... hopefully ... will be our most meaningful project in our life!'

JJ heard about the email and texted: 'Nice thing for the Chinese guy to say [about your being a great dad]. What was his source of reference? Oh, just what you told him ...'

Banter had always been a feature of all our relationships. No one was allowed to take themselves too seriously and certainly not be boastful. Once, when Daniel was five, I was on the news after an important court case about disability benefits. 'What did you think about seeing Dad on TV?' His reply: 'It was just like watching any other programme.' That set the pattern.

This time he groaned: 'Why are you contacting Chinese doctors now?!' He was amused that anyone would use me as a French interpreter.

I hoped that this chance meeting would open some new doors. Coley's, I knew, was used at one centre in China and I had an open mind about traditional Chinese medicine. Mum's response when I told her was: 'As if it was meant to be.'

I met with Drs Gentet and André in the poetically named Hôpital d'Enfants de la Timone. They were both eager to help, though Dr Gentet, the older of the two and a dead ringer for Fabio Cappello, the former England football manager, struggled a little with his English (like Cappello). They essentially agreed with Dr Mora.

We discussed various options and drug combinations, my head, as usual, spinning with so much technical information. They refused to take any money for the consultation.

Back at Marseille airport I had a multi-handed work conference call, sitting on the floor of the departure lounge.

We were due to have a meeting with Colin a week later. Petra was anxious we do something quickly. We all felt exposed when Daniel was off-treatment. Daniel meanwhile, wanted to know how to respond to his tutor Felix's idea of sixteen essays during the summer term – twice the normal number – to avoid re-taking the year. We thought that would be too much.

It's difficult to portray the emotion of important clinical meetings about Daniel. In my career and voluntary work, I have appeared loads of times on TV and radio, conducted the advocacy in important legal cases in this country and abroad, had countless meetings with ministers and civil servants and at the EU, taken part in debates and given many talks, given evidence to several parliamentary committees and a Royal Commission, taught over many years, presided over some fraught meetings as chair of a leading national charity. I now sit as a judge, after getting through the next time. Before all these I get nervous, no matter how many times I do them: I need adrenalin to flow for full concentration.

Yet none of these comes close to the anxiety of meetings with Colin, because of what was at stake. It often felt like we were to learn if Daniel was going to live or die. The complexity of the science and the impossibility of knowing the right course of action, simply added to the general feeling of helplessness. We weren't waiting for scan results this time, but I still felt tense.

Anna joined the meeting because she was intrigued by Daniel's pain pattern. Making my pitch for low-dose chemo as maintenance therapy, I said our objective was to keep the cancer chronic for as long as possible. Colin confirmed that it was rational to strike while the cancer was weak but, to my surprise, baulked at my suggestion that Daniel inevitably had some cancer. He probably did but one couldn't be certain, he said. This was unexpectedly melodious music to our ears. UCH did use maintenance chemo, Colin explained, for example for rhabdomyosarcoma, though he didn't agree with my impression that rhabdo, a nasty paediatric cancer, was biologically similar to Ewing's.

'Intellectually', he said, 'I'm not persuaded that maintenance chemo is appropriate and interruptions due to platelet depletion, although not catastrophic or irreversible, would rather defeat the rationale.' But he added: 'However, I ask myself rhetorically: but why not do it?' It wouldn't be irrational or irresponsible. I stressed that we wouldn't do something for the sake of it, or to address Daniel's anxieties (Colin was convinced that the various pains were in part psychosomatic and suggested counselling).

The meeting closed with Colin promising to contact the Barcelona and Marseille doctors, in about a week.

Petra and I left in a really upbeat mood, the earlier tension dissipated. It had gone far better than expected. The suggestion that Daniel might, after three relapses, be free of cancer didn't sit easily with Colin's certainty, on first relapse, that Daniel wouldn't be cured. I had noticed over the years that, when I reflected back to Colin his dire pessimism, he sometimes responded with shafts of optimism, however thin. This wasn't intentional on my part, but it seemed to be the way to extract hope.

Daniel picked up the positive vibes. He later took Jess for a walk by himself, I think for the first time.

That weekend, as agreed, I passed on to Colin the contact details for the doctors. I added a paragraph, copying in Anna:

'Since Tuesday marks the fifth anniversary of Daniel's diagnosis, it's an appropriate time to express our gratitude for the expertise and conscientious professionalism which you and Anna have shown throughout and for the excellent care he has received at UCH. I know that it must sometimes appear that, if you told me the time, I would want a second opinion but given Daniel's very serious condition I feel I owe it to him to cover all the bases. Five years may hold little statistical significance given the relapses but it's a still a milestone we didn't think we would get anywhere near and we are very grateful.'

Sadly, this was to prove the high point of our relationship with Colin over the latter part of Daniel's cancer journey. The problem was he didn't get in touch with the doctors. I sent him two polite chaser emails, but heard nothing, even after relaying worrying symptoms. Colin wrote to Daniel's GP, Dr Carty, promising to explore the option of further treatment. He said the evidence of benefit was limited but there was no doubt what he had promised to do. It would have taken minimal effort to kick-start the process. At no point did Colin offer any explanation for his failure, still less an apology. If he'd changed his mind, he should have said so.

On 4th May Daniel relapsed again. Whether low-dose chemo after radiotherapy would have made any difference is not the point. Dr Gentet later said he didn't think it would, given how aggressive the cancer obviously was. Perhaps he was being kind; more likely he was being realistic. But, inevitably, one wonders.

During the hiatus, Daniel's pain got progressively worse. It was intermittent – some days he didn't take any pain relief – but the general trend was bad. One day, towards the end of April, he suggested bringing forward the CT scan planned for 6th May. I said: 'Dan, you know I would get you an x-ray or scan if I felt it was necessary but nothing seems to have changed since the meeting with Colin and Anna and they weren't concerned.' Daniel replied: 'You want to think that.' He was right and in retrospect we should have acted earlier.

By this time, Daniel was feeling quite unwell, with some sort of virus, and had a hacking cough. A cough and fever were symptoms of pneumonitis, one of the radiotherapy side-effects. I fervently hoped it was pneumonitis. On 1st May, Mum and Petra went to see him in Oxford. He had, unusually, not got up for the traditional Magdalen Choir May Day singing on top of the tower at 6am.

He got increasingly worried. He again thought he had a lump around his heart. He wanted to have an x-ray at UCH but didn't want to travel on the tube because Osama bin Laden had just been killed!

Amidst all this anxiety, he sent me an essay about the poet Lucretius. It was really good, amazing considering the pressure he was under and how ill he was - there were times even he couldn't work. We went to see *To Kill A Mocking Bird*, Harper Lee's great parable about racism and empathy.

Tough times

May 2011 turned out to be a horrific month, one of the worst on this horrific journey. At UCH, we saw Anand

Sharma, Colin's new registrar. He confirmed there was nothing palpable around the heart. The cough was consistent with pneumonitis, he said. Daniel's oxygen level was excellent at 99 per cent.

Daniel had an x-ray. We left it that Dr Sharma would call me if it showed anything sinister. Daniel had decided to come home. It was six o'clock when we pulled into the drive. I thought we had got away with it. But then my mobile rang. Number withheld, so it could be UCH. I took the call away from Daniel. It was Dr Sharma. My heart sank. His voice was sombre. The x-ray showed some fluid. He wouldn't speculate about the cause. There was no visible tumour but the pleurodesis made it hard to read. I wasn't reassured. I said nothing to Daniel.

I did feel I needed to tell Mum who was still staying with me. I couldn't hide my worry. Petra was shocked how much worse Daniel's cough had become in a few days. He would be devastated if he was told there was no more treatment. So much was clear. Later, Daniel asked if Dr Sharma had been in touch. I hated lying to him, but I did. I needed to sort out my own emotions and thoughts, but I'm not sure it was the right decision. I made some telephone calls to the States about Coley's toxins and relayed the conversations to Petra, to help her mood. I kept to myself news that yet another Ewing's teenager had relapsed.

Katie and Annabel tried to be as positive as they could, Katie from New Zealand. Annabel's flatmates, all medical students, knew that radiotherapy causes inflammation which in turn can cause effusions, especially at high dose.

That evening, I bumped into Daniel at the polling station. It was the referendum on the alternate vote system. It was clear the system would be rejected, which disappointed me. But Daniel's cough was better and he wanted to take Jess home with him.

Two days later, back at UCH, Dr Sharma said we had to assume it was cancer. He hadn't wanted to tell me on the phone. He didn't know if the cancer was in the lung or pleura but radiotherapy had failed, probably in a high-dose area. This was massively disappointing. Colin wanted Daniel to restart irinotecan/temoz. His platelets were just high enough at eighty-one.

Daniel asked later: 'So how much of a setback is this?' We went into reassurance mode, yet again. I told him about Coley's and other options if we moved off chemo. He had been larking around with Sasha.

Annabel asked whether she should send Daniel a text. I asked her to say that the effusion was small and resolvable. Sian thought Mum should go home: it would be too much for her to deal with yet another relapse head on. I was ambivalent but thought it might help her to stay, for a while at least, because she felt she was doing something.

I had hoped that the following day, a Saturday, would bring just a little light relief for Daniel. He was a massive fan of the radio show *Just a Minute* and enjoyed playing Chopin's *Minute Waltz* on the piano (amusingly, I would call out 'deviation' if he made a mistake...). I had never managed to get tickets through the random draw. However, this was to be a special recording, marking the inauguration of Radio 4 Extra. I had booked tickets on the telephone. But they hadn't arrived and with so much going on I hadn't chased. That morning I eventually got through. There had been a mistake, I was told – there was a random draw and we had failed. I explained Daniel's situation. Nothing doing.

Over the next few weeks, I pursued the matter. Fortunately the ticketing agency recorded telephone calls and confirmed I was right. But they would offer no more than an apology. So I wrote to the producer. An assistant producer called: 'We get loads of requests like this but in the circumstances we can give two tickets for a recording in July.' This was good news and I expressed gratitude, but it was not given with good grace. The producer was concerned about Daniel being ill at the show. There was no sympathy or understanding in her voice: 'This has to be your risk. We don't have the facilities to deal with very sick people.' I felt like replying: 'I expect the BBC to lay on a fully-equipped operating theatre, with at least two anaesthetists.' But I knew to quit while I was ahead.

That was later. Back on that Saturday in May, things got worse. Daniel developed blurred vision. 'I get blurred vision quite a bit', I said. 'I don't', he replied. He seemed to have just a slight focusing problem and I decided to do a booked Samaritans session. It transpired that my co-Sam had studied Classics at Oxford and her daughter was studying philosophy at Godalming Sixth Form College, as Daniel had.

When I got home, my neighbour Alan said he'd never seen me looking so down. As if on cue, Petra rang to say that Daniel's vision was worse. He wanted to go to UCH. There, his vision deteriorated further. At midnight he vomited copiously. I had earlier assured him, when he wasn't nauseous, that one would expect vomiting if there was anything sinister – i.e. cancer in the brain. Daniel's comment now was: 'So this must be bad then.' I had no answer. He had a headache in several places. But thorough neurological tests by an SHO, who hailed from near Chobham, were encouraging. She persuaded a nurse to let me sleep on the floor next to Daniel.

The next morning he could barely read newspaper print, or the banner advertisement along the side of a London bus. The neurological tests were again good and a fundoscopy – to see if there was a mass at the back of the eyes – was negative. The registrar said it was good that the condition was fluctuating. He arranged an urgent CT brain scan. Daniel was nervous and clingy. Sasha feared he would go blind.

A nurse told me the neurologist would look at the scan in the morning. This panicked me because the radiologist had said his report would be on the system within thirty minutes. Had they seen anything sinister? I was so relieved when Marco, one of the best nurses on T16, chased and reported back that the scan looked normal. Daniel, unusually, wanted to know the result – he seemed to draw a distinction between cancer in his brain and cancer elsewhere.

I was buoyed by a positive email from my friend Norbert about visualisation (using the mind rather than the eyes) but disturbed to read that blurred vision was a side-effect of many types of chemo used for Ewing's: would this mean that Daniel would not be able to have chemo?

At the eye clinic the next day, Daniel performed badly in a test about differentiating colour and, more importantly, in one for peripheral vision. He began to cry, which set Petra off. The registrar told me the only rational explanation was a mass (i.e. cancer) in the brain. She was asking the neurologist to take another look at the CT scan. Here we go again, I thought. It was my turn to break down as Petra and I waited for blood results.

The plan was that Petra would take Daniel out to lunch. I went up to the ward, to check some things. I bumped into Antonio, Colin's former registrar. This was close to Daniel's bed, around which the curtains were drawn. I told Antonio what was happening. He confirmed that it sounded bad. I then went to Daniel's bed and to my horror found him there. Luckily, he had headphones on though he told me he'd heard every word. I'm not sure from his demeanour that he did but I was so angry with myself.

An SHO, who was with the neurologist examining the CT scan, promised to report back. I was trying to maintain outward calm for Daniel's sake while going through various scenarios in my mind. I waited for several hours, anxiety levels high again. The SHO never came. Perhaps she was waylaid by some emergency, but doctors should do what they promise, especially when the stakes are so high, or send a message if they cannot.

Palma Dileo, a pleasant and experienced Italian sarcoma doctor, later told us the CT showed no major abnormalities, with no bleeding or oedemas (swelling). However, they wanted to do a brain MRI, which would look for different things. So still no respite from worry.

I went to make Daniel's tea. Colin came to find me. It was around 7.30pm by now and I appreciated the gesture. He was pretty relaxed about the brain: 'We see vision problems all the time.' However a chest CT scan was really bad: there was a great deal of cancer in both Daniel's lungs, as well as the pleura. Colin had asked Ian Judson of the

Marsden (to whose talk about clinical trials I had gone four years earlier) for his views. Ian suggested a phase 1 trial but Colin wasn't convinced and preferred more of the same chemo. I said I needed no persuasion. Phase 1 trials are crucial for research, but the results for individual patients are extremely poor, certainly in cancer (I had read an article that the Marsden's direct success rate with phase 1 cancer drugs is no more than 1 per cent).

The news about the lungs was awful, much worse than expected. I had hoped this was still a left pleura problem. And yet my primary sentiment was one of relief. We were so terrified of cancer going to Daniel's brain that anything else seemed almost manageable, even though logically I knew cancer in the lungs was almost certainly fatal at this stage. 'The chemo needs to work', Colin added, almost superfluously.

Back on the ward, Daniel had been worried about how long I was with Colin. He had struggled reading a newspaper. Another interminably long day. But Annabel had been researching brain mets and was upbeat, too.

Petra was with Daniel early the next morning, pushing for the MRI and chemo starting. At 10am she texted: Daniel's vision was worse and he was really upset, thrashing around in his bed. She wanted me to come in. Daniel took diazepam for the MRI and had calmed down by the time I arrived. I had a chat with Anand Sharma about consenting Daniel and he just got Daniel to sign the form. Just as well: it said chemo was simply for symptom relief.

Melanie later told me the brain MRI was clear. Huge relief again. She understood the stress we were under. I was so happy to give Daniel the news. He was discharged after chemo. He was pleased to see Jess but said she looked different, as did Puzzle, his cat. But he watched *The Apprentice*, a favourite.

Once again, the respite was short-lived. Daniel was in excruciating pain overnight. As fate would have it, the traffic to London was terrible. I asked a police motorcyclist if she (yes, I was surprised too) could give us an escort to the hospital. She explained the bureaucracy involved in getting permission but suggested, unofficially, that we use the hard shoulder. So we did, dirty looks aplenty from the other drivers. At least it lightened Daniel's mood.

Anand Sharma was warm with Daniel, pressing his hand as he left. He thought it best to continue with chemo, which we were pleased to hear. Petra rang at 11.10pm. My heart jumped, as it always did when the phone rang. She wanted to tell me that Daniel was a bit better so I would sleep easier.

Daniel's vision problems continued for two weeks. I did my usual research and got contradictory replies about whether micromets could cause symptoms of the sort. It was a relief, naturally, when Daniel's vision returned to normal but I wasn't completely reassured. There might still be micromets, diminished but not banished by the chemo Daniel had now had.

The report of the MRI scan, when it came, didn't allay my concerns:

'...there could be some doubtful, and more prominent than expected, faint contrast enhancement around the optic nerves, immediately posterior to the globes, and in the midportion of the orbits, bilaterally. This is only seen on coronal images, and thus doubtful. If real, leptomeningeal pathology [cancer via the spinal fluid] cannot be excluded.'

I didn't tell Petra or Daniel about the report.

The month didn't get better. Even with vision restored Daniel was not at all well. His cough was bad and he experienced shortness of breath, which naturally made him panicky. He struggled to walk and often felt nauseous and he lost weight. Leaving the Rosenheim one day as I fetched the car, he was sick on the stairs and sat slumped there. Two people walked right past him, re-enacting the parable of the Good Samaritan. Mario from the Philippines, one of his favourite nurses, assumed the title role.

We implored Daniel gently to try to eat but it's hard when you're feeling sick. I was shocked to see how he looked one day, recreating the image of concentration camp victims. He had weird dreams, perhaps a side-effect of analgesia and woke up shouting. His voice was weak and his eyes sunken. He developed thrush. His weight was down to 7 stone 4lbs.

Then towards the end of the month, as if all this wasn't enough, he had serious diarrhoea, a symptom of the irinotecan. UCH wanted him to go to St Peter's because of possible dehydration and depletion of bodily salts. Daniel agreed, unhappily. We played Hangman as we waited for results. Joy, the pleasant SHO from Nigeria, reported that the chest x-ray showed no sign of an effusion; his platelets, amazingly, were 154, just within the normal range; and his kidneys were fine. All good. Joy's provisional diagnosis was gastroenteritis, not particularly serious in itself. But there was a sting in the tail, once again. Two of his liver enzymes, ALP and ALT, were raised. This was a new one for us. Daniel's liver enzymes were frequently assessed as part of a battery of biochemistry blood tests but there had never been a problem.

So we went into hospital with one problem and came out with another. After dropping Daniel off at 2am, I did some research. Raised ALT could be caused by cancer or the chemo (amongst other reasons). The former would obviously be extremely serious (my father died when his cancer spread to the liver). But the latter would be serious too, if we had to stop chemo.

In the morning Daniel was happily feeling and eating a little better and the diarrhoea seemed to be receding. At clinic the following day, he was annoyed with me for bringing up the raised liver levels, but I explained Colin needed to examine his liver. Colin didn't think it was cancer but we might have to adjust chemo. Liver breakdown could lead to nausea and diarrhoea.

It was another difficult meeting. Colin showed us the chest CT scan, after Daniel left. When I asked how many cancerous nodules it showed, he asked, rather drily: 'Do you want to start counting, David?' It wasn't a sensitive answer. 'Daniel has had a good response to the latest chemo, but there's no chance of chemo curing him', was his take-home message. 'Our objective', I said, 'is for Daniel to see the Olympics next year.' Colin looked at me, paused and replied: 'Look David, the Olympics seem a long way off even for me.' He brought the meeting to an abrupt end, such that I forgot to ask a couple of questions.

I had a sad conversation later with Petra when she picked me up from the station. She had tears in her eyes when she handed me the CT report, which was dreadful. She had never seen Daniel looking so ill and worried that his weight loss was putting pressure on his heart, as with anorexics. Everyone was struggling.

A challenging day – how many did we have over Daniel's cancer journey? – but one bit of good news was that JJ had passed his medical finals, a real achievement after suffering his own ill-health.

Control

My current strategy, always evolving, was to get the cancer under some sort of control, move onto low-dose chemo without a gap, use some form of local control such as chemoembolisation or laser surgery, then Coley's or some other type of immunotherapy with low-dose chemo.

Laser surgery was practised at the Brompton by George Ladas. This was a recent development and it was still pretty experimental. It was also used by a German doctor in Dresden, Alex Rolle. He claimed impressive results. A German anaesthetist whose son had testicular cancer recommended him. More relevantly, Dr Rolle had treated a nineteen year-old Ewing's patient, who lived in Brussels, thus far successfully.

Dr Rolle, unfortunately, explained that laser couldn't help Daniel because his disease was partly in the pleura. I felt despondent when I received his email: there were so many knockbacks along this journey. Cryosurgery too was out, though I had invested less hope in it. Cryosurgery involves freezing the tumour.

Chemoembolisation - which targets chemotherapy to the chest or liver - hit the buffers too. I had heard good reports from patients of the leading practitioner, again in Germany, but found him frustrating to deal with. His emails were terse to the point of useless. He seemed incredibly busy. A 5am call one day yielded virtually nothing, with monosyllabic answers. OK, can I come to see you, I asked, so we can have a proper discussion? No, that would not be possible. We would have to bring Daniel for treatment and have the discussion then. That was clearly unacceptable. I wasn't going to drag Daniel to Germany, especially in his present condition, to have highly experimental treatment without carefully evaluating the pros and cons and discussing them with Colin.

Daniel knew nothing about these disappointments – he didn't know that they were possibilities in the first place – but this was a terribly anxious time for him. He sought reassurance, though could be sceptical when it was given. One day when his pain was better, he said to me: 'That's the important thing, isn't it?' Yes, it was, I replied – but didn't want to say too much because the pain would probably reappear. 'My eyesight would have got worse if this was serious, wouldn't it?' he asked, as he read the *Metro*, to prove that he could. On another day as he lay in bed, nauseous, with stomach cramps and frequent bouts of diarrhoea, he asked me plaintively: 'Am I going to be ok, Dad?' I cannot have done my calming job well on this occasion because I was soon kicked out for Sasha.

On another occasion in the middle of May, I made things worse. Daniel was in bed in the Rosenheim – still too weak to have chemo sitting up. I was reading about brain and spinal mets, a little distance from the bed. To my surprise, Daniel was able to read the material, upside down. As far as he was concerned, the vision/brain problem was solved, so why was I still reading about it? I mumbled something but was so annoyed with myself. At least, if he was able to read upside down, his eyes were ok.

As ever, the best way to reassure Daniel was to talk about the future. I have never met a bigger Olympics fan. He managed to obtain tickets via the German association and made sure I was up at 6am for the second ballot. By this time Katie, his cousin, had decided to nominate him to carry the Olympic Torch. The people chosen would be those who had inspired others. Daniel thought he had no chance – what had he done? He insisted on seeing the draft, so we could not say how serious his cancer was. The reference to his latest relapse had to come out, because Sasha and Florence didn't know about it. The final version, bang on the 150-word limit, read:

'I nominate my cousin Daniel, diagnosed with metastatic bone cancer at only seventeen. Now twenty-two he has overcome numerous obstacles and setbacks. Despite years of aggressive treatment and countless hospital procedures and admissions, Daniel has, remarkably, achieved: four As at A-level, an Oxford University scholarship (Classics) and grade 8 in piano, clarinet and saxophone. He has line-judged at three Wimbledon championships and umpired matches on chemotherapy, debated in a national competition and travelled globally watching sport (continuing to play whenever possible). Daniel's attitude and achievements are a beacon to other young cancer sufferers, encouraging them to fulfil their dreams. He inspired my family and me to cycle across England for children with

cancer in the developing world, raising over £13,000. Daniel rarely complains and has retained his gentle, good-humoured, compassionate nature in the face of unimaginable adversity. A real symbol of hope and determination, he deserves this opportunity to shine.'

Daniel felt it was a bit OTT.

In the summer of 2011, Wimbledon also provided a focus for Daniel. For as long as possible, he kept alive the hope of line-judging at that year's tournament, and at Queen's. He worried about letting the tournaments down by pulling out late. My view, somewhat selfishly perhaps, was that the importance of sustaining the dream justified giving late notice. The reality, I assured him, was that the LTA had to cater for officials becoming unexpectedly unavailable. The tournaments wouldn't fall apart if he pulled out.

He was hoping to go on a line-judging course, as well, to enable him to officiate on Centre Court. He didn't want to block someone else by withdrawing late. I admired him for thinking about others even as he was struggling.

In the event he only went to Wimbledon as a spectator. On one of his visits, with JJ, he managed to get lost driving home. Some things never changed. He even got lost, again with JJ, walking from the Rosenheim to Planet Organic, a distance of no more than 400 metres. Daniel could get lost going to his bedroom; frequent were the times he would call, in a panic but laughing, on an apparently straightforward car journey.

Daniel and I hit a few tennis balls on the drive after chemo one day. It was gentle stuff, but Daniel loved feeling the ball on the racquet. The hope of playing tennis again one day sustained him, I think. Watching a test match at Lord's against Sri Lanka provided another antidote to chemo.

Daniel went back to Oxford for the final week of term and had a wonderful time. We were so pleased. He demonstrated unsuspected initiative by organising a group of friends to see the Oxford Revue and its Cambridge and Durham counterparts at the Oxford Playhouse. He went punting. He was concerned about the risk of infection to his PICC line if he fell in – not unknown with student punting, especially post-exams and peri-alcohol. We said he should go for it. He was touched when his friends clubbed together to buy him an iPod. I suspect that, at times, he felt disengaged from his friends and all they were doing, so this affirmation that he was still part of their circle must have been comforting.

A week later he played in the swing band at a summer ball and in July went to the Magdalen ball, making it to the survivors' photo at six in the morning, as he had two years earlier. This time it was more of an achievement, given where his health had reached.

He was honoured to be at Magdalen and pleased, I think, when Mum and I attended Evensong one Sunday. When Mum said she felt privileged, he replied 'So you should!' On other occasions, he was a proud guide to his cousin Holly and her Mum, my sister Sian, and to Tobias from Germany.

Compassionate use

Towards the end of June, Daniel began to experience a high heart rate. Various tests, including at the London Heart Hospital, proved negative, but was it a portent of things to come?

The symptoms eased and once again, he responded well to chemo, so much so that towards the end of June, Colin mused about moving him onto a low-dose regime, despite his doubts before the latest relapse.

And there was more promising news. Colin told me that Pfizer, the drug company, were going to release figitumumab, their IGF inhibitor, for serious Ewing's cases on a compassionate use basis.

Compassionate use is where a company is prepared to give a drug to a patient who doesn't qualify for a clinical trial and there is no full licence. Usually it's for seriously ill patients who are out of options. Pfizer had decided not to proceed with figitumumab, because the results weren't good enough, but trials were continuing for patients doing well.

I had kept abreast of developments with IGF inhibitors. I knew that they weren't a silver bullet. Most Ewing's patients didn't respond at all. Durable responses were only around 2 per cent. In any other situation, a 2 per cent chance would be regarded as derisory, not worth considering – and it wasn't even a 2 per cent chance of a cure, only of a response as short as six months. But in our situation, you latch onto anything. At the outset, Daniel's chances of surviving for five years were probably less than 2 per cent. But he had survived for five years.

By this time I had come across Debbie Binner whose daughter Chloë, a delightful and spirited teenager, was at UCH. Strangely, Debbie and I 'met' via a Ewing's support group in the US. Debbie told me about Peter, another Ewing's patient, a couple of years older than Daniel and from Plymouth, who was doing well on figitumumab. He had relapsed twice and his prognosis had seemed grim. I also read about a multiple-relapse Ewing's patient in the US who had been on IGF inhibitors for over five years. These were rare cases, but the important point was that they existed.

Enrique de Alava in Salamanca, supportive as ever, had arranged with a leading Ewing's lab researcher in Italy to analyse Daniel's tumour, to help establish if it would be responsive to the inhibitors. The science was in its infancy but there seemed to be some reason to believe that Daniel's tumour was of a favourable profile. The analysis might yet prove useful if we had a fight – even a legal fight – to get Daniel the drug.

There were still plenty of other options I was looking at, both conventional and complementary, but with each there were either safety concerns, insufficient evidence of benefit or quality of life issues. The evidence since IGF inhibitors were last prominent on my radar screen was they still seemed pretty safe. Peter, indeed, was working and taking accountancy exams.

There was a moral dilemma, which I discussed with Petra and Debbie. Should we alert other Ewing's parents? We knew supply of figitumumab was limited – Pfizer appeared to have a small quota for each country. We agreed it was better to be open. Although I was confident that we would get figitumumab for Daniel if Pfizer released it, no patient should have to compete with other patients for potentially life-saving treatment.

In early August after a special blood test, Sandra Strauss, standing in for Colin, secured Pfizer's agreement that Daniel have figitumumab and persuaded them to give it with another type of inhibitor, mTOR, as I had asked. They were not willing to combine with low-dose chemo, but this was progress (I discuss more about compassionate use in Annex B).

Sandra thought that figitumumab would be available for Daniel in around three weeks, which would tie in with his irinotecan/temoz cycle. She seemed to be really trying, and negotiating effectively.

* * *

This positive development pushed Coley's down the pecking order. I had already been to Norfolk to meet Henry Mannings, who'd begun to administer the toxins. Henry was a GP but lectured at the University of East Anglia about cancer and has worked at a cancer hospital. He'd set up a charity promoting an integrative approach to cancer. Prominent on Star Throwers' website is the story, told by the anthropologist Loren Eiseley, of the man who comes across a young boy throwing stranded starfish back into the sea. 'What can you hope to achieve?' the man asked, 'there are hundreds of beached starfish.' The child picks up another starfish, throws it back in the water and replied: 'I made a difference to that one.'

I love that philosophy and had used the story in a talk. It reminds me of the political philosopher Edmund Burke's aphorism, which I shared with Daniel more than once: 'Nobody made a greater mistake than he who didn't do anything because he could do only a little.'

I immediately took to Henry. He was friendly,

thoroughly dedicated to helping people with cancer, keen to impart information. I was able to share some information with him, too, which he lapped up. When I said that Daniel trusted me with decisions, Henry generously said that he would too.

By this time I had learnt that Daniel didn't qualify for the trial in Frankfurt – his tumour didn't have a protein called NY-ESO – but I wasn't too concerned because Henry now had a supply of Coley's toxins, albeit a different kind.

I had been speaking to researchers in the UK, Italy and Israel about tumour necrosis factors, cytokines which can cause cell death. TNF seemed to be linked to Coley's mechanism of action. I was encouraged that there was hard science around the toxins, even if it was poorly understood. A scientist at Queen Mary's in London was looking specifically at Coley's. David Wallach, a professor at the Weizmann Institute of Science in Israel, was especially helpful and opened his email: 'I kept thinking of your [email] since receiving it yesterday, trying to see what advice I could give you.'

Henry was treating his first three patients with Coley's (none of them Ewing's). The treatment wasn't easy even for someone less seriously ill. Henry described it like a really bad dose of flu, though the worse symptoms lasted only for a few hours. Conversely, the toxins could be an effective analgesia. Henry thought it was definitely the right thing to get Daniel back on chemo. The less disease there was, the more chance the Coley's had of working.

Henry wanted to meet Daniel. We went in early July, after I'd spoken to the Canadian manufacturers of the toxins for some background information. Henry was as kind with

Daniel as I knew he would be. There was no guarantee that Coley's would work, he explained, but he was a big fan and it worked best with sarcomas and Ewing's in particular. He found other optimistic noises to make.

Despite this, Daniel found the visit difficult. He was upset to meet a young patient with advanced bowel cancer and at Henry's remark that chemo rarely cured. Daniel worried that Henry might be too radical, a comment that surprised me. I assured him that, in my judgement, his oncology knowledge was excellent and he was a careful doctor, albeit a creative one. The debrief came to a sudden halt, when I noticed in my rear mirror smoke billowing out of the exhaust. Daniel took one look and implored me: 'Dad, let me out!' By this time, the bonnet was smoking as well. Fortunately there was a layby at hand and we pulled in there, with smoke everywhere. I called the fire brigade. Embarrassingly, the smoke (or was it steam?) had pretty much died down by the time they arrived. The car was a write-off and later became my first eBay sale.

Daniel agreed I could tell the AA about his illness but even so it was three hours before they picked us up. It was 11pm by the time we got home. Daniel still wanted his wheatgrass juice.

It was the day that Rupert Murdoch announced the closure of the *News of the World,* after the phone-hacking scandal. I was sorry in light of the paper's important undercover investigations (amidst not so worthy journalism). Daniel later sent JJ a text: 'Please leave a message and the NoW will call you back.'

A week after our visit to Norfolk, Henry told me that he was giving up on Coley's. It's highly labour-intensive and he found it emotionally draining too, given disappointing results. But, shortly afterwards, he agreed to give Coley's to Daniel subcutaneously, which would be much easier than intravenously.

I had in fact come across a patient in the UK using subcutaneous Coley's, Pauline Clark. It was one of those strange coincidences. Pauline is a friend of my friend Robin. Pauline seemed to be just about the only person on Coley's at that time. Amazingly, she was a patient at UCH under Dr Seddon, whom we had met on ward rounds. Pauline was diagnosed with leiomyosarcoma in 2008. She had refused chemo, offered to her on a palliative basis only and instead went to the Issels Clinic in Mexico, which claims expertise in sarcomas. The Issels is one of the many integrative cancer centres just south of the US border, out of reach of the Food and Drug Administration. Josef Issels was a German who had used innovative cancer treatments. I had spoken to his son, Ralf, a leading hyperthermia practitioner in Germany.

Pauline had a variety of treatments at the Issels, including dendritic cell vaccine (which I had discussed with Dagmar Dilloo in Bonn in 2010) and had just started taking wheatgrass juice. However, she attributed her remarkable progress to the Coley's. She wasn't cured, but there had been a marked shrinkage in the size of her tumour. Pauline told me that Dr Seddon had been 'gobsmacked' at the effect of her treatment and asked for details for another sarcoma patient.

I was also reading about unexplained recoveries from cancer. There is a well-recognised phenomenon called spontaneous remission (or regression), where a patient does far better than expected and the doctors cannot explain why. Often there is a cure, other times the patient is in remission for much longer than statistics would suggest. At one time, the medical profession was sceptical about spontaneous remission, putting apparent recovery down to misdiagnosis. In the days when cancer diagnosis was rudimentary, that was an understandable reaction perhaps, but now that diagnostic techniques are far better – if still far from perfect – that get-out for the closed medical mind is not available.

But still little attention is paid to the phenomenon – too little, I thought. If someone's cancer suddenly disappears in a way that defies conventional wisdom, therein may lie vital clues to the pathology of that type of cancer. But the response of most oncologists is to shrug the shoulders: 'We just don't understand why this happens.' Perhaps the incidence is just too rare – one in a million cases or one in ten million, depending on how one defines spontaneous remission – to merit research attention.

A German epidemiologist has found a significant correlation between spontaneous remission and bacterial infection. This would tie in with the case of the seventeen year-old Japanese boy I mentioned earlier and with the apparent success of Coley's toxins, which consist of killed bacteria.

Michaele, my friend in Germany, recommended a book called *Remarkable Recoveries*. It does indeed contain some remarkable case-studies, with positive thinking a recurrent theme. Even more remarkably, two of the case-studies were of Ewing's patients, confirming the impression that, for some reason, Ewing's seems particularly susceptible to spontaneous remission, albeit that the incidence is extremely rare.

For a young Sicilian girl, Delizia Cirolli, one of the cases discussed, prognosis was dismal and the family and wider community prepared for her death, in the way only Italian families can. But Delizia went to Lourdes and got better. This was in 1976. At the time *Remarkable Recoveries* was written, in 1995, Delizia was the latest of those Lourdes pilgrims whom the Catholic Church accepted as a bona fide miracle. The list was only twenty-five long. That seemed remarkable restraint by the Church, given the millions of sick pilgrims who have been to Lourdes. It appears to investigate cases thoroughly and to recognise the distinction between recoveries which are unexplained on the basis of current medical knowledge and those which are inexplicable in human terms. A sceptic would no doubt put everything into the unexplained category and assume that the unexplained will one day become explained.

It seemed astonishing that one of the few Lourdes 'miracles' – the inverted commas are a matter for personal taste – was a Ewing's patient. True, if one accepts that there had, up to then, been twenty-five Lourdes miracles, they have to be from some disease or other, so why not Ewing's? But, as the parent of a seriously ill Ewing's sufferer, it still struck home. Another of the twenty-five also had a sarcoma. I don't know what sort, but like Daniel's the patient's originated in the pelvis, so it could well have been Ewing's.

Michaele who had breast cancer, wanted us to accompany her to Lourdes. I certainly thought about it. My worry was the message that this would give Daniel – that he needed a miracle. On our trip to see Henry, I explained the background. 'So you want to take me to Lourdes now?' he asked. 'I will if you want me to', I replied.

My response was lame because Daniel looked to us for direction. I rationalised that, if God wanted Daniel to get better, he could cure him in Chobham. Why did we need to go to Lourdes? But perhaps I was too rational, or perhaps not rational enough. Debbie, from Irish Catholic stock, wanted to take her daughter Chloë to Lourdes but didn't think she would agree. She knew of another UCH patient who had been immersed in water there (I don't know what happened to his cancer).

Pain once more

Through all this Daniel was still experiencing pain. There seemed to be a pattern: after a few days of a new chemo cycle, the pain would subside but then return during week three, when he was not getting chemo. In mid-July 2011, I wrote to Colin asking whether Daniel could have low-dose chemo during week three, even if that necessitated reducing the dose during weeks one and two. He didn't reply.

Despite worsening pain and shortness of breath, in early August Daniel visited the library in Oxford, and Crystal Palace with Sasha and Florence to watch athletics. Sadly he was too exhausted the next morning to see Katie and Annabel. Katie was home after eight months, latterly holidaying in South America (including cycling down the infamous Road of Death in Bolivia: she told her parents only later).

It was the time of the London riots. It was awful to see people behave in this feral way, whatever genuine grievances some had.

But it was Daniel I worried about most. Our world was

closing in on us. With Daniel convinced the cancer was back yet again, I felt beaten down. In his autobiography, Rafa Nadal describes his long period of depression when a toe injury threatened his career. He feared 'tennis death.' How I wished that tennis death was the only variety Daniel faced.

Like many I have striven, at times more successfully than others, to view what's happening in my life in a wider context. It helps for tolerance of other people's perceived failings and of my own real ones and is a necessary corrective to self-obsession. By any objective measure, I knew I was more fortunate than most. One might think that faced with a life-threatening illness to one's child, little else - good or bad - would matter. Grave situations certainly sharpen perspective and I read many comments by cancer parents that normal preoccupations now took a back seat and they were grateful for it; they found irritating the priorities of 'normal' parents, the priorities they themselves had once possessed.

But my experience was that this was only partly true. The things that would have irritated me before – small things – continued to irritate me, if perhaps for shorter. And the things which gave pleasure before continued to do so, albeit overshadowed by the dark cloud which forever hung above. When Daniel was diagnosed, I would jokingly tell people, in a conscious echo of Steve Redgrave's famous remark on winning his fourth Olympic rowing gold medal: 'If anyone hears me complain about anything in future, you have permission to shoot me.' But I knew even as I said it that I would still worry about inconsequential matters, still allow my blood pressure to edge up in traffic jams. It's one thing to know that the trick is to wedge open narrow perspective, another to manage the trick.

As Daniel had settled in at Oxford, news came that at least ninety children had died in a school in Haiti. It brought back childhood memories of Aberfan, where 120 primary schoolchildren were crushed by a toxic combination of an unstable coal heap and bureaucratic indifference. A few years ago, I visited the cemetery, scarred by too many tombstones for eight and nine year olds. As a curate, my maternal grandfather had buried most of the 439 miners – many younger than Daniel – killed in the Senghenydd disaster in 1913, the starkest of reminders of the fragility of life and the seeming arbitrariness of it all. That fragility and that arbitrariness were constant companions on Daniel's cancer journey.

Fast forward to the summer of 2011, I found a woman slumped in a London churchyard. 'I don't have a home and you should go to yours, if you have one', she told me, bitterly. 'No one cares.' I rang social services and hoped that they did. Another victim of life's vicissitudes, barely visible to society. I realised that so many led difficult lives.

But still Daniel dominated my thoughts. How to avoid self-absorption in the midst of evolving personal tragedy? I had no blueprint for the weeks I knew lay ahead.

Countdown

Dad: *Do you like it when Mummy is on mothers' duty in school?*
Daniel (aged four): *No, because I can't do so many things*

In retrospect, the countdown had begun.

Saturday 13 August 2011
Petra, too, seemed beaten down, hardly surprisingly. But we all went to the World Badminton Championships at Wembley, with the British pair, Imogen Banker and Chris Adcock unexpectedly reaching the mixed-doubles final. Daniel was in buoyant mood.

Sunday 14 August
A fellow dog-walker told me a friend's cancer had spread to her brain – she was thirty-five with two kids. At lunchtime,

Daniel wanted me over straightaway: Petra and the girls had left for a short camping break in Wales. He was not at all well and spiked a temperature. He was semi doubled-over through the pain. Thinking aloud in despair, I asked him what he thought was going on, as though he could give me any comfort. He got irritated with me, rightly so.

UCH needed an anaesthetist to get the cannula in for bloods, so weak were Daniel's veins after so many draws. The chest x-ray was ok but he was tachycardic and shivery. Jo the nurse said I could stay but Daniel was concerned about my dog Jess, on her own for a long time.

Monday 15 August
Jo rang first thing to say Daniel was ok, a thoughtful gesture. He later had bouts of diarrhoea. He was pretty miserable and ate little. There was a fight in the corridor involving a patient. It broke up the afternoon but Daniel, the opposite of macho, hated it. All life is laid bare in hospital. The staff dealt with the incident well.

Tuesday 16 August
Today brought yet more bad news. The CT scan showed new cancer in Daniel's left lung with a slight thickening of the pleura. There was less cancer than in May. But I knew that what mattered was that the cancer was back (in truth it had never gone away). The chemo was no longer working. Daniel questioned me closely but I was vague with him until I gathered my thoughts.

A mother on the teenage cancer ward said to Daniel: 'My son looked like you a year ago. It will get better.' She probably thought Daniel had just started chemo. I'm not sure what message it gave him. Back in his room he did some work, asked me to read career leaflets and discussed (for the umpteenth time) what options he should take next year. Was there going to be a next year, I wondered silently.

Petra was back from the Gower. Daniel roared with laughter when she related that she'd missed a green light through stroking Jess and then stalled, so that no car got through. It was just wonderful to see him laugh. His pain was better and he had no diarrhoea.

Daniel was discharged that evening, always a cause for celebration. 'Am I now an animal lover?', he asked. He was careful to say that he loved Jess, Sweep and Puzzle (the two cats) equally, though there was no doubt who was now his favourite. Jess had a whale of a time in the Gower, probably her first experience of camping.

The irony was that now that Daniel had visible cancer, he should be eligible for figitumumab, the IGF inhibitor. In the mad world of experimental cancer treatment, a little visible disease is better than no visible disease. Sandra Strauss hoped that Daniel would be able to start treatment within a couple of weeks. Two weeks seemed an eternity and I asked whether Daniel could at least start on Rapamycin (sirolimus), the mTOR inhibitor, straightaway, to try to keep things in check. No reflection on Sandra, but Daniel said he wanted Colin to remain his main doctor.

Wednesday 17 August
I slept fitfully. Daniel's pain was very bad. He wasn't able to do anything and described the situation as 'annoying', typical Daniel understatement. Had I seen the CT report? He was anxious that I shouldn't be away from home too long.

Thursday 18 August

Daniel listened to *Test Match Special* on the radio and watched Wales play Argentina at rugby. He noted that the Welsh centre, Jonathan Davies, whom Annabel had just started going out with, wasn't having a great game.

Friday 19 August

Charlotte and Katie told Mum the cancer was back. There was no point trying to hide anything now. Daniel was downbeaten in the evening. I tried to reassure him and suggested seeing Brazil play Ghana at Wembley in a couple of weeks. Petra was feeding him on the sofa.

Saturday 20 August

Petra rang at 11.50pm. Daniel had acute pain in his right chest and had difficulty breathing. He wanted me to call 999 – that was a first. At A&E at St Peter's - familiar territory for us - Rachel, an SHO from Skipton initially diagnosed a pulmonary embolism. A PE had killed a girl in Annabel's year a few weeks earlier and nearly killed Serena Williams, the tennis player. Rachel took a blood gas reading, a painful procedure. This measures the amount of oxygen in the blood.

Something showed up in his right chest. The senior doctors changed the hypothesis to sepsis. But this had all the hallmarks of rampant cancer to me. Daniel's breathing was shallow. 'Is it safe for me to go to sleep?' he asked - gut-wrenching to hear. At 3am he wanted to play cards. He needed a wheelchair to get to the car.

Sunday 21 August

'If it's not a PE causing the pain, what could it be?' Daniel asked. When I talked gently about the cancer being back, a look of real concern washed over his face. 'I might not want to come to see Colin tomorrow in that case', he said. I hoped he wouldn't, but didn't say so. 'Dan, whatever it is we'll get you through this – there have been so many twists and turns.' I didn't convince myself and I doubt I convinced him.

Monday 22 August

Daniel decided he would come to see Colin. He felt rough so was given a side-room, next to the main waiting-room in the Rosenheim. He was struggling to walk.

This was Colin's first day back after his summer holiday. Tanya, an oncologist from Canada, was with him. He asked Daniel lots of questions and examined him but said little. That was a good thing because his thoughts were probably not ones Daniel wanted to hear. IGF was a reasonable option, he told Daniel. I had learnt that 'reasonable option' in the advanced cancer world is a euphemism for 'We don't have any answers, treatment x makes some biological sense, but we don't expect it to work for long.' But it had a positive enough ring for Daniel.

I have a clear recollection of the exchange that followed:

Me (to Daniel): 'Dan, I have some questions for Colin about IGF while you stay here, ok?'
Colin (interjecting): 'I have nothing more to say about IGF'
Me: 'Well, I have a couple of questions'
Colin (impatiently): 'It will have to be quick because I have lots of patients to see'

I was furious with him. He was too busy apparently to answer questions about the treatment in which Daniel – all of us – was investing such little hope as remained. Colin wasn't rude to Daniel and I didn't particularly care about him being rude to me, even though he must have realised, if he'd stopped to think, that Petra and I were under huge strain as well. But I cared very much about the message he was giving Daniel. Goodness knows what Tanya thought. Presumably she had come to learn how oncology was practised in the UK.

As we walked down the corridor to Colin's room, I vowed to stay for as long as it took to answer my questions. And we did. Not that things got much better. Petra asked Colin how long it would take for the IGF to come through. Colin's reply was: 'It shouldn't take weeks. We're in the hands of Pfizer.' There was no sense of urgency, no thought of putting pressure on the company. It brought back memories of my battle for IGF in 2008. Again, the message was: you just have to accept whatever the company decides. Except I was not prepared to. At least Colin said Daniel was clinically ready for figitumumab. I asked about an mTOR inhibitor in the meantime.

Colin thought that the pain on Daniel's right was cancer, maybe in the fluid. There might be an effusion.

Petra and I went to see Daniel, smiles on our faces as ever. Yes, Colin thought the pleural thickening was probably cancer, I told Daniel. 'The chemo hasn't worked then?', Daniel asked. 'It has but it has stopped working', I replied. 'I'm excited about the IGF – it's more targeted and Ewing's-specific than chemo', I continued, trying to sound upbeat. Daniel was sceptical: 'Are there other options if this doesn't work?' 'Yes there are, plus Coley's.' It was clear he didn't have much confidence in Coley's.

Melanie had a long chat with him: 'I have patients on much higher pain relief than you.' I wasn't sure that telling Daniel his pain could get much worse was the right approach, but she was trying to reassure. It was important, she explained, that he was up and about as much as possible.

At home Daniel did some filing, of all things. He was disorganised with his paperwork. But filing meant that he was thinking about his studies and that was good, even though he told Petra he was concerned that things weren't working. Petra and I agreed that we'd only mention the left pleura, because Daniel knew that that was a problematical area. We didn't want him to realise the cancer was more extensive.

Tuesday 23 August
I was awake for a long time in the night, angry at Colin. Perhaps it helped divert my worry about Daniel. Daniel had an ok night. He was concerned that I didn't dry Jess properly when it rained.

Lang Lang, the brilliant Chinese pianist, was due to play the Beethoven piano concertos in London in March 2012. We discussed which Daniel would like to hear. I doubted he would get there, but that wasn't the point of the discussion.

I had a frustrating time trying to get through to Pfizer, manufacturers of figitumumab. An employee in the US said she would pray for Daniel. The founder of the Abigail Alliance, which campaigns for access to experimental drugs for seriously ill patients in the US, was helpful, too.

Daniel's pain was worse by the evening and he was

anxious to get going on the figitumumab. He asked for his wheatgrass. I had still not heard from Colin about an mTOR as monotherapy, so I sent him an email. I showed a draft to Petra. She knew how angry I was about yesterday's clinic appointment and worried that Colin would refuse to treat Daniel if I was too critical. But she was happy with the draft. After discussing mTOR, I wrote:

'*More generally, I wanted to convey that we are not happy about communication over the past few months. I'm explaining this because we want to have a candid and positive relationship with you. When I wrote to you and Anna in early April, on the fifth anniversary of Daniel's diagnosis, thanking you for getting him this far, I meant it. But there has been a marked deterioration since.*' [After mentioning Colin's failure to follow-up the low-dose chemo option with the Barcelona and Marseilles doctors and reply to my suggestion of LDC in week 3 of a cycle, I continued]:

'*I was very angry at your reaction when I said to Daniel yesterday that I had some questions for you. After interjecting that you had nothing more to say about IGF you said that I would have to be quick because you had patients waiting. It's simply unacceptable for a desperately ill young man like Daniel or his parents to be made to feel that they are trespassing on your time or that of other patients. Daniel has just relapsed for the umpteenth time and has been in very considerable pain. He is very scared. Of course we had questions – about the significance of the pain, future treatment options (if any), which mTOR inhibitor, side-effects etc. – and we should not have been made to feel guilty about asking them. You had only been with Daniel for around fifteen to twenty minutes. We have often been kept waiting for a couple of hours or longer (that is not a complaint). I appreciate that it might be tiresome for you that Daniel refuses to discuss anything touching on prognosis or treatment options and that meetings therefore sometimes have to be split into two, but that is the way he wants things.*

I freely acknowledge Colin that you have been very generous over the years with your time and that I probably ask more questions than most parents and quite often challenge advice (to satisfy myself as best I can that we are getting the very best). This simply reflects the seriousness of Daniel's condition from day one. I appreciate that you have lots of patients, some of them no doubt as ill as Daniel and that there are many demands on your time, no doubt reflecting the reputation you have built up. But we are clearly at a critical stage. We understand the reality, but we are not ready to give up on Daniel and I'm sure that you are not either. We are determined to squeeze every last drop of potential out of treatment, which is why we are so concerned at the present treatment gap...

*Best wishes
David.'*

Perhaps I should have just focused on his behaviour yesterday, but the frustration I had been feeling for some months was welling up. This was the first time I had made a complaint about Daniel's care and even now it was to Colin rather than about him (Daniel asked me once not to complain about Colin following some incident, but I had never wanted to.)

I asked for an urgent reply but didn't expect one quite so quickly. I sent my email at 11.37pm. Colin replied at 11.54pm:

'Dear David
I am sorry that you are finding aspects of Daniels care unsatisfactory. I and everyone will try to rectify that. We have had an email this evening to say that the drug [figitumumab] should be delivered to UCH tomorrow. I have been at an outside clinic all day but have sent a message to book slots in daycare for Daniel for Thursday and Friday. I will be able to follow this up when I get back to UCH tomorrow. I think this addresses the issue of immediately introducing an mTor inhibitor. Had we heard nothing today then I had planned to contact you tomorrow to pursue this as it's a perfectly reasonable suggestion… I have been back from leave for three days and done three large clinics. I haven't been able to answer all messages and emails at the same time. However, I completely apologise that I was rude and dismissive on Monday. That was unacceptable.
Colin'

The response to the general complaints felt formulaic

– 'I'm sorry that you are finding aspects of Daniels care unsatisfactory' – but the apology for his behaviour the previous day seemed genuine. I admire anyone who is big enough to apologise; saying sorry is a sign of strength not weakness. I did wonder why I was having to make treatment suggestions (mTOR as monotherapy) but a conciliatory response felt right:

> *'Dear Colin*
> *Many thanks for your prompt reply. I accept your apology, of course. And I fully understand the pressure that you are under - not just from what seems from the outside an unreasonable workload but also through constantly having to confront seriously ill children and young adults, which must be incredibly emotionally taxing. Your commitment is not in doubt. Anyway, let's put this behind us. We'll await confirmation from UCH that we should bring Daniel to daycare tomorrow.*
> *Best wishes*
> *David'*

Wednesday 24 August

I also had an apology from Sandra Strauss this morning. I wasn't expecting that (like London buses, you wait for ages for one apology from a UCH doctor …) and didn't think it was needed. She had made several calls that morning; IGF would start tomorrow. We discussed analgesia and she seemed genuinely concerned about Daniel. I asked her not to discuss prognosis when consenting him.

Daniel was pleased about the IGF but sounded down and wanted to know when I would be back from London.

Maria, my Nicaragua friend and her family were sure this was a God-sent opportunity. All her Facebook friends, even people she didn't know, were praying for Daniel.

I realised I was investing hope in something with only a small chance of working. But that smidgeon was so important for all of us. In the evening, I contacted someone about Traditional Chinese Medicine in Serbia, a new country on my list.

Daniel watched *Toy Story 2* yet again and heard he was on a long shortlist to carry the Olympic Torch.

Meanwhile, in the world outside, Colonel Gaddafi was about to fall.

Thursday 25 August
For the first cycle, Daniel would have figitumumab for two days. He seemed to assume it would work and was more worried about not doing a thesis by the end of the holidays.

His face was red, maybe as a result of the increased pain relief. He took a photo with his mobile phone so that they wouldn't think later this was the IGF - he didn't want to stop treatment! He was technically an in-patient but would be allowed to stay at Paul's House provided he followed some rules.

Daniel asked Sandra to feel around the drain scar from his pleurodesis. He was concerned about a swelling. Sandra told me separately that it was asymmetrical: the left side of the chest was out of sync with the right side. The swelling could be the drain scar or the cancer growing, she said. I assumed cancer and so did Daniel. He thought it had grown over the past two to three weeks, perhaps even since the beginning of the week. Not a good start but I told myself that it all depended on the figitumumab. A relatively small growth shouldn't matter.

Daniel had no shortness of breath despite climbing three flights of stairs and his weight was pretty good. He asked me to read information about careers in international development and academia. He was frustrated about not being able to do voluntary work and internships which could help him onto the career ladder and not being able to travel.

While making food for Daniel I had a chat with a student from Uzbekistan. He had leukaemia and was waiting for a bone marrow donor. His parents had been over but now he was on his own. Imagine having cancer as a youngster far from home. I gave him my mobile number.

Daniel was proud of Florence for doing so well in her GCSEs, as he'd been proud of Sasha with her A levels a week earlier. The girls, too, were under enormous pressure, even if they didn't realise the full seriousness of Daniel's condition and it's a real tribute to them that they continued with their school work and whole host of extracurricular activities, including the Duke of Edinburgh awards scheme. Daniel was looking forward to having Sasha with him in Oxford, especially during his final year when his friends would have left.

Friday 26 August

Daniel woke me at 5.30, in agony. He was thrashing around. I'd rarely seen him like this. It was so distressing to witness. He topped up with OxyNorm and the pain subsided quite quickly. We watched quiz programmes until it was time to go to UCH for round 2 of figitumumab.

Daniel seemed particularly vulnerable and didn't want me to leave him. He was sullen with me but rude to Petra and Sasha later. He became frustrated waiting over an hour for a porter and smashed his bleep down on the wheelchair. This was so out of character. What was causing it? Was it the earlier pain episode? The strong painkillers? The steroids? Did he think he was dying? Were over five years of frustration spilling over?

Debbie, Chloë's Mum, later texted that he was smiling coming out of the lift with Sasha. His mood, with his pain, was fluctuating but even on a really bad day his default position was positive. Debbie had never met him but guessed he was my son from the eyes. Sasha was adept at cheering Daniel up and Debbie remarked how attentive she was.

However tough things were for us in a London hospital, they were much worse in a Tripoli hospital where there was a terrible massacre. Such unforgivable savagery.

Daniel was in terrible pain when he got home. He couldn't bear the thought of weeks more of this.

One of Mum's friends Joan Orchard, had arranged a prayer for Daniel at her chapel. I picked up the *Big Issue*, something I only occasionally do and did the crossword. One of the vertical answers was 'orchard' and the horizontal answer beginning with the 'd' of 'orchard' was 'dad.' I wanted to believe it was more than a coincidence.

Saturday 27 August
I slept well. Daniel was scared to death that the new treatment wasn't working. Colin emailed that, from the CT scan, there was cancer in Daniel's right lung. The report of the scan itself talked only of disease in the right pleura. Contradictory

information like this was becoming the norm.

Sunday 28 August
Daniel was up much of the night watching the athletics from Daegu, Japan. In the afternoon I sent several emails to doctors about temsirolimus, the alternative mTOR inhibitor to sirolimus: I'd heard it was a better option. Daniel's pain was better. Could this possibly be a response to the IGF/ mTOR? The only problem, he said, was that his heart raced on mild exertion. Soon his pulse was 130-140 when resting, pretty high.

AT UCH, Daniel was given oxygen. This was ominous. I knew oxygen was sometimes given as temporary respite for an acute problem, but had noticed that moving onto oxygen was a seminal moment in the final decline of sarcoma patients. We watched highlights of Man United beating Arsenal 8:2, an extraordinary result. Our SHO, an Arsenal fan, thought Daniel had an infection.

Neither of us slept much: the hospital plumbing kept us company and much worse, Daniel had a terrible hacking cough. Each splutter was a dagger in my heart. I knew this wasn't good.

Monday 29 August
But this morning Daniel was reasonably well, despite pain all over his back and we had another discussion about careers. 'Do I have an effusion?' he asked. I knew I was only allowed to answer in the negative, so kept quiet.

As Petra took over, I went to the office to prepare for a forthcoming case. A doctor, ignoring Daniel's expressed wish, told him he had fluid on his right lung. Daniel was vulnerable and looked awful in the early evening.

We had an unexpected conversation about his sperm taken at diagnosis (chemo can make one sterile). He told me they had asked whether a partner could use the sperm if he died. I don't know what was on his mind. (They had collected enough sperm for three infusions and Daniel had asked: 'Does this mean that I will be able to have three children?' We laughed, but there was logic to the question).

We watched *100 Best Gadgets*, hosted by the ubiquitous Stephen Fry. Number one, bizarrely, was the cigarette lighter. Daniel began struggling for breath and quickly became the centre of medical attention. The three nurses exuded calm efficiency, but it was obvious this was an emergency. Daniel's oxygen was raised from 3 to 12 and then 15 and he had to wear a mask for greater efficiency. That made him feel claustrophobic. He was scared and so was I; several times I thought we might be losing him. It was nearly the anniversary of my dad's death from cancer. Could this be cruel symmetry?

I rang Petra for her to come up. Daniel wanted to text her while she was en route to say he was ok.

Still in the early hours, two nurses from ICU came to assess the situation. Teach, senior of the two, brought a lightness of touch which was much needed. Daniel's oxygen remained high but things calmed down by 3am, so Petra went home.

Now we had a randomly bleeping machine to contend with. Each time the nurse came in, it had stopped: 'Well I can't hear anything', she said the last time, as though she didn't believe us. 'Well, we're hardly likely to make it up?', I responded, a bit sharply. It was a reasonable debating point but when she left Daniel told me off. I was proud that even in extremis he was maintaining his standards, even if mine were falling.

Tuesday 30 August

I apologised to the nurse in the morning. She wasn't gracious.

If the night had been awful, the morning was simply dreadful. Daniel's oxygen was low and his heart rate high. He was short of breath, and frightened. 'Am I going to be ok?' he asked, once again. He was crying. He was worried they wouldn't be able to address his breathing problem - I'm not sure he was even thinking about cancer. The ICU nurses came round again. I broke down talking to them in the corridor.

An oncology registrar thought Daniel probably had pneumonia. His right lung had collapsed. Pneumonia for him was life-threatening. I wanted him to have pneumonia. Pneumonia might be reversible; aggressively growing cancer, I knew, was not.

There was a short respite while we played cards and watched TV, before Dr Sohal an ICU registrar, came in quickly followed by Colin McMaster. We weren't expecting Colin. He let Dr Sohal have control of the examination. Dr Sohal explained that it was a marginal decision whether to move Daniel to ICU. He then went outside for a chat with Colin. I should have followed but didn't.

Colin returned. At first the conversation was jovial – well, as jovial as it could be in these circumstances. 'Were the steroids helping?' Colin wondered. 'Not really', Daniel replied. Colin looked disappointed. 'That's the wrong answer', I joked. 'Would I have a room by myself in ICU?' Daniel wanted to know, probably naively. Colin smiled. 'Yes and a flat-screen TV please', I chimed in, trying to keep the mood light. It didn't work. Colin started talking about Daniel possibly needing a graduation of breathing assistance, culminating in a ventilator. He would have to be involved in some decisions, he explained, and ICU wouldn't admit him without a clear steer about what to do under particular scenarios. Daniel began to get agitated and Colin noted that he was, but he didn't stop. I should have intervened to protect Daniel, as I had done so many times. It all happened so quickly and I had barely slept for two nights, but I offer no excuses. I let Daniel down. 'Can I have diazepam to ease my anxiety', Daniel wanted to know. 'No', Colin explained, 'because it could affect your breathing.'

I left with Colin to continue the conversation in a side-room. I knew what was coming. I had been dreading it ever since Daniel was diagnosed. 'Daniel has rampant, incurable cancer', he said, 'and you're going to have to make some decisions as a family.' He didn't buy the pneumonia hypothesis. He thought the overnight x-ray showed cancer rather than an infection, although there could be an infection as well. There was cancer in both lungs and both pleura. The planned ultrasound would tell us more.

And then came the words which drove deep into my soul: 'Daniel might only have a few hours.' I just hadn't anticipated that things would deteriorate so quickly. He wasn't saying the IGF and mTOR were not working, but would they work quickly enough? Sometimes they did work quickly. We should keep with the mTOR, he thought, contradicting the registrar. So he wasn't withdrawing treatment. That was something.

I asked about the pros and cons of going on a ventilator. 'I wouldn't advise it', Colin said. 'Is it painful?' I asked. 'No, but it's not a dignified way to die', came the reply. I didn't think Daniel would care too much about dignity, which often is really about the sensibilities of onlookers. There was no time-limit as such for being on a ventilator, Colin continued, but other organs would begin to break down.

I assured Colin: 'I have never supported life for life's sake and am a strong believer in voluntary euthanasia.' I meant it, but knew acknowledging defeat with Daniel would be so hard.

As was the pattern during difficult discussions, Colin was purely functional, patiently answering my questions but expressing no emotion. This must be the worst part of a doctor's job.

I had somehow managed to keep my own emotions in reasonable check during the discussion. But I was shaken to the core of my being. I might be about to lose my precious Daniel, that very day. Even if not, he clearly had little time left. I had twenty seconds to compose myself, walking back to his room. I failed. As soon as I saw him, I broke down. Thinking quickly, I said: 'Dan, it's because I love you so much and don't like to see you suffer.' The reply was pure Daniel: 'You're making me angry now, Dad, you're annoying me.'

He'd been anxious anyway but Colin's earlier comments had made him worse. I simply have no idea why he thought it was appropriate to talk to Daniel about ventilators. Daniel knew exactly what that meant. Just six days earlier in my complaint email, I had reminded Colin, yet again, that Daniel didn't want any discussion about prognosis and yet here he was ignoring his patient's wishes. If I'm to be charitable, perhaps he thought that with end-of-life decisions, the patient has to be involved. But the correct approach would still have been to take Petra and me aside and let us broach things with Daniel. I was really angry with Colin and began seriously to muse about asking a QC specialising in health law for a written opinion that Daniel's wishes had to be respected. In the end, I resolved to manage the situation as best I could, but I should never have had to consider the option.

We had more immediate concerns. Somehow I had to relay to Petra that Daniel might have only a few hours and we had to be ready with decisions. The problem was that Daniel was so agitated that he wouldn't let us leave his bedside, even to go to the loo. The clock was ticking towards 2pm, when he was due to have the ultrasound which would determine just how appalling the situation was. It was already past 1pm. How to communicate with Petra, without making Daniel even more distressed? The only option was text. Imagine having to conduct the most difficult conversation parents could ever have - *by text*. I hadn't even learnt predictive texting, much to Daniel's disdain.

I kept a record of the exchange:

Me: *'CM thinks it's mainly cancer not infection. US [ultrasound] will tell us if solid or fluid. If cancer he wants us to make end of life decisions. I want to give inhibitors chance if we can, maybe back on chemo to buy time, maybe low-dose w inhibitors. I think he wants us to make DNR [Do Not Resuscitate]-type decisions before ICU will accept. Im not willng to be bounced into massive decision tho nature may take its course'*

Petra: 'Will dan need to give consent? Is it likely to be imminent? I need to get girls back if it is. I don't want him to suffer any more'

Me: 'He wld hv to consent, eg not to go on ventilator. Cld be hours or much lnger. IGF needs time so we need to hold posn if we can and price not too high 4 Dan. CM agreed pain decr is good sign though not determinative. I don't think Dan ready to give up'

I told Petra she did need to get the girls back. We were both concerned that Daniel shouldn't suffer any more than he could tolerate, but I worried as the porter came to collect him that Petra thought we had reached the end of the road. We would soon know anyway. I have rarely felt so nervous. Daniel wanted me in the room as they prepared him, so that I could make sure the doctors didn't tell him anything – there is often a running commentary during ultrasound scans. He was panicky but the doctors were compassionate. Daniel then wanted Petra to take over. He was anxious that if there was fluid, draining it would be painful. I waited outside, pacing up and down, like an expectant father but in the diametrically opposite context.

Eventually one of the doctors, an American, came out. There was lots of fluid, she said. They couldn't see on the ultrasound whether there was also a solid mass (cancer). But the fluid was good news – or rather less bad news. Things were obviously extremely serious, but not quite as desperate as Colin had assumed.

The fluid began to drain – a bright red because of the blood it mingles with. Around 1.3 litres came off quickly, and Daniel's heart rate decreased significantly. There were several phone calls, one with Adam Sandell, about a case we were doing. A practising GP as well as a barrister, Adam had insight into what was going on and kindly offered to take over the case. I had to bring my Mum into the picture, too. She had guessed that something was up.

Angela, Petra's sister arrived with the girls and Sian, my sister, came too. We went to the chaplaincy.

Anna, who had ably led the nursing team during the crisis overnight, said she'd been thinking about Daniel off-duty. I'm sure that nurses and doctors do think of their patients off-duty. I had supportive messages, including from Debbie, Chloë's Mum:

> *'I … want you to know that Daniel is continually in my thoughts. I haven't met him, but I feel such empathy for you for obvious reasons, but also because you seem such a considerate, caring and lovely father.'*

That, too, made me feel better, though only slightly.

Daniel was feeling better and upbeat by the early evening, testimony once again to his remarkable capacity to recover psychologically. He thought I should go home. I was hesitant, knowing I would never forgive myself if he died when I was not present, but did as bidden so as not to worry him. His breathing was easier and I felt we were over the immediate crisis.

Wednesday 31 August

My instinct was right. Daniel was better. Sandra Strauss admitted missing the effusion in his right chest a few days earlier. But encouragingly, she added that the fact the cancer was growing didn't mean the IGF wasn't working. Colin later said that Daniel was looking better than the previous day. He ate well. We watched an old *Have I Got News For You?*

Thursday 1 September

A CT scan showed that the abdomen, pelvis and spleen were clear but there was disease in the soft-tissue near the ribs, on the left. The effusion was caused by cancer, Sandra said. The lung wasn't re-filling but it might do so if the inhibitors did not work. If so, another pleurodesis was an option but it was borderline whether Daniel was up to a general anaesthetic. At least he was now stable and we should have a few days to assess the situation. Sandra suggested we should give the inhibitors a chance to work, with low-dose chemo in reserve. I was happy with this.

Petra was furious with Colin about the ventilator discussion and dreaded his coming to the ward, afraid of what he might say to Daniel. I said Daniel's symptoms were nowhere near those of many dying Ewing's patients I had followed. I wanted to keep her spirits up, but it was true. His oxygen was down to 3. However, we agreed we would prefer him to go quickly if he was dying.

I had arranged a meeting at the hospital with my colleague Katy. As I waited for her in the foyer, two violinists played *Danny Boy*. It was too much to bear. Katy said she would continue to pray for Daniel. I found myself worrying about a case and marvelled about the way the mind works – my son was ebbing away before my eyes and yet I was fretting about work.

Late afternoon, Daniel had a painful procedure to

remove the drain. He wanted me to give him a foot/ calf massage. He took his supplements last thing – still determined to help himself get better.

Friday 2 September
Petra and Sasha came up early for yet another drain procedure. They were already in the room when I woke.

Daniel's mood was fragile but he laughed when I kissed him on his forehead. He touched his old childhood comfort blanket earlier, a sure sign of his vulnerability. 'Will I come out of hospital when I'm off oxygen?' he asked. 'You have taken a big hit and it's going to take a while', I replied. Privately I didn't know whether he would ever come out of hospital. He looked so thin and ill.

Saturday 3 September
They reduced his oxygen to 1 after draining more fluid. Daniel was nervous at first – how quickly he had become dependent on oxygen, psychologically as much as physically. His SATS were 100 and his heart rate high but not that high.

Sunday 4 September
Today was less good. That was how it was. There were no good days - how could there be? - but there were less bad days. Daniel came off oxygen altogether but didn't feel he was making progress. I arrived at the hospital to find that he'd gone down for yet another CT scan, to check that he hadn't developed blood clots through immobility (he couldn't have warfarin, the blood-thinning drug, because of low platelets). I was nervous it might show worsening

cancer. How I detested scans.

Angela, Petra's sister, was there with her daughter Helena, about to start student life at the Royal College of Dance. As ever, I felt lonely when they all left. Evenings in hospital were difficult. During the day, scans apart, it wasn't so bad, with the bustle of hospital life. There were still medical staff during the evening, of course, and visitors for other patients, but a melancholy atmosphere descended. Daniel never wanted visitors during any of his hospital stays, not wishing people to see him ill. I wished he had wanted visitors, for my sake.

I couldn't show him how I felt during these long lonely hours. I had to be upbeat. However bad I was feeling, he was feeling worse. That evening he was highly insecure and wanted me to stroke his arm. 'Is everything going to be ok?' came the plaintive cry, yet again. 'It's ok, it's ok', he kept repeating to himself, but wouldn't open up to me. He groaned as he drifted off to sleep.

At midnight, I fed him potato and broccoli. He couldn't really feed himself. 'It's nice sitting up, isn't it?' he said.

At least we still had Daniel. Sarah, a Ewing's patient in Illinois, diagnosed with pelvic cancer not long after Daniel, died today, aged sixteen.

Monday 5 September

This morning, I should have been at a case trial but couldn't leave Daniel – he began to have panic attacks.

He wanted me next to him and assurance that things were going ok. I lay my hand on his rib tumour and prayed for him, as a friend had suggested. He felt calmer; I didn't - the rib lesion had grown noticeably. When had this happened? I said nothing to Daniel. I noted in my journal that I still had faith. Was I trying to convince myself that I had faith?

Much more important than my anxiety was Daniel's. 'I'm scared, Dad.' He would not or could not articulate why. He told me he loved me, a sure sign, as previously on the journey, that he was vulnerable.

Tuesday 6 September
Daniel's cousin Holly's birthday. Holly, an IVF miracle and acute observer of human nature, was now studying politics at Nottingham.

Daniel was fragile. He liked me touching his chest. He insisted I remained in his line of vision, so kneeling on the floor, which was more comfortable, wasn't allowed. He didn't want me to have a shower, just five metres away. The new registrar said Daniel might be discharged in three days' time. I worried that he was being discharged for palliative care, to die, but decided I was being paranoid (I probably wasn't).

We watched Wales unluckily lose to England at Wembley, with Robert Earnshaw missing a sitter. A middle-aged Welsh fan died following an unprovoked attack. For Daniel getting into a fight was as alien as being an astronaut.

We did the *Times 2* crossword together. He didn't like the two clues about anxiety but was pleased when we completed it. He had been a little confused earlier in the day, rabbiting on about some game the previous week, but for the most part had lost little of his sharpness.

My last journal entry for the day was 'Dan fine.' Everything in life is relative.

Wednesday 7 September

Daniel was so anxious in the morning that he wouldn't let me go to the loo. 'How is my tachycardia going to get better?' he asked. 'The remaining fluid is holding things up', I suggested. His lung was reinflating, not perfectly but ok. Pain levels were good. There was usually something positive to hang onto, even during the darkest times.

Daniel's platelets were down to seventeen, too low for sirolimus, the mTOR inhibitor. He would need a transplant if they went below ten. He wouldn't be going home on Friday but I didn't tell him. Marco, the nurse, discussed community support, including a hospice. Daniel asked about Macmillans. Petra and I had been careful to explain to him that Macmillans were not just if someone was dying. Holly, Daniel's cousin, had done some research for me about the charity.

While I was briefly at the office and Petra was making him lunch, Daniel called in a panic. 'Dad, there are doctors outside the room. What shall I do?' he pleaded urgently. I asked Sasha to get them to come back later – I would be there in twenty minutes. As it happened, it was a false alarm but it exemplified the phobia Daniel had developed of doctors if Petra or I weren't there to protect him from things he didn't want to hear.

I felt pretty desolate. Daniel was agitated for two hours. 'Dan, after all this you will be able to cope with anything in life', I said, trying to buck him up. His answer was a sharp blow to the solar plexus: 'Only if you or Mum are there with me.'

Here he was, just short of his twenty-third birthday, when he should have been preparing to strike out in the world as an independent young man, about to graduate from one of the great universities, love in his heart, dreams in his back pocket, escapades of fun and more earnest endeavours on his horizon, career choices to prevaricate over. Instead he was trapped in a hospital bed and felt completely dependent on his parents for psychological sustenance, barely able to see beyond the next struggle to the toilet. I should, I suppose, have been pleased that he had so much trust in us, but the moment was too poignant for that. He said he would need to speak to us for an hour a day back at university.

Poor Daniel. I wanted so, so much to sort things for him. I began to compose an email to Sandra Strauss with some treatment ideas.

Thursday 8 September
We were told that Daniel had MRSA. It was the less serious kind, it seems, but it was still another thing to worry about, another medication to take, via his nose this time. Hospitals are amongst the most dangerous places.

Beatrice Seddon, on ward duty, was pleased that there had been no real deterioration for three days but thought Daniel was a bit more breathless. She suggested he went back on oxygen. The level was only 0.5 but it was a sad moment. It was awful to see the mask back on. It exacerbated Daniel's agitation, I suspect both because of claustrophobia and the symbolism of oxygen dependence.

I arranged for recent scans to be couriered to Jaume Mora and Uta Dirksen. A driver delivering oxygen to Daniel's home was annoyed about a wasted trip, seemingly not understanding the difficulty of organising someone to be at home with a child desperately ill forty miles away in hospital.

Daniel, meanwhile, was getting obsessed with his readings – SATS, heart rate, blood pressure – and insisted on having the machines near him all the time. They were his crutch, I suppose. In fact, he was becoming quite OCD in general. He would obsess over which DVDs to watch overnight, and in what order. Tasks were allocated to Petra and me. One of mine, when fluid was draining, was to unpeg and repeg the bag to his sheet when he went to the toilet. It had to me who did this, not Petra. Normally, Daniel wouldn't let me do anything practical, for good reason. I was allocated other tasks, too.

Daniel's psychological state was fast deteriorating, with panic attacks – really bad panic attacks – more and more frequently. Sometimes they would last for three or four hours. They puzzled us. The only suggestion from medical staff was lorazepam, which helped to begin with but soon did nothing.

We assumed that he was panicky because he realised he was so ill. What could be more natural? Being short of breath, dependent on oxygen, is also extremely scary. Sometimes going a few yards to the toilet used to leave Daniel gasping and he would then panic. That could make his breathing worse – the archetypal vicious circle.

This all made sense, but not complete sense. 'I don't know Dad, I don't know', he would tell me with meaning when I tried gently to elicit what was really on his mind.

These were tough days, the toughest I have experienced. Some nights, when I had finally got Daniel settled, after midnight, I would lie on my makeshift bed, waiting for the next 'Toilet, Dad' or 'Dad, come over here to sit with me.' It was the run-up to the tenth anniversary of 9/11. Daniel's ward was on the sixteenth floor – the top floor – of the UCH tower block. I would fantasise about a plane crashing into our floor, taking us both out of this world and all its suffering. I didn't literally want a plane to crash: it was a metaphor for how I was feeling. I didn't want to live if Daniel wasn't going to live. The fantasy had to be of a joint cessation of life: I couldn't die leaving Daniel alive, because he needed me.

As a Samaritan, I have asked hundreds of callers whether they feel suicidal. I have shared with people what might be the last moments of their life, a rare privilege. I have learnt that there is a spectrum of suicidal people, from those who are fundamentally not unhappy but are going through a crisis from which they can discern no escape, to those whose life seems so awful and hopeless that, frankly, you understand why suicide seems the only option. The terminally ill often fall into the latter category, with cancer sufferers a dominant subset.

Up to now I always had hope that things could get better. Now hope was being submerged by despair, its antonym. By any objective standard, I still had hope for a rich and meaningful life. I had my health – that priceless gift we should never take for granted but always do, until we lose it. I had my work, which I love for all its frustrations, and the things I believe in and sometimes fight for. I had goals and ambitions, mostly unrealised and perhaps unrealisable, but an important driver nonetheless. I had a wonderful family and lots of friends, to whom I knew I could turn even if I rarely did. I still hoped for another fulfilling relationship. I had money, not riches certainly, but unlike so many around the world enough not to worry about survival and a sufficient surplus for sport and other forms of entertainment and books and some travel and pizza with friends.

But as I lay there, I knew in my heart that I would not have Daniel and that outweighed all the other blessings of my life. The thought of living if he didn't live was just unbearable.

These were dark thoughts but these were dark times. I never allowed the thoughts to paralyse. When the call from Daniel came, as it inevitably did, I was at his bedside in five seconds, helping him to the toilet, cleaning up, watching some obscure match in the Rugby World Cup together in the early hours. I still followed and noted the minutiae of his health, day and night. I kept trying to find a solution for him, even as the odds hovered between massive and insurmountable.

But our joint deaths did seem an attractive option. Another Ewing's parent, then still in the midst of the journey with all its twists and turns and obstacles and steep climbs and plummets and all-round rollercoaster nauseating hairiness, told me of an occasional fantasy of being killed in a car crash, parent and child together. Childhood cancer does that to you.

Friday 9 September
Daniel was distressed going on the commode. He hated standing up during an x-ray, short of breath. He went onto humidified oxygen, at level 2, on his return. He started to watch *Chariots of Fire*, but concentration was difficult.

The fluid was back, with a vengeance. Daniel didn't know if he could handle another procedure, but he did. Nearly three litres was taken and he felt much better and calmer. Dr Seddon explained that lungs sometimes refill after the first draining and this didn't necessarily portend progressing disease. Something to hold onto.

'Was it a positive discussion?' Daniel asked me. We watched a rugby edition of *Come Dine with Me*. He had a bad hacking cough.

Saturday 10 September

Daniel had a good night. In the morning he had an accident using the commode, the second occasion. Normally, this would have been the subject of merriment, but Daniel wasn't seeing the funny side of things. In fact he rarely smiled, let alone laughed, during these weeks.

My sister Charlotte managed not one but two accidents on a new bike. Katie her daughter had hers stolen. Life was on hold in Room 1 on T16 at UCH but elsewhere it went on, if not always serenely.

Sunday 11 September

Daniel's platelets were 60, improved but not good enough for sirolimus, a disappointment. There was confusion about how much fluid was left and whether it was old or new. We desperately wanted it to be old fluid. Daniel was concerned about the rib swelling but Petra managed to reassure him.

I gave Daniel a CD of Lang Lang playing Liszt. 'Today was a good day', he announced. He watched Wales lose narrowly to South Africa in the Rugby World Cup – he thought Jonathan Davies, Annabel's boyfriend, played well this time. I couldn't help comparing Daniel's fate to that of Sam Warburton, the Welsh captain who made such an impression. Sam, born the day before Daniel, had the world at his feet; was Daniel about to lose his precarious toehold on the world?

Monday 12 September

Daniel talked in his sleep. At 4.30am he sent Petra a text to check she was ok (she would have been but for the worry of getting a text from Daniel in the middle of the night ...).

George, our competent SHO told him that the fluid was back. That worried him. More positively, Dr Seddon said he could restart on sirolimus. He took it before the planned blood test. Our fault.

Daniel was vulnerable and agitated during the evening. He kept feeling his rib swelling. He was upset hearing a crash call on the ward and didn't like seeing an injection on a programme about drugs in football. Normally, neither would have bothered him. 'Am I going to be ok?' came the repeated plea.

Daniel went for a walk around his room: George had said exercise was important for his lungs.

Tuesday 13 September

Daniel was in a lot of pain during the night. But he had a good breakfast.

Florence was missing Jess, now in Cardiff with my family. Dogs can bring real comfort at times of stress.

Daniel told Petra: 'I have had enough.' That was so painful to hear, even if it was just temporary despair. Over the cancer journey, I had resolved that, if Daniel ever said to me 'Dad, I can't handle any more, please end my life' and there was clearly no more hope and he was incapable of killing himself, I would put a pillow over his head.

Whether I would have the guts to do so, I didn't know. I would have worried, certainly, about arrogating God's role and making things worse for Daniel (or myself) in the afterlife. I would have worried about acting prematurely in that there might, in fact, have been hope and about making a mess of it. But I wouldn't have worried about the fact that I would face a life sentence for committing murder, even by shortening Daniel's life by just a couple of minutes.

I didn't share these thoughts with anyone. I hoped I wouldn't be put to the test.

Wednesday 14 September
Natalie, another of the SHOs – like George, ever helpful and efficient – showed me the x-ray, which showed some improvement. But there was still fluid in the lower part. Draining too much could cause an infection or lung collapse.

The team later said no to pleurodesis. Daniel was relieved: 'I don't think I could face another operation Dad', he said. What were we going to do? No one had a solution. I asked for a second opinion from the Brompton, the specialist lung hospital.

Later, we had a possible breakthrough. George had been having lunch with his mentor, Fraser Brims. Dr Brims was a respiratory consultant and also a Surgeon Commander in the Royal Navy. Fraser suggested Daniel could have a permanent drain fitted, which would mean that we could drain off fluid whenever necessary. It would take a few days to set up.

I later mentioned this to Colin and Beatrice Seddon. Neither seemed to know about permanent drains, which surprised me given how frequently fluid appears on the lungs with cancer. 'Daniel remains very sick', Colin said, 'and things could change quickly.' I knew he meant deteriorate.

But Daniel sat up to write some emails.

Thursday 15 September
Daniel wanted to reduce the oxygen level, so that he didn't become addicted. 'Will I have to be on oxygen for the rest of my life?' he asked.

Dr Seddon said he wasn't well enough to be discharged but weekend leave was a possibility. We were pleased: he desperately needed a change of scene. There were two things to address, she patiently explained to Daniel: the effusion and what was causing the effusion.

Fraser Brims came to see Daniel. He too, had an excellent bedside manner. There was a 50:50 chance of getting at loculated (trapped) fluid, he felt. 'Some patients have permanent drains for several months', he told Daniel. It was good for Daniel to hear a doctor projecting several months ahead.

Later he became agitated again. 'Change affects me', he explained. This is common with people suffering from anxiety. He was worried about being at home. He had two more panic attacks. He asked for but didn't take lorazepam.

He calmed down and told me he wanted to live in France for a year after graduating. He made me read more information about careers, this time in the civil service. Daniel loved word games so we did some. He ate well.

Friday 16 September
I postponed a scheduled hospital procedure (for me) yet again. The consultant's secretary understood: she had lost her son to cancer.

Daniel's right lung was refilling. It accounted for Daniel's pain. He described pain on the left as cancer pain. I knew he was right and it made me feel sick. I said it really upset me to see him in pain. 'You have got to stay positive, Dad', he replied.

He had two panic attacks; this time he took lorazepam. He smiled when Petra did *Five Little Pigs Go to Market* on his hand and I did *Round and Round a Garden*. How he used to love those when he was a young child. That is where he was regressing. It made me think again adults are but older children and children but younger adults.

And then Danjiela, one of the senior nurses dropped a bombshell. Daniel wouldn't be able to go home. The hospital, she explained, would no longer transport patients for weekend leave. Daniel needed an ambulance because he was on oxygen. 'OK, we'll take him in the car, with portable oxygen', I replied. 'No, that's not possible either', Danjiela said, 'because we can't let you take the hospital's oxygen in the car. It's too dangerous.' We were stuck. Our own oxygen hadn't arrived.

I wasn't about to concede defeat. Though Daniel was worried about coming home, we thought it really important for him to escape from the hospital environment, to try at least to address the panic attacks. I knew that public bodies were entitled to have policies on all kinds of things. But they weren't entitled to have inflexible policies: they had to consider each case on its merits. I fully appreciated that UCH's budget was under pressure and that weekend leave would normally be of low priority. But Daniel, so we considered, had a pressing clinical need for a break because of the panic attacks. He wasn't going home to see his mates. It felt like a classic example of bureaucratic mentality overriding clinical judgement.

So I asked to speak to whoever had made the ruling, to press for an exception. Danjiela did her best. Out of Daniel's earshot, she said she appreciated that his time was precious. I knew what that meant, and it made me feel nauseous. Petra and I discussed hiring a private ambulance. It would have cost nearly £400 just one way, but we would have paid it. I assured Daniel that he would be going home.

The wait extended into hours. This was eating into the weekend. I had the idea of checking if UCH's transport policy was on its website. It was. UCH's policy incorporated that of the Department of Health, which advised that transport for home leave should be approached case-by-case, guided by the patient's clinical needs. That is exactly what I would have expected.

I rang Mary in the transport department. She said there was no policy against weekend leave. What was going on? I went to see the ward sister. She contacted her boss: Daniel could have an ambulance.

But then there was a further complication. The hospital was on red bed alert (nothing to do with communists). There was an acute shortage of beds that weekend. Dr Seddon would only discharge Daniel if he was guaranteed a bed on Sunday and he wasn't. A compromise was wrought: Daniel could have an ambulance home in the morning (Saturday) and a bed would await his return on Sunday. Melanie suggested he could decide, unofficially, to come back on Monday instead.

Daniel calmed down and we went for a wheelchair ride to the canteen. Later, he got agitated after going to the loo.

Saturday 17 September

Daniel's SATS were down to 92 at 5.30am and he panicked again. During tennis visualisation, he rebuked me: 'I will tell you if anyone comes to the net' – I had rashly suggested that one of us was volleying. Tennis visualisation was no longer working and he wanted to discuss careers in the law instead. So I went through the different types of law one could do. It seemed to help (I'm fairly confident that this was the first use of legal careers as an antidote to panic attacks...). 'I want to make a difference and help people', he said in his understated way, before adding, almost apologetically: 'But I want to earn some money as well.' He knew I did freedom of information cases and liked the idea of fighting for greater transparency in public affairs. Petra always thought Daniel would become a lawyer (my neighbour Harvey once related how much he enjoyed overhearing Daniel and I discuss law in the garden).

As we waited, I chatted with the father of a young Ewing's patient, himself the father of an eleven month-old baby. The cancer had recurred within six months of frontline treatment, not a good sign. The (grand)father was clearly struggling.

The ambulance arrived two hours late, further truncating the weekend. Daniel was anxious about the journey but coped. The driver touched Daniel on his arm as he said goodbye, a kindly gesture.

Daniel looked scared after climbing the stairs at home – a real challenge – but quickly calmed down. In fact, he was calmer than we'd seen him for weeks. He wasn't out of breath going to the toilet. He did have a minor panic attack in the evening but overall he was so much more at peace. I wouldn't have believed the difference had I not witnessed it.

There was general excitement when Jess arrived after two weeks in South Wales. Usually the most understated of dogs, she bounded into Daniel's bedroom and he craned his neck to see her.

True to his word, Colin was exploring options about the fluid with the Brompton. In his letter, he described me as 'extremely [well-] informed and highly motivated' – I smiled wryly to myself that this was probably doctors' code for 'Give this guy a wide berth.' Colin said that Daniel was in a fragile situation but there might be the beginning of a response to the inhibitors. That surprised me and cheered me up.

Sunday 18 September

I slept until 9am but was soon shaken from any feeling of complacency.

Daniel had managed to go to the toilet three times by himself but was having a panic episode as we spoke. He wanted me over. He decided to return to hospital today. The ambulance was supposed to arrive at 8pm but came at 5. Daniel couldn't cope with the short notice. He needed to prepare for things, a symptom of his fragile state of mind. So we sent the ambulance away.

Daniel was frequently feeling the lump on his ribs. It didn't look obviously different to me, though Petra thought it was bigger. He asked me: 'I have had a good day, haven't I?' I assured him he had; actually, it had been significantly worse than yesterday. He knew he looked awful, a gaunt shadow of his former self. I would catch him looking at himself in the mirror. Petra was struggling too.

Monday 19 September

The hospital rang, concerned that we were bringing Daniel back in the car with oxygen. I explained the mix-up with the ambulance; we took responsibility for the risks, I said. The nurse rang back – they were sending an ambulance.

Back at the hospital, Daniel's oxygen was increased to 3.5. The permanent drain would be fitted tomorrow. The registrar explained the procedure to him gently, but it started him off.

'I'm so scared', he told me. He claimed it wasn't about his illness or the drain procedure. Perhaps his thinking was that, if he didn't acknowledge that the cancer was back with a vengeance, it wouldn't be.

We watched *University Challenge* and *Dragon's Den*, two of his favourites.

Tuesday 20 September

We took Daniel down for his drain procedure, to be followed by a CT scan. What a shock when we saw his swelling. It had grown massively. There was little point having the CT – we knew what it would show.

The procedure went smoothly and Petra picked up quickly how to drain in future.

I was on edge for the rest of the day, waiting for the CT result but it didn't come. Daniel agreed to see a counsellor. I asked Jane Elfer, whom I'd seen back in 2006, whether she be willing to talk to him, even though he was no longer a child. She would, in two days' time. I suggested that, though it was entirely up to him, it was unlikely he would want to discuss death and dying.

We thought we were losing Daniel at one point in the

early evening. He stopped breathing for a few seconds. He quickly recovered. We laughed at the thought of the doctor, whom we had summoned urgently, arriving to see Daniel playing cards. She hypothesised that Daniel had suffered a mini-stroke.

I slept uneasily.

Wednesday 21 September
In the morning Adam, the third of the triumvirate of supportive SHOs, thought the CT showed no change. I was surprised but told Petra I would grab no change. By the afternoon, Adam had the report. It wasn't good. There was disease progression everywhere in the pleura and lungs. The rib tumour had grown to 10cm x 5cm. The spleen, pancreas, adrenal glands and kidneys were all normal, as were the liver, abdomen and pelvis. There was no lymph node disease. That was all good, but, to state the obvious, there's no point in parts of the body being healthy if there's fatal disease elsewhere. This chest disease was really serious and I was devastated.

But there was no time for self-indulgence. I went to the internet café to compose an email to Colin and Sandra. I was really afraid they would say that there was nothing more they could do. Maybe that was the correct course, maybe we just had to accept that we were going to lose Daniel and soon. But I was still not ready to give up. I tried to put as positive a spin on things as possible in the email:

'I guess the obvious question is whether there is evidence that the disease has slowed down from what might otherwise have been expected - given how

aggressively it grew between the scans of 16 August and 31 August - such that it's worth continuing with figitumumab/sirolimus. My big fear was always that Daniel's disease would be biologically responsive but that it was just too aggressive for the inhibitors to cope with in the short term...'

I continued:

'The next question is then, if there is reason to think that the tumour is biologically responsive, whether it would be better for him first to have a blast of chemo - whether gem/docetaxel, continuous infusion high-dose ifosfamide, trabectedin or something else - with a view to going back on the inhibitors after the hoped-for debulking. As you know, Daniel has always been very responsive to chemo, apart from low-dose etoposide on second relapse. I appreciate that it's the law of diminishing returns but might debulking be enough for the inhibitors?'

(Debulking means reducing the amount of tumour).

I discussed some other options and then concluded:

'We are just exploring options at present. We know that one option is simply palliative care. It's his call ultimately.

As ever Daniel is very clear that he does not wish to discuss anything and is very vulnerable psychologically at present with numerous distressing panic attacks.'

That last sentence was for Colin's benefit. I emailed

Jaume Mora at the same time. For the first time, he didn't reply. He must have realised the game was up.

Colin left a message. He was away in Italy for a couple of days, but Sandra would explain the favoured treatment option in the morning. I was relieved he was still talking about treatment options.

Daniel wanted to walk around the ward, to help his lungs. So off we set, with me carrying his oxygen cylinder. I joked weakly to the nurses that this was our escape attempt. Daniel kept going for twenty-five minutes, head down, breathing heavily, trudging up and down the corridors. I have never felt so proud of him. He had lost none of his resolve.

Thursday 22 September
Daniel was due to be discharged, after round two of figitumumab but I didn't expect that to happen.

I prepared for the meeting with Sandra and I also prepared Daniel. This was really difficult. I'm afraid I lied to him. He was in such a fragile state mentally. Anticipating that chemo would be the option, I told him it had always been the plan to interrupt figitumumab with chemo to help get things under control and he would then move back onto the inhibitor. It was not a complete untruth – it had been my goal to get him onto low-dose chemo with figitumumab, if we could persuade Pfizer, and even now I hoped he would go back onto figitumumab if the chemo could only get the cancer under control. But I was dissembling and loathed doing so. Daniel seemed satisfied. Petra and I had earned his trust over the course of the journey, over his whole life perhaps, and I was able to redeem some of the credit now.

It was Dr Le Grange, the South African consultant who saw us in fact. We went into a side-room while Petra stayed with Daniel. I asked my questions. The preferred option was gemcitabine. Normally, it's given with docetaxel but this would be too toxic, she explained. She made it clear that the chances of the gemcitabine working were very small.

We talked about end-of-life sedation. Our priority I stressed, was to protect Daniel from suffering, even if that precipitated loss of consciousness. I had a job keeping my emotions in check. Dr Le Grange was kind, as was Melanie. A registrar, however, looked bored and yawned. Here we were, about to lose our beloved son and a doctor couldn't even be bothered to listen, or so it seemed to me.

I was worried what Dr Le Grange would say to Daniel. I acknowledged she had to answer questions truthfully, but asked her not to volunteer bad news. When we went back, Daniel asked: 'Is there any reason to be concerned about this?' pointing to his rib tumour. My heart was in my mouth. 'I'm not concerned if you're not', Dr Le Grange replied. I was so grateful to her. Daniel looked relieved.

To my surprise, Dr Le Grange said that Daniel could go home after the chemo. I suspect the chemo dose was low.

A little later, I noticed her team laughing as they continued their ward round. I didn't blame them in the slightest. Doctors need a safety-valve and can't allow one patient's desperate circumstances to dictate their interaction with other patients. I didn't expect people to don sackcloth and ashes just because we had. But this morning the laughter heightened my feeling of isolation.

So home we went. By this time we had our own oxygen

supply, so didn't have to bother with ambulances. Daniel was anxious the oxygen would run out.

As Petra drove, I had the chance to reflect on the past few weeks in hospital. Daniel had so much excellent care – really excellent care – at UCH for over five years, led by Colin McMaster. There was much that was excellent, too, during this stay. The vast majority of doctors, nurses and health care assistants, and porters and other ancillary staff, were efficient and compassionate. Other scientific disciplines, some unseen, contributed their expertise.

It may seem churlish, therefore, to criticise Daniel's care during this stay. And yet. The motto of my father's school in Ystalyfera, in the Swansea valley, was 'Nid da lle gellir gwell' – 'It is not good if it could be better.' That sums up my approach to things which matter. (I once used the motto in a talk and was surprised that there was an Ystalyfera alumnus in the audience – what were the chances of that?) For all the plus points, Daniel's care could have been better during this stay. Colin's conversation about ventilators caused him unnecessary anxiety. In the recent political vernacular, the weekend leave was an omnishambles. None of the oncology consultants knew that UCH fitted permanent chest drains, or if they knew failed to suggest it. Daniel couldn't have been discharged with a constantly refilling lung and the consequent morbidity.

But my biggest criticism of UCH during this period relates to his panic attacks. A nurse from Spain, Laura, and a health care assistant from Portugal, Ana, sat with Daniel and were brilliant but no one else seemed to take the attacks seriously. The response was simply to offer lorazepam. Only later was I to learn what probably caused the attacks.

Daniel would tell us that the anxiety was worse than the pain (which the staff did, to their credit, keep under pretty good control). The psychological suffering of the dying should be taken every bit as seriously as the physical; it must surely be a frequent interloper on cancer wards.

UCH, I have no doubt, wants to be measured against the highest standards. Those standards were attained so often during Daniel's cancer journey. But they were not always met at the time when he needed them most. One can rarely prove cause and effect with disturbances of the mind but I fear that Daniel suffered more than he needed to.

I put those thoughts aside when we reached home. A hospital bed had been delivered to make him more comfortable – another cause for real gratitude. He soon settled down. I did some research into appetite stimulants and nutrition boosters.

What would the next few days hold? I barely dared to think.

Friday 23 September
Daniel's sleep patterns were all over the place. He was concerned about his shallow breathing. Symptomatic of his general anxiety, he channel-hopped and was intolerant of adverts.

I had a chat with Henry Mannings about Coley's. He thought that the permanent drain might be a blessing in disguise because the toxins could be given directly into the tumour. The evidence was that they worked best intratumorally. Similarly, one could inject into the rib lesion. He was willing to come down from Norfolk, which was incredibly kind. The call cheered me.

As usual, reality soon slapped me in the face. Daniel's wheelchair arrived – another poignant moment – and after a ride downstairs he had a panic attack lasting over three hours. We had to increase the oxygen to 5. It was truly horrific and a horrible evening. Daniel looked dreadfully ill. He talked gibberish on waking from a brief sleep. Later, he was groaning – was this pain from the cancer or his position in bed, or anxiety? He did eat quite well and had some green tea. He was still trying so hard.

Melanie at UCH had explained to the district nurse that Daniel didn't like discussing anything, that I had to be at every meeting and that I was a solicitor. I laughed but in truth hated the thought that UCH were doing anything different because I was a lawyer or so hands-on.

Saturday 24 September
Daniel asked me over to watch some rugby. He wanted Jess on the bed to stroke her.

Petra drained some fluid and thought she had got most of it. Would it come back? We had to assume it would.

I had arranged to visit Pauline who was doing well on Coley's. She had been about to get in touch when I contacted her. An omen, perhaps? I was clutching at any passing straw. To be honest, I was happy to get away for a few hours. It was so upsetting being around Daniel. I had never expected to look on an afternoon in Luton as light relief.

Pauline's partner Walter is an alternative medicine practitioner. Both are strong believers in wheatgrass juice. They were informative. I came away resolved to try Coley's, if Daniel was up to it.

Back in Chobham, I felt worse after failing, again, to hide

from Mum how I was feeling.

Daniel didn't want me over initially, once more because change was difficult. But he did want to speak to me. His voice sounded weak. He had been for a ten to fifteen-minute walk around the house, but hadn't made it to the garden. I told him the meeting with Pauline was really positive and broached the subject of his having wheatgrass, maybe tomorrow. It was to convey that we were carrying on as normal.

Jess helped herself to Daniel's meal when he wasn't looking.

Sunday 25 September

Daniel's appetite wasn't good but he ate as much as he could. Another long panic attack followed a fifteen-minute walk around the house. Petra was going shopping and Daniel worried about the transition. It had to be done in a certain way and I even had to place the toilet roll in a particular position.

'Dad, I don't understand how I'm going to get better', he pleaded. 'I'm not surprised', I felt like saying, but in fact replied 'as the treatment works and we sort out the fluid problem.' It was gut-wrenching.

At about 6.30pm, Daniel started shouting at the cancer. This was a first. As I had done before, I encouraged him to visualise attacking the disease. 'I'm scared', he told us a little later.

Petra asked whether I thought UCH expected to see Daniel again. Melanie had given us several blood forms and wished Daniel happy birthday, for 6th October on one, a nice touch.

In the evening I spoke to Marie Issels, widow of Josef Issels who had used Coley's in Mexico. Now well into her eighties, she was knowledgeable and supportive. I sent some emails too.

Monday 26 September

More research on Coley's, with a helpful reply from California where a sarcoma patient was using it. Henry thought we should get on with the treatment, though he seemed doubtful whether Daniel was up to it.

Petra drained some more fluid. Daniel sounded weak and breathless but said he was ok. He went for a walk downstairs.

I emailed a friend explaining I wouldn't be coming to the party to celebrate his appointment as a High Court judge.

Daniel wanted me back at 7.30pm as he had another panic attack. It didn't last long. We watched *University Challenge*, a *Despatches* documentary and *The World's Strongest Man*. The programmes summed up Daniel's wide range of interests, from the serious to the trivial.

He looked so ill and helpless, and developed another cough. He got a bit panicky when it was time for me to leave but then said I should. He wasn't willing for Michael Johnson's *Gold Rush*, which Petra had got autographed for him, to count towards his birthday presents!

Supportive emails arrived from old school friends I had been due to meet.

Another long, long day.

Tuesday 27 September

Petra thought Daniel was a bit better this morning. Colin wrote that the Brompton had nothing to suggest about the fluid. In any event, Colin added, this was only a small part of Daniel's problems. I knew he was right. Dr Carty later told me that Colin had been helpful, spending a long time on the phone.

Daniel went for a twenty-minute walk. We started to do a crossword. He thought he had put on some weight. But then came another panic attack, lasting nearly four hours. Simply awful. But he was calmer in the evening and had a good tea.

My friend Robin lit another candle for Daniel in Gloucester Cathedral. Debbie sent a blog of a Ewing's patient still alive after multiple relapses. Sadly, we were beyond even that stage but I appreciated the gesture.

I read a circular email on the Sarcoma UK support list. A patient had posted a message criticising a doctor at the Royal Marsden. Bizarrely, it seemed that another list member had forwarded the message to the doctor, who had reacted furiously, claiming that the email was defamatory. Some doctors have an inflated ego, housed within a thin skin.

List members were understandably upset about this gross breach of confidentiality. A mole hunt was instigated. In a funny way, the episode provided a welcome diversion from what I was dealing with.

Sasha did wheelies with Daniel in his wheelchair.

Wednesday 28 September

Another tough, tough day. Mum was crying a lot this morning.

The day had started well enough. Petra thought Daniel was considerably better. This is a common feature of dying from cancer – deterioration does not follow a linear path and the patient may perk up for a while. I had seen it with Dad and read about it with several other Ewing's patients.

But it cheered me that morning and I even managed a long, and rather difficult, work call.

The more upbeat mood didn't last.

Daniel became sleepy and talked gibberish. Petra thought he was losing consciousness. And yet he answered a few questions on *The Chase*, the ITV tea-time quiz and watched the *Champions League*.

A couple of times he said: 'I'm scared, Dad.'

Petra drained nearly 500ml of fluid. The rib swelling definitely seemed bigger. But he was eating, which surprised the district nurse. I hand-fed him some pasta, but he refused an extra helping because it had cheese. He had it firmly in his mind that dairy was bad for cancer and wasn't prepared to compromise, even at this stage. I was glad his determination remained intact, but worried about lack of protein. I did some research into cachexia, which causes people to waste away and ordered some diet bolsterers.

We had a visit from Jane, from Community Palliative Care. She spent twenty minutes alone with Daniel and surmised he was trying to protect us. The thought was there, she believed, that he'd had enough. However, he had indicated that if he had an infection, he would want to go to hospital.

Jane explained the rule of thumb that, if a cancer patient deteriorates from one week to another, they have weeks to live; if the deterioration is from one day to another, they have days. Dr Pilai from the surgery thought death could be imminent but more likely was a little way off. Petra and I agreed that confusion was better than panic attacks.

What to do about Coley's? Henry Mannings was coming to see us in a couple of days. Petra was doubtful. Katie, Daniel's doctor cousin thought we should go for it.

I tried to explain the reality gently to Katie's sister Annabel, who had just qualified as a doctor. She was angry that we were giving up. 'You can't do that, Unc', she insisted. I reassured her we weren't giving up but things were not good. Annabel really loved Daniel. She thought the confusion was caused by morphine-based analgesia, but she was trying to persuade herself. UCH didn't think the cancer had spread to the brain, Daniel's worst fear. It hardly seemed to matter now.

Norbert sent me a heartfelt email about talking to Daniel about death.

Thursday 29 September

This was the day when any last vestige of hope might be realised. Henry Mannings was visiting.

I slept badly and broke down telling Mum I thought I had failed Daniel. She still hoped for a miracle. She recalled his advising her, a few months earlier, to rest before Annabel's graduation and was touched by his concern for her. Daniel didn't always articulate the compassion he felt.

I bumped into Tabs, one of several supportive neighbours. 'He is dying', I said. It was the first time I had uttered the word. But I wasn't giving up, even after a call from Dr Carty suggesting that we agree to DNR – Do Not Resuscitate. We decided we wouldn't sign the form until we were sure.

I took a blood sample to the path lab to get the results in time for the meeting with Henry.

Daniel looked awful. He was confused and kept repeating himself. But he was able to find 'Dad mob' on his mobile and knew his name and mine. And astonishingly, a little while later he was conjugating Latin verbs with Sasha. He had enough insight to know he had slowed down.

When I was alone with him, I said that God and Jesus loved him. He replied: 'God loves me.' And again: 'God loves me.' This was a really important mini-conversation for me. A few weeks earlier, Daniel had told JJ he was an atheist. Perhaps there was an element of youthful bravado in the comment (not long before he opined that it was almost inconceivable that the world was just an accident). One could hardly blame him for struggling with the concept of a loving God after all he had been through.

I always wanted Daniel to be a free thinker, to read widely and deeply, to enquire, to probe, to challenge assumptions, to unpick arguments. I was glad that he enjoyed philosophy so much. Parents, inevitably, hope their children will absorb their values. I would have been gutted if Daniel had turned out a racist, or if he thought that cruel exploitation of the weak, human or animal, was acceptable, or if his main purpose in life had been to make shedloads of money. But I wanted him to formulate his values, his worldview, through his own reasoning and in his own time.

But religion is qualitatively different to any other topic.

Whether religious beliefs are true is, axiomatically, the most important question of all, transcending worldviews. The central questions of religion really matter even in the flush of carefree youth. But they take on a special urgency in the face of impending death, when life has become anything but carefree. I wanted Daniel to believe in God, for many reasons, but mainly because if he was to die I wanted him to pass into a happy and peaceful afterlife – Heaven, if you like. Pascal's wager – which weighs the risks of not believing against those of believing – is the weakest of arguments for theism, owing everything to opportunism and nothing to intellectual rigour. And the Christian injunction that belief in Jesus as the Son of God is a prerequisite for paradise, whilst a brilliant recruitment and retention policy, strikes me as terribly unfair on those led by reason to a different conclusion, or who are simply ignorant of Christianity (such as those around in the BCE era).

Questioning, surely, is not a bad thing. Galileo said: 'I do not feel obliged to believe that the same God who has endowed us with the sense, reason, and intellect has intended us to forgo their use.'

However, for all that logic told me that Daniel's fate on death shouldn't depend on whether he believed in God or Christianity, how could I be sure? I was slipping into my own version of Pascal's wager. I desperately wanted Daniel to be safe when he passed.

I would never have imposed my views about religion on him and it wouldn't have worked anyway, not least because of the doubts I struggle with. But as I looked at him, his life ebbing away and as he repeated 'God loves me', I wondered whether he believed it or whether he was confused or whether he was trying to please me. I hoped, really hoped, that he believed. I added: 'I'm confident Dan that, when the time comes – a long way off – you will go to heaven because you are so lovely.'

By coincidence, my friend Romana texted from Prague:

Romana: *'Dan definitely is going to be happy. I saw his soul folded with light, smiling.'*
Me: *'How?'*
Romana: *'By my inner vision in meditation. Please pray to God: Thy Will be done. God loves Dan infinitely more than we can imagine. When you surrender your will to God it will bring peace to Dan's soul …'*

I found the words comforting and hoped she was right. But still I wanted Daniel to stay in this world. I thought of the Latin phrase my father uttered when he was dying, 'dum spiro spero' – 'while I breathe I hope' – changing it to 'dum spirat spero' – 'while he breathes, I hope.'

The blood results seemed surprisingly normal. Katie, JJ and Annabel thought they were really good. Daniel's creatinine was a bit a low but JJ thought that was because of muscle wastage. His potassium was a bit high but Annabel put that down to dehydration. She had expected his calcium to be elevated and his renal function was brilliant. What did it all mean? How can you be dying and yet your blood markers be normal?

Dr Carty was surprised, too. I worried that UCH were giving up on Daniel too early. He confirmed they had not asked for i/v fluids.

I told Daniel that Henry was coming and asked him to trust us with decisions. He said he would.

Henry spent a few minutes with Daniel. He was as gentle as I expected him to be. He remarked about the rib swelling.

The debrief was also as depressing as I had expected. Henry was shocked at Daniel's decline since early July. We were talking about days. He thought Coley's would kill him. I said: 'I'm not finding it easy to separate my self-interest from Daniel's' and asked him to speak to Petra separately. I knew she was sceptical about Coley's and seemed to have accepted the inevitability of Daniel dying. I was trying to assess what he would want, had he been able to think rationally, but it wasn't easy.

As he left, Henry said he would be willing to try Coley's if Daniel's breathing improved – in other words, if there were signs the gemcitabine was working. He would visit again in two days' time. I knew he didn't expect any improvement, but was nevertheless grateful for the slither of hope.

Daniel was a bit anxious after the visit. Too many visitors, he said. But he ate a plate of fried potatoes and amazingly, managed a game of knockout whist with us all. He struggled a bit but we made sure he won.

I told Petra I hadn't given up hope, faint though it was. I'm not sure I believed it. She had told the girls earlier that their beloved brother was probably not going to make it. Just horrific.

I did some research, late at night. With Daniel's breathing pretty good, just maybe he was having a mixed response – tumour reduction in his lungs (which we couldn't see) but tumour growth in his ribs (which we could see but which mattered a lot less).

Yet more straw-clutching, I knew. It had been another horrendous day. I realised things were almost inevitably going to get even worse.

Friday 30 September

Daniel deteriorated markedly overnight. His breathing was bubbly and he had coughed up some blood. He did recognise me, however, and stroked Jess. A friend sent me a technique about panic attacks but in fact Daniel was generally much calmer now.

We needed his breathing to improve for there to be any possibility of Coley's. His SATS were only 92 when Margaret the district nurse removed his nasal tube temporarily, but 98 with oxygen at 4, which wasn't bad. His heart rate wasn't that high at 105. He walked to the loo, which was incredible.

Sian collected the end-of-life combination prescription – for pain, sedation and fluid secretion – from the chemist. She had never seen a chemist move so fast. Margaret told me that Daniel's time was short.

I discussed funeral arrangements with Petra. I was happy to have a family funeral but she and the girls thought that he would want a public funeral because, for all his love of privacy, he enjoyed a fuss being made of him. Apparently he had told Sasha some months earlier – not, I think apropos his own impending demise – that he would want to be buried. I would have preferred a cremation, but naturally we had to respect his wishes. What a desperate conversation to have about your child.

Daniel had asked Petra on Wednesday whether he was

dying. She had answered 'No' and thinks he believed her. Were we right to protect Daniel in this way?

I'm sure many people – many professionals – would say it's best to be honest with the dying. Certainly, there are powerful reasons in favour of honesty. It gives the person a chance to come to terms with what is happening, to prepare for the transition to the afterlife if that's what they believe, to make their peace with their Maker. It gives them a chance to tell loved ones that they love them and make up with anyone they have fallen out with. It gives them a chance to put their affairs in order, to prescribe what they want for their funeral, as my Dad did.

There might have been some girl that Daniel wanted to say something to, or friends to bid goodbye to. As it happened, a text arrived for him, from a girl he was close to at Oxford: 'Hey s…, why haven't you been in touch?' Daniel couldn't reply now, but a little earlier he might have wanted to prepare her.

The other reasons were much less applicable. We didn't need telling that Daniel loved us and he knew we knew. He had few affairs to put in order. I would be surprised if there was anyone he had fallen out with.

It's conceivable that Daniel would have been more at peace, less confused about what was happening and less prone to panic attacks if he had known, rather than suspected, that he was dying. But I don't think so. My guess is that his psychological state would have been even worse.

Where lies the boundary between hope and acceptance? Pema Chödron, a Buddhist nun, extols the benefits of hopelessness so that 'we can have a joyful relationship with our lives, an honest direct relationship, one that no longer ignores the reality of impermanence and death.'

In truth, we lacked a vital piece of information – whether death really is the end. How can one judge how to ease a loved one's exit from this life without knowing what he is exiting to?

I had thought long and hard about what to tell Daniel. The clincher for me was the message he had given us throughout the journey, loud and clear: he didn't want to know bad news. He simply couldn't handle it. Whatever our personal views, we were respecting his wishes. I'm glad that Petra answered as she did. Like Daniel, I preferred the dishonesty of hope to the honesty of hopelessness; like Desmond Tutu, I was a willing prisoner of hope.

In the evening, Petra and the girls sang some songs to Daniel. At one point he asked: 'Is Daddy David here?' I can hardly bear to type those words. He was so vulnerable, a small child again. He even had his old cot blanket – personified by Daniel as 'Cover' – and his toy Snoopy in bed with him.

At 11pm, Daniel again shouted 'Get away' at the cancer. I said the Lord's Prayer to him and we settled down for the night, all of us together. We knew the end was near.

I slept on the floor next to Daniel. Eight or ten times a pair of legs suddenly appeared over my face. He had no idea what he was doing, but if he wanted to get up, then I would help him to get up. Petra was exhausted and was fast sleep, as was Florence, but Sasha would jump up each time. She was great with Daniel, aping the reassuring things she had heard Petra and me say many times. Immediately Daniel had sat up on the side of his bed, he would want to get back in. He was restless but not, I think, agitated.

On one occasion, however, he wanted to go for a walk, so we went for a walk. Only a couple of faltering steps, baby steps, supported by Sasha and me, but it was a huge achievement. His legs were so thin. His oxygen tube came off and it took us around forty-five seconds to reattach it. Just a day or two earlier, this would have been cause for real panic, but Daniel was by now too far out of it to worry. He told me he loved me, and then said 'Let's go to Guildford.' That was one wish I didn't respect.

Twice during the night I thought we were losing him. There was a gurgling sound in his throat. But he survived.

Saturday 1 October
It was a minor miracle that Daniel had made it into October. Could he make it to his birthday, in five days' time? It seemed unlikely.

Daniel was chuntering. 'Why is Mum sleeping?' he asked early in the morning. 'Do you mean how is she sleeping, considering the din you are making?' I joked. 'How is she sleeping?' he repeated. He still retained some level of comprehension, some of his magical sense of humour.

Petra drained another 250ml of fluid, on top of the 400ml yesterday. Then she read the Macmillan's end-of-life booklet. I couldn't.

Henry was due back at 6pm. Had there been an improvement in his breathing? Daniel's SATS were 98 late morning on oxygen level 4 and his heart rate 127. I reduced his oxygen to 3.5, but had to increase it. Daniel was breathing easily for most of the time, but there was no real improvement. His general condition was worsening. Hope was disappearing. In truth it had already all but disappeared, short of divine intervention. I still hoped and prayed for that.

Katie and Annabel had arrived in Chobham with Charlotte, my sister, and my Mum. They wanted to see Daniel but Petra was clear about respecting Daniel's wishes about no visitors.

Henry took one look at Daniel and said it was hopeless. He was looking even worse than on Thursday. 'David, if I thought there was a one in a million chance, I would give him Coley's, but there isn't', he said. I knew he was right and didn't try to persuade him. I felt guilty even about considering the option. There were tears in Henry's eyes as he said goodbye. This was a doctor who really cared. I felt raw desolation as his car pulled away. Medically, there was now no hope.

At 8pm, we again thought we were losing Daniel, as his breathing became laboured. Petra asked him to squeeze our hands if he was in pain. Daniel's response was a bit equivocal but he seemed ok. We then told him for the millionth time how much we loved him and Petra said: 'Dan, squeeze our hands if you love us back.' He took each of our hands in turn, Petra's first and then mine and gave each a really big squeeze. There was nothing equivocal this time. I have no idea where he got the strength: he must have been under six stone by now (it upset him too much to be weighed).

It was, quite simply, the most precious moment of my life, worth all the other ones added together. I thanked him.

A little later, I read the passage in Philippians about living and dying. I was desperately looking for solace. 'Everything is going to be ok, Dan', I told him. I meant in this life or the next, but was happy for him to think I was talking about this life, if he could understand me at all.

Daniel continued chuntering until the early hours and then shouted at the cancer once again: 'Get away!' If these were to be his last words, they lacked the pithy resonance of Caesar's 'Et tu Brute?', or the humour of Voltaire's 'Now, now, my good man, this is no time for making enemies' when implored by a priest to renounce Satan, or the acceptance of Jane Austen's 'Nothing, but death', when asked whether there was anything she wanted. But they summed up perfectly Daniel's strong desire to live. It gave me some comfort that I was right to continue looking for options for him.

Sunday 2 October

Daniel was peaceful throughout the day. He didn't change position and was non-responsive, although Mary and Shirley, two of the district nurses, thought he could probably hear. I hope he didn't hear anything which upset him.

The nurses drained over a litre of urine. We were annoyed that none of the other district nurses had suggested doing this. Surely this must be a standard thing to check? Daniel didn't seem to be in discomfort, but maybe he was but couldn't express it.

The waiting, oh such agony. Waiting is such a feature of cancer. Waiting for diagnosis to be confirmed, waiting for chemo to start, waiting to see if Daniel was well enough for each successive chemo and each radiotherapy blast, waiting around hospitals for tests and appointments, waiting for results, waiting for relapse and then further relapses, waiting for the dreaded 'I'm sorry, there's nothing further we can do.' It felt as though I had spent five and a half years waiting. And now I was waiting for Daniel to die. The Stoics taught that one should recognise what is under one's control and what is not and not worry about the latter. I wished that I could be so stoical.

My mind went back to my Dad, as his life ebbed away, saying to his cousin, in Welsh: 'Rydwy'n aros' – 'I am waiting.' Was Daniel waiting too?

Watching Daniel die is what I dreaded the most from the outset and I was right to do so. It's simply horrific watching one's child die. The nausea-inducing feeling of helplessness, of emptiness, of anticipatory grief, of frustration that he would miss out on so much, of desiring to stop the clock, of wanting the end to come but not wanting it to come, of wishing Daniel's suffering to be no more but silently imploring him to continue breathing, of confusion about the meaning of it all, of enhanced sense of spirituality yet disappointment at prayers unanswered, all the time mingled with all-consuming love and an overwhelming desire to protect, to give physical and psychological comfort to ease the passing but with a nagging guilt that I should still be trying to find answers for him (yet knowing, rationally, that I couldn't) – this maelstrom of emotion compares with nothing I have experienced.

Even in the midst of something so awful, many aspects of normal life still carry on. I still interacted with people, family and strangers as I normally would, I still shaved, I still ate (not much, but I actually enjoyed the food), I was still thinking up strategies to help him get better: that had become very much my normal. There was even some laughter as I enjoyed some rough and tumble with Jess on the bed next to Daniel and told the girls that he was forever chiding me for being too rough with her.

I guess that's how human beings survive awful experiences. Even in the most extreme circumstances, there are crutches of normality that we lean on. People who don't find those crutches go mad. Watching Daniel die was at the same time both extraordinary and ordinary and I found that extraordinary. It brought to mind Hannah Arendt's evocative phrase 'the banality of evil' to describe Nazi bureaucrats like Adolf Eichmann.

Hope, even forlorn, illogical hope, is humankind's principal crutch. Late in the afternoon that Sunday, I noticed that Daniel's rib tumour had become highly vascularised (there were lots of veins showing). What did this mean? The tumour seemed to have stopped growing. I did some quick internet research, and spoke to the three doctor cousins. They were gentle with me but realistic. I fired off a text to Henry, apologising for disturbing him on a Sunday, but realised as soon as I sent it that vascularisation was actually a bad sign: the cancer had its own sophisticated blood supply to feed its avarice. Henry, too, was gentle in his prompt reply and suggested the cancer was still growing inwards even if outward growth had ceased.

Still I couldn't let go. I worried that, just possibly, the chemo was having some effect but we couldn't detect it in Daniel's lungs and pleura. He was breathing so easily and his SATS were good. I say 'worried' because Daniel wasn't getting any fluids or food. What if the chemo was beginning to work but he died of dehydration? Maybe, just maybe, the rib tumour wasn't growing inwards and the lung and pleura cancer was also responding to the chemo. Long shots had become de rigueur in this journey.

At 10.30pm on a whim, I rang Siwan, a palliative care registrar who attended my Mum's church. Again, I was apologetic, but this was no time for social nicety. It might be too late by the morning.

We spoke for half an hour, Siwan patiently explaining what she thought was happening. Her guess, based on my description, was that Daniel could live for another few days. She told me about terminal agitation – panic induced physiologically by the body breaking down. It all suddenly made sense. From what she could tell, giving Daniel fluids might cause problems with his breathing. The last thing I wanted was to disturb Daniel's present comfortable state.

Nevertheless, I decided to get in touch with Colin first thing in the morning and composed the email in my mind. I wanted to be as sure as possible that we were doing the right thing by Daniel. Leaving no stone unturned, as I had so often been advised when he was diagnosed. I didn't expect to find anything under this particular stone, but had to lift it just in case.

As I settled down beside Daniel, I set the alarm for 6am. Maybe we did have a few more days. I had to use them to maximum effect. I felt surprisingly serene, having managed to manufacture some hope again.

At 12.50, Petra woke me in a panic. Daniel had stopped breathing. This time he didn't start breathing again. Daniel had died. There would be no email to Colin. Hope, earthly hope, was extinguished

I'm not certain that I was awake at the moment of death, but something had woken Petra, some instinct perhaps, as he breathed his last. The important thing is that one of us was awake. Presumably, in fact, it took some minutes for brain death to happen.

One never knows how one is going to react at a moment of profound sadness. Each of us loved Daniel more than words could possibly articulate but we reacted differently. Petra and Sasha were in floods of tears, inconsolable. Florence didn't cry then. She just sat there looking at her beloved brother, unable, it seemed, to take her eyes off him. I didn't cry either. There had been so many tears during the cancer journey. But that night I didn't cry.

Petra had been more realistic than me during the last few days, accepting that we had lost and focusing solely on making Daniel as comfortable as possible. But now she couldn't accept. She wouldn't let me turn the oxygen off until the doctor had been. 'Has he definitely died?' she asked a couple of times.

I rang the out-of-hours GP services, to report Daniel's death. It would be a couple of hours before anyone came because they were busy. The living take priority over the dead, I suppose. The doctor I spoke to didn't express any sympathy.

Dr Zarif, the doctor who came to certify, was kind. He switched off the oxygen. Daniel didn't need it any more.

My new reality was that Daniel – my precious, precious son – was dead. But there was another new reality for me, which I hadn't expected. Almost immediately, I found my perspective, still inevitably anchored in what I knew, nonetheless changing, subtly but noticeably, to one that extended beyond this world. I had spent the previous years doing everything I could to keep Daniel in this world. I had failed. Now I wondered: 'Where is Daniel now, not that useless body but the real Daniel, his spirit?' Was he gone, really gone, or was he transitioning to some new place that we couldn't begin to understand?

As I looked at him, lying on the hospital bed which had become his death-bed, this was the thought which dominated. Like everyone, I had often pondered whether there is an afterlife, but now the question was overwhelmingly pressing. A worry, ever-present, about whether Daniel would live had become a worry about whether he was safe now, indeed whether he still was. I could no longer help him, other than (I hoped) by praying for his soul, but the worry had not disappeared, merely metamorphosed into something different.

To state the obvious: it was a strange night. But some things didn't change. Daniel had been in the same position for over twenty-four hours. He was no longer breathing – a fairly important detail, admittedly – but he looked no different. We still told him that we loved him. We still held his hand. We still kissed his forehead. And, because it was still only four in the morning by the time Dr Zarif came, too early to call the undertaker, we settled down to sleep beside him. It might some odd but it seemed the natural thing to do.

I felt strongly that Daniel was still with us and hoped it wasn't the self-delusion of wishful thinking.

* * *

One final cruel blow Fate delivered that fateful day. It was due to be Sasha's first day as a student at Oxford. There is no good day to lose an adored brother. But this of all days. 'Men are not prisoners of fate, but only prisoners of their own minds', mused Franklin D. Roosevelt. Sasha, who had already lost her father when she was five, could be forgiven for disagreeing.

Farewell, Daniel

Dad: *Do you like parsnips?*
Daniel (aged three): *No I don't like them because I've never tried them*

The next few days were filled with things no parent should ever have to do. Imagine registering your son's death. Imagine having meetings with the vicar about your son's funeral. Andrew Body was accommodating (even if he didn't get my joke about putting down the side of the church the tennis officials who had contacted him). Imagine having to pass on news of your son's death. Outside family this was initially by text, that most modern of forms of communication. My friend Dominic replied that tears were streaming down his face.

I sent round an email, saying something about Daniel and how he had dealt with his illness. It inspired an amazing reaction, far beyond the kinds of things people say on these occasions. Daniel's age and the broken dreams had something to do with this, I'm sure, but it seemed more than this. Because, I suppose, I had been open in my email, many people opened up to me. I finished the email with 'I hope and pray with every fibre in my body that Daniel is now in a better place', a line which Rev Body picked up on at the funeral. A number told me about their own conviction about the afterlife, in a way I doubt they would normally have done. It told me that more people have religious convictions – using that term in its broadest sense – than one sometimes supposes in our secular age.

People sent poems which had helped them during bereavement. Helen, a barrister friend, told me about her father, a leading civil servant who like her had been to Magdalen and was dying of prostate cancer. Kindly but unnecessarily, she expressed guilt about the depth of her grief when he did die: she had lost 'only' her father, not her child. A work contact took his phone off the hook to read the email properly; others re-read it.

In addition to all the emails, I received some wonderful, handwritten letters, composed it seemed, from the heart. Handwritten letters are an anachronism in the electronic age, but somehow they convey deeper emotion.

All these messages were - and are - a real comfort, in a way that I wouldn't have expected. It has redoubled my determination to communicate solidarity with anyone going through a hard time.

I sent the email to Colin and other UCH staff. I wanted

to acknowledge that a great many people had been involved in Daniel's care. I also wanted them to know something about him, the person not the cancer patient, especially given how private he had been during his illness. Dr Seddon acknowledged the importance of doctors seeing the person behind the patient.

Colin wrote a letter of condolence, which we appreciated. Melanie, Daniel's specialist oncology nurse, liaised actively with the community team during his last few days, but when he died we didn't hear a word. I thought that was poor. Specialist oncology nurses are not ordinary nurses. Their job is to support patients and their families in all ways. A young man had lost his life. Would a phone call, an email, even a text, have been too much trouble, to acknowledge his family's enormous loss? Perhaps, unbeknown to me, Melanie faced pressures in her own life. But the message she communicated by her failure to communicate was that Daniel was just another patient and now that he was an ex-patient we were of no concern to her.

We chose a coffin called 'The Oxford'; it seemed the obvious choice.

Petra and I visited Daniel in the funeral home. I wasn't sure why I went. I didn't think of Daniel as inhabiting his body any longer. This is why I rarely visit his grave. But irrationally, I felt I would be letting him down if I didn't go. I'm glad I did but the image of Daniel in his coffin disturbs me greatly. Petra and the girls wanted him dressed in his special clothes and for Cover and Snoopy to be with him.

On the morning of the funeral, I went with Jess to Chobham Common for some solitude and to practise my eulogy. On the way back, I passed a hearse, parked outside the home of Graham, a neighbour. His daughter Lindsey, in her early forties with two young children, had a facial cancer. Graham and I used to update each other on our children's progress. Some coincidence that Lindsey and Daniel, from the same village and both dead far too early from the same disease, would be making their last earthly journeys on the same day.

I worried about how I would cope with the eulogy and had one wobble during the week about doing it. But it had to be me or Petra and Petra didn't feel strong enough. I faced one obvious difficulty. Daniel was exceptionally modest and hated any hint of parental boasting. Within the inner family, he was proud of his achievements, certainly, but didn't shout the odds outside it.

The problem was that eulogies need to eulogise, otherwise they're not really doing their job. The task I set myself was to try to capture the essence of Daniel's personality. There would be no solemn recitation of achievements, like some glorified school report. Equally, however, they couldn't be ignored. You cannot separate the man from his achievements, particularly when forged in such adversity. The eulogy went through several drafts.

Every time I practised it, I broke down. I had arranged for JJ to be my substitute, in case I couldn't carry on. When he read the eulogy, he apologised: 'Unc, I'm really sorry, I just can't do this.' Katie, his sister, agreed to be sub for the sub.

It's a strange thing but a kind of serenity came over me during the funeral. There were tears, certainly, but not as many as I'd expected. Delivering the eulogy was easier than I feared. I have heard similar tales: my neighbours Alan and Andy experienced the same thing giving the eulogies of their fathers. Maybe strength came from above, maybe Daniel was with me (a wonderful thought), maybe the unreality of the situation had a calming effect. As I stood at the lectern, I just couldn't imagine Daniel in the coffin next to me, even with the beautiful Wimbledon floral tribute made by a friend of Sian's.

I addressed the last few lines of the eulogy to Daniel directly rather than the congregation. It seemed natural because I wanted to thank him for being such a wonderful son. It was only a couple of weeks later that I learnt, while reading a book by Sam Leith, that there is a term for this rhetorical device: 'apostrophe.' Daniel would have been interested in that.

As I sat down, the congregation broke into spontaneous applause. I knew it was primarily for Daniel.

Apart from Felix, Daniel's tutor, who gave a heartfelt eulogy of his own, the other participants were all youngsters which seemed appropriate. The pall bearers were Tobias, who came over specially from Germany, JJ and two of Daniel's cousins on Petra's side, David and Richard. Paul, a Magdalen friend, read Canon Scott Holland's beautiful poem about the dead just slipping away into the next room and read it beautifully. Annabel struggled to get through St Paul's majestic hymn to love in 1 Corinthians 13. People came from far and wide and some who couldn't attend held their own services.

The funeral seemed to make a real impact. No doubt Daniel's age played a part, but there was more to it than that. Perhaps it was because he had so much to offer, perhaps his character shone through, perhaps the playing of his sonata struck a chord.

Over the next few weeks I sent the eulogy to people not at the funeral, including the many doctors who had helped me along the way. Again, the reaction was astonishing. So many doctors took the trouble to communicate how they felt. Some opened up about tragedies in their own life, about their own cancer. Others told me about their religious beliefs. One said she looked forward to meeting Daniel in the afterlife and quite a few wished they had got to know him in this life. Many were in tears as they read the eulogy (one example: 'I'm at a scientific meeting … and the people in the room are probably wondering why I was tearing up reading [the] email. If I am touched so deeply I can't imagine how you feel'). One or two said they had printed it, or the poem at the end, for re-reading. Many said Daniel's story would provide extra inspiration in their research or clinical work and asked permission to share it with colleagues who had not known of Daniel. Idriss Bennani-Baiti, a research scientist in Austria, kindly offered help with this book. One doctor sent me an editorial entitled *Carpe Diem* he had penned and carpe diem – Daniel's approach to his cancer, to his life – resonated with many.

Uta Dirksen in Münster sent me not only an email but also a card by post. Beate Stöckelhuber remembered us at Christmas. Jaume Mora encouraged me to write this book. Peter Bader in Frankfurt wrote a beautiful handwritten letter. Marciana Duma, the young Romanian radiotherapist in Munich, told me she still found it difficult to leave her work at the hospital after a duty. I suggested that, although a certain distance was necessary for objectivity and sanity, perhaps the best doctors were the ones who thought about their patients outside work.

One of the most moving replies was from a doctor hailing from Greece, Giannoula Klement, originally a vet but now a sarcoma doctor in Boston:

'I feel incredibly honored that you shared with me your sad news ... I rarely find out much about the outcomes of my encounters with families like yours and I rarely have such an opportunity to learn about the person behind the disease. Reading the eulogy I realised what a privilege my vocation is and how fortunate I am to get to know people like you. I realise that I must be really grateful for the window you offer me in expanding my quest to help patients like Daniel. As intense as cancer therapy is, we (physicians) play a very small part in the individual lives. We get to know so little about the children who, like Daniel, become our patients. Reading the description of Daniel's life, the extent of his ambitions and accomplishments and the strengths and love of his family, has allowed me to know more about you, about him and hopefully about my future patients.

I am treating a number of other patients with Ewings; all of them are facing the odds that Daniel faced. They are on novel therapies, so our relationship is intense and supportive, but there are things we do not know about each other. After reading Daniel's eulogy, I feel I want to know them – THEM – not their disease and for that, I thank you. I promise to take the time to benefit from the insights and dreams of my patients and to let them know my dreams. I promise to make the time, because you took the time to let me know and to share your love

for Daniel.
  Thank you for making me part of your (and his) life,
  I am genuinely honoured.'

Wow. Giannoula, in fact, had always struck me as an empathic doctor.

It must be so difficult for doctors to see such suffering every day, particularly of children, to experience frequent helplessness and yet retain sanity and humanity. I gained renewed respect and admiration for the medical profession during Daniel's journey, with extraordinary help from so many. I read of a doctor who contacted a young girl dying of Ewing's every day and another who told his dying teenage patient that he loved her. Does that cross the line? Some will think so, but I find it hard to criticise an excess of compassion. Doctors like Pete Anderson, a creative paediatric oncologist who gives so much time helping parents around the world, really understood the importance of conveying hope.

Typically, perhaps, despite the reaction it inspired I wasn't all that happy with the eulogy. I had told myself not to focus too much on the cancer years: there was so much else in Daniel's life worth telling. But I still focused on those years, I suppose because they had been so dominant and were still so fresh. There were stories I wish I had included, but didn't think of them. One from Daniel's time at Winston Churchill School in Woking summed him up so well. Petra and I were used to his teachers telling us how much they loved teaching him, how he was a model pupil, how they all wanted him to do their subject at GCSE or A level. So much so that we were taken aback when, at one parents' evening, his physics teacher began the conversation: 'I'm very angry with Daniel.' 'Why?', we asked. 'Well, we have been studying waves and every time I say the word Daniel and his friends start the Mexican Wave.' 'We'll have a word', we replied. Secretly I thought: 'That's my boy!'

I wish I had related that, when as a toddler he cried, a fairly rare event, I would say to him: 'Dan, whatever you do, don't laugh' and within three to four seconds a big grin would break out and the tears would melt away. That would have encapsulated what an easy child he was, with contentment his default position.

But these were small regrets. Much more relevantly, I was beginning life without Daniel. I didn't know how I would cope, if even I wanted to cope.

Reflections

Dad: *Shall we ring Grandma today?*
Daniel (aged three): *No*
Dad: *But she likes speaking to you on the phone*
Daniel: *Tough*

One more kid dies of cancer. One more young person loses his life long before his time. One more drop in the ocean of suffering which laps unceasingly against the shores of our precarious existence. We hear so much bad news, sometimes close to our own lives, more often in the wider world. We acknowledge the sadness, we think of those affected, we may feel a spasm of referred pain. And then we move on. We have to, not just because we have lives to lead and our own worries to address, but because we cannot take on board all the world's ills and at the same time retain our sanity. Those directly affected cannot move on, or not easily. We know that but in most cases we have to leave them to their suffering.

And so it is that, most of the time, most people have had to leave those of us mourning Daniel to our suffering. That is how it has to be; it's no criticism. I have noticed that some people find it harder, now, to ask how I am than they did when Daniel was still here. But that's no criticism either. It's easier to identify with a child's illness than with a parent's grief. Besides, I used to open up more about Daniel's cancer than I do about my own grief: to say 'I'm doing ok, thanks', my stock reply is not to invite in-depth discussion. None of this, in any event, is to denigrate the wonderful support I have had and I know there is plenty more available if I ask for it. My good friend Martyn wrote: 'Your loss is my loss', a wonderful example of empathy expressed with economy.

Daniel was simply delightful as a toddler.

Coping with grief

Grief has brought surprises. I have not noticeably gone through any of the classic stages – numbness, denial, anger, acceptance and so forth. True, there is coping on the inside and coping on the outside. The latter enables one to function as part of society; the former gives inner peace. I suspect the analogy of the swan gliding serenely over the water whilst paddling furiously beneath the surface fits the lives of more people than we realise.

However, even below the watermark my paddling has, on the whole, been more controlled than I expected. I have heard bereaved parents talking about grief physically hurting; I haven't experienced that. I have found it easier to say that Daniel has died than I expected and I talk about him easily. I have been able to throw myself into my work and this book. At times – not often, admittedly – Daniel's life being really well lived and my privilege in sharing it have combined to give quiet satisfaction. I hadn't expected that. Yes, Daniel's life was largely unfulfilled, his character was still developing and many of his dreams were scattered on the winds before they could take proper shape. But that is so with all our lives. Had Daniel lived to a hundred, his character would still have been developing and there would still have been dreams unfulfilled. It's just a matter of degree.

I haven't come close to mental meltdown, as some experience, though at times I have seen how it could happen. Apparently, the amount of transporter variant in the serotonin produced by the brain correlates to depression after a major stress event; maybe I have less

Mum has always been the fulcrum of the family.

than some. Daniel and I shared the same ability to relegate psychological pain to a place where it can do less visible damage.

Human beings rapidly adjust to new reality. This had first struck me in my mid-twenties in India when I was disturbed how quickly the sight of beggars and of children deliberately mutilated to improve their marketability, became my new reality. There is a danger in adjusting too quickly in this way. If one isn't careful, it can lead to a dulling of sensibility to the suffering of others, even to brutalisation. It's what enables otherwise decent people to behave out of character in war, for mob rule to take over if the conditions are right, for the demonisation of minorities to become the norm.

It's perhaps not surprising that we adjust so readily. As children, we suddenly find ourselves in this extraordinary world in this extraordinary universe. Noam Chomsky has postulated an innate sense of language and Steven Pinker an innate sense of morality, transcending culture, but there's no denying that life is strange and yet we adjust to it seamlessly. Only gradually do we begin to question what it's all about.

I should add 'so far' to this assessment of my grief. Grieving is a long and winding road; who knows how I will feel next week let alone next month or next year? A bereaved Ewing's parent wrote that her counsellor warned about delayed grieving: she had been so worried 'about keeping the wheels and cogs going that I can't seem to take the time to have that nervous breakdown I so desperately need.'

It's all relative, anyway. Suppressed pain is not dissipated pain. There have been plenty of tears, most in private, some in public. There have been nights when I didn't care whether I woke up and some – not many – when I wished not to wake up. There have been several bouts of existential angst, at times bordering on nihilism. Longevity for longevity's sake holds no attraction. Grief is debilitatingly tiring, I have found. I rarely feel rested, even after a good night's sleep. Nothing in life tastes quite the same any more. In March 2012, as I watched Wales win the Grand Slam at the Millennium Stadium, I felt inured to the mounting excitement – lonely in a crowd of delirious Welshmen.

I miss Daniel terribly. The moment he died was the moment I was denied the opportunity of loving the way I had loved him. Loving romantically is different to loving a child. It's corny, and anatomically perverse, to say that he has left a Daniel-sized hole in my heart, but it's how I feel.

All those things we would have shared. Not just the big life events – graduating, career, family – or even all the sport, music and theatre we would have gone to together, the films we would have watched, the sport we would have played, the books and newspaper articles we would have read, the TV and radio programmes we would have chatted about. Watching him grow as a human being. Discussing his cases if he'd become a lawyer.

But little things too – the jokes, the ribbing, the card games, the telephone calls. His endless questions in the face of my endless ignorance (as he would remind me while asking yet more questions). So many times I have found myself wanting to chat about things with him and imagining his reaction. In fact, sometimes I do share them. I talk to him every day and tell him I love him. I have taken part in a couple of university debates since Daniel died and found it difficult to be among students. One delightful lad, a fan of Jeremy Bentham's philosophy, reminded me of Daniel. A few months after Daniel died we planted a tree in his memory in the grounds of Magdalen College. It was my first time back in Oxford and it upset me more than the funeral. Perhaps it was because his contemporaries were about to graduate and were talking excitedly about their futures.

To me the idea of finding personal happiness – that elusive crock of Eldoradan elixir at the end of the Nirvana rainbow – seems absurd. How could I be happy when the most precious part of my life has been torn away? There are pleasurable times, thankfully, and fulfilment from work and extracurricular activities and in relationships of various sorts. Reading gives me the solace which, strangely, it didn't during Daniel's illness. I have my health, for now at least and that is cause for genuine gratitude.

I have memories, too, so many happy memories. When, before Daniel died, bereaved parents said how memories sustained them I used to think they would be no good to me. I thought the past would be a foreign country, as the novelist LP Hartley put it and that I would visit as rarely as possible. There would be too many landmines, the climate would be inhospitable and the food unpalatable. I expected peremptorily to remove photographs of Daniel and delete his number from my mobile. Well, many of the memories are painful, but there are some I can retrieve; they often bring a smile to my face. I'm able to look at his photograph and his number remains on my mobile. Recently at the Royal Albert Hall, I chanced upon a photograph of the 2007 *Last Night of the Proms* and could just make out Daniel. The moment was poignant but the memory is precious. Unlike parents of a stillborn child, I have a treasure trove of memories.

But happy memories don't equate to happiness. People say: 'Daniel would want you to be happy, to get on with your life.' I'm sure he would. But it's not as simple as that. I'm of a mind with Paul, one of the sons in DH Lawrence's *Sons and Lovers*, who, faced with his mother's plea that he be happy, insisted: 'So long as life's full, it doesn't matter whether it's happy or not ... so long as you don't feel life's paltry and a miserable business, the rest doesn't matter, happiness or unhappiness.' Like Paul, what matters is that my life is full and has some meaning.

Grief, this kind of grief, is a life sentence. I know that. And I don't want the sentence to be commuted, because what would that say about my love for Daniel? I have no masochistic tendencies, but raw psychological pain feels right because it reflects the depth of my loss. I sometimes feel guilty when I laugh, because Daniel is not laughing, at least not here. It was a while before I hit a tennis ball and playing still feels uncomfortable because Daniel should be the other side of the net. I'm not sure I could play table-tennis: table-tennis was when we talked about everything and nothing. Bouts of temporary amnesia give welcome respite but the sudden jolt back to reality is, equally, a necessary corrective. As CS Lewis commented on the death of his much-loved wife: 'The pain I feel now is the happiness I had before. That's the deal.'

We all need coping mechanisms for life's challenges. In the early months after Daniel's death, I would sometimes pretend that I still had treatment decisions to take. I would imagine that we were doing something together, like going to the Olympics. This wasn't denial – I knew the reality – but a technique to get over a difficult moment. Some might regard it as unhealthy but coping strategies, provided they don't take over, can be a bulwark against mental disintegration.

I have found that trying to turn adversity into something positive has helped. Writing this book is part of that. Mark Matousek, in *When You're Falling, Dive*, recounts the inspirational tales of people who have achieved great things following tragedy. No one should feel guilty for not being able to build on the ruins of personal disaster, and serious illness, physical or mental, is understandably more than enough for many to deal with. As with all things in life, we should applaud the small steps that people take rather than condemn them for not taking bigger strides. There are days, many of them, when I feel wholly inadequate to apply the lessons I have learnt. But on the less bad days the challenge remains one to which I feel I must try to rise.

It helps me, at any rate, to think that I'm not wasting all the pain. I recently heard Terry Waite talk of his determination not to waste the lessons from his captivity in Beirut. In *Agamemnon*, the play I saw with Daniel, Aeschylus wrote that humanity is fated to learn by suffering. I have tried to learn from my suffering.

Dreams

Human beings have a wonderful capacity to think that bad things will not happen to us, only to other people. It helps us cope with life's many bear-traps if we can persuade ourselves that they won't ensnare us. We know it's irrational, and we take measures to reduce or avoid obvious risks, so the confidence is not absolute. But, though we vaguely know the road casualty statistics, improved but still horrific, we don't imagine they apply to us as we get behind the wheel. Cancer is what happens to other people's children.

Dreams are more honest. For me bad dreams are routine, as they were during Daniel's illness. Vivid, fast-moving dreams. The unconscious mind is still a mystery but perhaps dreams are the best guide to inner well-being. Freud and Jung would have had a field-day with some of mine. I have dreamt about Daniel a lot, and I'm grateful for that. For that fleeting slumberous moment, Daniel has been alive again. I haven't been too troubled by the sense of disappointment on waking up. I know of bereaved parents desperate to dream about their child but unable to. Most of my dreams about Daniel have been sad, it's true. A typical scenario is that he is really ill but I'm still looking at treatment options, so there's still hope: a metaphor for the whole journey. One night I was holding him in a swimming-pool (in fact, he was a much better swimmer than me). Occasionally the dreams take on more of a nightmarish quality. In one, Daniel turned over in his coffin and asked for a cup of coffee (he never drank coffee, as it happens!).

Evidence of a troubled mind or portent of something deeper? Who knows, but I have discovered that dreams, in all their ephemeral confusion, can ease the pain. Even with nightmares I'm glad to have the connection.

Some dreams are uplifting. Soon after he died, I dreamt that Daniel was introduced to God. I had never dreamt about God as far as I can remember. How did I know it was God? I just did. My religious/spiritual friends eagerly told me: 'That was no dream.' Others have joined in on the dreaming act. On the night the Olympic Torch arrived in the UK, my sister Charlotte dreamt that Daniel told her: 'Tell Daddy I'm ok.' The next day, she opened a book at a chapter headed 'Carpe Diem', the motto I had assigned to Daniel in my eulogy. On the night he died, Barbara, a supportive friend in the States who has had a near-death experience, kept dreaming of an unidentified young man (she had never met Daniel).

Losing a child

Why is losing a child the worst kind of bereavement? Joseph Kennedy, patriarch of the American dynasty remarked:

'When the young bury the old, time heals the pain and sorrow, but when the process is reversed the sorrow remains forever.' I loved my Dad, but losing him doesn't compare with losing Daniel. It would have been the same for Daniel had he lost a child. I'm struck by how often people say 'I can't imagine what you are going through', not 'I can imagine how difficult that must be', the usual response to someone's problems. It's as if the human mind cannot make the leap of empathic imagination for the tragedy which we dread most of all. Or perhaps it dare not try because it knows the pain, even imagined, will be too great.

People say that a child predeceasing disturbs the natural order of things. Edmund Burke, the 18th century philosopher politician whose two sons predeceased him, lamented: 'I live in an inverted order. They who ought to have succeeded me are gone before me. They who should have been to me as posterity are in the place of ancestors.' But I'm not sure that the inversion of order is an adequate explanation. An evolutionary biologist would argue, I suppose, that the pain reflects the need our genes have to replicate. However, I'm not aware of any evidence that parents suffer less at the death of a child who has already reproduced. Perhaps the answer lies in a parent's pain at what the child has lost.

Daniel's loss, indeed, matters so much more than mine. *The Old Testament* patriarch Isaac died 'old and full of days.' Daniel died young and full of dreams. Viewed from his diagnosis, at seventeen, Daniel increased his longevity by only 30 per cent. Much better than so many other Ewing's patients, but a fraction of the 500 per cent he could reasonably have expected pre-diagnosis (in fact, life expectancy will presumably be much higher for his generation).

Daniel had so much potential for fulfilment, for enjoyment, for achievement, for friendship, for love. He had such a zest for life: a cliché, perhaps, but like all clichés containing much truth. Not for Daniel the narcissistic death-wish of the poet Frank Thompson, who lamented: 'I am too brilliant … I shall be burnt out at twenty-three. I must seek an early death to keep my flame untarnished and immortal' (he had his wish, mown down in Bulgaria during the war). Daniel was more in tune with another Ewing's patient, in her mid-twenties and the mother of twins: 'I have too much life left in me to waste in the darkness of a coffin.'

My frustration at Daniel's loss is tempered in two respects. First, we don't actually know that he would have had a happy life. This is the assumption always made when a young person dies, but it may not be warranted. Even if Daniel had survived his cancer, there's a good chance he would have got a different cancer – osteosarcoma or a leukaemia – as a result of all the toxic treatment. That would have been just awful. Secondary cancers usually occur with Ewing's a few years after treatment, though they can hit soon after frontline treatment finishes. Gage, a delightful boy in the US diagnosed with Ewing's when three, developed leukaemia soon after chemotherapy (and then died, aged nine and paralysed, when his Ewing's returned).

There is a litany of other long-term physiological effects Daniel could have suffered. Psychological trauma resulting from childhood cancer is well-documented, too, and for all his equability, who's to say that he would have been immune?

Beyond cancer, any of the disasters which lurk at every corner could have befallen Daniel as they could befall any of us – car accidents, assault, other physical illnesses, schizophrenia, depression and so much more. He may have been unlucky in love. He might have lost his own child.

And at a more global level, one doesn't need Jeremiahan pessimism to feel gloomy at the prospects for humanity. Professional optimists such as Matt Ridley and Bjorn Lomborg may have faith in human ingenuity to solve existential problems in time, but I'm not alone in thinking it likely that the human race will eventually self-destruct – through nuclear attack, untamed climate change or some medium thus far uninvented. We have, in the West at least, moved on from Thomas Hobbes' assessment in *Leviathan* of life as 'solitary, poor, nasty, brutish and short', and child mortality now represents far less than the 50 per cent plus of all mortality it historically has, but there's still plenty to fear in today's world, more in some ways. The Oxford philosophers Julian Savulescu and Ingmar Persson even argue for moral bioenhancement - using neuroscience manipulation to increase our moral capacity - because people are unlikely to alter behaviour to address problems like climate change, where potential catastrophe is too distant in time and place and our own individual responsibility too minor.

What if we cannot find antibiotics to replace those made redundant by resistance? The global population explosion and the pressure on water and other resources and the waves of refugees which it brings, is the elephant in the room which few politicians will talk about; indeed, some governments are actually trying to increase their populations, oblivious to the misery outside their affluent borders, or, prisoners of misguided religious fervour, engage in a macabre numbers games. The toxic alliance of religious fanaticism – and no religion is exempt, sadly – and evermore destructive technology will remain an ever-present threat. Some not only predict the Apocalypse but wish to bring it about. One day they may succeed. On that day, or myriad other days, we may see that Daniel was the lucky one.

He is now protected from the kaleidoscope of earthly tragedy and there's real comfort in that. And yet he would have taken his chances with all the slings and arrows of fortune, personal and global, such was his embrace of life. I have no doubt about that. In that sense, I can discount the precariousness of life from my reflections about Daniel's loss.

The other respect in which concern about Daniel's loss is tempered is more profound. If, as I fervently hope, he is in a better place now, at peace and happy, it seems counterintuitive to talk about his loss. It's not loss but huge gain. It's just that we cannot know and so with our narrow, materialist perspective it still makes sense to talk about Daniel's loss.

Regret

With grief and loss comes regret. Regret is normally a futile emotion, if there's no useful lesson to be learnt. Regrets come in two types: things one has one done which are clearly mistakes, even if that is only apparent in hindsight, and things one wishes one had done differently, even if no criticism can be made of the choice made given what one knew at the time. For Daniel's pre-cancer life, I wish Petra and I had been able to stay together. That would have been better for Daniel and it's a big regret.

But my focus here is on regrets about cancer decisions. I don't have many regrets of the mea culpa sort, though I certainly blame myself for the delay in diagnosis.

For the most part, my regrets are in the second category. There were so many decisions to take during those five and a half years, decisions which I wasn't prepared simply to delegate to Daniel's doctors. I researched everything exhaustively (and exhaustingly). We collected a large amount of diagnostic information, significantly more than is collected for most patients and at only a slightly increased burden for Daniel. And of course, we listened closely to what Daniel's doctors advised. I was satisfied that every decision was rational, based on what we knew at the time. There is no treatment decision of which I say to myself: 'Come on, you should have done better than that.' And that is a comfort. When we decided not to have particular additional treatment, there was a very good reason. Many things I would like to have tried but the evidence wasn't compelling enough. Daniel couldn't be a guinea-pig for speculative treatment which would carry more than a minimal price for him.

I do regret that Daniel didn't have a CT scan in the latter part of 2009; that would surely have picked up the relapse and might have given the eventual radiotherapy a better chance of working. Again, however, regret has to be tempered with realism. CT scans contain a high level of radiation and a study of 180,000 records of children and young adults published in the *Lancet* in 2012 suggested that multiple CT scans could triple the risk of secondary leukaemia or brain cancer. There was good reason for Colin's cautious approach and many Ewing's doctors, though not all, were similarly cautious.

I certainly regret that the system wasn't responsive for Daniel to have an IGF inhibitor when he was in remission, when it would have stood the best chance of working. The cancer was too advanced and had become too heterogeneous, by the time he had the Pfizer inhibitor in 2011.

I certainly can't say that, had Daniel had the inhibitor when in remission, it would have made a difference. But nor can anyone say that it would not have. With extremely life-threatening illnesses, the dynamic of statistics changes. Assume there is a 5 per cent chance of cure from an experimental treatment administered when a cancer is at microscopic level (remission). If the chances of cure from established treatment are, say, 70 per cent, clearly one wouldn't be much interested in the experimental alternative. But assume, instead, that the chances from established treatment are 1 per cent (much closer to the reality for Daniel). Suddenly 5 per cent becomes attractive. It may well be that an IGF inhibitor in 2008 wouldn't have increased Daniel's chances fivefold. But the point I kept coming back to was that the inhibitors seemed safe and easily tolerated, so there was no reason not to try.

But the biggest treatment regret lies with radiotherapy to Daniel's lungs, whole lung radiotherapy (or WLI) as it's called. Back in 2007, the choice presented to us was high-dose chemo or WLI but not both and Colin's recommendation was the former. By contrast, Jürgen Dunst, the radiotherapist I went to see in Lübeck, was a strong advocate of WLI even after high-dose chemo. A comment Colin made, in March 2008, worried me. He said that if WLI was given and Daniel remained in remission, we wouldn't know if it was the WLI which did the trick or all the chemo. I could understand why Colin wanted to know this with his other patients, present and future, in mind. However, Petra and I would not particularly care whether the WLI had been the crucial factor. We cared about other patients, very much, but as Daniel's parents our responsibility was to him and which treatment was decisive would have mattered little.

When Daniel eventually relapsed, it was to his pleura, the lining around the lungs. WLI would have encompassed the pleura. Might lung/pleura radiotherapy have staved off relapse, even killed the cancer which we know now was lurking in his pleura? We can only speculate. Daniel did eventually get cancer back in his lungs, although we don't know whether that was residual cancer after frontline treatment or migration from his pleura. WLI (actually just to his left lung) failed in 2011, but by that time his chest cancer was much larger and more virulent than it would have been in 2007/8. Were Daniel's doctors too conservative in advising against WLI on top of high-dose chemo?

The judgements were excruciatingly-balanced and I don't criticise Colin and Anna Cassoni for their caution. But not having WLI earlier is still a major regret. Colin told me that the lungs were the least of Daniel's problems, given how relatively quickly his initial lung mets had disappeared.

He wasn't saying that the lungs were not a problem, simply that Daniel's bone disease was a much greater problem. So this regret is not of the self-flagellating sort. But it's still a regret.

The problem we constantly faced was: how to differentiate between a genuine opportunity and a mere hypothesis? How to pull off impossible balancing tricks? You need the wisdom of Solomon. I didn't possess it, clearly. The only wisdom I had was the Socratic sort – awareness of my own ignorance. I had no experience to draw on, no refined instinct and pathetically inadequate knowledge about cancer. But nor did Daniel's doctors really possess wisdom. They had knowledge and judgement, but wisdom occupies a higher plane and it was wisdom we needed, the sort which often only comes with hindsight. In fact, even their knowledge was far from complete. There were so many known unknowns, let alone all the Rumsfeldan unknown unknowns. I respected doctors – Colin was one – who, where appropriate, were candid about their ignorance, echoing William Osler, the Canadian often dubbed the father of medicine: 'Medicine is the science of uncertainty and the art of probability.'

A final regret is about Daniel's panic attacks during his last weeks. No one mentioned terminal agitation, even though we told all the doctors about the attacks. Daniel could have had stronger sedation. I recognise that doctors have a dilemma with terminal patients – they have to balance the desire for continued consciousness with symptom relief – and there was still a chance Daniel would respond to the inhibitors. But there should have been a proper discussion with us.

I also blame myself. I spent hour after hour, day and night, trying to calm Daniel, reassuring him, stroking his arm, touching his chest when he asked me to, visualising with him, telling him how much I loved him, giving him hope, always giving hope. And so did Petra. He said we were the best at calming him down. But my research focus was still on finding an answer to his cancer. I should have insisted that a palliative care doctor came to see him.

I sometimes wonder if we should have taken Daniel elsewhere for treatment. The relationship with Colin McMaster was mixed, cordial and even light-hearted when things were going well, less good when he had bad news to impart and I wanted to discuss decisions closely. My assessment of Colin is that, if someone had a complicated illness, which required deep scientific knowledge and sound medical judgement from a dedicated doctor, where the indicated treatment was available, where the prognosis permitted hope and the patient wanted to know just how things stood, Colin would be your man, with few peers. He was less good in Daniel's desperate situation: he still had the requisite knowledge and judgement and the dedication, but, I thought, lacked the creativity to look beyond the tried and trusted. He wasn't prepared to fight as hard as I would have liked to access treatment which wasn't readily available and wasn't sufficiently sensitive about what Daniel didn't want to know. He didn't see it as his job to identify hope. That was our experience, at any rate; others may have had a different experience.

But for all that, I don't regret staying with Colin or UCH. It was always important to balance the needs of treatment with Daniel's quality of life, minimising disruption to normality as much as possible. Daniel liked Colin and had confidence in him and one shouldn't underestimate the importance of that. Despite what I see as his shortcomings, he is a very good doctor. There is no such thing as the perfect doctor, any more than there is the perfect lawyer or perfect gardener or perfect anything. I thought I could help provide creativity via expert doctors around the world. Perhaps I should have been more decisive in following through with ideas, but these were incredibly difficult decisions.

For all the retrospective analysis, the bottom line is that I set myself the task of getting Daniel better. Not by myself, of course. Compared to expert medical input, my role was only ever going to be relatively minor. But I still regarded restoration of Daniel's health as my responsibility, ultimately. And I failed. I failed Daniel. He really looked to me. To Petra too, but principally to me because he knew I was leading on the research. Whether I'm blameworthy for the failure is beside the point. With the things that matter to me, simply doing my best isn't enough (how can one know what one's best is anyway?). Only succeeding lets me off the hook on which I impale myself. Glorious failure, putting up a good show, brings little comfort. And nothing has ever mattered to me as much as Daniel being cured. My failure is a burden I will carry forever.

The personal credit column

But it's right to record that the sense of failure doesn't monopolise my personal ledger. There is a credit column too. These pages recount that there were everyday judgements I got wrong. This is no surprise. Not only was I way outside my scientific comfort zone, I was also in unchartered emotional territory. The fact that Daniel wanted to be protected from all bad news complicated things and called for plenty of snap judgements at a time when I wasn't in the best shape to make such judgements; some inevitably went awry. But for all the imperfection, I'm proud that Petra and I worked so hard, not just on things medical, but on protecting Daniel, on allowing him to breathe, on helping him to get on with his life and pursuing his dreams.

Above all, on giving him hope. Hope is so important for a cancer patient – of any age, but particularly a child. *The Anatomy of Hope*, by American oncologist Dr Jerome Groopman, implores doctors to give hope. Not false hope: he was critical of a doctor, well-meaning but misguided, who told a patient things were going well when patently they were not. The chickens soon came home to roost for the doctor when confronted by an angry daughter. But as much hope as one can possibly identify. Dr Groopman recounts the story of *Pandora's Box* from Greek mythology: hope as the necessary antidote to disease, pestilence and other ills.

Human beings cannot survive for long without hope. Victor Frankl, a concentration camp victim, described in his seminal work *Man's Search for Meaning* that fellow-prisoners without hope died. *In Three Minutes of Hope*, Rabbi Hugo Gryn, another concentration camp survivor, recounted his father's musings:

> *'You and I have seen that it's possible to live as long as three weeks without food. We once lived almost three days without water. But you cannot live properly for three minutes without hope.'*

Outside a concentration camp, the periods may be longer – I once visited someone on day sixty-three of a hunger strike – but the sentiment holds true and it's a lesson which not all doctors have absorbed. I couldn't have traversed Daniel's cancer journey without hope and, speculation though this has to be, I suspect he would have died much earlier without it. Within the suffocating constraints imposed by the cancer and the brutality of treatment, Daniel, infused with hope, survived for a number of years and prospered. He was the one doing the physical suffering and facing mortality far too early, but I'm confident that we eased the burden for him. For all my mistakes, I think we got right hundreds, thousands, of decisions, of human judgements. I hope, I believe, that for Daniel this made those difficult years, first as bearable and then as enjoyable and fulfilling as possible.

And perhaps, who knows, we also helped to extend his life through conventional and complementary medical and dietary decisions. I was surprised when medical professionals involved with Daniel's care said they thought my research had made a difference to how long he lived. It's impossible to know. But I'm convinced, for example, that it was right for Daniel to have extra radiotherapy to his bone metastases, in 2008. There was such a high expectation of early, fatal relapse in his bones that the decision could have added years to his life.

I'm proud I tried so hard and proud, too, that every single decision touching on Daniel's care and quality of life I took with his welfare as my sole motivation. Dissecting human motives is always a delicate task; they nearly always congeal into a complex mixture, even if the ingredients are not all the same weight. Determinists argue there's no such thing as altruism, that we are compelled to act in the way we do, even when it seems to be against our self-interest. As I get older, I do think we often enjoy less free will than we realise. It's an intractable debate, but I can confidently say that everything was geared to giving Daniel the best chance and to making as happy as possible whatever time he had left. I subsumed my interests to his for those five and a half years in a way I might not have thought possible. I'm sure the same is true of Petra. My decisions may not always have been right, but my motivation was and that brings comfort.

So, for all the regret, I feel relatively at peace with my efforts for Daniel.

Profound effect

Daniel's cancer years were years of unceasing anxiety. Not for a single moment between diagnosis in April 2006 and death in October 2011 did I feel able to relax fully. Damocles' sword was forever poised, often menacingly and in full view, always at least in peripheral view. Worry gnaws away at the soul. Waiting for endless scan and other results, looking out for symptoms, hoping not to find them, trying to understand their significance when they appeared anyway, anticipating relapse even when, in retrospect, Daniel was doing well, agonising over treatment decisions, assessing his state of mind, dealing with doctors and other health professionals (usually a pleasure but occasionally not), challenging drug companies and regulators – all this was bound to have a profound effect on serenity. The endless research, the analysing of scan reports, added to the stress because I learnt about possible problems about which I would otherwise have been ignorant, and with constant reminders about Daniel's dismal prognosis. (The irony is I would give my right arm and quite a few other limbs to have that anxiety back).

One often hears people say that a really bad experience has changed them, given them a different perspective on life. I don't think that my experience with Daniel has altered my values or worldview; if anything, it has underscored them. It has nevertheless had a profound emotional effect on me; it could hardly be otherwise. The fear and uncertainty of death, of loss, are closer to the surface. I feel less able to take knocks and at times am more pessimistic than I would like. Doris Kearns Goodwin, in her recent biography of Abraham Lincoln, describes the effect losing their three year old son had on his wife: 'deepening her mood swings, magnifying her weaknesses, and increasing her fears'. Perhaps not the first, but I can identify with the second and third.

For five and a half years, I inhabited a world drenched in suffering. I saw Daniel's suffering up close, Petra's suffering, the girls' suffering, the suffering of the wider family, the impact on friends, especially the more sensitive ones. But it went wider than this. I saw so much anguish in hospitals, here and in Europe. I learnt about cancer in the developing world, something I had known nothing about. I followed so many stories of children dying and saw what it did to their families.

I was also frequently reminded of the suffering of millions of animals used in cancer research. Whatever one's view about the ethics, or the efficacy, of cancer animal research (discussed on my website), one should acknowledge that lab animals pay an enormous price and that their suffering matters as much to them as ours does to us. Many people sadly leave it out of account, confusing what they regard as the moral acceptability of the suffering with the suffering not mattering.

Empathy

I confess uneasily that the pain of Daniel's illness affected me just as deeply as all this torrent of suffering put together, perhaps more so. It set me thinking why that should be so. Objectively, Daniel's suffering and death was no more tragic than the suffering and death of, say, a child with cancer in Malawi. Part of the explanation is that we feel greater empathy for those closest to us. JBS Haldane, the evolutionary biologist, put it crudely when asked if he would give his life to save a drowning brother: 'No but I would lay down my life for two brothers or eight cousins.' Presumably it would have needed a great many Malawians to induce the same sacrifice.

But I think that Haldane was only partially right. Human beings are capable of empathising with those a long way away, with people of different races, religions or cultures, indeed with members of different species. Proximity to suffering does, I'm sure, influence emotional response. I have no doubt that, if the Malawian child had been in the next hospital bed, if I had witnessed his shattered dreams, it would have caused greater pain than when he was little more than a statistic. Watching Daniel die would still have hurt more, but the disparity would have been less and I hope I would have been motivated to help the Malawian boy, if not to the same extent.

Adversity does, or should, sharpen empathic instincts. A few years ago I began writing a book about empathy as a basis for ethics (one of many unfinished projects). Psychopaths apart, perhaps, I believe empathy can be developed, taught even. One of Daniel's doctors said he had become a better doctor since his own daughter was diagnosed with cystic fibrosis. 'Only the wounded physician heals', as Jung put it. In her bestseller *Hannah's Gift*, a moving account of her three year-old dying from kidney cancer, Maria Housden wrote:

'I knew there had been a time in my life when I had been oblivious to suffering – my own and everyone else's. I believed that people brought suffering onto themselves. I had felt superior to them and thought that compassion was about feeling sorry for the fact that their lives weren't perfect like mine …'

I find the notion that one develops empathy and compassion only through a bad experience profoundly depressing for humanity and I'm not sure how typical it is. But that being close to cancer helps to nurture empathy I have no doubt, and that's a real benefit. Maria now tries to help others through her writing and speaking.

The great challenge for humankind is to use our imagination to understand the suffering of those who are not proximate. The 2nd century Stoic philosopher Hierocles pre-empted Haldane by urging people to treat strangers as cousins and cousins as brothers and sisters; Hierocles was himself echoing the universalist Chinese philosopher Mo

Tzu, who taught that Confucian ren (loosely, empathy) should be distributed without favouritism. It's rare that one disagrees with a saying in popular currency, but I do disagree that 'charity begins at home.' I believe charity begins where it's most needed. Responsibility starts at home, but not charity. I helped bring Daniel into the world and so I had a responsibility to help him, not that it felt in the least burdensome. Even so, it feels uncomfortable that I spent so much money on Daniel when the need, in Malawi and elsewhere, was just as pressing and the potential recipients just as deserving. Because money goes so much further in the developing world, the thousands of pounds I spent on Daniel could have helped so many children. My bike ride helped a bit, but I could have done much more.

And yet I don't regret focusing primarily on Daniel. Perhaps I should. The answer to my mild crisis of conscience, I believe, is that most of the responsibility rests at a communal level. Governments and international institutions should do everything in their power to diminish inequalities, to focus on what unites rather than what divides, to make trade rules fairer, to make war truly a last resort, above all to place compassion at the heart of policy. I applaud David Cameron for sticking to his pledge that the UK should devote 0.7 per cent of its GDP – hardly a king's ransom – to international development. But we should support policies of compassion much closer to home as well.

The most famous expression of empathy as the basis of morality lies in the Golden Rule in *St Matthew's Gospel* – 'Do unto others as you would have them do unto you' – but it's found in all the major religions, in Confucius even.

Sometimes it's expressed as a positive and sometimes as a negative obligation and sometimes both, as in the Prophet Muhammad's injunction in *Kitab al-Kafi*: 'As you would have people do to you, do to them; and what you dislike to be done to you, don't do to them.'

The Jewish scholar Hillel, an older contemporary of Jesus, put it like this: 'What is hateful for yourself, do not do to your fellow man. This is the whole of the Torah and the remainder is but commentary.' A verse in the *Letter to Hebrews* gives succinct practical context: 'Remember those who are in prison, as though you were in prison with them; those who are being tortured, as though you yourselves were being tortured.' Karen Armstrong, in her book *Twelve Steps to a Compassionate Life*, finds compassion – empathy's sibling – at the heart of all the major religions. Her analysis may be a little optimistic, but we have a deep-seated need to believe in a compassionate God (captured by the Taize prayer 'ubi caritas et amor Deus est': 'where charity and love are, there is God'). Racism, sexism, homophobia, discrimination against the physically disabled and the mentally ill, the abuse of animals, represent above all, a failure to imagine what the victims are feeling. Instead of institutionalising and justifying exploitative behaviour, we should ask ourselves the simple question: 'If I would not want done to me what I'm proposing to do to another, what gives me the moral right to do it?'

The steps are small and uncertain and sometimes backwards but humankind is, I believe, becoming more enlightened, giving the lie to Calvin's pessimistic description of man as a 'vile polluted lump of earth.' Steve Pinker, in his book T*he Better Side of My Angel*, shows convincingly that we are becoming a less violent species, relative to population, and he attributes this in large measure to a better understanding of other people. Global trade and the greater contact it brings and the internet have played major parts but he also cites the popularity of novels from the 18th and 19th centuries and the encouragement to empathise with the lives of even fictional characters which they brought. The sizeable fly in his soothing ointment, in my view, is that the development of technology with the potential to cause terrible suffering (nuclear weapons, drones, factory farming methods), the concentration of power in the hands of barely accountable corporations such as Big Pharma and the secrecy which still pervades so much of our public life mean that the forces of reaction can still be more powerful than those of enlightenment. Individuals can feel powerless to effect positive change in the face of such forces.

It's a crucially important subject. I wish that Daniel could have lived to see whether increasingly enlightened attitudes do win through in the unceasing war between good and evil.

Thinking about religion

The cancer years caused me to think ever more deeply about religion. Why are we here? Is there a God? Is there an afterlife? Why, indeed, is there so much suffering in the world (Tennyson's 'Nature, red in tooth and claw' hardly seems an adequate description)? Why was Daniel taken so young? Why do any of us die? Why did God create a world where all life decays? Is Christianity the true religion? Or Islam, Buddhism, Hinduism, Sikhism or Jainism? Or none of the above? Are we reincarnated? Despite pretty fundamental doctrinal differences, can the core messages of religions be synthesised into a coherent whole?

Although I know I will not find definitive answers this side of the grave, that doesn't stop the search. I want desperately to find solace that Daniel is safe. It's not an obsession – Daniel wouldn't have wanted that – but these are subjects I find myself returning to time and again.

I have read widely since Daniel's death, books from very different traditions, books about traditional Christian teaching, about theodicy, about hypnosis enabling people to regress to previous lives, about near death experiences (Pope Gregory the Great had one, it seems, and so did Jung and a Catholic teenager with Ewing's, and they are mentioned in Plato's *Republic*). But I have also been interested in the views of 'ordinary' people: no one has a monopoly of wisdom in these matters. Much of what I have learnt gives hope.

None of it gives definitive answers but then faith and doubt are handmaidens, not antitheses. *The New Testament* places heavy emphasis on faith but in *St Mark's Gospel* the father of a healed boy cries: 'Lord, I believe; help thou mine unbelief.' For Paul Tillich, the German theologian, doubt was an element of faith. In my view, the greatest contribution religious leaders could make to spiritual debate and certainly to societal harmony, would be to admit to the doubts which they must harbour if they retain intellectual honesty.

They would be in good company. In his *Confessions*, St Augustine of Hippo confessed: 'The notion began to grow in me that the philosophers whom they call Academics were wiser that the rest, because they held that everything should be treated as a matter of doubt and affirmed that no truth can be understood by men.' Religious belief is more than blind faith – it's based on diverse strands of evidence, however incomplete and sometimes flimsy – but nevertheless it cannot be about certainty. The same is true about lack of belief. Richard Dawkins, in *The God Delusion*, admitted that he couldn't be certain that there is no God, which by some definitions makes him an agnostic, not an atheist. A wise scientist will harbour doubt about the material world, too: it's always possible that new evidence could lead to a change in thinking.

Religious leaders, sadly, will continue to profess conviction. Reinhold Niebuhr, the Protestant theologian, wrote acidly in 1939: 'The truth, as it's contained in the Christian revelation, includes the recognition that it's neither possible for man to know the truth fully, nor to avoid the error of pretending that he does.' (It was Niebuhr, incidentally, who composed the beautiful prayer: 'God grant me the serenity to accept the things I cannot change, the courage to change the things I can, and the wisdom to know the difference.' During Daniel's cancer journey, I was not bad at the courage bit, not so good at serenity. I had a pretty astute idea of the difference but carried on regardless.)

Hope in death

For all the healthiness of scepticism, we yearn for certainty. Bereaved parents often say they are desperate for signs that their children are alright. The signs they often identify seem pretty flimsy to me – butterflies, rainbows, that kind of thing – but sometimes they are more impressive.

I would like to share three stories after Daniel died which have given me hope. One is Petra's and two are mine. Before I relate them, some grounding in realism. Astonishing coincidences happen all the time. When you pass a stranger in the street, imagine the infinitesimally large number of decisions, going back millennia, which had to be taken in one way rather than another for the encounter to take place, even for the two people to be born. The odds against the encounter, even viewed from the perspective of a hundred years ago, are many billions to one. And yet there are millions of such encounters every hour. Similarly, the chance of a pack of cards being dealt in a particular order is 80,658,175,170,943,878,571,660,636,856,403,766, 975,289,505,440,883,277,824,000,000,000,000:1 (I haven't checked the calculation) – or 52 factorial. And yet every time a pack is dealt, those exceptionally unlikely odds are realised.

So, when people say 'That can't be a coincidence', the answer, almost certainly, is 'Well, actually it can.'

Petra's story is this. A few months after Daniel died she went to see a psychic named Frances, recommended to me by a friend. Petra's expectations were low but she was desperate for reassurance. Frances said she made contact with Daniel. Much of what she said could apply to him but to many others, too. Other comments were more particular to Daniel; some things made no sense. At one point Frances said: 'Daniel was trying to get a message to you before Christmas that he is ok. Did you give your sister a dog, no a china dog, for Christmas?' A pretty random question.

Petra had indeed given Angela a china dog. It's not the sort of present she would normally buy her, but she had seen this ornament and thought it looked like Angela's dog, so she bought it. The display dog had a label round its neck with the name 'Lucky', a pretty standard dog's name. Petra assumed they were all called Lucky. There was nothing to indicate that different dogs had different names. The assistant pulled one off the shelf, packed in a box.

When Angela opened the box on Christmas Day, the label around the dog was 'Daniel.'

Whenever I have related that story, even atheist friends have gasped. I have never heard of a dog with the name Daniel, or even Dan or Danny. It doesn't feature in any list of popular dogs' names, though there might have been some personal reason why the manufacturer chose Daniel as one of the names. People are with justification often sceptical of psychics and the way they pick up what people say, their body-language, to make them think that they have made contact with someone who has died. There are undoubtedly shysters out there, preying on the vulnerable. But Frances could have known nothing about this unusual gift, or had any control over what it was called.

My own story is this. Nearly a year after Daniel died, I was staying in a hotel. Flicking through TV channels, I chanced upon *University Challenge*, a programme I like but rarely watch (Daniel loved it). It was half way through the episode. Aficionados will know that the two teams are given a starter question and the team that gets it right then has three bonus questions. The first starter I heard involved identifying a hymn tune. The team that buzzed got it wrong. They got a later starter right and were asked to identify three other hymn tunes.

Of the four hymns, we had had three at Daniel's funeral: *Guide Me O That Great Jehovah, The Lord is My Shepherd and Dear Lord* and *Father of Mankind*. These are popular hymns, but even supposing the programme was only choosing hymns from the fifteen most popular and that included these three hymns, the chances of all three featuring approached 2700:1 (allowance has to be made for the fourth hymn slightly contracting the pool if it came up early in the selection). Odds of 2700:1 are not that remarkable. But what really grabbed my attention was that both the starter and bonus questions were answered by Magdalen College, Oxford: Daniel's college. Even on the basis that Magdalen was appearing on that particular episode, the chances of its answering correctly the starter question which led to the bonus questions significantly lengthened the overall odds. And, in fact, Magdalen is one of twenty-eight teams in any year's competition and on average appears only every two years. A further twist was that *The Lord is My Shepherd* is sung to a number of different tunes. The one the programme used was the one we had, the great Crimond, admittedly the most popular of the melodies.

I wrote to the producer to ask how often contestants were asked to identify hymn tunes: in fact, the only time since the programme reappeared in 1994 was about sixteen years ago. One has to make some assumptions, and statisticians might bridle about artificially creating a statistical scenario retrospectively (a bit like retrospective clinical trials are frowned upon), but I estimated that the chances of Magdalen answering these particular starter and bonus questions, during the second half of the programme, was of the order of 5m:1 to 10m:1. And then one has to factor in the unlikelihood of my watching at all. I would see perhaps only one episode in two series. In fact, I had noticed in a newspaper that Magdalen were on that evening and had made a mental note not to watch, because I thought it would be too upsetting.

The third story is that, just prior to Christmas 2013, I was watching a video of the performance, by a five thousand-strong choir of the public, of a beautiful song, *Clouds*, composed by Zach, a seventeen year-old with osteosarcoma. I was barely concentrating, when the camera suddenly zoomed in on a six or seven year-old boy in the choir. The image took my breath away: he was identical to Daniel at that age. If I had not known the context, I would have said 'That's Dan', without a moment's hesitation. Rationally, I know that Daniel having a double is not that surprising. The fact that he was in a sarcoma fundraiser and that I chanced upon it (those two factors are linked, I acknowledge) is far less likely.

Does any of this prove that Daniel still exists? Sadly, no. And the proposition that he or some other force had something to do with the *University Challenge* questions or the *Clouds* video and my watching both, or china dogs, would raise the most profound questions, not least about free will and determinism. But there the stories are. Other sarcoma parents have told me of their remarkable experiences after the death of their loved ones.

There was an amusing footnote to the *University Challenge* story. A former winning contestant, Sean Blanchflower, runs a website about the show. Sean remembered the previous occasion when teams were asked to identify a hymn tune. On that occasion, too, *The Lord is My Shepherd* had featured. But the contestant, being Oxbridge, gave the Latin name for the hymn, *Dominus Me Regit*. This flummoxed Jeremy Paxman, the quizmaster, and they had to stop filming to check the answer (in fairness, *Dominus Me Regit* does not translate as *The Lord is My Shepherd*).

This is not the place to expound my views about religion. But I do, on balance, believe there is more to life than the finality of death. Voltaire remarked: 'It is not more surprising to be born twice than once.' Confirmation bias, but I prefer the hypothesis that there is meaning to life and to suffering to the hypothesis that we are all descendants of some bacterium in some primeval pool, the product of an extremely random confluence of factors enabling life to exist and that Daniel just bought the wrong ticket in the genetic lottery.

For each of us, only time will tell whether St Paul was correct: 'For the perishable must clothe itself with the imperishable and the mortal with immortality.' I hope so passionately that Daniel's spirit lives on, freed from the perishable body which let him down so badly. It would be simply amazing to 'meet' him again, but ultimately what matters is that he still exists and is at peace. That is more important to me more than anything I could possibly conceive.

The benefits of cancer

There is a poem which does the rounds on cancer support websites:

'Cancer is so limited
It cannot cripple Love
It cannot shatter Hope
It cannot corrode Faith
It cannot destroy Peace
It cannot kill Friendship
It cannot suppress Memories
It cannot silence Courage
It cannot invade the Soul
It cannot steal eternal Life
It cannot conquer the Spirit'

All true, no doubt. There is so much that cancer leaves untouched.

A Ewing's teenager in the US, Samantha, captured the benefits of cancer beautifully:

'... [Cancer] taught me so many lessons. ..... Instigator because it shocked me into living for what life is really about and to stop worrying about stupid and petty things. It has been a little sooner than I would have liked, but still a welcomed and appreciated kick in the butt. Gift because it was a present, made to mould me into who I was to eventually become ... There will forever be a part of me that belongs to cancer. I don't ever want that piece gone. That part makes me unique, special and different from other people my age. It has made me realize just how gifted I am to be here, how wonderful my life truly is.

Would I ever ask for cancer? Of course not, not in a million years. Would I ever wish cancer out of my past? The answer is incomprehensible for someone who hasn't gone through it, but it's the same nevertheless: Of course not, not in a million years.'

Out of the mouths of babes such wisdom. Andy Ripley, the former England rugby player said of his prostate cancer: 'My life has been enhanced: I have never loved so much or been loved so much, since I had cancer.'

Many cancer survivors say it's the best thing that has happened to them. It's a variant on the Nietzchean aphorism that what does not break you makes you stronger. There is one little catch: to enjoy prolonged benefit from cancer's largesse, first one has to survive. That immediately excludes swathes of potential beneficiaries, including, sadly, Daniel. But he still did benefit in some ways. Had he not had cancer, he wouldn't have rehearsed with the BBC Symphony Orchestra for the *Last Night*, or met his tennis heroes, or travelled to sporting events around the world, or, perhaps, realised that quite so many people cared so much about him. Someone mused that 'life is not measured by the breaths we take but by the moments that take our breath away.' Daniel was fortunate to have more such moments than most even during his cancer years. The disease taught him fortitude and must have opened his eyes to the suffering of others; I see that as a benefit. It gave him the chance of showing his extraordinariness, even while denying him the chance to build on it.

The credit column is fuller for me than for Daniel. I have learnt so much, doors have opened which would otherwise have remained shut or undiscovered. Daniel was my greatest teacher: he taught me that it's possible to deal with horrific adversity and yet retain the essence of one's character. But I have learnt from many others too. I came across so many wonderful people. I think of Victor's story. A young girl in Minnesota had Ewing's. Corinne's parents, a deeply religious couple, noticed that Victor rarely had visitors. He too had Ewing's. It transpired that he was in a care home. So Deb and Mike adopted Victor (who was of a different race), adding to an already large family. What an amazing thing to do, a true Christian act. Victor eventually succumbed to the cancer, a month before Daniel. But he had wonderful years of love and was able to face his death with faith and equanimity.

Like Daniel, I have visited places I wouldn't have visited and experienced things I wouldn't have experienced, had cancer not come calling. I remember after a visit to a Munich hospital, a wonderful Italian string quintet (anomalously including an accordion) playing Pachabel's *Canon* in the street. I remember Table Top Mountain in Cape Town and the submarine in Barbados. I remember the children I met on my bike ride. I remember the kindnesses shown by so many people, in so many countries, a reaffirmation of all that is good in humankind and a necessary antidote to all the negativity the media drip-feeds us. Kindness, the Roman Emperor-philosopher Marcus Aurelius said, is mankind's greatest delight. We were shown more than our fair share. Angela, my hairdresser from Ukraine, refused to accept tips: I needed the money more, she said. A London cab driver, dropping Daniel at UCH one Christmas, waived the fare. Small acts, but magnified by the kindness which inspired them.

Because I have lost Daniel, I can now empathise with

all the other parents who have lost a child. That is a routine occurrence in the developing world, sadly, but is all too common even in the developed world. I don't pretend to know exactly what it's like for other parents. I don't even really know what it's like for Petra. But I have some insight into what other bereaved parents are going through. If life is about experiencing the range and depth of emotion available to human beings, about understanding the challenges and the joys of other people's lives, about building empathic bridges across continents and cultures, I now know what it is to experience perhaps the rawest emotion of them all. That doesn't make me a better person, but it does make me a more emotionally-educated person.

In short, I'm not sorry that I have experienced real psychological suffering; I'm only sorry that Daniel had to be the catalyst.

But the greatest gift cancer bestowed on me was to forge an unbreakable bond with my son. I had always felt that Daniel and I were close – enough people remarked on our relationship – but I harboured doubt about what he felt about me as his Dad. This was partly because of a temperament which needs frequent affirmation and partly because I didn't live with him: the curse of the 'absent parent'. That insecurity raised its head when Daniel passed his driving test, in considerable pain and barely able to walk, just a few days before he was diagnosed with cancer. He hadn't mentioned he was taking it. My immediate reaction was: 'Your not telling me has taken some of the shine off.' That was I believe, the only unmasking to Daniel of my insecurity but it was still truly pathetic and I regretted the words as soon as I uttered them. My philosophy as a father was always to encourage, to praise and to reassure.

Long before the end of the cancer journey, all doubt about our relationship had been removed. There was a trust which was unspoken but unmistakeable. Someone suggested that my eulogy demonstrated a 'wonderful mixture of "Dad and son" and "best buddies"' and maybe that was true. No doubt there were topics which Daniel didn't broach with me. Some he will have discussed with Petra or with Sasha or Florence or his friends or with no one. Some things he discussed with me but probably not with anyone else. We all need to decide when to share, and with whom, and when to internalise.

But what matters is that, despite his need for private space, I knew that Daniel knew he could come to me, or Petra, about absolutely anything, important or trivial and that we would listen sympathetically and try to help, never trivialising, though lightening with humour where appropriate. The cancer years would also, I think, have reaffirmed that we would go to the ends of the earth (and beyond) for him. I'm grateful that he survived long enough for us to demonstrate the depths of our love for him

Perhaps all this is a metaphor for love forged in adversity. The love I thought I had for Daniel pre-cancer moved into a whole new dimension. I learnt that I was capable of unconditional love (well, as capable as any human being is). I would have claimed that prior to the cancer, but now I knew it experientially. This love is the Greek *agape*, selfless love, the altruism which presents such a challenge for evolutionary science; or the Buddhist *ahisma*. If I get cancer, I cannot imagine investing even 1 per cent of the effort I invested in Daniel's struggle. His life meant more to me than my life. It's as simple as that.

I still got things wrong as Daniel's father, naturally. I continued to stumble over my lines and at times wasn't even sure what script I was supposed to be reading from. But about the strength of my relationship with Daniel I came to harbour no doubts. That was some gift and at low moments, I pull it out and it helps. Cancer chipped in generously with buying the gift; that is the greatest irony. How awful it would have been had he died estranged from Petra or me. My heart bled for Chris Huhne, the former cabinet minister (and Magdalen alumnus), when those searingly hurtful texts from his son were made public. At least, I suppose, he can hope for reconciliation.

Do the benefits from cancer make the suffering, the loss of Daniel, worthwhile? The question is strictly rhetorical. I would a thousand times prefer to have Daniel and to forego the benefits. Of course I would. But life is what life is. It's full of contrast, every shade of grey, good versus evil, good coming from evil, evil lurking unsuspectingly behind good. It's a futile exercise trying to imagine what my life would have been like had Daniel not contracted cancer and died young. Life's experiences, whether sought or not, leave a permanent imprint on our souls. The lessons Daniel's cancer journey threw up are my companions for life. So I might as well learn from them.

A magical personality

As I continue my journey through life without Daniel, he sustains me with the memory of his wonderful personality. Even if I had the expressive powers of a Dickens or a Jane Austen, I couldn't come close to capturing that personality.

We are all far more than the sum of our character traits and abilities, but somehow that seems particularly so with Daniel. To those who knew him well, he was just Daniel.

One of the things I admired about him the most was that he never tried to be anything that he wasn't. That is a much harder trick to pull off than may appear, with all the

Cancer removed all doubts about my relationship with Daniel.

conflicting pressures, peer and otherwise, that descend upon us in the modern world of unrelenting pace, complexity and imperative to succeed. 'Just be yourself', seems such empty advice. What is one's true self? We are all a smorgasbord of nuance and degree. To give an example: when should one stand up for what one believes and when should one instead let things go, for greater harmony? Each is likely to be an aspect of the one personality; to know when to give prominence to which can be difficult. I feel I'm conveying a slightly different aspect of my personality to everyone I meet. I suppose this is because no personality is an island (to paraphrase John Donne) and any given personality only has full content when interacting with other personalities, each of which is unique.

Philosophers have argued that the most we can achieve is partial or transient authenticity. Perhaps Daniel's apparent authenticity was an illusion. Perhaps like so many he struggled to find the true essence of his personality. All I can say is that, from the outside, he seemed comfortable in his own skin and felt no need to project a character that wasn't his.

That doesn't mean that he was open with everyone. Quite the opposite. As a toddler and young child he was an open book but as he got older more of the pages stuck together. His illness had much to do with that, no doubt, but he was more introvert than extrovert anyway. But however much or little he chose to reveal of himself, it seemed to be the real Daniel. Although naturally honest, like the rest of us he occasionally succumbed to the temptation of saying what was easier to say, whether to cover up some personal failing, to avoid embarrassment or to spare the other person's feelings. Sometimes he stayed silent when it would have been more honest to speak. But even when he wasn't telling the truth, I felt that he somehow managed to retain the essence of this character. That is some trick to pull off.

I cannot hope to be objective in my assessment of Daniel and I don't feel a particular need to try. I cannot tell how much my admiration of him is due to parental bond, how much to a rose-tinted perspective on a deeply loved son, how much, having lost him, I now need to bathe him in the most flattering light. I'm conscious that parents are prone to see in their children those qualities and values they would like to possess. But I think I would have really liked Daniel even if I had not been his father.

Daniel, inevitably, was in large part the product of the genes Petra and I had passed onto him and the way he was brought up. But, whatever the respective roles of nature and nurture in forming his character, it's Daniel who deserves the credit for his many, many attributes. In truth, he was a better person than me. And that is how it should be. If humankind is to progress spiritually and ethically, each new generation must build on lessons from those preceding it.

Of course Daniel wasn't perfect and to idealise any human being is to invite hubris and ridicule. Iconic figures never live up to their iconic status and it takes only a breath of scandal to topple from their pedestals celebrities who never deserved to be put there in the first place. Like the rest of us, Daniel was work in progress. Like the rest of us, he could be selfish. He was more follower than leader and you wouldn't pick him out in a crowded room as a figure of charisma. Although he would have approached whatever he did in life enthusiastically and conscientiously and probably for the most part successfully, who knows whether he would have ripped up many trees, oak trees anyway, or have even wanted to?

He was even-tempered, but very occasionally during his illness he acted out the huge frustrations he must have felt. Petra would then ask me to have a word with him. They were never difficult discussions because he hated falling out with us. All I would need to say was 'Come on Dan, you know you can't behave like that', and we would move on. Even when he was young, the idea of hitting him – I refuse to use the euphemism 'smacking' – was preposterous. I would have felt an utter failure. I can only remember raising my voice to him on a couple of occasions. Once was when, as a fourteen year-old, he was tossing my mobile phone around on a station in Paris. He looked so hurt that it was me who ended up feeling guilty and telling myself I had to do better in future. He was such a joy to be with.

Given my own lack of objectivity, perhaps the best thing is to quote some of the things people said about Daniel when he died. Tributes from his Oxford tutors are included later but here are some other comments from people without a parental axe to grind:

'Daniel was a witty, gifted, sweet and loyal friend … I do not have a single memory of Daniel without a smile … Daniel was an exceptional man. I can only ever remember him with a smile on his face … I played in Magdalen Swing Band with Dan, I only knew Dan through the band but I knew him as someone who was always friendly, cheerful, and a pleasure to talk to. I wish he was still here, because even though knowing him briefly I knew he made the world better … Daniel was a superb lad [one of his teachers] … He always knew how to make me laugh … The world has lost one of its brightest stars … I remember Daniel as a lovely boy of about ten. He was so sweet and such fun to be with … I knew Daniel as a line umpire – he was a pleasure to work with, delightful in every way … Amazingly talented person with a wonderful sense of humour, I'll miss Daniel greatly … Daniel was a delightful pupil who had a great future in front of him … I wasn't an especially close friend, but the time I spent with him was always cheerful and enjoyable. I never heard Dan complain about anything …'

And some more:

'Daniel was simply the nicest person I knew, I will always

remember him with a smile on his face, and a joke ready to deliver ... Magdalen is very proud of Daniel. We will remember him as a very popular, cheerful and talented student. He packed so much into his time at College [the President of Magdalen] ... He was a great friend ... A lovely person I will never forget ... Dan was a truly lovely guy, who never had a bad word for anyone. We had the honour and pleasure of playing with him in the Magdalen Swing Band, where his great talent was abundantly obvious ... I knew Daniel only briefly through his occasional visits to Woking [Mencap] Club with David but he seemed a lovely guy, happy to join in with all our folks ... I remember him as a clever, sincere little boy with a cheerful smile ...

I was one of his philosophy tutors. I always admired his courage and his cheerfulness. He was extremely able at philosophy and I'm sure he could have done graduate work in it if he had wanted to – but then that was true of his other subjects as well ...Daniel was always a source of humour, inspiration and fun. Forever at the centre of whatever we did whilst at Winston [his school until sixteen]. A true friend in every sense of the word ... I will always remember his smiling face – forever positive and a pleasure to have met... Dan was a dear friend to me and will always be remembered for how much fun he was. He is a true inspiration to me ... Such a happy chap and always polite ... I have always thought that angels like Daniel are sent to teach the rest of us what is possible and just what we can overcome ... I was bowled over when I met Daniel ... The world is full of parents who believe their child to be something special. Unfortunately it's rarely true. However you clearly have a right to believe that … Daniel will always be remembered by us as a very good tennis official but more importantly, as a friendly, kind and courageous young man … I knew him only briefly but he made a great impression on me. A truly lovely human being … Thanks for being such fun. We loved having you in Naxos – keep winning at table tennis … I will never forget his sense of humour, enthusiasm and table tennis serve.'

This from his friend Joe, born as it happens on the very same day:

'I considered Daniel one of my closest friends throughout those formative years of secondary school. Your [eulogy] encapsulated everything we remember: the formidable intelligence (especially as a peer!), the sporting and musical talent, but most of all that sense of humour (unforgettable, particularly if you were directly on the receiving end)!'

And, finally, Tobias wrote from Berlin:

'I am sure that, if a place like Heaven exists, Daniel lives there! He has been such a loving, caring and good character, if he should not be there, [then] who'

I hope so, Tobias, I really hope so.

Naturally, people say nice things about people who have died, especially the young. My father was fond of quoting the Latin saying 'De mortuis nihil nisi bonum': 'Of the dead, [say] nothing unless good.' (Jimmy Savile, who died the same month as Daniel, might think an exception was made for him.) But clear themes emerge from these messages: Daniel's humour, his sense of mischief, his cheerfulness, his enthusiasm, his loyalty as a friend, his determination, his general niceness.

His Oxford tutors were at one in admiring his intellect, his restless inquisitiveness, his ability to spot new things in the literature he was studying, his rigorous challenging of assumptions, his skill in assimilating evidence, his expressiveness. I knew he was good, but I didn't realise just how good until he died. He was bright even by Oxford Classics standards.

Daniel was a pretty talented musician, too. My favourite comment about his A level sonata came from my friend Edwina, who also plays the clarinet:

> 'Words that came to mind - Parisian, romance, decadence, but a quiet humility, spring time, hopeful, wanting, mischievous ... I can see the music being the backdrop to a short silent film.
>
> I really loved it, I'm awestruck, I'm so sorry you never got to see him do the great things he was destined to do. I'm so so sorry. All I can say from the bottom of my heart is he has already produced a work of art in this music that people don't get around to doing with eighty years to play with. I can see why you are so proud ... I'm going to take inspiration from him and create, whatever that may be.'

(I told her she should be a music critic instead of a lawyer.) I learnt recently that children at the special needs school Daniel's cousin Amy used to attend, really respond to the piece.

And yet Daniel was the epitome of modesty. His extravagant all-round talents must have helped to shape his character but they never caused his head to grow or his lips to brag. I suspect those who knew him only through academia, music or sport would have been surprised to hear about his abilities in the other disciplines. He would not have felt the need to tell them.

Alongside the modesty – and the gentleness and kindness – Daniel's sense of humour was central to his character. His humour was irreverent, laughing when he shouldn't, but never nasty or prejudiced.

I often think of things happening now which would have made him laugh. The Magdalen tree-planting ceremony took place on a filthy day. The college chaplain, Michael Piret, conducted a brief service and we then all stood in silence, contemplating, waiting for the nod from Michael. It was an eternity coming. Charlotte, my sister and I had the same thought: Daniel would have said 'What on earth are you all doing, standing in the pouring rain, looking at a tree shrub?!' Because of the weather, my mother had to stay inside and Annabel stayed with her. Annabel then missed the reception, when two talented musicians sang and there were brief talks. Annabel left to see the tree but missed that too, because it had been taken away for re-planting later in the year. She had taken the day off work to come to Oxford and had missed everything. Daniel would have laughed at that as well.

One day, Daniel had left a note saying 'You have been burgled' by my front door (I hadn't). He had considered tipping over some chairs for authenticity ... And he could laugh at himself too and frequently did. He was generous in laughing at other people's jokes, unless there were mine. He

Daniel's tree in the grounds of Magdalen College.

would not laugh at mine on principle (and perhaps because he thought they weren't funny, theoretically possible I suppose). After getting no reaction, I would stare Daniel out, until he cracked. He would then deny vigorously that it was the joke he was laughing at; indeed, there was no joke to laugh at, he would say. On my fortieth birthday, when Daniel was nine, he told me: 'Right Dad, you're going to have to start acting your age now.' I loved that he felt he could make fun of me and never missed an opportunity.

When he was four, I asked him one night if he had come straight home from school. 'No, I came round a few curves', came the reply (he meant bends), an early indication that his humour could revolve around language and of his love of language. There was much laughter even during the cancer years, unless things were really bad. It was his default position. Laughter sustains; some even use it as a therapy for cancer. I hope it sustained Daniel.

His demeanour during the cancer years was usually positive, perhaps borne of youth's sense of indestructibility. He was phenomenally determined to get better and did everything we suggested, from extra radiotherapy to diet to supplements to wheatgrass juice to diagnostic trips abroad. He had always been determined, keen to do things well. Cancer determination was simply the clearest manifestation of a more general resoluteness, all the more praiseworthy because he was vulnerable and sometimes scared.

In his eulogy, Felix, an Oxford tutor, used the word 'courage' and others did too. It's funny, but I never regarded Daniel as being courageous. Perhaps this is because, wrongly, I associate courage with physical courage. Daniel wasn't physically courageous in the conventional sense: I cannot imagine him on a battlefield, or as a have-a-go hero. But there is mental courage, too. In fact all courage is ultimately mental, I suppose. 'Courage is not the absence of fear, it's the ability to act in the presence of fear', as someone said. Daniel had the sort of courage which endures set-back after set-back and still bounces back, without corruption of personality or values. He didn't give in to his fears. He endured so much physical pain, nausea, extreme fatigue and other unpleasant symptoms and for the most part handled them heroically. They had become an unwelcome companion on life's journey but they couldn't stop him living out his dreams. Andrew Hobson, his tutor on the Naxos trip in 2009, only realised then what Daniel had to put up with. I broke down when I was told that: in relative terms, Daniel was actually well at that time.

Dostoyevsky once remarked: 'There is only one thing I dread: not to be worthy of my sufferings.' Daniel would have scoffed at such pretension, but courageous or merely determined, he truly was worthy of his sufferings.

Perhaps he was helped as well by a certain naïveté. Daniel had always been an innocent abroad, trusting amid all life's cynicism. Fiachra, another of his tutors, told me that Daniel thought he could keep his cancer keep from them. Maybe it was that innocence which enabled him to persuade himself he was going to get better, in the face of overwhelming evidence to the contrary.

One or two people have suggested that Daniel was just too good for this world. I don't actually believe that. I think he had a temperament for life. He was able to acknowledge and absorb all the sadnesses and injustices and want to do something to address some of them in some ill-defined way and yet still find so much to enjoy and be fascinated about. He was very much of this world and loved life. Not in a hedonistic, get smashed on a Saturday night kind of way - there might have been some of that had he not been so strict with himself about alcohol during his illness - but as someone who was inquisitive, genuinely interested in people and in issues and who understood instinctively that life has so much to offer if one has a modicum of luck and above all, good health. Wittgenstein may have asked 'To what problem is immortality the solution?' but Daniel had heard about scientists who thought humankind would soon be able to live to a thousand and was excited that it could apply to him – late into his journey, he would joke that I had been born in the wrong generation. Shortly before he died, he described his ambition in the Magdalen year book: 'Live for ever or die trying'.

But health was the one gift which was denied Daniel. He was living proof, and dying proof, that all the talents in the world, all the love, all the friendship, all the opportunities, all the material comforts, count for precisely nothing, if one doesn't have good health. Daniel's cancer journey has underscored my cherished belief that health, including sanitation, should be an absolutely key priority for any government and that it's meaningless to talk about freedom unless people have access to essential medicine and decent housing.

This is my take on Daniel. In my eyes, a very, very special human being. As well as the usual problems of growing up, he had to deal with a debilitating disease and face his own mortality. That is some triumvirate. How do you cope with growing up when you don't know whether you will grow up? The pressure must have been intense but Daniel continued to chase his dreams and just remained Daniel throughout it all.

Amidst all the doubt about paternal bias clouding judgement, there are two things of which I'm certain. The first is that I have been incredibly blessed to be Daniel's father. Daniel has lit up my life as brightly as the brightest star ever could. If I'm allotted my biblical three score years and ten, I will have shared less than a third of my life with him, and yet those twenty-three years are worth a thousand lifetimes. There is no other child I would have preferred to be parent to. Nearly all parents feel that about their children, I'm sure, but the fact is that I'm the only person to have been Daniel's father. That is a unique privilege of stupendous good fortune. This is not to suggest that Daniel is any better, any more precious, than any other child, simply that I'm so grateful to have been

Smiling came naturally to Daniel.

Daniel retained his youthful innocence into adulthood, refusing to bow to all the cynicism around him.

the one chosen to be his dad. All the Midasian riches could not begin to match that gift.

And, if it was Fate's decree that this child, this young man, was to be afflicted with cancer and to leave the world early, I'm so grateful that Petra and I were chosen to share the journey with him. Many, many times the pain was searing, and it will remain my shadow for the rest of my life, but I'm glad I was allowed to share the road with Daniel, strewn with rocks and craters and mines though it was destined to be. I would not have wanted the burden, the privilege, to be anyone else's.

The second thing of which I'm certain is simply this: the world was a better place with Daniel than it is now without him.

And that, in the final analysis, is the best epitaph any of us can hope for.

www.danielmyson.com

Eulogy and tributes by university tutors and students

Eulogy by Felix Budelmann, Daniel's Tutor

'Many of my memories of Daniel, in tutorials and elsewhere, have him ask questions. He had a restless mind, always pressing on. He also had an uncanny way of cutting to the chase. Being in tutorials with Daniel kept you on your toes, as he was always liable to interrupt, to home in on what really matters and to undo the best-laid plans of arriving there on a circuitous route. I suspect my philosophy colleague was only half-joking when he once remarked that Daniel's first essay of a course of eight had pre-empted several that were to follow. This is very much how I think of Daniel – inquisitive, sharp, never content to stay still, always going for what matters.

As a result, Daniel excelled across all subjects he studied at Magdalen. He was awarded a Classics prize after his second year and without doubt would have excelled further if he had had the opportunity. All this he did without any kind of showiness. Daniel was too intensely focused for there to be space for immodesty.

Continuing with his studies, despite everything, must have meant a great deal to him. Several of us last saw him in the summer, coming to Oxford in the middle of the vacation to borrow books from the library for a piece of work next term. In the previous year he sat his exams while undergoing chemotherapy, toing and froing between hospital and the exam room. And he did that without ever hinting that it's an extraordinary thing to do. Daniel had a great reluctance ever to get special treatment because of being ill, special treatment, that is, that would have been more than appropriate in his case. He didn't even mention the cancer to me for the first six months and I thought he was trying to forget about it. But that was wrong. When he did speak about it, he spoke about it with great frankness, in the same no-nonsense way in which he spoke about everything else. It was never awkward talking with him about how he felt or what the illness and the treatment allowed and didn't allow him to do, about arrangements that had to be put into place, about treatment he had to undergo.

One word, therefore, that keeps coming to mind and that several of his friends have used in the past few days is courage. It must take enormous courage to experience what Daniel experienced and to continue in such a normal way and to be such good company.

Another word is cheerfulness. 'He was always cheerful, despite it all', somebody said last week. He must often have felt very, very low, but it's true that the image of Daniel that I carry in my head, too, is one of somebody who retained a remarkable capacity for cheerfulness. Of the many wonderful things about Daniel, to me, this is perhaps the most wonderful.

All of us at Magdalen, students and tutors, will remember Daniel with admiration and very great affection.'

Letter from Fiachra MacGorain, former Magdalen tutor, October 2011

'I wish to express my most sincere and profound condolences on the death of your son, whom I taught at Magdalen in his first and second years while Latin lecturer. I will always treasure vivid memories of him.

The first of these is from the day his admissions cohort took the language tests in college. Some of the candidates were in contortions with nerves, but Dan was placid and may I say, there was a radiant stillness about him and he smiled at me as he took his paper. Later I came to know him as a focused, vigorous, indefatigable and voraciously curious student of the highest calibre. Typically his essays were three-in-one. He would nail the issues in a matter-of-fact, methodical and unpretentious way, pushing the analysis as far as the evidence would possibly allow. His intellect had an uncompromising and penetrating clarity which always saw right into the core of a subject. Quite often there were typos, signs of his great haste to finish this point and tear into the next one. He was the same in discussion and with him there was nowhere to hide! His way of dealing with his illness and especially of having a rich and full life despite it, was an inspiration from when I first knew him. Because he would have put most people in their full health to shame, I would often think of his tenacity when there were little causes to grumble or be lazy. He was never either of these things and this stays with me as a source of inspiration. His frankness and honesty were remarkable.

On a few occasions he was unselfpityingly direct about how he was feeling (in his second year). But I remember also his playfulness and his sense of humour, as when he told me once, in Celtic solidarity, in an exaggerated Welsh accent, that he was originally from the Valleys!!

He was very greatly admired at Magdalen, more than others - and differently from others - and I take your point [in your eulogy] that his response to his illness determined his way of being. Felix, Al, Ralph, Andrew and I often talked with agreement about his exceptional intellect and industry and there was a tacit acknowledgement that his circumstances and illness were part of what made up his character. Tutors at Oxford (because the subject-year groups are so small and the contact can be quite close and intimate) tend to always debrief colleagues after a first session or two with a new cohort, and my recollection is that Ralph said that Daniel had anticipated the whole term's arguments in his first essay on Plato. (And Ralph has been teaching this paper and ones like it to the most talented students for forty years.)

Another thing which I'm sure you know is that when Daniel was thinking of (or indeed agonising over) what papers to choose for finals, his difficulty was that he was talented in all areas: obviously in philosophy, but in literature and historical texts too. Usually students excel in one but not in all three. He knew Horace's first book of Odes like the back of his hand and would often cite pertinent details from it for comparison with Virgil and Catullus in a very mature way.'

Tribute by Paul Goulding, fellow Classicist: June 2012

'Dan was the most unassuming, positive and friendly of people, whom we sadly never had the chance to get to know well enough.

We remember a young man with a sparkling, mischievous sense of humour. Dan would never shy away from asking his tutorial partners exactly the question which would see their argument unravel, all the time retaining his composure as that partner simmered with confusion. We remember his endless supply of football-based, groan-inducing, pun-intensive jokes which could brighten up any occasion. We remember a young man whose wit and warmth made every tutorial with him a prospect to cherish.

We remember a young man of immense sporting talent. While we were never able to see him express fully his talent during his time at Oxford, his exploits on the table-tennis tables of Naxos left none of us in any doubt as to his true ability. Dan 'The Baseline' Thomas could play alternately-handed and even sitting down, all the while manfully tolerant of those opposite and beside him. We remember his passion and love for music: we all enjoyed his performances for the Magdalen Swing Band, in particular.

We remember a young man who was endlessly patient and winningly self-deprecating when interrogated about the glamorous life of a Wimbledon umpire. We also remember a man who could spot 'the wrong/awful/shameless call' of every unfortunate line-judge on TV!

Looking back, Dan still makes us smile, especially when we remember his particular fondness for potatoes and the ovens in which he would cook them. He would never (ever) complain about his restrictive diet and was often eager to involve others in his efforts in the kitchen. For someone so ferociously bright, when wrestling with the oven of 62 High Street, temperature over time was an equation that he often misconstrued, resulting in a plaintive text to his friends to rescue the now blackened and otherwise unidentifiable object from the oven.

We remember a young man who was an unfailing support to his friends. His was a shoulder to cry on; he would listen to problems, large and small, responding always with warmth and loyalty. He was patient, calming, smiling and comforting – a true friend to all of us.

These are only a few lasting memories of Dan from his friends at Magdalen. It's impossible to do justice in only a few words to someone whose personality was, of all his many talents, by far his most extraordinary quality.'

Simon Perrot Oration

An oration has been given, in Latin, at Magdalen College in commemoration of Simon Perrot since the 16th century. In 2012, it was given by Marcus Field, a Classics undergraduate, and contained this excerpt:

ORATIO

in honorem Simonis Perrot
a M. Alexandro Agro habita
e munere Annae Shaw stipendiario
in aula collegii beatae Mariae Magdalenae apud
Oxoniensis
pridie Kalendas Maias anno domini mmxii

aures tuae scilicet fatigatae
sunt a rebus gestis tamquam
praecone relatis; sed quod
ultimum attingam, quod
extra huius orationis
consuetudinem iacet,
diligenter, quaeso, attendite.

Naturally your ears are tired
of hearing achievements
reported as though by an
auctioneer; but I ask that
you listen carefully to the
last point upon which I shall
touch since it lies outside the
accustomed scope of this
speech.

gaudium vero post
hominum memoriam
talium verborum calx esse
solet et materies: cum in
ludis, in doctrina, in nescio
quo studio Magdalensis
aliquis floruit, nos communi
animo laetamur; cum
unus e sapientissimis sociis
nostris collegium reliquit,
tamen pracepta ac benefacta
eius, non exitus tristitiam,

Since time immemorial, the
bricks and mortar of such
a discourse have been joy:
whenever a Magdelenite
has flourished in sport, in
learning or in whatever
pursuit, we are all alike glad;
whenever one of our wise
fellows has left the college,
still it is their teaching and
their kindnesses, not the
sadness of their departure,

libenter recordamur; sed in hac clade victoriae gaudio aut multitudine annorum levamento uti nequeo. haec de Danieli Thomas morte dico

which we fondly remember; but in the case of this misfortune I cannot bring to bear the joy of victory or the length of years as a palliative. I am speaking of the death of Daniel Thomas.

non in animo habeo laudationem pronuntiare, cui neque locus neque tempus videtur idoneum; at cum is nobis ademptus sit cui ingenuim in litteris, in musica, in ludis stabat tanti, cuius benignitas totiens hic et alibi videbatur, quem tot maerent, hunc non tacitus praeteribo.

It is not my intention to give a eulogy, for which neither the setting nor the occasion seems appropriate; but when we have lost a man, whose talent in Classics, in music and in sports was so great, whose good will was so often to be seen both here and elsewhere, whom so many mourn, I shall not pass over him in silence.

hoc vespere, Magdalenses, virtutes plurimas audivimus. nam alius industriam, alius spem, alius constantiam cotidie exhibit. virtutem quandam autem non memoravi – nec hinc, ut scio, abest – quae, quod in virtutum numero

This evening, Magdalenites, we have heard of many good qualities. Every day one or other of you displays hard work, hope, determination. But there is a quality not mentioned – and, I'm sure, it is not absent from

praesat, nullum nomen
habet nisi virtutem; hanc
vero Danielus ante omnia
possidebat.

sed, quia nullum verbum,
nulla oratio a me habita
memoriae huius aut
vestrae luctui proderit,
nunc desinam

Sed in his omnibus
unum restat: nam nobis
in periculis hortatori,
in dolore consolatori,
in victoria laudatori,
in gaudio participi fuit
collegium nostrum cum
suis omnibus, surrexi igitur
huic propinemus, uno
animo verba clamentes,
quibus Magdalenses per
omnia saecula conexi sunt
– floreat Magdalena!

here – which because it is
prominent amongst these
qualities, has no name but
'courage'; this, truly, Daniel
had especially.

But, since no word, no
speech of mine will be of
any benefit either to his
memory or to your grief,
let me now leave off...

Yet in all these events
one thing has remained
constant: in adversity
our college and its
members have offered
us encouragement; in
grief, consolation; in
victory, praise; and in
joy, fellowship. Therefore
let us rise and drink to
it, crying out with one
heart the words by which
Magdalenites through all
ages are untied – floreat
Magdalena!

My eulogy

How can one possibly sum up Daniel and his life in just a few minutes? All I can do is give a glimpse into his wonderful character.

Daniel was diagnosed with an extremely serious form of bone cancer in April 2006, when he was seventeen. The latter years of his life were inevitably dominated by cancer and all it involves, but it never defined him as a person. How he responded to the cancer did, however, very much define him.

I well remember the morning after the diagnosis. Daniel was, typically despite the devastating news, studying the Latin poet Horace and wanted to discuss the poems with me. As you can imagine, it was the very last thing I wanted to do, but it was always very hard to say no to Daniel.

Daniel's favourite Horace ode was *1-XI*, the one about carpe diem – seize the day:

'Ask not — we cannot know — what end the gods have set for you, for me; nor attempt the Babylonian reckonings Leuconoe. How much better to endure whatever comes, whether Jupiter grants us additional winters or whether this is our last, which now wears out the Tuscan Sea upon the barrier of the cliffs! Be wise, strain the wine; and since life is brief, prune back far-reaching hopes! Even while we speak, envious time has passed: seize the day, putting as little trust as possible in tomorrow!'

Carpe diem became Daniel's motto. He really did carpe the diem. His determination to live life as fully as possible – with all the huge constraints imposed by cancer and the extensive and often brutal treatment he had to undergo – was extraordinary. His doctor told him to forget about AS levels for that year, in two months' time, as he would be in the middle of chemo with all its nasty side-effects and hospital stays. Daniel took the exams.

The following year, he took his A levels just weeks after a lengthy stay in hospital after really aggressive and dangerous chemo which wiped out his bone marrow. He took the exams on time despite missing a great deal of schooling through a year of heavy treatment.

He then took some more AS/A levels for good measure. He started to learn the sax, to add to the piano and clarinet. He represented his school in a national debating competition and played in orchestras. He took his driving test in considerable pain. He qualified as a tennis umpire, later umpiring tournaments while on chemo. And, Daniel being Daniel, he did everything conscientiously and to a very high standard.

But his proudest achievement was getting into Magdalen College Oxford to read Classics. Daniel always loved Latin and Greek and other languages and the evolution of language and was conjugating Latin verbs with Sasha his sister even on his death-bed. He was so determined to get to Magdalen and loved his time there, severely interrupted and impaired though it was. He was so touched when ten of his friends clubbed together to buy him an iPod this summer.

He was thrilled to be awarded a scholarship by the

College last year, soon after he had suffered a very bad relapse and been very very ill but still taken some major exams and to be following in the footsteps of Cardinal Wolsey, Oscar Wilde, Lord Denning, CS Lewis, Ian Hislop and so many others. He would be amazed that Magdalen has been flying its flag at half-mast since he died.

In his first term at Magdalen, Daniel was invited to the prestigious President's Dinner and invited to sit next to the President of the College, a great honour. After the dinner, there would be a tour of the college library, which holds the oldest surviving fragments of *St Matthew's Gospel* and centuries of other history. They were kindly going to make a separate meal for him because he was on a special diet.

During the evening, I was in a meeting. I had a message from Dan – 'Dad, I need to speak to you.' Whenever we got a call from Daniel – and sometimes that was a few times a day – our hearts missed a beat, fearing some new pain or other worry.

Anyway, I came out of my meeting and called Daniel. It transpired that he had been playing table-tennis and - this is typical Daniel - had actually forgotten to go the dinner ... He wanted to know what he should do.

This is Daniel's charm, I think. On the one hand, you have this exceptionally determined and courageous person, with, as you will have picked up, very special academic and musical talents – and throw into the mix his sporting abilities as well. On the other hand, his head was sometimes in the clouds, he was unsure of himself, trusting, always asking us for advice, about small things and big things. Maybe it was because of this unusual combination - talented and driven but vulnerable and exceptionally modest - that he was loved by all who got to know him.

Daniel loved sport, all sports – tennis, football, table-tennis, cricket, rugby, hockey, badminton, athletics and so on. Playing a great deal when healthy as well as watching, most recently the Rugby World Cup in hospital. He was lucky enough to have seen a great deal of live sport all over the world as well as this country.

His biggest love from an early age was tennis. I used to love playing tennis, table-tennis, any sport with him, as did all the family – he was very competitive but always great fun to play with.

Last November, he was thrilled to meet his heroes Federer, Nadal, Djokovic and Roddick and sit in on their TV interviews for the Masters tournament in London. He was fascinated by the media and lapped up the whole experience.

Daniel was one of the youngest line-judges ever at Wimbledon, when he was sixteen and just loved the tournament.

On one occasion his line-judging and his college life clashed. In 2009 the grand Magdalen summer ball fell on the Friday of the first week of Wimbledon. I picked up Daniel from Wimbledon. He was determined to dress the part for the ball – white tie, top hat, even a cane – I made sure I walked a good few paces behind him ... Daniel made it to the survivors' photo at 6 the next morning (as indeed he did this year, when he was pretty ill).

Then after hardly any sleep Petra took him straight to Wimbledon. It was a baking hot Saturday and not surprisingly, by the evening Daniel was wilting and put in probably his worst ever performance as a line-judge.

He was asked to explain himself. Daniel feared being downgraded – he wanted to be upgraded so that he could do the Centre Court one day. He wanted to say 'Ah, but there is a good reason for my bad performance – it's because I pulled an all-nighter at the summer ball' but of course knew he couldn't. I think there may be tennis officials here today – I hope you will forgive Daniel this one transgression. He was always so professional, conscientious and willing.

When I think of Daniel, it's mainly of all the laughter we had. From a toddler, he was always so happy, with a smile that could light up a room and a wonderful personality and the priceless gift of being able to laugh at himself. When he made fun of you, as he often did, it would make you feel special. He retained that humour right up to near the very end, whatever adversity he faced (and he had faced real adversity even before the cancer).

He had so much fun with Sasha and Florence, whom he adored and with his various cousins when he could see them – Daniel was always the centre of attention, it seemed to me.

The other day he recalled one night I stayed with him in hospital in 2006 or 7. Petra or I stayed countless nights in hospital right up to ten days before he died and though one would not have chosen them they were very special times, with the late-night chats, the card-games, the crosswords, the privilege of helping to look after him. They brought ever greater closeness.

On this occasion, Dan and I were going up in the lift, alone, late in the evening to the Teenage Cancer Ward which is on the twelfth floor of University College Hospital in London. Just before we got out Daniel decided to press the button for all sixteen floors – time can be very long in hospital. A man rushed to catch the lift as we got out – I'm sad to say that we laughed at the thought of this poor man, probably headed for the ground floor, having to stop at each floor for no reason.

That was Daniel's mischievous sense of humour – but he was never malicious. In fact, there was not a malicious or cynical bone in his body. He hated confrontation and any form of violence, to people or animals and was developing a very compassionate and caring aspect to his personality, with really good values. One of the reasons I admired him so much was that he never tried to be anything he was not.

As you will have gathered, Daniel loved music – classical music but jazz, ragtime and the *X Factor* too. We went to many concerts together. He really enjoyed playing in various orchestras and the swing band at Oxford. He loved playing the piano and composing. Hearing him play a nice piece I would sometimes ask him what it was and he would shrug his shoulders and say 'I just made it up.' I only wish that he had been willing to transcribe these informal compositions.

And, in 2007, he was given the wonderful opportunity to play clarinet with the BBC Symphony Orchestra for the final rehearsal for the *Last Night of the Proms* and then we all went to the concert itself which Daniel had always loved. It really was a magical day.

We are going to miss Daniel terribly, more than words can possibly convey. I know the trick is to focus on the million happy memories we have – even at the very end just before he lost consciousness for the last time he gave Petra and me the most precious memory we could possibly ask for.

I know we should focus on how incredibly blessed we

have been, rather than on what we are to be denied, all the laughter we will not have, wondering what he would have done with his career (probably law) and whether he would have made a difference and helped people as he told me shortly before he died he wanted to (before adding that he wanted to make some money too!), whether he would have had a family as he also wanted.

I know I should focus on the fact that Daniel was, I think, secure in the knowledge throughout his life that he was surrounded by a deep love from his immediate family and his wider family and friends and that we would do absolutely anything for him. There are so many kids who sadly cannot say that, of course.

I know that's the trick, to focus on what we have had rather on what we have lost. But I also know that I will fail, every hour of every day. And part of the reason is that Daniel was interested in just about everything. So there are reminders everywhere. He enjoyed everything from:

- *EastEnders* and *Corrie* to intellectual programmes such as Melvyn Bragg's *In our Time* and discussing ethical issues

- From TV quizzes like *University Challenge* and *Countdown* and *Catchphrase* to science and history programmes and films and plays and musicals

- From comedy shows like *Just a Minute* and *Have I Got News For You?* both of which he saw live, to current affairs

- And just chucking a ball around – including in the house

I loved our discussions. From a very early age he was so inquisitive and he was still asking questions about all manner of things very shortly before his death – it never seemed to bother him that, in my case at least, I didn't know the answer half the time.

Daniel tried unbelievably hard to get better, embracing whatever we suggested – nutritional and various complementary therapies as well as additional conventional treatment over and above what his doctors recommended. There were several trips abroad. He really seemed to trust us, which I found very touching.

Daniel hardly ever complained – and believe me there was plenty to complain about. A member of the hospital staff wrote to me on Monday: 'Daniel was just always so nice and pleasant and undemanding and gentle.' (Very kindly, she didn't add 'unlike his dad'!)

Our priority was to protect him as much as we possibly could and always to nurture hope and I hope we succeeded in that.

Only in the past few days have I come to appreciate how many people Daniel inspired – I did already know that he had inspired his cousins Katie, Annabel and JJ and other family and friends to take part in a bike ride for kids with cancer in the developing world two years ago and that he had been shortlisted to carry the Olympic Torch, which he would have loved even though he didn't think he deserved it.

Above all else it was his family that mattered to Daniel. Unusually for someone of his age and perhaps partly because of his illness, he still loved spending much of his time with us and with his pets, at home, on holiday or doing various things. He gave so much love often, I think, without realising it.

I really believe that in spite of all the difficulties and its short duration, it was predominantly a very happy and fulfilled life.

I would like to end with a short poem. I don't know who it's by but it's called *The Chosen One*:

*If before you were born, I could have gone to Heaven
and saw all the beautiful souls, I still would have
chosen you...
If [God] had told me "that one day this soul may make
my heart bleed", I still would have chosen you...
If He had told me "this soul would make me question
the depth of my faith", I still would have chosen you...
If God had told me "this soul would make tears flow
from my eyes that would overflow a river", I still
would have chosen you...
If He had told me "this soul may one day make me
witness overbearing suffering", I still would have
chosen you...
If He had told me "all that you know to be normal
would drastically change", I still would have chosen
you...
[And], if He had told me "our time spent together here
on Earth could be short", I still would have chosen
you...*

Danny, if we had known about all the heartache, all the worry of the past few years, the thousands upon thousands of hours spent in hospitals and looking after you and desperately trying to find answers for you, if we had known the horror of the past few weeks in particular, if we had known the utter desolation we now feel and the pain we know that lies ahead – if we had known all that at the outset, we still would have chosen you, without so much as a nanosecond's hesitation.

It's just the greatest privilege anyone could possibly have to be your Dad, and I'm sure Mum and the girls feel the same way.

Dan, I have learnt so much from you and you have given us all so much joy and love. Thank you from the very depth of my soul.

We love you so so much.

Annex A:
How to research and advocate for your child

This annex is not intended as a blueprint. There is no 'right' way to act as a child's advocate or research their cancer. Indeed, parents shouldn't feel guilty about simply leaving decisions to the doctors. Cancers such as Ewing's sarcoma are immensely complicated and the vast majority of cancer parents are not scientists, let alone oncologists.

Certainly, the landscape is forbidding. Despite the hype one sometimes hears, cancer research moves at glacial speed, with progress measured over decades rather than years. Where cure rates have improved, it's often at least in part due to better and earlier diagnosis. Research into Ewing's advanced little over Daniel's five and a half year journey (indeed, for metastatic Ewing's, there has been no real progress for thirty years). Researchers have learnt more, certainly, but will that knowledge convert into effective treatment? It's unfair to say that researchers and clinicians have simply rearranged the deckchairs on the Titanic, tweaking protocols here and there, testing a few hypotheses with limited success - but not that unfair. It's possible that the new pieces of the jigsaw will eventually enable the full picture to emerge, but that is speculation at present.

I had always assumed that medical science would eventually find the answer to each disease. It might take a long time, with many knock-backs along the way, but researchers would eventually get there, step-by-step. Medicine was different to physics, I thought. Many physicists acknowledge that not only is there so much we don't know about the universe (or multiverses, if one prefers), but so much that is unknowable. Einstein actually delighted in the impenetrable – 'the highest wisdom and the most radiant beauty, which our dull faculties can comprehend only in their most primitive forms.'

But I assumed that the finite set of problems of the self-contained human body was solvable. I began to harbour doubts as Daniel's journey progressed. Perhaps the human body is just too complicated for the human brain, a paradox given that the brain controls everything. Trial and error may come up with partial solutions for some intractable diseases, with effective symptom control and perhaps prolongation of life, but whether we will ever fully understand the diseases is questionable. I read once that there is presently no cure for two-thirds of the world's diseases; all doctors can do is ease the suffering. Occasionally, medical science may hit the jackpot with complicated illnesses, but that may require a big dollop of luck to accompany persistent and intelligent research. Indeed, some doctors believe that the focus with difficult cancers should be on making them chronic rather than curing them – living with cancer, in the way that people live with many physical disabilities.

This may all be a counsel for unnecessary despair. But more relevantly, the task for the engaged cancer parent is not to come up with cures but to help choose the best treatment and to give treatment the optimal chance of working by complementary lifestyle adjustment and psychological support. My approach, in a nutshell, was: to ascertain the full range of options (much fuller than those presented by Daniel's doctors), to canvass opinion as widely as possible, to learn enough to be able to ask intelligent questions, to be able to understand the answers and to be able to challenge them where appropriate. The topics of research encompassed efficacy, side effects and the risk of making things worse, all too real with cancer. This all added up to cost:benefit analyses of some sophistication.

Clearly, my research didn't achieve what I wanted because Daniel died, even if he lived far longer than expected. I believe it comforted him that I was seeking answers for him. Importantly, the fact that I ultimately failed doesn't mean that other parents cannot make a real contribution, especially if their child's illness is less serious than Daniel's.

I was an extreme researcher. I wanted to know everything. I trawled the world and read more articles about cancer than was good for me. One way or another, I must have spent thousands upon thousands of hours on Daniel's illness. But a more modest research effort can also pay dividends; indeed, my efforts would probably have been as effective had I ignored the more outlying stretches of the expansive research tableau. I truly believe that parents can make a difference, and a number of doctors agreed.

For good or ill, this was my approach, in twenty-four steps:

Step 1: Get the diagnosis as early as possible
It may seem a bit incongruous to start with this. By the time you know you are a cancer parent, cancer is already diagnosed. This step is directed at parents who are concerned about their child's persistent but undiagnosed symptoms.

Early diagnosis is absolutely crucial, because with

most cancers the best, perhaps only, chance is when the disease is relatively immature, with fewer genetic changes. Unfortunately, cancer is often diagnosed too late. A large-scale study published in 2012 found that nearly a quarter of UK patients were diagnosed in A&E, when they presented with serious symptoms. The picture is even worse with sarcomas. Just about every case I came across was diagnosed late, with GPs not spotting the symptoms. Usually, it's not their fault: they are not trained to differentiate between common symptoms indicating relatively benign conditions and those indicating a sarcoma. Doctors are taught to make the obvious diagnosis rather than the exotic, an application of Occam's Razor (look for the simplest explanation).

The key message is that if symptoms, especially pain, aren't clearing up as anticipated, you should insist on being seen by a specialist, with appropriate scans. As the adverts say, it's probably nothing, but if it's cancer early action may just save your child's life, and avoid much suffering.

Step 2: **Make sure you are at the right hospital and have the right doctors**
It's of the first importance that your child is treated at a specialist centre for the particular cancer, with studies showing that it makes a real difference. I used to wonder about this, because of the standard treatment protocols which every hospital in a country uses. The answer is that with relevant expertise, adjustments can be made to the protocol, the doctor is more likely to know about clinical trials, the other members of the multidisciplinary team (MDT) (for example, surgeons, radiologists and pathologists) will understand the cancer and the nursing

and other support staff will know how to deal with side-effects, some of them highly dangerous. Plus the hospital is more likely to have the relevant scanning and other equipment. All this adds up. In 2008, a study in Germany of 600 patients with soft-tissue sarcoma reported that, in well over two-thirds of cases, private clinics and non-specialist hospitals got the diagnosis wrong.

It's so important to feel comfortable with the main doctor – the oncologist. One mother posted this message about their experience:

'We find a decent person along the way and think they are a hero merely because they behaved decently to us - they held our hand when they gave bad news, or didn't dump bad news on us unexpectedly right in front of our child, or actually responded promptly to a worried phone call instead of having us call over and over again.'

I came across other horror stories, but far more positive stories, it's fair to say. Vitally important though the human side of medicine is, it goes without saying that the key attributes in a doctor are technical knowledge and clinical judgement. As another mother said: 'I'd rather have a great surgeon with terrible bedside manners than an okay surgeon with great bedside manners.'

Parents shouldn't assume that they are stuck with the doctor initially allocated. The stakes are just too high. (However, I'm not sure I agree with the parents who rejected a particular surgeon because his hands were too big, given the dexterity needed for the procedure!). One should be prepared to go to another hospital for part of the treatment if appropriate.

Step 3: Make sure the doctors use all the relevant diagnostic techniques

There are two elements to this: first, the techniques used at diagnosis and second, those used later.

It's important to get a full and accurate picture at diagnosis. It didn't occur to me to ask whether Daniel needed more than the pelvic MRI, bone and chest CT scans he had. I knew nothing then about those in the Ewing's community advocating for whole-body PET/CT and MRI scans. Daniel eventually had those scans, but we laboured under the disadvantage of not having baseline scans at diagnosis, making assessment of progress and decision-making more difficult.

A full picture at diagnosis is also needed for staging (grading the seriousness of the cancer), which can sometimes determine treatment choice, for example under a clinical trial.

Scans are the obvious diagnostic technique but there are several lab ones too. I felt that the more we knew about Daniel's tumour, at diagnosis and relapse, the more informed treatment judgements would be. We had to treat the results with care because they might be poorly understood then, but my approach was to collect as much information as possible in case it became relevant as medical understanding improved.

Tests during and following treatment are also extremely important, again both imaging and lab. For example, the RT-PCR, though not perfect, can detect cancer at a much earlier stage than traditional techniques and therefore act as an early-warning system. Other techniques to improve detection of tumour cells circulating in the blood – there may be only a few in a local cell population of billions – are being improved.

There is, however, a balance, as with all things cancer. Some diagnostic techniques carry risks. I have already mentioned the risks from CT scans. The contrast fluid used for some scans, to aid readability, carries its own risk. A biopsy – taking a sample of the cancer – often involves a general anaesthetic with children. I was acutely conscious, too, of the burden for Daniel of trips abroad for special scans and RT-PCR procedures.

On the other hand, while ignorance of lurking post-treatment cancer may be bliss, it's unlikely to serve one's child well.

The take-home message is: find out if there are additional diagnostic tests which might help. If the doctor says there is no point using them, ask why (and check with other doctors); if they might help but are not available at the hospital, consider having them done elsewhere, even abroad, if practical.

Step 4: **Know the statistics but don't get hung up on them**
It's a mantra of some practitioners, driven to counteract doom and gloom oncologists, that patients are not statistics. Statistics are only averages and anyone can buck a trend. I told myself that, if only 2 per cent of Ewing's patients with lung and bone mets survive for five years, we had to do everything to ensure that Daniel was one of them. Not by pushing anyone else out, of course, but by choosing the correct approaches.

At diagnosis, Daniel could realistically have expected to live for twelve to eighteen months at most. Another lad at

UCH with a strikingly similar Ewing's profile survived for only a year; some children live for just a couple of months. (The irony is that, because Daniel survived for five years, his treatment would be considered successful. Successfully treated but dead. The mad, mad world of cancer, where language is inverted: a positive scan is bad, a negative one good, a patient hopes to make good progress but disease progression is bad.)

Studies about Ewing's statistics are often contradictory, largely because as a rare cancer, data has to be collected over a period of years and from several hospitals or even countries, with the consequent widespread variation in treatment and diagnostic techniques.

But statistics obviously do matter. They give a good indication of the seriousness of someone's condition, and what is likely to happen. They inform decision-making and crucially, how much risk to take. I couldn't do my best for Daniel if shielded from reality.

For all the caveats and their generally depressing nature, statistics could also give flashes of hope, as when studies indicated that Daniel might be in a less unfavourable subset.

Step 5: **Prepare thoroughly for meetings with the doctors**
When Daniel was in remission or part way through a long cycle of treatment and there were no scan results pending, meetings with Colin McMaster were often routine and required little preparation. Many others, however, required extensive preparation, sometimes running into hours or even days.

Doctors will discuss patients at key stages at MDT meetings and no doubt on other occasions too. The reality, however, is that often the only time a busy doctor will think about a patient is when the previous patient leaves. If I had questions beyond the routine, I would send them beforehand by email. I wanted the doctor to mull over the issues. Email is a real boon to patients/families. Potentially it's a real burden for doctors, so it should be used judiciously (not sure I always got that right).

With appointments when we were expecting results, I would often prepare two sets of questions, one contingent on a good result and the other on a bad result. Whenever possible I would try to get the results beforehand. I could then prepare my questions on the basis of an actual rather than a hypothetical result and, as importantly, could steady myself emotionally.

It wasn't easy getting results in advance: the UK way is to give results at the next appointment. In other countries, the system is different – patients are often given results the same day, by telephone. That can cause its own difficulties, because the result may not be black and white, but I much preferred pre-meeting notification.

With someone like Daniel who didn't want to hear bad news or discuss options or prognosis, it's also important to be clear beforehand whether they're going to attend and if so, when they will leave and then stick to that.

Step 6: Get everything you need out of meetings

The objective is to get the information one needs. This can be harder than it sounds, because of the emotion and the complexity of the information. For this reason, it's important for another adult to come wherever possible. Two memories and two questioners are better than one.

But the best way to compensate for unreliable memory is to take notes at all meetings (and phone calls). I cannot stress too highly how important this is. I know from the early encounters – when I didn't take notes – how apparent understanding at a meeting metamorphoses into confusion and amnesia the moment one steps outside.

One Ewing's patient in the US tape-recorded meetings. I wouldn't necessarily suggest that, because it could make the doctor defensive and monosyllabic, but I understand the rationale.

It's really important to make sure one understands the answers given. Some doctors are better at explaining things than others. In his book about his son Damon's heart disease, Doron Weber wrote:

> 'I have one rule: if we can't understand an issue or a medical approach makes no sense to us, it's the doctor's problem, not ours. No mumbo-jumbo. We must always know exactly what's going on so we can help ensure the best decisions are made. The most capable physicians supply the clearest explanations – equally clear about what they don't know as what they do – and only the mediocre take refuge in obfuscation or omniscience.'

A bit strong, perhaps, but the general sentiment holds true. Persist until you get an answer you understand.

In cricket, teams up against a massive total are said to face scoreboard pressure, inducing mistakes. We were often conscious of waiting-room pressure, where one feels uncomfortable about asking too many questions because of patients waiting their turn. The waiting-room at the

Rosenheim at UCH was often heaving. Again, resist such feelings. One should keep questions focused, certainly, and avoid discussion just because an issue is interesting. But the bottom line is that a patient and their family are entitled to the information they need to make decisions. If the doctor is too busy, or isn't good at managing his or her time, there is no reason why patients should suffer.

Step 7: Make notes after the meeting

I mentioned earlier the importance of taking notes. I would always type up my notes as soon as possible. Occasionally, if I'd forgotten to ask something important, I would email Colin. There might well be a 'to do' list as a result of the discussion.

Step 8: Ask for reports of scans and other results

I felt it really important to get all the reports of Daniel's scans and other diagnostic tests. Sometimes, the report didn't reflect what we had been told. The confusion then needed resolving.

I was able to quote from the reports when writing to other doctors, to give them a better flavour of Daniel's condition and progress.

Step 9: Ask for a copy of the scans

At UCH, we could get a patient's scans for £20 a go (though I was often given them cheaper). The scans were meaningless to me but I would often send them to other doctors.

Step 10: Buy a medical dictionary

I found my *Oxford Medical Dictionary* so useful, in

conjunction with online dictionaries. Cancer, medicine generally, has its own language, usually derived from ancient Greek and sometimes Latin and understanding suffixes and prefixes helps to demystify.

Step 11: Use the internet wisely

The internet is both a wonderful and a frightening thing. It provides a window to information one wouldn't otherwise know existed. But the information can be of Pacific proportions and it can be seriously problematical to differentiate the useful from the useless.

Given the dismal prognosis of metastasised or relapsed Ewing's, one might suppose that there were few options to explore. In a sense, the opposite was the case, because intractability spawns creativity. When Daniel relapsed, I prepared a table of possible options, including various chemo combinations, stem cell transplants, radiotherapy and allied techniques, biological therapies, surgery techniques, a long list of types of immunotherapy and many other categories. Each was used or suggested by a Ewing's doctor somewhere and then there were countless complementary therapies, too. The table was constantly evolving, and included the contact details of patients trying or looking at an option. Every single option came with complicated and uncertain science.

I nevertheless found the internet an invaluable way of ascertaining the direction of research travel and the right people to speak to. I'm sure useful internet research can be done with less time than I was able to devote, but it does need the hard yards (even an email address could take a couple of hours to track down).

Step 12: Develop your skills in assessing evidence

This could be a book by itself. As a lawyer, assessing complicated evidence wasn't new to me. With both medical and legal evidence, the key imperatives are to test the evidence rigorously, to give it appropriate weight and not to jump too readily to conclusions.

I faced a number of difficulties. First, there is precious little which is certain with rare cancers. To a greater or lesser extent, that is true of all medicine and science. Thomas Kuhn, the 20th century American physicist and philosopher of science, argued that scientific laws are forever provisional – they only hold true until new evidence requires a paradigm shift. There are countless examples of received wisdom proving not so wise, from the Aristotelian paradigm of the sun circumnavigating the Earth onwards.

Linked to this, most science involves drawing conclusions from observations – the so-called inductive method, developed by Francis Bacon. Only if a consistent pattern emerges can there be confidence of a causal link between remedy and cure (or side-effect). Even then, patterns may become less distinct as more evidence rolls in, a particular problem with rare diseases.

Epidemiology – the study of patterns in a given population – is particularly inconclusive with environmental and lifestyle factors, which many think are important with cancer. Epidemiology looks for association or correlation but not proof. In the real world outside the lab and clinical trials, there are too many variables for proof. The epidemiological link between smoking and lung cancer was disputed for a long time and vested interests are adept at exploiting the inconclusive nature of the link between, for example, fossil fuels and climate change or red meat consumption and cardiovascular and cancer mortality.

In addition most cancer researchers, in my experience, don't follow the stricture of Karl Popper, regarded by many as the greatest philosopher of science of the 20th century, that researchers should set out to falsify a hypothesis rather than verify it. It sounds counter-intuitive, but Popper maintained that one cannot prove a theory, irrespective of how many examples one may find to support it. Identifying an example which doesn't fit destroys the hypothesis, or at least requires it to be adjusted. If attempts to falsify fail, the hypothesis is more likely to be correct.

Popper's approach is now generally accepted by scientists. I'm sure many relish picking holes in a hypothesis developed by a rival. And yet most of the articles I read during Daniel's journey seemed intent on proving a hypothesis. This was particularly so with complementary remedies but it was also common with conventional medicine: many researchers had a pet theory they were keen to promote (granted, a hypothesis has to be erected before it can be dismantled).

There is then the question, which I touched on earlier, of the extent to which one can trust data presented in articles, given the pharmaceutical industry's inglorious history of suppressing and massaging inconvenient facts. Even when data is presented fully and fairly, to assess whether treatment A is better than treatment B one needs a statistical comparison between the two and this is often absent.

The result of all this is that so much of what one reads is preliminary, even if not presented as such. That makes assessing evidence a hazardous occupation. I received so much contradictory advice.

So, what to do? My approach was as follows:

i. View the evidence as rigorously and objectively as possible, questioning everything and then double- and triple-checking it with independent sources. The more outlandish a claim, the more sceptical one should be.

ii. Work out who to trust, recognising that a layperson will not understand enough about the science for independent judgement. It may take some time to develop this instinct, but there are short-cuts: is the person a specialist in the relevant cancer?; how experienced are they?; what is their position?; do they work, or did they train, at a leading institution?; what is their publication record (not failsafe because not every clinician publishes and conversely senior doctors are often included as authors when, in truth, they have contributed little to the study)?

iii. What patient data is there to support a proposition? I learnt to distrust hypotheses based on preclinical research, however logical the argument might seem. The gap between bench and bed is just too great.

iv. How rigorous does the data appear? Do the results pass the threshold of statistical significance and do they justify the conclusions or is there a non sequitur or overclaiming?

v. What level of consensus is there amongst experts, albeit that it may only be emerging uncertainly? Canvass as many views worth listening to as possible.

vi. Be aware of confirmation bias: cherry-picking evidence to suit the conclusion one wishes to reach. The risk lurks in all areas of life but it's particularly high when one is looking for solutions for a seriously ill child. It's so tempting to latch onto a hopeful claim because we want it to be true, but it does a grave disservice to one's child to view evidence through rose-tinted spectacles.

vii. Be prepared to look beyond clinical trials. At the experimental stage, clinical trials are undoubtedly the best form of evidence – particularly large-scale, randomised, placebo-controlled, double-blind, phase 3 studies (RCTs) (or, better still, systematic reviews – meta-analyses – of multiple RCTs). Clinical experience, once a treatment has been approved, is then obviously hugely important. However, the big mistake which many oncologists make, I believe, is to reject therapies which fall short of the clinical trial ideal. Remedies which have not been subjected to this level of scrutiny must be viewed with particular caution, but it doesn't follow that the evidence should be rejected. Sometimes the best is the enemy of the good. The key question is what weight should be attached to particular evidence.

viii. A doctor's experience with their patients, though often pejoratively dismissed as 'anecdotal', can be valuable.

ix. Understand that treatment doesn't have to be identical for everyone with a particular condition. There is room for individual adaptation, if that's what the evidence and the doctor's intuition (itself nurtured by knowledge and experience) suggests. Targeted therapies are seen as the future.

x. With rare, life-threatening illnesses, look for the spark of creativity, but supported by as much hard evidence as possible.

xi. Try to rank the available options.

Step 13: Be prepared to go down blind alleys

At least 95 per cent of my research alleys proved to be cul-de-sacs, though often only after considerable expenditure of effort. In a strange way, it could be a relief when something failed, because it eased the burden of decision-making. Equally, an alley would often divert to somewhere unexpected and promising (the justification traditionally given for 'blue skies' research).

Step 15: Be willing to look abroad

Petra and I were clear from the outset that our search for Daniel would be global. Cancer services in the UK have improved significantly over the past few years, with increased spending. But the base was relatively low for a leading economy and there's still a lag with some countries. I cannot point to statistics showing a better outcome for Ewing's in other countries but some types of treatment or diagnostic techniques, available in some European countries, aren't available in the UK. One young man with a nasty sarcoma had proton radiotherapy (not generally given in the UK) in Switzerland at the NHS's cost. The law also entitles patients to NHS-funded treatment in other EU countries if delay is the problem (rare with paediatric cancer, in fairness).

As importantly, information from abroad can be used to push for treatment in this country. I learnt about radiotherapy to bone metastatic sites from Germany, but Daniel then had the treatment at his hospital. Similarly, I pushed for PET/CT scans at UCH because they were commonplace in some other countries.

Step 16: Make use of the different ways of communicating with doctors

There are three ways to communicate with other doctors: by email, by telephone and face-to-face. Email is incredibly useful and free and the easiest.

By far the most effective, however, is face-to-face. One can pick up so much from body language and the nuances of spoken language. It's easier to ask supplementary questions and to probe. Doctors may be willing to say something they wouldn't wish to commit to writing. Some showed me scans of patients to illustrate a point. One builds up a personal relationship, too, which may be useful for the future.

As well as all the meetings in this country, often with complementary practitioners, there were numerous trips abroad, some with Daniel (if he was having a diagnostic procedure), some by myself. Only a couple of the trips proved a waste of time. I appreciate that going abroad is not practical for everyone.

I was amazed how easy it was to pick up the phone and speak to a doctor, especially abroad. If a doctor was not available when I called, they would call back promptly – and sometimes apologise for their earlier unavailability! Although I would ration myself to a limited number of questions, I rarely felt rushed. Every offer of payment was turned down.

Step 17: How to email

I had some self-imposed rules for email communication:

i.   Always be polite (apart from being appropriate, this is far more likely to produce a response).

ii.   Understand that the person you are writing to owes

you nothing.

iii. Give a brief background of your child's condition, with relevant recent scan or other findings.

iv. Show you know what you are talking about – you are more likely to get a useful answer.

v. Ask specific questions, rather than 'what is the best thing to cure my child?'

vi. Ask only a question or two: doctors want to be able to answer quickly (although some gave detailed expositions).

vii. Do not ask for specific advice: doctors will be aware they don't have the full picture and won't wish to second-guess the treating doctor. They may also be sensitive to a possible negligence claim if something goes wrong. I would say something like: 'I appreciate you cannot advise in Daniel's case without much more information. We will discuss matters in detail with his doctors, but in very general terms would you think that, in this sort of case ...?' That would usually do the trick.

viii. Where possible get over some of the human side – many doctors started their reply 'As a parent myself ...'

ix. Immediately express appreciation if they reply, even if the reply is not helpful.

x. Keep supplementary questions to a minimum.

xi. If necessary, send a chaser email, expressed even more politely – 'I would greatly appreciate a reply, if you have the time.'

xii. Where appropriate, ask for a telephone discussion (and offer to pay).

I would have expected doctors, especially in the litigious USA, to hide behind medico-legal concerns but this was extremely rare. One American doctor offered to give me Coley's toxins – which were then in short supply – if I waived legal liability. I would unhesitatingly have agreed - I had no interest in suing anyone for anything. It's to the credit of the medical profession that so many doctors, in so many countries, were so willing to help Daniel.

Step 18: How to get hold of articles for free

I found that emailing authors was an effective way of getting articles for free. There is a move these days towards open access (where full articles are published on the internet), encouraged by major UK research funders. At present however, one has to pay for most articles; only the abstract (summary) is free, though this in itself can be useful. Typically, articles cost around £30 to buy, which soon mounts up. So I would ask one of the authors for a copy, explaining my interest. It nearly always worked. Apart from a natural desire to help, doctors were pleased at the interest in their work.

Step 19: Do not hesitate to get a second opinion

Doctor: I'm sorry to tell you, Mrs Smith, you only have six months to live.
Mrs Smith: Well, I would like a second opinion
Doctor: Ok, you're ugly as well.

Mrs Smith was right to ask for a second opinion. Patients are often reluctant to do so, because it feels like lack of trust in one's doctor, on whom one is so reliant. I recognise that feeling.

However, Daniel's life was in the balance and I had to put to one side any fear of causing offence. Doctors always say they have no problem getting a second opinion and the good ones will not mind their judgement being scrutinised. A second opinion helps doctors, too, and oncologists often obtain their own.

One Ewing's parent blogged:

'My wife and I didn't believe everything any doctor told us. We got four opinions on everything they wanted to do, and then we decided on what we thought was best since the four doctors didn't even agree. … My son would not be alive today if we had listened to the first two doctors we had seen, they pretty much just wrote him off…'

I obtained two types of second opinion: informal and formal. I sought informal opinions without reference to Daniel's doctors. I must have asked for hundreds in all. Informal opinions are not as good as formal opinions, because the doctor will not have the full picture (although scans can be sent). A reply may be off the cuff. These are important caveats. However, informal opinions are quick and free and multiple opinions on an issue can help establish where broad consensus lies and can point to new line of inquiry.

Formal second opinions are usually arranged by the treating doctor, who chooses the independent doctor. The patient's role is passive. However, I knew from whom I wanted second opinions and found it really useful to visit the doctor.

Although there's no legal right to a second opinion under the NHS, a request is rarely refused.

Step 20: **Try to understand the cause of the cancer**

As with step 1, in a sense the horse has already bolted by the time of diagnosis. However, logic suggests that addressing what caused the cancer, where that is possible, can help the remedial process.

The World Health Organisation (WHO) estimates that a third of cancers originate in environmental or lifestyle factors; some put the figure considerably higher. Environmental factors include pollution and exposure to radiation and lifestyle factors include excessive alcohol, smoking, diet and lack of exercise. Carcinogenic chemicals are pervasive but, with many of the other factors, it should be possible to effect change.

The cause of many cancers is unknown. With Ewing's sarcoma, there have been suggestions of environmental factors playing a part, with some remarkable clusters for such a rare cancer: two in a school of only thirteen pupils in Texas, three children from the same graduating class in North Carolina, another cluster near a US military base. There have been isolated cases of siblings contracting Ewing's, with no real suggestion of hereditary factors (thereby strengthening the case for environmental factors). I read epidemiological studies reporting a significantly increased risk of a child getting Ewing's if their father was exposed to pesticides at work. Strangely, a child's direct exposure to pesticides barely increased the risk.

Some believe that stress can trigger cancer. Daniel had a calm temperament and coped with all that life threw at him with remarkable stoicism and equanimity. Fittingly for someone who loved Wimbledon so much, he took to heart the advice given to the young boy in Kipling's poem

If, posted at the entrance to Centre Court, to treat alike the twin impostors of Triumph and Disaster. But he experienced real stress in his pre-cancer life, not least the loss of Mike his stepfather to whom he was very close, when ten.

Daniel also nearly died at childbirth. During a difficult labour, his head pressed the umbilical cord against the wall of the womb, thereby cutting off the blood supply to his brain. He was delivered by emergency caesarean. The staff were brilliant: seconds mattered. Could the trauma have played a part in converting his chromosomal translocation into full-blown Ewing's?

Might stress then have some influence on survival from cancer? Removing stress is easier said than done – and, of course, cancer and the financial worries it often brings are themselves highly stressful – but it makes sense to control it if possible.

The fundamental message is: if environment or lifestyle might be a factor with your child's cancer, it's advisable to alter them wherever possible.

Step 21: Be open-minded about complementary and alternative methods (CAM)

There is not the great divide between orthodox and complementary medicine some would have us believe. Indeed, some two-thirds of conventional drugs are plant-based: periwinkle, found in Madagascar, is the base of two standard chemotherapy drugs, Vinblastine and Vincristine; aspirin is derived from the willow bark.

A surprisingly large proportion of cancer patients take CAM remedies or are on special diets. Many oncologists are sceptical. One of Daniel's doctors used to joke with him about

'Dad's magic potions.' US authorities even remove children from parents who wish to ditch chemotherapy in favour of a CAM approach. There have been legal causes célèbres about Ewing's patients, one involving a doctor for whom I developed great respect. In another case, the child's oncologist gave evidence against the parents, not great for relationships.

There is an assumption that, whereas conventional medicine is based on rigorous research, building up from exhaustive laboratory studies to strictly-controlled clinical trials, complementary medicine is a research-free zone, relying (at best) on anecdote and cod science. There is certainly truth in this. But it's only part of the picture. There is often painstaking research into CAM remedies too. For example, I read numerous articles by serious researchers, about curcumin and ashwagandha (remedies from the Ayurvedic tradition). The science was as dense as anything I read about conventional treatment. There is a branch of mycology – the study of mushrooms – looking at how they can attack cancer. I also read a well-researched book by Josef Beuth, a professor of complementary medicine at Cologne, and Ralph Moss. Like so many others, Prof Beuth freely gave his time to speak to me. Dr Moss, a guru of CAM and a strong critic of chemotherapy, produces a useful, free weekly newsletter (though his expensive report about Ewing's was far less useful).

The problem is that traditional or diet-based remedies are usually not patentable and therefore there is insufficient incentive for pharmaceutical companies to run clinical trials, which are extremely expensive. Occasionally, Big Pharma does see the potential of a CAM cancer remedy, as when the British company GlaxoSmithKline paid an astonishing

$750m for a small Boston company which had activated the gene SIRT1 in resveratrol, the molecule found in red grapes. Some think that the gene holds the key to longevity (the cancer link is that ageing cells are more prone to cancer). GSK later closed the company.

This is a gross generalisation but, whereas conventional cancer therapy introduces external agents into the body to attack the cancer (chemotherapy and radiotherapy) or cuts out the cancer (surgery), complementary therapies seek to use the body's own healing powers, in particular the immune system. I was surprised to learn that all of us have cancerous or pre-cancerous cells from time to time. The immune system usually deals with them before they become dangerous. One often hears the phrase 'boosting the immune system' in relation to complementary therapies, including diet. The immune system is exceptionally complicated and it's naïve to think that 'boosting the immune system' can by itself cure cancer. But the immune system remains key, it seems to me. Similarly, there is legitimate criticism of conventional medicine that it looks at symptoms and only the part of the body manifesting disease, whereas CAM looks at the whole person. Since everything in the body is interrelated, that seems the correct approach, even if it inevitably adds to complexity.

Some of the larger cancer hospitals in the US, such as MD Anderson in Houston and MSKCC, have helpful websites, summarising the evidence about particular CAMs in a measured way. This presumably reflects the questions they get from patients but it shows a degree of open-mindedness which I didn't often find among UK doctors.

I looked into everything, including faith and spiritual healing, but I retained healthy scepticism, too, resisting the temptation to jump too readily onto the many CAM bandwagons encircling the cancer world. This is my advice:

i.   As ever, research as thoroughly as possible and find out the people to trust. There are many genuine, knowledgeable people but unscrupulous practitioners too.

ii. If someone has something to sell, be especially cautious about the objectivity of their advice. To engender hope is important; to engender false hope is to prey on the vulnerable and is particularly reprehensible where there is financial gain.

iii. Do not be blinded by science: some practitioners deliberately deploy complicated-sounding science, confident that the mystique of incomprehensibility will persuade some of efficacy.

iv. Avoid the logical fallacy captured by the Latin phrase 'post hoc ergo propter hoc': 'B was caused by A because B happened after A' (it was one of the logical fallacies Daniel studied in his Critical Thinking AS and is well-known in both law and medicine). Many people fall into the trap: 'I took x, I got better, therefore it was x which made me better.' They might have got better anyway, and indeed x might conceivably have slowed recovery. Correlation is not the same as causation. Overclaiming by proponents of particular CAM approaches is a frequent problem.

v.   Success stories are great for morale but may not give the full picture and may not be replicable.

vi. Be cautious about websites and magazines that do not give references.

vii. Check with the doctors that a CAM remedy wouldn't interfere with conventional treatment. CAM remedies –

which are, after all, made up of chemicals – can interfere with chemotherapy, radiotherapy etc, by reducing efficacy or increasing risks. For example, some oncologists argue that the antioxidants found in many CAM supplements interfere with chemo and, especially, radiotherapy. This was a real concern: for obvious reasons, we needed to maximise efficacy. Equally, many believe that antioxidants can enhance chemo and radiotherapy. My eventual compromise was that Daniel didn't take certain remedies during radiotherapy or chemo infusion days. I'm not sure how scientific it was. As with everything else with cancer, the science of the interaction between remedies is complicated and incomplete.

viii. As the journey progressed, I would go direct to the always helpful UCH pharmacists, because they knew more than the oncologists. In truth, judgements were speculative, because the science was so rudimentary. For example, there was a suggestion in a preclinical study that curcumin reduced a patient's platelets. By this time, Daniel's platelets were a real concern, so I took him off curcumin while he was on chemo. By the end, I would sometimes bypass even Pharmacy and rely on my own research. I felt I should take full responsibility.

ix. Be careful about dosing. One of the problems with CAM remedies is knowing the appropriate dose. Dosing is key with conventional medicines – Paracelsus, the German Swiss Renaissance scientist, noted: 'Poison is in everything and nothing is without a poison. The dosage makes it either a poison or a remedy.' Scientists want to know the appropriate ADME – how the body absorbs, distributes, metabolises and excretes a substance. There are complicated disciplines called pharmacokinetics and pharmacodynamics. With CAM remedies, it's largely guesswork and not particularly educated at that. If the dose is too small, any efficacy will be lost; if it's too large, there are risks to safety or of interfering with other treatment. I listened to manufacturers and practitioners and spent ages researching, but it was all a bit hit or miss. At one point, Daniel took piperine (black pepper) to aid absorption of curcumin. Goodness knows whether it did any good.

x. Don't be put off by the fact that the evidence about a particular remedy is incomplete. The evidence with conventional treatment is incomplete, too; less incomplete, perhaps, but still incomplete. There was, by contrast, any amount of evidence about the failure of the conventional treatment on offer to Daniel; that was the whole point of complementing with CAM.

xi. Ultimately, make a harm:benefit assessment as best you can. Every decision in medicine is about weighing harms and benefits. The benefits of CAM remedies, where they can be established, usually fall short of a cure. In the vast majority of cases, the most one can hope for is a positive contribution, perhaps just the easing of treatment-related symptoms. Might a remedy enhance – 'potentiate', as oncologists say – conventional treatment? Equally, a patient may derive psychological benefit from taking something he believes is helping (the placebo effect).

xii. On the other side of the equation, with most CAM remedies and approaches, the risk of harm seems small. For me this was crucial. The smaller the risk, the less evidence about benefit I was willing to tolerate. But I wasn't complacent about harm, checking out everything with manufacturers and experts around the world, for example once speaking to the WHO about the level of metals in a particular supplement. Burden for Daniel was a harm, too and financial cost would, sadly, be a factor for many.

xiii. Focus on the complementary rather than the alternative in CAM. With serious cancers, you need the blockbuster conventional treatments. I spoke to a teenage girl in the US who, encouraged by her father, relied on diet and something called PolyMVA. She had a bad experience with chemo (as he himself had had with his own cancer) and so abandoned it. She died not long afterwards.

I rejected countless CAM remedies, though some simmered on the back burner rather than being cast into the incinerator. For the record, this is what Daniel took: curcumin, ashwagandha, astragalus (a Chinese herbal remedy), lycopene, echinacea, resveratrol, agaricus blazei (mushrooms), maitake (ditto) and various homeopathic remedies

My overriding objective was to make Daniel's body an inhospitable environment for the cancer. The remedies may have helped to keep it at bay and even if not, they may well have eased side-effects. Daniel generally tolerated treatment better than most Ewing's patients and that in turn kept treatment on track. The objective was a virtuous circle of nutritional and other immune-enhancing measures, weight gain, treatment tolerability, reasonable quality of life, positive thinking - all of which could in turn have some effect on his prospects. With cancer, vicious circles abound, so we were keen to fashion a virtuous one.

At any rate, I have no regrets about the approach we took and would do the same again. I discuss two unconventional approaches, homeopathy and Ukrain, in Annex C.

Step 22: **Be prepared to change your child's diet and encourage exercise**

Diet can be seen as a form of CAM and most of the same considerations applied. I'm convinced that diet has a real part to play with cancer.

Unfortunately there a huge number of cancer diets and I looked at a good many of them. Many are flatly contradictory; some are highly, and surely unnecessarily, prescriptive. One diet excited controversy and some vituperative comments on the Sarcoma UK website, where patients divided between those open to the role of diet and those unwilling to contemplate change (understandably enough, since food can be a real comfort when so much else is going wrong).

Drink is as important as food. As well as wheatgrass juice, Daniel had green vegetable and fruit juices. He took red grape juice until I discovered that pasteurisation would kill any benefit from the resveratrol. He also had Acai berry juice, from the Amazonian forest and described as a superfood, full of nutrients, though the label is used lazily. Daniel also drank green tea, which is extolled in many parts of the world for its health benefits, including cancer. He would try to drink two litres of bottled water a day to flush out his system.

Allied to diet, studies suggest that exercise, with the increased oxygen it engenders, is an important part of the armoury against cancer. It can certainly help psychologically.

Step 23: Be open-minded about positive thinking

Many regard positive thinking as important with cancer, although again traditional oncologists usually dismiss it. The link between mind and body is little understood but undoubtedly exists, in my view, with some empirical evidence in addition to reams of anecdotal. In an experiment by Dr Fabrizio Benedetti in Turin, volunteers who thought (wrongly) they had been given morphine didn't react to previously painful stimuli. Dr Benedetti hypothesised that the volunteers' belief that they were getting morphine triggered the release of endorphins and enkephalins, which then did the work of the morphine.

In a study of breast cancer patients at UCH, Daniel's hospital, those with a positive outlook did better than the pessimistic. Other studies show similarly impressive results. One has to be careful about this sort of study, it's true: the categories are not exact and the picture is not uniform - a study in Australia involving lung cancer patients showed that positive thinking made no apparent difference.

We worked extremely hard to keep Daniel as positive as possible. If nothing else, I'm sure it enabled him to cope better with the horrible treatment and to embrace the dietary and other complementary approaches we suggested.

Step 24: Adopt an efficient system of filing

This is really boring but important. During Daniel's five and a half-year journey I amassed an enormous amount of information; filing was time-consuming. I'm afraid my approach was not kind to Amazonian rainforests. I don't like reading anything of any length on the computer screen and feared losing everything stored on my hard drive.

By the end I had around forty lever arch files, crammed full of articles, meeting and telephone notes and emails. This was on top of all the books. The categories were fairly random, because everything overlaps in cancer, but an index enabled me to locate things easily using a word search.

I also had numerous tables, setting out the pros and cons of various options and contact details. There were tables for CAM and diet. I kept a record of the numerous blood results. I copied and pasted passages from CarePages and Caringbridge pages, so that I knew who had tried which treatments and to record personal insight.

One of the tables was of the emails I sent. During the early months I was firing off so many that it was difficult to keep track of who had replied. The table enabled me to do so.

Naturally I kept all communications with Daniel's hospital – meeting and telephone notes, scan reports, diagnostic reports, emails, copy letters to GPs, information sheets.

My system would not have won any prizes for office administration but it worked pretty well for me and enabled me to access information quickly.

Conclusion

If you follow some or all of these steps, or adopt your own, it will not guarantee that your child survives. But parents can undoubtedly help to maximise their child's chances. There is plenty of good advice out there. It's just a matter of identifying it and differentiating it from the less good.

Annex B
Compassionate use access to drugs

Towards the end, Daniel received figitumumab, an IGF inhibitor, on a compassionate use basis. For a while it wasn't clear that he would. Some background may help other families running out of options and wishing to access unlicensed drugs.

The received wisdom is that compassionate use lies completely within the discretion of the drug company. I found out that this isn't true. There is a specific European law, Regulation 726/2004. Article 83 defines 'compassionate use' as 'making [relevant medicines] available for compassionate reasons to a group of patients with a chronically or seriously debilitating disease or whose disease is considered to be life-threatening and who cannot be treated satisfactorily by [a licensed medicine].' The drug in question must either be in a clinical trial, as figitumumab was, or awaiting a full licensing decision. Daniel and figitumumab clearly both qualified. Article 83 goes on to say that the decision whether to allow compassionate use rests with EU member states, such as the UK, after taking into account any views expressed by a particular EU committee.

So drug companies do not have a free hand. It's doubtful whether a government could force a company to make a drug available on compassionate use, but it would have to ensure that the terms on which a drug was made available were fair.

I wanted to ascertain the approach of the MHRA, the UK regulator of medicines. They told me compassionate use was not formally regulated. I knew that was wrong – at least, it should be regulated. The reply also seemed to confuse compassionate use with so-called 'specials', which are imported unlicensed medicines for identified patients. An MHRA guidance note about specials explicitly said that it didn't cover compassionate use. There were no guidelines about compassionate use. I was told that only if a drug is imported did they need to give consent for such use. Consent could be given within twenty-four hours. I couldn't see why it mattered for compassionate use whether the drug was imported or manufactured in the UK. It would be pure chance whether Pfizer happened to manufacture figitumumab here.

Pfizer themselves had no guidelines about compassionate use specific to the UK, but global guidelines recognised quadripartite involvement: Pfizer, treating doctor, governments and patients. There had to be meaningful human clinical trial data to support an assessment that the potential benefits to the patient outweighed the risks. I noted a statement I could use publicly if need be:

> 'Pfizer is ... committed to making reasonable accommodations so that seriously ill patients who have exhausted other appropriate treatment options may, under the conditions described in this policy and in accordance with applicable local law, have appropriate access to investigational products before they are commercially available.'

I had to prepare the ground in case the company was uncooperative. I came across another little-known EU law, Regulation 1901/2006, setting out special rules for medicines for paediatric use. It wasn't directly relevant, but, as always with EU legislation, it contained general statements – 'recitals' – which could be used to support a case. It recognised that many medicines used for children had not been through child-specific clinical trials. 'Market forces alone', it continued, 'have proven insufficient to stimulate adequate research into, and the development and authorisation of, medicinal products for the paediatric population.' The regulation aims to facilitate the development and accessibility of medicines for children, by a carrot and stick approach, with a requirement for drug companies to disclose paediatric data.

There is a further piece of EU legislation, dealing with so-called orphan drugs. These are drugs which the pharmaceutical industry would not normally develop because of the rarity of the conditions in question. Regulation 141/2000 provides incentives for the development of orphan drugs.

I resolved, if necessary, to use the legislative recognition that paediatric patients and those with rare conditions were ill-served by the drug development process. Many paediatric cancers are rare. In the UK, the Rarer Cancers Forum fights for better access to treatment. It's a charity but has semi-official status and has been instrumental in persuading the Government to establish the Cancer Drugs Fund, which provides additional money for cancer drugs.

I saw the RCF as a potential ally in accessing figitumumab, should there be problems. But one thing concerned me. Most of the large drug companies, including Pfizer, are sponsors of the charity. No doubt there is much common ground – it is, after all, in drug companies' interests that funds are made available to buy their products. But coincidence of interests was not inevitable. If Pfizer refused to make figitumumab available on compassionate use basis, or drew their criteria in such a way as to exclude Daniel, or refused to allow the drug to be given with other treatment, would the RCF be prepared to speak publicly against one of their sponsors? It seemed unlikely.

In the US, the Abigail Alliance fights for early access to cancer drugs. Frank Burroughs' daughter, Abigail, died of cancer in 2001, after being denied a drug (not dissimilar to IGF inhibitors) which her oncologist felt strongly could help her. The Alliance has had considerable success. Frank offered to smooth the path with Pfizer.

In the event, Pfizer came up trumps, and we were very grateful. It's not always so easy.

Annex C
Homeopathy and Ukrain

It might be useful to discuss two alternative approaches which I researched. We embraced one, homeopathy, and rejected the other, Ukrain.

Homeopathy

Daniel received homeopathic treatment at the Royal London Homeopathic Hospital in Great Ormond Street, next to the famous children's hospital. It's under constant threat of closure, because of the persistent assault of the orthodox medicine establishment on homeopathy. Daniel liked our doctor at the RLHH, Dr Sosie Kassab, who trained with Colin McMaster, at Bart's. They were as different as two doctors could be. Whereas Colin is precise and data-driven, Sosie is much more intuitive. She would sometimes ask me what I thought we should do, prompting Daniel, laughingly, to ask 'Why are you asking him?' a reasonable question. We used to enjoy our visits.

Homeopathy is a strange one. To the rational mind, it makes no sense (which is why so many doctors dismiss it). It's based on the principle 'Let like be cured by like', developed by the German Samuel Hahnemann in 1796. As far as it goes, there is nothing particularly remarkable about the concept – vaccines, too, work by giving a person the relevant disease and provoking the immune system to respond.

What's strange about homeopathy is that the patient gets only the minutest trace of the substance in question.

It will have been diluted to the nth degree. The theory, as I understand it, is that the water is able to 'remember' the energy of the substance.

I read a book about homeopathy for cancer, based on the experience of an Indian doctor, Dr AU Ramakrishnan. The book is unusual because homeopathy doesn't usually focus on specific diseases, as allopathic (traditional western) medicine does. I was excited when I saw Ewing's get a couple of mentions. With 'viable' cases of bone cancer, Dr Ramakrishnan claimed a success rate of 74 per cent. But what did 'viable' mean and how did he judge success? The book explained that viable cases excluded those with no expectation of cure. So Daniel wouldn't be considered a viable case. Some cases were considered successful even though the normal cancer yardstick of five years had not expired. So there was some statistical sleight-of-hand. More reasonably, Dr Ramakrishnan and his co-author pointed out that many patients seeking homeopathic assistance for the first time are in the later stages of cancer and have already exhausted traditional Western treatments. That is a frequent bugbear of complementary medicine practitioners – the remedies have much less chance of working by the time they are tried.

For bone cancer, Dr Ramakrishnan strongly recommended hekla lava, from an Icelandic volcano, and also recommended carcinosin. Carcinosin worried me because it's derived from breast cancer. I knew the amount in a solution was vanishingly small but it still felt uncomfortable giving Daniel something containing cancer. I spent ages looking into it. Daniel himself was unconcerned and wanted to know why I had delayed.

Daniel also took Iscador, popular in Germany with many oncologists. Some studies claim an increase in survival time.

Sosie told him silica could improve mood and indeed at one time he thought it made him happy. So, take more of it, she told him. It was a great approach to medicine, a welcome relief from all the nastiness and regimentation of chemotherapy.

I met Dr Ramakrishnan once. He billed himself as the homeopathic doctor to the President of India and his fees matched: £250 for the consultation, serious money in India. It was clear he didn't think that Daniel would survive – he was not one of his viable cases – but suggested that homeopathy could increase his survival time and ease symptoms. Who knows whether it did? We didn't do the labour-intensive method Dr Ramakrishnan recommended – it was just too much of a rigmarole – but Daniel was assiduous in taking his homeopathic remedies, at least until the latter stages when he grew pretty sceptical.

My overall approach to homeopathy was: ok, it's not going to cure Daniel by itself and may be nonsense, but might it just help? Crucially, homeopathic remedies carry hardly any side-effects, so there is not the usual cost:benefit assessment to be made (other than financial cost).

Ukrain

Ukrain is on the fringes of conventional medicine. It's a combination of a chemo drug, thiotepa, and a plant, greater celandine, traditionally used for liver and gastrointestinal complaints. Ukrain was said to be far less toxic than thiotepa. The drug was developed by a Ukrainian, Wassyl Novicky, who had been nominated for a Nobel Prize more than once. That seemed to give him scientific credibility, but campaigns for Nobel Prizes can artificially boost a candidate's credentials.

As with other treatments, my appetite was whetted by the claim that a Ewing's patient had got better after taking Ukrain. Standard treatment had earlier failed. The Austrian authorities, however, were not convinced. They thought that efficacy were overblown and refused a licence. That was a concern, clearly, but it didn't put me off investigating further. Regulators are often highly conservative.

Dr Novicky was so convinced of the potential of his product that he took the Austrian Government to the European Court of Human Rights. No doubt he saw the commercial potential too. The case was about the process which the Government had followed – the court was not being asked to say that Ukrain worked – but inevitably Mr Novicky's lawyers, who sent me the court papers, led considerable evidence about the alleged benefits of the drug. The evidence seemed impressive, but I knew how good lawyers can be at presenting their client's case. It's only when you see the other side's arguments that you can begin to form a view.

I read a review by a professor of complementary medicine at Exeter University. He concluded that there seemed to be something in it, but there were serious methodological faults with the seven clinical trials he reviewed.

Unlike homeopathic remedies, Ukrain carries side-effects. And it's not cheap. The overall cost:benefit analysis was negative and so I rejected it.

A Greek Ewing's teenager did try it, but unsuccessfully. His father, Robert, was a fellow-traveller, literally and metaphorically, along the global highways and byways of Ewing's research. When Erik died, he penned a beautiful tribute, with the halting English somehow enhancing poignancy:

'I never believe that my son was going to be for me son, teacher, brother and sometime father. He learn me how to fight for the life, how to love with heart, how to cry, how to kiss, how to be a man in this dirty world. I'm so proud for him.'

Postscript

by Allison Ogden-Newton, CEO World Child Cancer

The life of every child is extraordinary, a gift and worth the struggle for survival. To lose a young life to cancer is a tragedy, not just for that child and their family but also for the society in which they lived because it is simply the case that children are our future, carrying with each and every one of them the hopes of the next generation.

On behalf of World Child Cancer, I am delighted to have been able to write this postscript to David Thomas's moving book. It is an opportunity to thank him for his commitment to our work and the inspiration we have all felt through the commitment and caring of his family and in particular his extraordinary son Daniel.

Daniel found out about the work of World Child Cancer after his struggle with cancer had begun. It says a great deal about him that even as he suffered what is always a difficult, debilitating and painful disease, his thoughts turned to others.

Daniel was inspired by our mission to reach out to children whose cancer would otherwise go undiagnosed and untreated. He was struck by the inequality of children in the developed world with those in poorer countries where treating cancer is still often perceived to be either too expensive or too difficult. World Child Cancer works to prove that it is possible to offer children cost-effective treatment; even in the most inhospitable places we can help children with some types of cancer to achieve up to a 60 per cent cure rate.

At World Child Cancer we think every child should have access to treatment for their cancer and where that is not possible they should, at the very least, have access to pain relief. Daniel agreed with this, happy for family and friends to join World Child Cancer challenges and raise money for our work.

Following Daniel's untimely and tragic death, his father David Thomas continues to be his champion as he was in life and supports our little charity by spreading the word.

At the time of writing, World Child Cancer supports nine projects working across sixteen countries that enable us to reach out to over 3,000 children a year suffering from cancer. Countries in which we work include Ghana, Malawi, Cameroon, Uganda, Ethiopia, Bangladesh, the Philippines and Myanmar.

Cancer is now an urgent international healthcare issue. Globally, it kills more people than HIV, malaria and TB combined. With the majority of cases occurring in low- and middle-income countries, it can no longer be thought of as a disease of affluent societies.

Margaret Chan, World Health Organization Director-General, has spoken of cancer in developing countries as an 'impending disaster.' Non-communicable diseases such as cancer have received far less attention from donors, the international community and international healthcare providers – largely because they were left out of the UN's Millennium Development Goals.

The fact is that cancer is a growing cause of death in the developing world. As people escape extreme poverty, the incidence of illnesses such as cancer, diabetes and heart disease grows. Significantly, as child mortality from infectious diseases, malaria and malnutrition is reduced across the developing world, childhood cancer is emerging as a greater threat to life. Cancer is a leading cause of death for five to fourteen year-olds in developing countries and is becoming an increasingly bigger killer of children under the age of five. This follows a similar pattern seen in the US and UK during the 1950s and 1960s.

There are very strong reasons for making sure more children have access to cancer treatment and care. Although cases of cancer in children represent only 1 per cent of all cancer cases, they are among the most curable. Children can be cured of most common cancers with generic drugs and relatively simple treatments that are affordable and sustainable. The knowledge to cure children exists following four decades of research in developed countries yet this expertise has rarely been transferred to developing countries. This massive global inequality must be addressed as a matter of urgency. This is what World Child Cancer does.

World Child Cancer specialises in creating and funding medical twinning partnerships between hospitals in developing countries and experienced childhood cancer units in high income countries. These partnerships create a two-way transfer of expertise and we build into our twinning partnerships our experiences and lessons learnt from five years of operational work. In this way we have been able to create affordable, sustainable and scale-able solutions to caring for children with cancer in the countries in which we work.

World Child Cancer also introduces specialist palliative care training for hospital and outreach nurses which together with access to the necessary drugs ensure children who cannot survive their cancer have a quality of life that should be the right of every child.

We were established in 2007 by a team of international specialists who wanted to redress the global inequality in the provision of cancer treatment for children, and we are the only charity dedicated solely to helping children with cancer in low- and middle-income countries on a global scale. Childhood cancer is becoming an increasingly urgent problem in developing regions and our vision is to see a world where every child with cancer has access to treatment and care.

To do this we rely completely on the support of wonderful people like David Thomas and his son Daniel; people who are willing to think about the suffering of children they will probably never meet.

David Thomas is one of few who has met some of the children we help when he underwent our extreme Malawi Bike Challenge in 2014. This endurance feat set out to cycle, in blistering heat, between two children's paediatric oncology units in Lilongwe and Blantyre, 450 kilometres apart, to raise awareness and funds for World Child Cancer. We know it was a gruelling challenge in a country where roads would not always be recognisable and the heat defines everything. David was courageous in joining the pioneers who completed this landmark challenge and described his participation as a privilege, which, given what they went through, was typically generous. Together David and the rest of the team raised a staggering £44,722 (after expenses).

It is certainly a privilege to have David's support, his dedication is a wonderful thing, borne out of love and destined to touch so many young lives.

www.worldchildcancer.org

Thanks and acknowledgments

I am very grateful to Phil Garner, one of Daniel's best friends at university and Ultimate Frisbee star, for permission to use his photograph of the Magdalen tree-planting ceremony; to Marcus Field for allowing me to quote from his Simon Perrot Oration (delivered in Latin); to Felix Budelmann and Fiachra MacGorain, who were more than tutors to Daniel, for their tributes; and to Paul Goulding, another good friend to Daniel, for his.

So many people have helped me get this book to completion, as I have aspired, no doubt unsuccessfully, to match Vera Brittain's ambition for her First World War autobiography *Testament of Youth* of making the story 'as truthful as history, but as readable as fiction'. If I have forgotten to mention anyone, it is because of temporary memory lapse (exacerbated by the ageing process), not because I have actually forgotten the contribution or do not feel real gratitude. Please forgive me.

Warm thanks to Shoba Vazirani, Director of my publisher, Splendid Publications, for guiding me patiently and wisely through the various stages of the publishing process. From the start, Shoba believed in the book when it would have been easy to say that the charmingly-named 'misery lit' genre was too crowded for another sad story, especially one penned by a non-celebrity. Shoba has done everything to accommodate my wishes, understanding what a personal book this is, and I am very grateful to her, and to her colleagues. Chris Fulcher is responsible for the excellent design of the cover and the layout of the contents.

A special thanks, too, to Fiona Palmer, an excellent professional editor, who kindly offered to read the book when it was at its most verbose (even I got bored reading it). Fiona helped me to understand that less is often more and provided several helpful examples of how to reduce length without losing meaning. She refused to accept any money for her painstaking work. Thank you.

A number of other people kindly read part or all of the book and provided valuable objectivity that I could not hope to achieve: my amazingly supportive sisters Charlotte and Sian, Annabel, Caroline, Caterina, Constance, Djuna, Gillian, Harvey, Lesley, Norbert, Richard and Tobias. Other family members kept me going with their enthusiasm for the project.

Debbie Binner not only read the book and offered sharp journalistic insight but generously agreed to write the foreword. Debbie has lost her magical daughter Chloë to the same horrible disease Daniel had but, rather than erect barriers around her grief, she now fights indefatigably and effectively for better access to treatment for youngsters with cancer. As she says, we became partners in crime and firm friends.

I am grateful, too, to Allison Ogden-Newton for telling us about the work of her excellent charity, World Child Cancer. Splendid Publications, of their own initiative, are donating a proportion of the royalties to WCC; a wonderful gesture.

Not just related to the book, but I wanted to thank all those colleagues, past and present, who have supported me throughout the whole journey, during many dark times. I started to write a list but it was just too long and, again, I feared omitting someone, so I hope that a heartfelt collective thanks will suffice. The same is true of all the friends, fellow Samaritans and neighbours who have shown they cared: I know who you all are, and am really grateful. I make a single exception in mentioning Doreen, who years ago bore the burden of being my secretary and who has just lost her equally wonderful sister, Rita. I know Doreen and Rita shed some of my tears.

Many thanks to Dominika and Jacob Flindt for their patient and helpful guidance with the book website (www. danielmyson.com).

A very special thanks, finally, to two people. To Claire, for not only giving comments – sometimes left field, always insightful – on various drafts but also for providing encouragement during the many times I needed it; and, most important of all, for teaching me to laugh again and not feel guilty about it.

And to Mum, for just being there with her love and compassion and self-deprecating humour, as she always is for all of us. She has experienced real pain, too: she loved Daniel as much as he loved her.

I finish with the usual author's disclaimer: many have contributed to any good points in the book; I am responsible for everything else.

David Thomas is a lawyer in the voluntary sector and a part-time judge. He has written numerous articles on legal and other topics and contributed to various books. He is a former chair of the RSPCA and campaigns for street children in Central America. He is a Samaritan. Like Daniel, he is a sports nut (playing and watching) and shares his love of language, music and ethics. David lives in Chobham, Surrey.